Principles and methods
of social psychology

Principles and methods
of social psychology

EDWIN P. HOLLANDER
State University of New York at Buffalo

New York
OXFORD UNIVERSITY PRESS
London   Toronto   1967

Second printing, 1968
Copyright © 1967 by Oxford University Press, Inc.
Library of Congress Catalogue Card Number: 67-15127
Printed in the United States of America

To Pat and Peter

Preface

This is a textbook for students in the first course in social psychology. It takes for granted very little prior preparation, though in most instances students will have had an introduction to psychology, sociology, or perhaps cultural anthropology. Where necessary, I have recalled and reviewed basic points from these fields in building toward an understanding of social psychology's distinctive approach.

My aims in writing this book are twofold: first, to show in a balanced way as much as possible of the totality of the field; second, to do so within the framework of a systematic treatment. As I see it, a textbook should convey the major trends of study, their theoretical origins, and the principles they sustain, without the need for an exhaustive catalogue of findings. My intent is to provide the student with what he needs to know concerning the range and shadings of research on a particular topic, and to discuss research studies with specific regard to some explicit point in the body of the text at a given juncture.

The prime concept in my treatment of the field is social influence. I see this as a central process common to many phenomena which are often treated quite separately in social psychology, among them attitude change, socialization, role behavior, conformity, and leadership. As a significant element in understanding this central process, time—and the human capacity to live in and react to a time dimension—is stressed throughout. The book's approach is therefore very much person-centered within a systematic scheme that looks at social influence in transactional terms. In this sense, it brings together the contemporary emphases on cognition, the perceptual features of social interaction, and concepts of social reward and social exchange.

Social psychology has substantial relevance to the world of affairs. To show some points of contact, I have drawn freely on findings from sociological, political, and economic sources, as well as newspapers and other popular publications, in dealing with such topics as social class differences, the language of advertising, voting behavior, and international relations. In so doing I have tried to enliven interest for relevancy and infuse a sense of the exciting and vital nature of the field and its subject matter. I have also employed examples of a light nature from daily life. These examples do not, of course, illustrate a point in the same way as a research finding, nor are they treated as such.

The organization of this book proceeds from the general and the historical through to the special place of attitudes, and of social interaction, and then on to the nature of particular social, cultural, and group influences and phenomena. In order, the first three chapters present a broad set of definitions and terms of reference, an historical perspective on the field, and a detailing of methods within the context of their relationship to theory. These chapters should provide a solid foundation for a better grasp of the import of issues and findings covered in the topical chapters which follow.

Because of the organic character of the field, I have made frequent cross-references between these topical chapters to show the kind of interrelationships that prevail over topical boundaries. I have not felt compelled, in this regard, to pigeonhole each and every topic in a single place. Broad topics, such as attitudes and social interaction, are variously treated in different juxtapositions though they are given a primary focus in their respective chapters. Prejudice is considered in the attitude chapters, then in further detail in Chapter Ten regarding personality, and again in connection with inter-group relations in Chapter Thirteen.

Suggested readings, with selected references, appear at the end of each chapter and are meant to be read after digesting the chapter itself. These materials should provide an expansion of points, as well as a useful continuity to and preparation for the chapters which follow; they are listed where they are most applicable, though they may be quite suitable for later chapters as well. Special care has also been given to identifying those books which are available in paperback editions.

My intellectual debts to colleagues and friends, in and out of the field, are considerable and I could not hope to repay them here. What I have put into this book also benefits from my own students and teachers, in whom I have been most fortunate. For their special help in reading and commenting on various portions of the manuscript, I am pleased to thank F. Kenneth Berrien, Stephen C. Jones, James W. Julian, Joseph M. Masling, and Marvin E. Shaw. While I take the usual responsibility for the result, I very much appreciate their useful criticisms.

Particular thanks are owed to Leonore Ganschow who helped enormously in seeing me through the typing of the several versions of the manuscript. I also greatly appreciate the work of Alison M. Bond in editing the manuscript and carrying it through production, the fine design of Frederick Schneider, and Frank Romano's illustrations. My wife, Pat, was my most diligent reader and greatest source of aid, especially in the final phases of work. I am delighted to note her invaluable contribution, as well as the supportive efforts of my son, Peter.

London, England   E. P. H.
January 1967

Acknowledgments

The following copyright holders are gratefully thanked for giving their permission to reproduce the material indicated:

The American Psychological Association for the figure on p. 98 from *Journal of Abnormal and Social Psychology*, 1947, *42*, 40; the figure on p. 80 from ibid., 1962, *64*, 139; the figure on p. 167 from ibid., 1964, *69*, 293; the table on p. 419 and the figure on p. 420 from ibid., 1961, *63*, 248 and 249; the figure on p. 165 from ibid., 1957, *55*, 247; the figure on p. 235 from ibid., 1961, *62*, 653; the figure on p. 74 from ibid., 1951, *46*, 42; the figures on p. 408 from ibid., 1954, *49*, 68; the figure on p. 105 from ibid., 1955, *51*, 673; for the figure on p. 186 from *Journal of Comparative and Physiological Psychology*, 1955, *48*, 394; for the figure on p. 291 from *Journal of Personality and Social Psychology*, 1965, *2*, 828; and the figure on p. 422 from ibid., 1965, *1*, 131; for the tables on pp. 412 and 432 from *Psychological Bulletin*, 1959, *56*, 247 and 260.

The American Sociological Association for the figure on p. 66 from *American Sociological Review*, 1950, *15*, 258; for the figure on p. 445 from *Sociometry*, 1964, *27*, 496; the figure on p. 447 from ibid., 1958, *21*, 330; and the figure on p. 424 from ibid., 1963, *26*, 501.

Columbia University Press for the figure on p. 69 from P. F. Lazarsfeld, B. Berelson, and Hazel Gaudet, *The People's Choice*, 2nd edition, 1948.

Harper & Row, Publishers, Inc., for the table on p. 64 from R. G. Barker and H. F. Wright, *Midwest and Its Children: The Psychological Ecology of an*

American Town, 1954; for the table on p. 450 from D. C. Cartwright and A. Zander (Eds.), *Group Dynamics: Research and Theory,* 2nd edition, 1960; for the figure on p. 46 from M. Sherif, *The Psychology of Social Norms,* 1936.

Holt, Rinehart and Winston, Inc., for the figure on p. 71 from T. M. Newcomb and E. L. Hartley (Eds.), *Readings in Social Psychology,* 1947; and the figure on p. 324 from Eleanor Maccoby, T. M. Newcomb, and E. L. Hartley (Eds.), *Readings in Social Psychology,* 3rd edition, 1958.

Human Relations for the figure on p. 72 in their issue of 1948, *1*, 522.

The Journal Press for the figure on p. 65 from *Journal of Social Psychology,* 1934, V, Fig. 1; and the figure on p. 128 from ibid., 1936, VII, 194.

Journal of Conflict Resolution for the figure on p. 459 in their issue of 1963, *7*, 588.

The Linguistic Circle of New York, Inc., and the Johnson Reprint Corporation for the figure on p. 254 from *Word,* 1958, *14*, 154.

McGraw-Hill Book Company, Inc., for the figure on p. 149 from S. Koch (Ed.), *Psychology: A Study of a Science,* Vol. 6, 1963; and the figure on p. 103 from C. T. Morgan, *Introduction to Psychology,* 2nd edition, 1961.

Personnel Psychology for the figure on p. 452 in their issue of 1962, *15*, 50.

Princeton University Press for the figure on p. 142 from S. A. Stouffer, L. Guttman, E. A. Suchman, P. F. Lazarsfeld, Shirley A. Star, and J. A. Gardner (Eds.), *Measurement and Prediction,* 1949.

Rutgers University Press for the figure on p. 221 and table on p. 222 from H. Cantril, *The Pattern of Human Concerns,* 1965.

The University of Chicago Press for the figure on p. 366 from W. F. Whyte, *Street Corner Society,* 1943.

Contents

Figures

Tables

Principles and methods
of social psychology

1

The contemporary field of
social psychology

The predictability of another person's behavior, especially someone we depend upon, is an important feature of life. The very fact that we expect this regularity makes us all the more aware of its absence. Thus, when we encounter a friend who fails to respond to our greeting, the continuity of the relationship is broken, for this meeting constitutes part of a series of interactions, not merely an isolated event. This sequence has caused us to develop certain "expectancies" regarding one another's behavior, based on our past encounters. We then seek explanations if these expectancies are not fulfilled. Indeed, the fulfillment of such expectancies is an important element in explaining social behavior.

One major reason why the scientific study of human behavior is different from the study of inanimate matter is precisely this quality of human experience. People remember and act on past events, and anticipate future outcomes or gains; they do not simply react to the present situation. This quality of *relationships over time* has been called "historicity," and it is especially significant in differentiating the study of Man from other scientific efforts (Homans, 1965).

The person concerned about an apparent snub from a friend is reflecting the kind of *everyday* interest in human behavior that all of us share. It is not the same, however, as scientific study on a more systematic basis. The differences lie in several considerations; the first is the obvious limitation imposed on any one person's unique observa-

3

tions. Another is the fact that, however unwittingly, our thinking is inevitably colored by persisting myths from the past. Finally, we all succumb to the subjective bias of personal feelings; in short, we may be judgmental, even without realizing it. Language itself is a vehicle which conveys our view of a given behavior and intrudes on understanding. Thus, if we dislike someone who is behaving in a given way, we may refer to this behavior as "boisterous"; the same behavior for someone we like, or dislike less, might be described as "colorful." And, in this same vein, none of us is completely free of the judgment exemplified in such statements as "You are obstinate and pig-headed; I am tenacious and resolute." "You are unprincipled; I am flexible." "You are acting on the basis of mere prejudice; I am acting out of reason."

It would be hard indeed to build understanding and develop generalizations about human behavior if we relied upon such individual observations and biases alone. To get around these limitations requires a degree of objectivity and related methods which help us go beyond this elementary stage.

What is social psychology?

Social psychology is one of the scientific fields concerned with the objective study of human behavior. In particular, social psychology directs its attention to *understanding* the influences producing regularities and diversities in human *social* behavior. It approaches its study through the systematic analysis of data obtained through rigorous scientific methods. The distinctiveness of social psychology arises from two major factors: first, its interest in the *individual* as a participant in social relationships; and, second, its emphasis on *understanding* the social influence processes underlying these relationships.

The term "understanding" includes several levels of meaning, from simple description, through analysis and accuracy of prediction, to explanation of phenomena. In achieving a systematic understanding of social behavior, social psychologists have increasingly obtained evidence from experimentation to test the validity of their predictions about *social influence*. As we shall see, most of the concerns of interest to the social psychologist are based somehow in influence relationships.

There are manipulators of behavior who have evolved successful techniques of influence for their own purposes; propagandists and politicians come readily to mind as illustrations of these. They will often have found certain regularities of behavior that they can induce for their own profit. In one sense, they have hit upon predictable relationships in human affairs; in another sense, however, such practices, whatever their successes, are limited by the superficiality inherent in knowing only that some appeal evidently worked, but not *why* it worked.

In contrast to these catch-as-catch-can approaches, scientific understanding tries to explain the root causes of behavior. It is in the nature of scientific study to break through the usual crust of subjective judgment that overlays everyday approaches to man's behavior. As "self-evident" as many of these commonsense approaches appear to be, they do not provide a sufficient basis for understanding. If we look at proverbs as generalizations from commonsense, for example, we find them notorious for their contradictions: "Birds of a feather flock together" vs. "Opposites attract." The obvious, then, is not enough, and indeed it often obscures the actual causal relationships by short-circuiting a more rigorous study of the underlying factors at work.

Several advantages are gained by the kind of systematic approach to human behavior represented in social psychology. The primary advantage rests in the essential value of any scientific enterprise—the rewards of broadening and deepening our knowledge. Once achieved, though, this knowledge can be helpful in many ways: in organizing our efforts as humans more constructively; in developing individual potentialities with greater effectiveness; in reducing the handicaps under which men often live out their lives; and in providing thereby a greater mastery of Man over his environment.

Features of social psychology

As with all scientific fields, social psychology has four basic features:

First, *a set of phenomena of concern*, in this case, those involving social influence. This covers person-to-person interactions, as well as those relationships prevailing between groups or total societies, or those of an individual with these broader social entities.

Second, *a body of theory* concerning influence phenomena, that is, concepts which help to explain them in part or in larger wholes. Basically, a theory consists of one or more functional statements about the relationships which produce phenomena. These may involve concepts such as "group cohesiveness," as in the functional statement: "Other things being equal, conformity to a group's standards is positively related to that group's cohesiveness."

Third, *accumulated findings* in the form of recognized knowledge about these phenomena; this is represented, for example, in scientific findings gathered together and summarized in textbooks, and is expressed in terms of research data and the principles they support.

Fourth, *a set of research methods* for obtaining evidence about these phenomena by recognized, objectively based procedures for gathering data systematically.

These features of social psychology necessarily depend upon one another, and are not fully separable. Thus, findings test theory, but theory often serves to direct research by providing one or more guiding hypotheses. Moreover, the methodology employed in social psychological research is often dictated by the theoretical basis for the research and what has been found previously by others applying a given method. We shall be returning to a fuller consideration of methods in Chapter Three.

Asking the right questions

Social psychology shares in the characteristic effort of science to get beneath simple description to the basis for phenomena. To achieve this with regard to social influence, a crucial step lies in framing the right questions to ask. Generally speaking, one of the main tasks in *any* science is asking questions which have the prospect of providing meaningful answers—in other words, questions that are revealing. Because social behavior is so often multi-determined, and only rarely the result of a single cause, this presents an even greater challenge in social psychology. Furthermore, terms have to be used with a view toward *which* standards or criteria will be used to define and measure them. Several illustrative questions that allow this kind of specification are:

> What are the conditions under which some appeals lead to attitude change and others do not, and why?
> What factors allow for greater effectiveness of a group

leader in, say, producing higher group cohesiveness, and why? How is this related to group productivity?

Under what conditions will some persons tend to act more independently of a given group?

What are the consequences of a conflict of values dictated by different groups with which a person is identified? For instance, what are the general circumstances in which a teenager will be more inclined to accept parental standards as against peer standards?

What causes the rise and spread of rumor?

Why do some organizations characteristically innovate while others remain inert and unchanging? In what features of their operation are they different?

Questions of this sort are studied by social psychological research to provide a better grasp of the sources and regularities of influences on behavior.

The study of social influence

The central concern of social psychology is with the process of social influence. Humans by necessity are oriented toward other humans in their environment and social influence occurs whenever one individual responds to the *actual* or *implied* presence of one or more others. This definition refers to several different kinds of events, some less obvious than others.

In the first place, social influence may have to do with the reciprocal effect of one person upon another in *social interaction*. As was exemplified in the situation where we encountered a friend, social interaction is a process basic to human experience, beginning with earliest childhood. It constitutes a model or "paradigm" of other social relationships. Most of the characteristics we possess are in one way or another affected by social interaction, including our personality and related values and attitudes.

Social psychology is also concerned with the wider play of influence relationships that prevail between a *group and an individual*—conformity, leadership, prejudice, morale, and other group phenomena. Several of these are pictorialized in Figure 1.1. In the *conformity* in-

stance, more than one individual exerts influence on another in terms of
a prevailing pattern of social behaviors or attitudes—what we will call
a norm. A counterpart to this exists where an individual affects a group
or larger social entity, such as an organization, political party, or nation,
as in the case of *leadership*. Here the source or agent of influence is an
individual who is able to direct and alter the behaviors and attitudes of
others. *Prejudice* is an inter-group phenomenon that has its origins in
the effects of group identification. Similarly, *morale* provides a convenient summation of a shared group attitude which affects other outcomes for individuals.

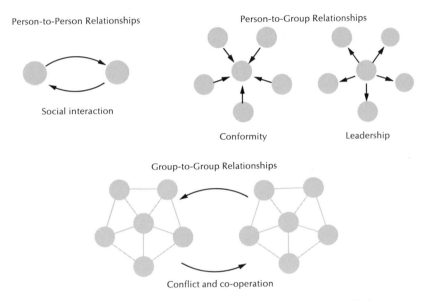

Figure 1.1: Some influence relationships studied in social psychology.

Social influence also has to do with the relationship that exists between *two or more groups,* which could be defined in the narrower
sense of cliques within a fraternity, or in the wider sense of inter-group
or international relations.

A pivotal point in any consideration of social influence is the recognition that behavior more probably will remain unchanged so long as
alternative modes of action are not available. This is not just force of
habit. For change to occur it is essential that avenues be perceived for

achieving desired outcomes. When we speak of social influence, then we should add: where there are alternative modes of response which are perceived to be available to the individual. Furthermore, these modes of response must be relevant to anticipated returns in the future.

Persons may be influenced not only by the existence of present pressures, but by past experience with others in society and the learning that this has produced. Humans have a vast capacity to learn from new experiences, to indulge in higher forms of symbolic thought, and to share in the behavior and experience of others. Accordingly, it is quite understandable that one dominating quality of social behavior is its responsiveness to social influence.

The individual as a focus

A distinctive attribute of social psychology resides in its study of the psychology of the *individual* in society. This interest carries with it a probing of the many features of the social environment which have an impact upon him. Social psychology therefore draws upon the storehouse of materials available from sociology and cultural anthropology, among other behavioral sciences. It also employs some concepts and terms from these older disciplines. On the whole, however, social psychology retains a primary emphasis on the *psychological* level of analysis.

There are still those to whom social psychology represents a halfway house between psychology on one side and sociology and cultural anthropology on the other. But this is an inappropriate metaphor for two reasons: first, each of these fields has its own level or levels of analysis, and second, social psychology carries its own distinctive approach to the analysis of social processes based in concepts requiring extensions from individual psychology to the level of social behavior. This does not mean, however, that social psychology merely takes over generalizations from work in the experimental psychology laboratory. Rather, it employs psychological concepts, and the insights provided by an understanding of psychological processes, to account for the dynamics of social phenomena. To take one example, we know that people are capable of modifications of behavior through learning; therefore, principles of learning have direct utility in understanding dynamic human relationships. The question of why we learn *some* things from our social environment and *not* others is a reasonable one challenging the social psychologist's interest.

Another example is represented by perception. Knowing how an individual perceives the social environment and is motivated to take action within it, affords an important insight into his behavior. A person's own interpretation of his world—his "psychological field"—provides a better basis for understanding than would a strictly literal description of the things or events in his environment. The evidence is also overwhelming that a great deal of the content of each person's psychological field from birth onward is determined by what he encounters in his society. It is useful, therefore, for us to devote some attention to the importance of this context.

The context of society and culture

All of us are born into an organized human society, a social environment. In the process of growing up within this environment we learn to adopt the manner and ways of others. The content of this process varies enormously depending upon the people and circumstances we contact during these years of development and after. It is not surprising, then, that the person brought up in a city apartment must necessarily learn modes of adaptation and acquire behaviors which are different from those of the person brought up, let us say, on the shore at a fishing village, even though in the same country.

The other people with whom we have contact are part of a *society*. Their *culture* represented in the patterns of life which they lead, consists of the ongoing practices and institutions passed on, though perhaps modified, from generation to generation. In our own society, some illustrative cultural patterns are represented in our language, the monogamous family, private ownership, and the four-year baccalaureate degree.

CULTURE AS AN OUTLOOK

There is another significant thing about a culture: it gives us an *outlook* on the world. The social psychologist, aware of culture as a context of experience, is interested in *how* the individual's perceptions, as well as his motivations, are affected by it. To expand our understanding of social behavior, then, we not only recognize that other people are important social stimuli to which we react, but also that collectively people *create* other socially significant stimuli that have symbolic value —words, preferred foods, money, flags, and so on. These bring about significant social responses, too. Accordingly, the social psychologist focuses attention not only on the relationship of persons but also on the individual's interpretation of and reaction to things which have socially symbolic meaning. This is part of the perceptual quality of culture which we will take up in greater detail in Chapter Eight.

THE "HUMAN NATURE" FALLACY

On the whole, people are inclined to think of the characteristics of those in their *own* region or country as "human nature." Their personal observation of how others behave leads them to conclude that somehow this has applicability to men or women in general, even though this behavior depends upon learning in society. Quite commonly, therefore, we may hear statements such as these:

> "It's only human nature for people to want to get ahead."
> "It's only human nature for people to want to take advantage of others."
> "What do you expect of a man?"
> "Isn't that just like a woman?"

The fallacy in this thinking lies in extending observations in one society to generalizations about the tendencies of people living elsewhere, under different social and cultural influences. We can see this in better focus if we imagine someone from the Orient contending that eating with chopsticks is "human nature" since after all it characterizes those he observes in a large share of the earth's population. The widespread belief in the essential similarity of other humans is an example too of the workings of the psychological phenomenon of perceptual constancy.

On the essential matter of overreaching from a limited perspective, the extensive field work of cultural anthropologists demolishes these simple notions. It reveals, for instance, that a concern with getting ahead, or achieving higher status, is not typical of all societies in the world, even though it may seem to be true of people in our own society. As a matter of fact, it is not even true of everyone in our own society, as we can recognize by recalling individual exceptions we have known. Nor is it true, as some would have it, that women universally are kitchen-bound, or that they must traditionally occupy a passive position. The well-known field studies of Margaret Mead and many other cultural anthropologists indicate that male roles and female roles are culturally determined (Mead, 1949). There are, in fact, some cultures of the world in which cooking is distinctively "man's work." And we need only mention the fact that chefs in our society are men.

"YOU CAN'T CHANGE HUMAN NATURE"?

Perhaps *most* misleading of all these myths is the commonplace that "you can't change human nature." This contention, that mankind possesses unyielding, inborn characteristics, denies the evidence of Man's greatest capacity, that of adaptability through learning. Imagine, for example, the reaction from adults if children were to use the argument that "you can't change human nature" in opposing their parents' guidance. Plainly, whatever Man's nature, it varies considerably as a result of the infusion of cultural experience through learning.

In Chapter Four we will consider some of those things which appear to be characteristic of Man's "nature." Now it is worth noting again two points of reference: the great diversity of human adaptation to varying social environments, and the vast capacity of humans to communicate and to partake of the features of organized societies with a continuity of patterned life through culture.

RACE, CULTURE, AND BEHAVIOR

Another widespread misconception is founded in the belief that observed differences in behavior between the peoples of various societies are the result of inborn racial characteristics. Sometimes this is captured succinctly but erroneously in the phrase "It's in the blood." Reproduction, however, involves only the germ cells, and since only these and these alone carry genes from both parents, randomized through the process of reduction-division, genes don't depend upon blood, nor does race. Any racial classification constructed will almost certainly contain persons who possess the usual blood types of man—O, A, B, and AB. Speaking to the issue of genetics and race, Dunn and Dobzhansky (1952) said:

> People differ in the color of skin, eyes, hair, in stature, bodily proportions, and in many other traits. Each trait is determined by several, often by many, genes. How many variable genes there are in man is unknown; certainly hundreds, possibly thousands. Because of this, some of us have blue and others brown eyes, some have prominent and others flat noses, some are tall and others short. Such differences are, of course, common among people of the same country, state, town, members of a family, and even brothers and sisters. We do not suppose that every person with blue eyes belongs to a different race from everybody with brown eyes. It would be absurd to do so because blue- and brown-eyed children are frequently born to the same parents (p. 117).

Nevertheless, because physical factors are more readily observed, it is frequently assumed that they must necessarily be associated with *genetically* determined dispositions toward some common behavior. Therefore, it is important in the first place to distinguish between physical characteristics and the cultural patterns we observe in a society such as a nation. Also, it is essential to recognize that neither societies or nations nor religions need be made up of people with common physical qualities. No less than Americans, Frenchmen, for example, are widely variable in physical "type."

A nation after all is a political unit; one is a "national" of a country by virtue of living within a political boundary. A religion is comprised of people who share a common faith and may live in various societies or nations, just as a society or a nation may be made up of people of differing religions or even different languages. Switzerland has three official languages, and Canada, not uniquely, has two. Many nations of the world have a diversity of religions. Buddhism and Mohammedanism are among the major religions, in addition to Christianity, having widespread adherents.

Yet races, religions, nations, and languages are often confused with one another—as when people speak of a "French race" or a "Jewish race" or a "Slavic people" or a "Catholic nation." Such usage in the first place presents an oversimplified, pigeon-holed picture of the great diversity of human life; more particularly, it totally disregards the wide range of *individual differences* that exist within any human grouping.

These labels or "stereotypes," as Walter Lippmann (1922) originally dubbed them, obscure the subtler origins of social behavior in the complex relationships between biological and social psychological factors. The phenomenon of stereotypes in itself has a legitimate place as an area of study in social psychology, especially in regard to prejudice.

With regard to race and behavior, even given some common physical attributes, no reasonable inferences can be drawn about any common psychological capacities or behavioral tendencies of a group since there is such an overlay of cultural influence in the complex determination of individual behavior. Two UNESCO statements on race, signed by eminent social scientists, and entitled *Human Rights* and *The Race Concept,* make these points, the first regarding intelligence:

> Wherever it has been possible to make allowances for differences in environmental opportunities, the tests have shown essential similarity in mental characters among all human groups. In short, given similar degrees of cultural opportunity to realise their potentialities, the average achievement of each ethnic group is about the same (1950).
>
> . . . it has never been possible to separate members of two groups on the basis of mental capacity, as they can often be separated on a basis of religion, skin colour, hair form or language. It is possible, though not proved, that some types of innate capacity for intellectual and emotional responses are commoner in one human group than in another, but it is certain that, within a single group, innate capacities vary as much as, if not more than, they do between different groups.
>
> It often happens that a national group may appear to be characterized by particular social attributes. The superficial view would be that this is due to race. Scientifically, however, we realize that any common psychological attribute is more likely to be due to a common historical and social background, and that such attributes may obscure the fact that, within different populations consisting of many human types, one will find approximately the same range of temperament and intelligence (1952).

When we focus on those distinctively "human" things, like speaking a language, we find them the most highly subject to the wide-ranging influences of diverse societies. This appears to be quite clearly an environmental effect and not a matter of genetic factors. The illogic of this latter view is illustrated by the fact that nobody would adopt, let us say, a French baby in the naïve expectation that when he grew up they could learn French from him. Common sense as well as the best scientific evidence indicates that all normal human infants are capable of learning any language spoken by humans, given sufficient exposure to it; they are not born with a tendency toward any particular language. Let us also be clear that, just as with language, a multitude of other patterns of behavior and outlook are available to be learned from the particular humans we encounter in the formative years. How these effects are produced requires some probing of heredity and environment.

Heredity and environment

Since the terms "heredity" and "environment" are still often pitted against one another in everyday discussion, it should be emphasized that they are *not* opposing forces. Any behavior depends in some degree upon the mutual effects of heredity within environment.

By definition heredity is that which is biologically based, usually in the sense of genetic determinants. Though heredity is sometimes bleakly viewed as though it were destiny, this is unnecessarily defeatist; it fails to take account of the environmental sources which can shape alternative outcomes. We may not literally change the genes with which we are born, but we can encounter or even seek environmental factors to which they will respond more favorably. Recent work on DNA, which provides an understanding of genetics in terms of biochemical coding, lends emphasis to Montagu's (1956) point that genes are

> . . . chemical packages which vary chemically under different conditions and tend to accelerate the chemical reactions of other chemical packages. Genes do not act as such in a vacuum, but they interact with the environment in which they occur . . . Development is the resultant of the interaction between the inherited pattern of genes, the genotype, and the environment in which those genes undergo development (p. 72).

Environment has to do with all of those experiences from the time of conception, including possible intra-uterine involvements, which can bring about physical or behavioral effects. One widespread misconception, which slights the environment, is to consider that shared behaviors within a family are the result of heredity. The fact that you can see them with your own eyes is supposed to be proof enough. Thus, the child, who is overweight and whose parents are also overweight, is obviously a victim of his genes—or is he? Since eating is a matter of family social patterns, which might include routine second helpings, the environment clearly pleads a strong case. If a father imbibes excessively and his son follows in this pattern, is that heredity? Or might it be environment? Plainly, "like father like son" can be equally apt as a reference to environmental learning. Just as children, in growing up, learn to speak the language of those around them, they learn the eating habits, as well as the many other features of behaving which are characteristic of those others. Parents, often blind to this implicit learning process, are too readily inclined to see the mannerisms their children share with them to be hereditary in a genetic sense. Visiting relatives are not excused from making the same error of observation.

Another recurring error in understanding heredity is the assumption that if a given physical characteristic which is genetically based is associated with a behavior, then the behavior too is genetic. It is still common to hear, for example, that redheads have very inflamatory personalities and tend to be easily excited. There is no scientific basis for this contention, yet, given the belief, the effect could follow. This is an example of the "self-fulfilling prophecy," a wide-reaching phenomenon about which we shall be saying more later. Where the members of a society among whom we live share certain beliefs about us as redheads, then act toward us in distinct ways, in turn leading us to defensive action, is that heredity? The very condition which is alleged to be genetic—a personality trait—can be environmentally produced by a social psychological process originating in beliefs. This process fits the circumstance of the so-called "minority group" in many human societies. Indeed, the same condition is true with respect to the differentiation of males and females. If young girls and boys are encouraged toward sex-typed behaviors, these are environmentally determined and hardly outcroppings of biological sex determinants, as many believe. In fact, in our society the social distinctions between little girls and little boys begin quite early, as the color-coding of pink and blue outergarments reveals. Accordingly, the doll-play of a boy past the nursery stage is viewed as inappropriate and the girl in the sandlot ball game may be tolerated but is a "tom-boy" to the gang, to her parents, and in the view of broader society.

Table 1.1: IQ differences of identical twins reared apart under conditions of different educational advantage. (After Newman, Freeman, and Holzinger, 1937.)

NUMBER OF PAIRS	AVERAGE AGE AT SEPARATION	AVERAGE DIFFERENCE IN EDUCATIONAL ADVANTAGES ON 10-POINT RATING SCALE	AVERAGE SUPERIORITY IN IQ POINTS OF TWIN WITH GREATER ADVANTAGE
6	15 months	Very unequal (5.1 average difference)	15.2
7	9 months	Somewhat unequal (2.4 average difference)	4.6
6	24 months	Relatively similar (1.6 average difference)	1.0

The clearest way to see the relationship between heredity and environment is to consider that heredity provides a capacity for a *wide range* of different behaviors which may then be encouraged and sustained by the stimulation of the environment. In psychology, for example, studies demonstrate that intelligence is not tightly determined by genetic factors. Nineteen pairs of identical twins reared apart were studied by Newman, Freeman, and Holzinger (1937). Since hereditary factors are constant for identical twins, any variations in intelligence can be attributed to environmental opportunities. As shown in Table 1.1, the greater the differences in educational advantages, the greater the superiority of twins with the greater advantage, using the IQ as a measure. Thus, intelligence is clearly found to be dependent upon the interrelationship of hereditary capacities and the environmental opportunities and enrichment. Learning is, of course, a central process affecting this outcome. Furthermore, in a society where doing well on some things is more important than doing well on others, the reinforcement provided by social approval, and the availability of relevant resources, make it more likely that those kinds of performance of the first, or valued, sort will out-run those of the latter, or less valued sort. As Gardner (1961) has put it:

> The virtues which flower in any society are the virtues that the society nourishes. The qualities of mind and character which stamp a people are the qualities that people honor, the qualities they celebrate, the qualities they recognize instantly and respect profoundly (p. 151).

Social interaction and social influence

Thus we come to the essential point that social behavior depends upon the influence of others. A key to this process rests in social interaction. If social behavior may be said to be a response to social stimulation from others, including the symbols that they transmit, then social interaction may be thought of as a sequence of such stimulus-response relationships. One person's behavior is the stimulus for the other's response and, sequentially, that response then becomes the stimulus for the first person's following response as shown schematically in Figure 1.2. Regularized interactions of this kind are the basis for many of the influence events within societies.

Whether we speak in terms of conformity to group norms, attitude change as a result of communication, or leader-follower relationships, all represent features of influence process. Moreover, that process is usually a result of social interaction, referring to those interdependent relationships we have with others from which we acquire our modes of behaving and our outlook on the world as represented in attitudes and values.

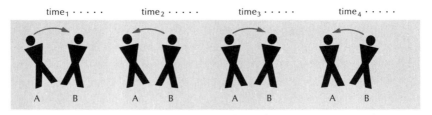

Figure 1.2: Diagrammatic representation of reciprocal quality of social interaction over time for two persons, A and B.

To what degree can individuals affect or influence one another through social interaction? There are of course limits set by biological factors. Men cannot fly like birds, however much they may be persuaded to do so. But the physiology of the individual can be affected by social factors. Most members of our society, even though hungry, will not readily eat socially disapproved foods—e.g. grasshoppers, whale blubber, or lamb's eyes—though other people consider them delicacies within their cultures. Indeed, the discomfort from eating them may result in illness and vomiting. The writer witnessed a graphic instance of this effect when several people at a party became ill after learning that the "delicious hors d'oeuvres" the hostess had just served were made of rattlesnake meat.

In a recent experiment, Schachter and Singer (1962) have shown that when subjects were given a drug without being aware of its effects, they were highly susceptible to emotional reactions parallel to those of another person there. Whether that person was instructed to behave in an angry or giddy way, there was a high rate of matching behavior by the subjects. Furthermore, the subjects tended to label their "feelings" in line with the other person's action pattern.

Many of the disorders we think of as being "psychosomatic" derive from social interaction. The actions of other people can make us laugh or cry, and feel pains of anguish. The person who is unhappy with his relationships, at work or at home, can develop quite real physical symptoms, such as a stomach ulcer or even a heart attack. In good part, this is evidence of Man's capacity to symbolize and to react internally to anticipated threats by unseen, but nonetheless significant physiological changes.

There are many other effects of social interaction upon the perception, motivation, and especially the learning and adjustment of the individual. These begin early in life as a neophyte in a particular society develops relationships with others. In infancy, it is clear that there is the necessity to obtain satisfaction for fundamental biological needs, the primary motives necessary to maintain life. But it is also true that the nature of Man's condition is essentially social. Therefore, it is not only that physical survival depends upon others but that others stimulate in us those qualities regarded as "human." Because the kinds of distinctly human behaviors learned may differ with varying cultures in terms of language, marriage, economic practices, art, religion, the use of techniques, tools, and other social artifacts, we are all subject to insistent social influences to learn some things very well and others not at all.

Variables of study in social psychology

In studying social influence, social psychology focuses on the relationship between particular kinds of *variables*. A variable is an attribute or condition which can vary in one or more ways and which can be systematically shown to affect or be affected by other attributes or conditions—hence the use of the qualifying terms "independent" and "dependent." In the case of theories, relationships are postulated between variables which can then be tested by research. This gives us a basis for their verification. Also, in the very act of testing theories, we gain by the necessity to specify variables clearly and measure them with care. This in itself contributes to understanding.

Perhaps the most widely studied variable in social psychology is the concept of *attitude*. A long history of work has been directed toward the investigation of attitudes, their sources and their effects on social behavior. Essentially, attitudes are perceptions about persons, things, or events in the environment. They also have motivational qualities insofar as they direct behavior. The most vital consideration in defining attitudes is the way in which they "set" the individual to view and respond to the world in certain ways. Studying attitudes is most useful since they help to account for individual differences in reacting to a given situation. In large measure, they conveniently sum up the past history of the individual's social experience to allow differential predictability of individual social behavior. In that sense, then, they are an important part of our personal orientation to the world, the "psychological field" which shapes distinctive reactions to social stimulation.

Associated with the concept of attitude in social psychology is the variable termed *values*. Fundamentally, values represent long-range motives which lead the individual to persist in choosing certain goals over others. As with most variables with which we deal in social psychology, they are learned as a consequence of exposure to others who hold these values. Furthermore they frequently underlie attitudes. Values have substantial directive force in human experience. Men die for values such as "duty," "freedom," and "honor."

Another variable is *group cohesiveness,* which essentially refers to the degree to which members of a group find it attractive. In terms of the specifics of deeper social psychological analysis, this attraction can be thought of as reflecting motivation to belong. And, in turn, this motivation to belong could be determined by several other factors or variables. This illustration points up a fact we shall be considering further in Chapter Three: when dealing with phenomena of social behavior, it is frequently the case that variables can be *either* dependent or independent and are not fixed permanently as one or the other with regard to the direction of effect. Thus, cohesiveness in a group may be an outcome of certain other processes, or it may be looked at as a factor producing certain outcomes.

A different kind of variable in social psychology is represented in *roles*, which refer mainly to a variation of quality rather than quantity. In essence roles are the different behaviors which we display in connection with a given social position we occupy; accordingly, there are behaviors associated with the role of mother, with the role of policeman, with the role of teacher, or with the role of employer. All of us have a multiplicity of roles which we must fill in the course of our daily lives. Indeed, in any one day we may be obliged to fit into a wide range of roles including several in the family circle alone. Roles are behaviors. Yet they have considerable *psychological* significance as is revealed by the social expectation in the co-ed's response to her boyfriend's ardor —"Let me be a sister to you." On the psychological level, then, roles can be defined as our perception of the expectations of others, which we shall be referring to as "social expectancies."

Expectancies play a part in another variable in social psychology that varies qualitatively—*norms*. Where there are general behaviors, including approved attitudes, which are socially prescribed in a given situation, we may speak of a norm, or sometimes a "social norm" or a "group norm." This mainly means a standard of conduct, but it also conveys the sense of matching behaviors to the expectations of others in that situation. Notice that both roles and norms necessarily involve a process of person perception. A study of that particular psychological process, therefore, gives us a good deal of leverage in understanding influence relationships producing social behavior.

A particularly important variable of study today is embodied in the concept of *reference groups*. This too has properties of a qualitative variable in terms of the different "psychological affiliations" a person may have with groups even apart from actual membership. It may also vary quantitatively in terms of the strength of affiliation or motivation to belong. While it was common in the past to consider individuals to be directly affected by groups to which they belonged, it was found that this did not account for many variations of effect. People might apparently be members of a group, in some descriptive sense. Yet a more analytic probing of the psychological significance of group membership revealed that they might or might not be motivated, in a psychological sense, to accept this group's standard of conduct or outlook. Furthermore, it became evident that even where an individual did *not* literally belong to a group he might be affected by it. In a socially mobile society, aspirations for achievement tend to encourage this identification process, and reference groups therefore represent those aspirations which may have high value.

Simply noting group membership is therefore not enough; we must also know whether the individual actually "refers" himself to a group, by using it as a standard for conduct, as a basis for evaluation, or as a source of attitudes. For the social psychologist, this raises the question of whether the person is motivated to retain identification with a group or reacts instead to a standard held by another group to which he aspires to belong. Herein lies one of the crucial points of study regarding social behavior, the *psychological meaning of group affiliation*. It represents a dominant theme about which we will have a great deal more to consider in subsequent chapters, especially in Chapters Twelve and Thirteen.

In the next chapter we will consider the historical traditions leading to contemporary social psychology, and then consider the interrelationship of theory and research methods in Chapter Three.

SUMMARY

Social psychology is one of a number of fields concerned with the objective study of human behavior. Its particular focus is upon understanding *social behavior* exemplified in the effect of one individual, or a group, upon another individual, whether in an actual or implied sense. Based on *social influence process*, these effects produce phenomena such as conformity, leadership, prejudice, morale, and inter-group conflict.

While people are interested generally in social behavior, social psychology seeks to achieve an understanding of its underlying causes through objective study and the use of scientific methods. A crucial step in social psychology is to frame the right kinds of questions about these phenomena.

A distinctive quality of social psychology rests in its emphasis on the *individual* in society. It employs psychological concepts and psychological processes to account for social influence. It therefore takes account of individual perceptions, motivations, and learning in understanding the dynamics of human relationships. Social psychology is also aware of the context of society and culture, in the sense of the other people in the social environment and their way of life. It goes beyond the confined view of any one culture regarding "human nature," to a broader conception of Man's capacities for adaptation to the diversity of cultural demands. It also recognizes the faultiness of generalizations regarding genetics and race, especially when applied to social behavior.

Social psychology emphasizes neither hereditary nor environmental determinants of social behavior but rather looks upon them as interdependent influences. Thus, the fact that many behaviors are assumed to be hereditary, when seen for example in a common family pattern, is recognized to be an incorrect inference which slights environmental effects.

Social psychology views *social interaction* as the core of social influence phenomena. Social interaction is essential to survival in early life, and to the development of characteristics which are distinctively "human" such as the learning of language. It can affect not only the overt behavior of the individual but his physiological states as well. Thus, we often find the cause of "psychosomatic" disorders in the stresses of social interaction.

In studying social influence, social psychology attends to the relationship between variables such as attitudes, values, group cohesiveness, roles, norms, and reference groups. Its research activity is aimed at verifying the effects of these upon one another as postulated in theories.

SUGGESTED READINGS

From E. P. Hollander and R. G. Hunt. (Eds.) *Current perspectives in social psychology.* (2nd Edition.) New York: Oxford University Press, 1967:

Introduction to Section I: *Basic issues and processes*
1. Robert B. Zajonc: *Social facilitation*
2. Solomon Asch: *The data of social psychology*
3. Roger G. Barker: *On the nature of the environment*
4. Jerome S. Bruner: *On perceptual readiness*

SELECTED REFERENCES

*Benedict, Ruth. *Patterns of culture.* New York: Penguin Books, 1946.
*Dunn, L. C. & Dobzhansky, T. *Heredity, race and society.* (Rev. ed.) New York: New American Library, 1952.
Lindzey, G. & Aronson, E. (Eds.) *Handbook of social psychology.* (Rev. ed.) Cambridge: Addison-Wesley, 1967.
*Mead, Margaret. *Male and female.* New York: Morrow, 1949.
*Montagu, A. *Human heredity.* New York: New American Library, Mentor Book, 1960.

  * All books thus indicated, here and in subsequent chapters, are available in paperback editions.

2

Historical and modern approaches to social behavior

Any study of human affairs carries a guiding image of Man. The assumptions underlying this image are often "tinged with the coloring of some secret, imaginative background," as Whitehead put it.

Though philosophers and other thinkers have been preoccupied with the sources of social behavior since ancient times, they have all too frequently been handicapped by their own assumptions. In approaching the modern field of social psychology, it is useful to examine the backdrop of these ideas to be aware of the legacy they have left.

Three stages in the study of social behavior

There have been three distinct stages in achieving knowledge about social behavior (see Figure 2.1). Each has added to the succeeding one so that today all are embodied in contemporary work. The oldest is *social philosophy*, which has its origins in antiquity. It is characterized by conjecture and speculation, usually in the absence of any systematic gathering of factual information, since it is most often based on authority or reason alone. The method of "rationalism" in earlier scientific efforts exemplifies one characteristic of the traditional philosophical approach, that is, reliance on the power of thought apart from testable data.

The next stage, beginning in the nineteenth century, is termed *social empiricism*. It represents the advance toward a fuller description of human attributes and the conditions of human society. In general, it is characterized by systematic data-gathering which goes beyond conjecture, though of course it may be and often is guided by it. A current example of social empiricism is seen in simple polling procedures aimed at indicating *how many* people intend to vote one way or another, without probing for the "why" of that intent.

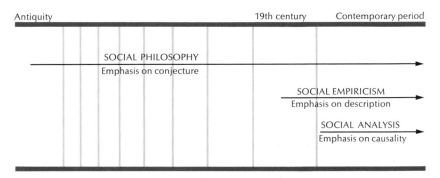

Figure 2.1: Stages in the emergence of three approaches to the study of social behavior represented in the contemporary period.

Social empiricism provides the basis for the next stage, *social analysis,* which is a twentieth-century development and the dominant emphasis in contemporary social psychology. It signifies a more penetrating study of underlying relationships aimed at testing and establishing theory. While the word "analysis" can mean several things, including some which apply to philosophy, we specifically intend to signify the search for causal relationships through the study of data gathered by systematic empirical research. The major feature of this approach is to go beyond simple descriptive data to the level of verifying relationships between variables; this quest frequently involves experimentation aimed at determining the validity of relationships postulated by theories.

Latter-day forms of social philosophy and social empiricism are still with us offering contending views usually devoid of procedures for verification. We see this in many reaches of life where a simple finding is generalized out of proportion to its validity. Such claims to being scientific must necessarily be viewed in the context of standards embodied in modern social analysis.

The backdrop of social philosophy

A central theme in social thought, as we noted in Chapter One, is seen
in the critical and long-standing heredity-environment controversy,
sometimes stated in terms of "nature-nurture." Two kinds of questions
flow from this dichotomy. The first rests fundamentally on the issue of
what mankind in general brings into the world as distinctive human
characteristics. This represents the vital core of the "human nature"
issue. The second question concerns the expansion of this issue to
whether these characteristics are "good" or "bad."

Classic responses to the question of the qualities of human nature,
and of the necessary conditions of human society, tended to share
several failings in common. First, readily generalizing about observed
behaviors in one society they applied the "human nature" fallacy to
mankind in general; second, they distilled out of the richness of human
relationships an all-embracing explanation for every facet of life, rooted
in some one factor, e.g. power, self-interest, imitation, and pleasure;
third, they emphasized a static view of Man devoid of any adequate
accounting of his great potential for *learning* and for *changing* in the
face of new experience. The tradition of "instinct" theories, the major
thrust of which lies in imputing an inborn tendency to all humans, illustrates all of these failings. In this section we propose to consider five
such viewpoints, each within its own social context.

INSTINCTUAL VIEWS IN GENERAL

Regarding the primary issue of "nature or nurture," the Greek philosophers Aristotle and Plato are often compared for their different though
not entirely opposite responses. They were not, however, the first to
consider this fundamental issue which is a feature within the Babylonian Code of Hammurabi dating from before 2000 B.C. Aristotle was
nonetheless a leading exponent of the view that Man's behavior was the
result of an instinctual nature, while in Plato's view Man was seen to
be more subject to the effects of organized society. In this respect,

Plato suggested various social innovations, including the reign of "philosopher kings," in order to render changes in human behavior in his idealized society. He also considered Man's relationship to society to be a "contract" in which Man received certain benefits by behaving within the regularities of an organized society. Plato thus signified his reliance on the social effects of learning, though he was interested as well in individual differences in capacity.

As to the "goodness" or "badness" of Man's inherent nature, many controversies have raged over the centuries. Perhaps best known as a spokesman for a dour view of Man, though by no means alone in his stand, was Thomas Hobbes, who lived in the seventeenth century and is known particularly for his social commentary, *The Leviathan*. Man, devoid of a regulated society, in Hobbes's memorable words, was given to a life that was "solitary, poor, nasty, brutish, and short." Among his other views which made a persisting impression was his advocacy of the pleasure-pain principle which held that Man would inherently seek pleasure and avoid pain. This idea, later elaborated by Jeremy Bentham and the utilitarians, also found its way into twentieth-century thought in the theories of Sigmund Freud.

In the eighteenth-century Age of Reason, Hobbes's views, which had gained wide adherence, came under assault from Jean-Jacques Rousseau, and such thinkers as Kant, Diderot, Goethe, and Condorcet. Man was innately good, they said; but society spoiled this "noble savage" and developed malevolent characteristics in him; there was no innate "badness" to Man's nature.

Followers of Hobbes and his later disciples scorned the "noble savage" concept, referred to its proponents as "the Romantics," and provided a resounding theme still echoed in political debates. The Hobbesians asserted that theirs was the "realistic" view of Man and in this they were abetted by the prevailing philosophy that accompanied the approaching Industrial Revolution. The nineteenth century produced an atmosphere that heavily favored the doctrine of justifiable dominance by some humans over others and fitted the insistent trends of "Darwinian" thought to which we shall be turning shortly.

There is of course no one answer to the complex question of whether Man is "good" or "bad." The terms themselves can be relative and often depend upon cultural standards. However, with broad regard to life-sustaining or life-denying tendencies, the history of mankind, including

recent times, affords evidence of both extremes. Given human susceptibility to the forces in the social environment, the best response seems
to be that Man has the capacity for extremes of high morality and
conscience as well as for the basest forms of degradation in his treatment of fellow Man.

On the positive side, the mere existence of organized societies indicates the presence of widespread co-operation and of trust in the essential good will to be expected and received from others. Moreover, individual men often show limitless efforts of a humanitarian and altruis-
tic kind. It is not merely a cliché but a fact of daily existence that people usually trust others and think that most other people are decent. In
1964 a survey conducted by the National Opinion Research Center
found that 77 per cent of a nationwide sample responded affirmatively
to the question, "Do you think that most people can be trusted?" In
1948 the figure had been 66 per cent (*Trans-action,* 1966).

On the negative side, however, Man as a species is the only one
known to maintain organized efforts to kill and otherwise harm its
members. Animals and insects engage in combat, but largely in un-
organized and reactive ways, when provoked (Lorenz, 1966). Human
history is written with the bloody pen of calamitous wars, including
the relatively recent spectacle of the organized brutalities and agonies
of death camps. Conquests, repressions, slavery, and other atrocities
and iniquitous social practices are still woven into the fabric of human
life.

There are abundant signs, then, of both extremes without undue
searching, so we must conclude that in general mankind has the capacity to be moved in either direction, providing sufficient environmental support. The implications of this for war were recently summed
up by a group of psychiatrists as follows:

> In the course of human history, deep-seated stereotypes have
> evolved around war that not only play a role in serving human
> needs, but also constitute an important psychological barrier to its
> elimination. The educational systems of all nations teach that war
> is right and proper under certain circumstances. War's destructive-
> ness and violence are sanctioned in the name of a greater good for
> the group, and thus what the individual might view as wrong or
> immoral becomes, by group sanction, not only right but supremely
> right. . . . War is glorified as brave, just, righteous, and honorable.
> . . . However, such a conversion from the "peacetime ethic" of

"love thy neighbor" to a "war ethic" that sanctions mass killing requires special training, indoctrination, and propaganda (Group for the Advancement of Psychiatry, 1964, pp. 233-234).

HEDONISM AND "ECONOMIC MAN"

Associated with the pleasure-pain principle was the doctrine of "psychological hedonism" or self-gratification, whose major proponent in the nineteenth century was Jeremy Bentham. In his view, Man searched for gain at the expense of others. Taking this viewpoint literally there would be no room for altruism, since the advocates of this doctrine looked upon altruism as another form of self-satisfying activity. Indeed, though Bentham did not see Man as an irresponsible member of society, but rather as one who practiced what he called "ethical hedonism" too, his viewpoint could make *any* act seem self-serving, as can be easily pointed out.

Put in simple logical terms, the prime failing of hedonism rests in the consideration that it provides for no alternative predictions about human behavior since it is predicated on the dual assumption that whether a person does a thing, or does *not* do the thing, the motivation is the same, i.e. self-gratification. This amounts to an "if A, then B: if not A, then B" proposition. It tells us nothing about how we might differentiate the two opposite outcomes. To say that the captain of industry who hoards his money is motivated in the identical way as the one who gives large sums to philanthropy, is to reach a logical absurdity and to provide no basis whatever for the differential prediction of behavior or an understanding of why it occurs.

Like the pleasure-pain principle with which it is linked, the doctrine of hedonism omits the range of social psychological relationships which may act on an individual to direct his behavior in one as opposed to another channel. Furthermore, it operates on one shaky premise which was fondly cherished as the basis for Adam Smith's eighteenth-century economic theory; that is, that individuals are continually alert to what is in their best interest regarding the return of gain or profit. Whatever the promise of a thoroughly rational view of Man's relationships, this was an untenable premise. Utter rationality in the marketplace, as a useful basis for explaining economic behavior, remains a shaky concept. In a comparable sense, the general utility of a simple hedonistic explanation for predicting and understanding social behavior is doubtful.

"SURVIVAL OF THE FITTEST": SOCIAL DARWINISM

Among the landmarks in the development of contemporary social sci-ence is the pronounced influence of the work of Charles Darwin. His theory of evolution, published in *Origin of Species* in 1859, altered the course of thinking and stimulated others such as Herbert Spencer and Karl Marx to apply his laws of natural selection to the development and course of society. His evolutionary viewpoint played a decisive part in shaping social theory. The "class struggle" element in Marxian ideology owes its origin in some measure to the "Social Darwinism" to which Marx was favorably disposed.

Laying overwhelming stress on the competitive rather than the co-operative aspects of life, Darwin attributed a natural aggressiveness to Man, hence the so-called "struggle." Yet he did recognize that apart from just natural selection there were social effects on Man's moral qualities. The concept of social transmission of cultural influences was therefore not foreign to his thinking. Darwin's popularized doctrine of natural selection had been construed largely in terms of physical evo-lution, despite the fact that he himself, in *The Descent of Man* (1871), emphasized his belief in moral and social evolution through social and cultural factors. Nevertheless, Social Darwinism, as developed by his disciples, led to an emphasis on "struggle for existence" in terms of con-flict between individuals and groups rather than with the environment.

It is clear that Darwin himself did not intend to suggest that this "struggle" necessarily meant a conflict between individuals. Indeed, he saw the "survival value" inherent in social practices such as co-opera-tion and interdependence. In *Origin of Species* he had said: ". . . I use this term [struggle for existence] in a large and metaphorical sense including dependence of one being upon another, and including (which is more important) not only the life of the individual, but success in leaving progeny" (Ch. 3, p. 62).

Followers of Darwin, such as Herbert Spencer, who had advanced his own evolutionary ideas in an 1852 paper anticipating Darwin's view-point, employed the "Darwinian" view to argue for the superiority of some groups and the inferiority of others, and thus justified war, colo-nialism, business ethics, and other social practices featuring implicit competition or conflict. Many nineteenth-century thinkers, concluding that human nature itself differed racially, ethnically, nationally, and between social classes, saw this as a function of biological factors determined by the evolutionary processes of natural selection. Montagu (1956) says that the concepts of "struggle for existence" and "survival of the fittest" led many distinguished intellectual leaders of the time to the persuasion that the bondage of "the lower classes" and the exploitation of the lands of "inferior" people were not only biologically justifiable but the clear judgment of Nature (p. 27). Though unsubstantiated, the consequences of such views linger today in many forms, especially in terms of an alleged "competitiveness" as a universal feature of human relationships.

INNATE AGGRESSIVENESS: FREUDIAN PSYCHOLOGY

A belief in Man's innate aggressiveness was central to the theories of Sigmund Freud, who grew up in the intellectual atmosphere of the Darwinian age. His towering conceptions, notably surrounding the effects of early experience and processes of the unconscious mind, stand with those of Darwin as significant landmarks in intellectual thought. That he made unparalleled contributions to the psychology of the individual is unquestioned. Along with these, however, he fostered an instinctual view of Man which led him to a conception of society as a hostile force imposed on Man's instinctual impulses which then produced frustration and repression in him. Furthermore, he postulated the existence of a "death wish" or "death instinct" which has found no substantive support in contemporary science.

With regard to sexual expression, Freud contended that society set restrictions on such impulses in the form of incest taboos and monogamy. The instinct of aggression, and the sexual drive which he saw on a par with it, had to be controlled for society to exist and these became absorbed and recast in terms of "character traits." He did not, however, treat these so much as outcomes of social experience, i.e. the restriction of one's impulses, as factors innate in themselves.

Withal the Freudian viewpoint, while influential on other grounds, added little to an understanding of Man's place in society. There are several reasons for this. First, along with others, Freud's views tended to be tightly bounded by his own subjective observations, mainly in a single society, and therefore were not generalizable to the broader world; second, he too readily accepted observed aggressiveness in Man as proof of its innateness when it might more readily be seen to develop as a consequence of certain social patterns; third, he emphasized Man's impulsiveness and irrationality thus underrating Man's rationality and his associated abilities to communicate and to share in a culture.

IMITATION AND THE "GROUP MIND"

A century ago Auguste Comte posed the paradox of how Man could at one and the same time *shape* society and yet *be shaped* by it. Often called the father of modern social science, Comte revealed in this statement a critical question surrounding the interrelation of Man and society: the way to reconcile the individual and social qualities of Man's life and experience. One answer to it was developed as a quite distinctive French school of thought during the latter part of the nineteenth century. Its explanation was simple: in groups or crowds, persons were influenced by a "group mind" which reduced their individual autonomy; with this went the notion of *imitation* as the essential vehicle by which Man was influenced by others in his society.

The most significant figure in this movement was Gustave LeBon, best known for his work *The Crowd* (1896) in which he presented this formulation:

> The most striking peculiarity presented by a psychological crowd is the following: Whoever be the individuals that comprise it, however like or unlike be their mode of life, their occupations, their character, or their intelligence, the fact that they have been transformed into a crowd puts them in possession of a sort of collective mind which makes them feel, think, and act in a manner quite different from that in which each individual of them would deal, think, and act were he in a state of isolation (p. 27).

Earlier LeBon had postulated that Man has a natural tendency to imitate. Imitation, he said, was a social necessity which could be observed in the powerful influence of fashion. This viewpoint was elaborated by the other notable figure of the French school, Tarde, in his book *The Laws of Imitation* (1890). Historically, both Tarde and LeBon were influenced by the "principle of suggestion" which grew out of Charcot's then current work on hypnosis. To their view, crowd behavior, which they often used interchangeably with the term "group behavior," was a reflection of the suggestibility found in persons who had been hypnotized.

Neither of the two key propositions in the views of the LeBon-Tarde school of thought—that Man had a natural propensity toward imitation, and that this operated through the presence of a group mind when individuals were together collectively—has any scientific standing today. However, their consequences remain in force. There are still those who mistakenly think of social psychology as the study of crowds and the group mind.

But why was the group-mind thesis put forward by men of acknowledged intellectual stature? Answering this in his discussion of the emergence of social psychology, Asch (1959) says that the conception of a group mind was a way of taking account of Man's social nature, and adds:

> It started with a serious problem—with the clarification of group characteristics and group membership. It had its roots in a formulation by no means strange today, namely, that one cannot understand an individual by studying him solely as an individual; one must see him in his group relations (p. 369).

Newcomb (1951) has pointed out that what the group-mind concept was intended to cover is better understood in terms of self-other perceptions as shared norms. In this respect, he says that a great shortcoming of this older viewpoint was that it "had nothing to say about the conditions under which such sharing took place" (p. 40). Where the individual gets caught up in a group or crowd, what happens, according to Newcomb, is that "what the individual wants to do and what he perceives as demanded by his role come to be identical . . . for once in his life others expect him to be exactly what he wants to be. His world of social reality perceives him precisely as he perceives himself" (p. 44). This view provides a way of putting aside the mysticism which for so long has tended to surround the conceptions of group and crowd behavior and see it in terms of systematic relationships.

And now what of the related matter of imitation? It too has proceeded through a line of continuity to the present day. In one of the first two major textbooks in social psychology, E. A. Ross (1908) used the imitation-suggestion tradition as a key principle for his work. In the other text of that same year, William McDougall presented a social psychology built on the concept of instinct, adding a forerunner of the attitude construct of today, his conception of "sentiments."

Though Ross, a sociologist by orientation, insisted upon imitation as a widespread social phenomenon, McDougall from a psychological vantage point rejected any such reliance on imitation. Indeed, even within his commitment to an instinct orientation, McDougall plainly stated that an instinct of imitation does *not* exist because, as he put it:

> Imitative actions are extremely varied, for every kind of action may be imitated; there is therefore nothing specific in the nature of the imitative movements and in the nature of the sense-impressions by which the movements are excited or guided . . . most important is the fact that underlying the varieties of imitative action, there is no common affective state and no impulse-seeking satisfaction in some particular change of state . . . further, if we consider the principal varieties of imitative action, we find that all are explicable without the assumption of a special instinct of imitation (1908, pp. 106-107).

Nonetheless, in one of his later works entitled *The Group Mind* (1920), McDougall offered the view that an important effect of groups is the "exaltation or intensification of emotion" which they produce in their members. He went on to say that those of lower intelligence bring members of higher intelligence down to their own level. This viewpoint has found little support from subsequent study.

So far as is presently known, there is no generalized tendency toward imitation as a social influence process. To the contrary, the evidence suggests that imitation is selective in terms of whom we imitate and what we imitate (see Bandura and Walters, 1963). In his critique of the doctrine of imitation, Newcomb (1950) has pointed out that no child imitates indiscriminately and that many a parent laments the fact that his child utterly fails to imitate the "correct" models set before him. Furthermore, he goes on, no individual acquires a completely conforming response to all of the "standard" behaviors of his society. Moreover, fads and fashions may appear to be good illustrations of widespread imitation, yet many fads simply fail to catch on or are short-lived, and only a few become incorporated in the culture. Finally, Newcomb concludes:

> There is a considerable body of experimental evidence indicating that imitation presupposes a process of learning . . . imitation, in

fact, is subject to the same range of conditions which are known to determine the many variations of learned behavior. People imitate or do not imitate, depending upon what they have learned, are capable of learning and are motivated to learn. It is this fact, probably, which accounts for the highly variable conditions under which imitation occurs (p. 11).

Thus, the concept of imitation fails on the grounds that it is overly general and neglects the important features of learning that arise from individual motivation and perception. It is these, as we shall be pointing out further, which provide a necessary foundation for an understanding of Man's social relationships. Equally unsatisfactory was the general doctrine of instinct which eventually had to give way to a more penetrating view of Man's propensities for learning within a social environment.

Social empiricism

Until the nineteenth century it was quite unusual to find systematic efforts to obtain information concerning the conditions of human life and Man's experience. The Darwinian revolution, among other forces, did however instigate several developments in this vein.

GALTON AND THE GENETICS OF MENTAL DIFFERENCES

Francis Galton, who was much taken by Darwin's views of natural selection, conducted an investigation directed especially at the genetic transmission of genius by tracing the genealogy of families whose members gained great prominence. His *Hereditary Genius,* originally published in 1869, is among his best known efforts. In some sense, Galton may be credited with the development of the study of individual mental differences, although he was inclined to a narrow focus which omitted the favorable environmental factors in the lives of his subjects. Nonetheless, Gardner Murphy (1949) has stressed that "Francis Galton grasped the implications of the evolutionary outlook for psychology and made his ingenious experimental contributions to this area of research" (p. 353).

BINET AND INTELLIGENCE TESTING

In France, during the 1890's, Alfred Binet began his attempts to develop measures of human intelligence. Working with Simon, he took as his immediate task the matter of detecting and measuring mental defects. While their eventual test of 1905 had failings, particularly in terms of standardization and the fact that some of the sub-tests were harder and others easier than they supposed, this opened the intelligence test movement and provided the forerunner of the modern IQ test. Terman's 1916 "Stanford revision," an American version, is with us even today in still more refined form known as the Stanford-Binet test. While this work said little about social effects on intelligence and could not specify the processes which produced it, it stands as a landmark in social empiricism. It provided a descriptive measure of a human characteristic and led to a fuller understanding of differentials and similarities among men.

Other works reported in 1903 and 1905 by two Americans, Kelly and Norsworthy, paralleled the Binet-Simon work. They gave sensory and motor tasks to feeble-minded children and normal children to measure ranges of performance. Though the feeble-minded youngsters tended to do distinctively less well than normal children, there was a fairly even transition from the lowest to the highest scores across both groups. "In Norsworthy's language, the feeble-minded were not a 'species'; the most intelligent of the feeble-minded could not be sharply distinguished from the least intelligent of the normal" (Murphy, 1949, p. 354). The significance of this early empirical work was of inestimable importance in terms of what it revealed about the faultiness of assumptions concerning "superior" versus "inferior" levels within the human species. Furthermore, as Gardner (1961) has observed, broad-scale use of objective intelligence tests made it clear that rich resources of intellectual capacity existed at every level of the socio-economic ladder.

COMTE AND DURKHEIM: SOCIOLOGICAL BEGINNINGS

Auguste Comte is perhaps best known for his comprehensive philosophy of the sciences, *Positive Philosophy* (1830). Among his important conceptions was the recognition that the individual develops his mental processes only through society and that he must always be considered in terms of his social setting. In contrast to other thinkers of his time, he also furthered a view of Man as a reasoning being. He urged a positivist approach in the scientific study of Man which represented a significant underpinning for the empirical movement.

Emile Durkheim gave further impetus to the interrelated developments of theory and research on social behavior. His general aim was to make sociology an empirical study, and his contributions to the methodology of the social sciences were of seminal importance. True to the positivist position, Durkheim insisted that for an empirical treatment of social data it is necessary to have "social facts." He rebelled against the rationalistic approach which had characterized so much of the work of other social thinkers.

In his doctoral thesis, *Division of Labor* (1893), Durkheim had cited the increased suicide rate in the nineteenth century as an argument against the rational emphasis of the utilitarians. Following up with his famous study *Suicide* (1897), he combined statistical description and theoretical constructs to isolate factors operating to produce suicide. Durkheim cited statistics from political, religious, and family life to support his analysis, and demonstrated, for example, that the suicide rate bore a significant relationship to marital and parental status. Married persons had a lower rate than single persons and parents had a lower rate than childless couples, with the parents in large families having the lowest rate of all. He interpreted these results as demonstrating the strong preservative power of group attachments. Apart from the empirical features of this work, Durkheim employed the concept of a "collective mind" to further his view that the individual has no existence except as a member of society. While he openly rejected the psychological level of analysis as a basis for understanding social phenomena, Durkheim nonetheless opened an avenue for the study of how social influences produced effects on "individual" features of human existence. His contribution to modern sociology is of redounding significance.

OTHER EMPIRICAL DEVELOPMENTS

Two other trends reflecting social empiricism are represented by the tradition of "demography" and in the field work of anthropologists describing pre-literate cultures. Both of these involve descriptions of human attributes and the conditions of life.

Demography is the study of population characteristics including numbers of people and their distribution geographically. Its recognized areas of concern have been birth rate, death rate, and migration. Today demography constitutes a distinctive area within sociology, and is perhaps best known to the public in terms of the population census. The first national census in the United States was conducted in 1790, and since then it has been continued on a total population basis every ten years. The modern census reflects the highly diversified quality of demography today by its wider concern with many facets of human society, beyond population size and movement, such as marriage and divorce, education, employment, income, and standard of living. These and many other characteristics of the population by area and locale provide a rich pool of descriptive data about significant aspects of the human condition.

The tradition of field expeditions in anthropology, coming down from Edward Tylor in the last century, and of Bronislaw Malinowski and Franz Boas in this, also reveals a great deal about the diversity of human life. Under the guidance of George P. Murdock, the massive array of data accumulated on the cultures of the world, and on their patterns, has been codified in the form of the Yale Human Relations Area Files. Use of these materials affords a significant link to social analysis by strengthening our understanding of general patterns of life and by revealing the weakness of glib assumptions about human nature.

Social analysis

If the tradition of social empiricism can be said to provide a description of human characteristics and attributes, then social analysis represents its extension toward establishing a scientifically valid foundation for what is described. In probing beneath the descriptive data to understand the nature of causal relationships, social analysis gets closer to social processes, including those of change, by taking account of the factors which interrelate to produce social behavior.

THE BEHAVIORAL SCIENCES

In the contemporary scene, the use of social analysis is characteristic of what have come to be called the "behavioral sciences." These are psychology, sociology, cultural anthropology, and to some extent political science and economics. The term "behavioral science" is a relatively new one in our vocabulary. We can describe it in one sense as a body of knowledge regarding certain describable conditions in the human being and/or his environment which lead to certain describable consequences in his actions, and in another sense as techniques or methodologies which typify the study of conditions leading to these consequences. A very comprehensive coverage of work in the behavioral sciences is provided in the recent book by Berelson and Steiner (1964) entitled *Human Behavior: An Inventory of Scientific Findings.*

LEVELS OF ANALYSIS

All of the behavioral sciences are to some degree concerned with social behavior, though they approach it at different levels and in terms of the specifics of varying social institutions. By levels, we means the essential unit for study. In the case of psychology, it is clear that the individual is the prime focus of attention. The psychologist is concerned with the differences as well as with the commonality in human behavior. The fact that some psychologists may also study animal behavior reflects a comparative approach which ultimately can have implications for humans. Sociology tends to be interested in behavior at the level of groups and organizations or social institutions; though these are comprised of individuals, the major thrust of study tends to be on the nature of social-structural features as they affect social behavior, for example, in terms of social class or the structure of organizations. Cultural anthropologists, sometimes called ethnologists, direct their attention to the cultural or societal level of analysis as do some sociologists. In the case of political science and economics, the study of social behavior is conducted within the context of political and economic social institutions. In fact, however, there is currently less separation between these disciplines because of an increasing adoption of a social psychological framework for analysis.

A SOCIAL PSYCHOLOGICAL FRAMEWORK

Among the more distinctive trends in the behavioral sciences today is the degree to which they reflect a coming together for purposes of empirical study, very often within a social psychological framework. By this we mean that they employ the variables and techniques which have been found useful in studying the relationship of the individual to his social environment. For example, roles represent describable social practices, in the form of appropriate behaviors; but in terms of underlying individual processes, they also have meaning as psychological expectations. Similarly, organizations may be established according to the structure of a formal organization chart, yet be far more affected by interpersonal relationships determined as well by the personalities of those involved.

Today we can find a good deal of research cutting across disciplinary lines and employing this framework. In the case of voter behavior, for instance, Angus Campbell and a research team composed of social psychologists, sociologists, and political scientists study such matters as the psychological basis of party identification through survey research on presidential elections (cf. *The American Voter*, 1960). S. M. Lipset, by training a sociologist, has been involved in studies of political loyalty and participation (cf. *Political Man*, 1960). Hadley Cantril, a social psychologist, has conducted research on the psychological sub-structure of needs for political affiliation (cf. *The Politics of Despair*, 1958). A psychologist, George Katona, is well known for his extensive research on consumer attitudes of optimism and pessimism as these relate to buying practices (cf. *The Powerful Consumer*, 1960, and *The Mass Consumption Society*, 1964). Furthermore, the physiological correlates of social behavior are being increasingly studied, as is exemplified by the recent volume *Psychobiological Approaches to Social Behavior* edited by Leiderman and Shapiro (1964).

Social analysis in the twentieth century has been shaped by a number of distinctive theoretical contributions which go beyond the tradition of social philosophy to lend themselves more readily to scientific test through research. Accompanying these was a technological advance in measurement procedures and in statistical analysis. Even more dramatic is the computer revolution. Thus, the interrelationship of theory and empirical efforts was established early as a characteristic feature in the evolution of social psychology, and its potential remains considerable. To better understand this trend, we will briefly review several major approaches to social behavior which have had a significant impact on social psychology today.

Forerunners of modern social psychology

In the more than half-century since 1908, when the first two textbooks on social psychology appeared, profound changes have occurred to displace the central theoretical views they presented. As we noted earlier, E. A. Ross writing in a sociological tradition continued to give considerable weight to the imitation-suggestion conception in accounting for social behavior; William McDougall, within a psychological tradition, presented a view heavily flavored with the concept of instincts. Both of these views proved unsatisfactory in themselves, at least partly because of their quality of overstatement. But neither man was so committed to a singular view as to reject other modes of accounting for social behavior. Thus, in association with his thinking, Ross was interested in the interpersonal effects of one person on another, and McDougall— whose book influenced more than a generation of thought through many successive revisions—helped to further the concept of attitude.

The instinct idea had been so overblown, it would have fallen in any case by its own weight. But it was pushed aside in the early 1920's in the wake of the burgeoning "behaviorism." The leader of the behaviorist movement was J. B. Watson who renounced the doctrine of mind, as well as that of instincts, as a basis for psychology. He asserted that the proper study of psychology was behavior and that the task of the psychologist was to determine the relationship between stimuli and responses, the so-called S-R link. His viewpoint was heavily environmentalist insofar as he felt that all behaviors, including social behavior, were learned through experience.

Within the framework of behaviorism, Floyd Allport in 1924 published a text in social psychology in which he emphatically stated that group concepts were unnecessary for explaining individual behavior in groups. To his view, there was no psychology of groups, but only a psychology of individuals. He contended that individuals reacted to group pressures in terms of their own motivations or perceptions and certainly not as a consequence of some "group mind." Yet, he felt that the context of the group, and in general the social situation, had an effect in shaping the motivations and perceptions of individuals and, in this regard, he acknowledged the importance of attitudes. His viewpoint had a profound effect on social psychology at the time and led to a line of systematic experimentation in social psychology.

SOCIAL FACILITATION

It is worth noting that Moede (1920) had previously been carrying out demonstrations at Leipzig on the effect of the presence of other subjects on individual performance in standard psychological tasks. Allport picked up this work as a source for his own experimental work on what came to be called "social facilitation," that is, how one individual's performance was affected by the presence of others. Still another line of experimental work, represented by Goodwin Watson (1928) and Marjorie Shaw (1932), considered whether individuals or groups did better on a task; the findings varied so with the task and situational conditions, that the primary issue was unresolved, though the way was opened for more specific research questions (see Zajonc, 1965).

ATTITUDE MEASUREMENT

In this period, the measurement of attitudes also gained a footing through the work on "social distance" by the sociologist, E. S. Bogardus (1925), and the attitude-scaling technique developed by the psychologist, L. L. Thurstone. This topic is considered more fully in Chapter Six.

By "social distance" Bogardus meant the degree to which a person would be willing to admit a person of a given group to more immediate contact with him, e.g. from "admit to my country" to "admit to marriage in my family." Today this work finds its extension in scaling procedures which determine a person's position on a continuum, usually of approval or disapproval, as in the Guttman scale. Thurstone's work encouraged the development of attitude scales which involved "weighting" attitudinal items on favorability. Illustrating this, Thurstone and Chave (1929) constructed a scale of attitudes toward religion which included items ranging from "high" to "low" favorability.

In the early 1930's attitude research was further facilitated through the development by Rensis Likert of a simpler form of attitude scaling which is still widely utilized today. All of these procedures relied on the advances in statistical methods which were becoming available at the time. These gave greater impetus to the use of subtler research designs and to the testing of hypotheses through refined statistical inference.

INTERACTIONISM

During the same era, others were concerning themselves with the social interaction of individuals. George Herbert Mead, a leading social psychologist, gave expression to a set of conceptions which led to what has come to be called "interactionism." His essential idea was that social interaction was not a literal matter of behavior alone but was enhanced by the capacity to "take the role of the other." The day-to-day relationships between people, he said, were based on their understanding of each other's role. Thus, he considered that we could go beyond awareness of our own behavior to a sense of what is dictated for a person in a role with which we are interrelated, a "reciprocal role." To take one illustration, if a person applies to a bank for a loan and is refused that loan by a bank official, he does not necessarily think of that official as unkind. The behavior usually is *not* seen as a consequence of the other's personal inclinations but as a *result of role*. Hence, in some symbolic sense his position is understood in terms of other demands made on his behavior, beyond personal inclination.

The fact that individuals are able to imagine themselves in the place of another, and to even see themselves as others might see them, was Mead's way of dealing with Man's capacity to transcend his own self and have experiences from a broader vantage point. This quality of human relationships was also very congenial to the thinking of another prominent sociologist of the time, Charles Cooley. He contended that individuals were able to experience social influences from various group sources in an imaginative way. This has its counterpart today in the "reference group" affiliation concept mentioned earlier. Cooley developed the concept of the "looking-glass self," conveying the idea of how we believe others see us. This was an early forerunner of the considerable emphasis today on the self-concept. It is also related somewhat to the importance McDougall attached to the "sentiment of self-regard" in human affairs (see pp. 283, 289-290).

Both Mead and Cooley gave prominent weight to the individual's reactions to symbolically realized phenomena, quite apart from actual external stimuli of the moment, and thus their position was distinct from that of the "behaviorists." There was a further difference which had its effect on the development of social psychology. The behaviorists tended to encourage the experimental method and this gave further impetus to the expansion of experimentation on social behavior in the 1920's. The "interaction" movement of that time did not have an experimental tradition but emphasized the refinement of theory; research in this framework was to come later. There was, however, one line of research on groups which had some of the quality of "interactionism." This was in the work of J. L. Moreno on "sociometry" beginning in the 1930's.

SOCIOMETRY

Moreno's most important conception was the idea that person-to-person relations, especially *choice and rejection,* were central features of life. His approach led to the development of a research tool, the "sociogram," which permitted the diagramming of the choice and rejection patterns within a group. It gives a picture of the structure of the group, for example in cliques, and indications of cohesiveness. Furthermore, patterns of choice were found to depend upon personal feelings, like friendship for an individual, or to be dictated by some recognized social standard set by a group. Thus, a person might select another as a friend on the basis of certain personal characteristics which he likes, or he may choose a person as a leader, independent of personal liking, in recognition of certain necessary "role demands" in that group. The special significance of Moreno's work resides in his early recognition of interpersonal evaluation as an implicit feature of interaction and as a useful basis for investigating social behavior.

EXPERIMENTATION ON THE PRODUCTION OF SOCIAL NORMS

Following on Allport's earlier experimentation, a major landmark in the 1930's was the Sherif study (1935) on the production of social norms. Arthur Jenness, a student of Allport's, had conducted a study (1932) in which individuals judged the number of beans in a bottle, then discussed this with others to arrive at a single judgment; then they made a second judgment alone which indicated a shift toward the group's standard. Other findings of a similar sort had been found by Münsterberg (1914) and by Allport (1924).

Sherif approached the problem in terms of the *creation* of "social norms" which he said are both (1) products of social interaction and (2) stimuli which are represented to any person who is a member of a group with those norms. In this particular work Sherif made use of the so-called "autokinetic effect." A spot of light projected in a totally darkened room will be seen to move, and this phenomenon is subject to wide individual differences. Such apparent movement is brought about by the fact that our eyes are never completely still; they show small, but continuous shifts. Sherif puts subjects in a darkened room alone in the first phase of his experiment. Over many trials, each was asked to look at the spot of light and report the direction and degree of movement. Then each subject was taken back to the room again, but this time in the company of others. Reporting their judgments aloud as they watched the spot of light, they soon converged toward a group standard of apparent movement. This effect is shown in Figure 2.2 for three

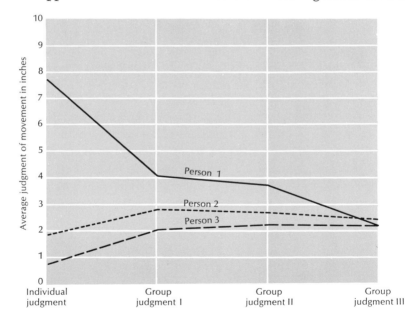

Figure 2.2: Illustration of convergence in average judgment of light's movement for three persons in the autokinetic situation, beginning with individual judgments alone. (From Figure 6, p. 103, in *The Psychology of Social Norms* by M. Sherif. Harper & Row, 1936.)

individuals making judgments alone and then at three intervals in the presence of others.

After this experience with the group of others, Sherif studied subjects again alone and found that they now retained the group norm rather than their own private standard as a basis for judging movement. This experiment did much to encourage further experimentation on the psychological aspects of group phenomena. It also showed the harmonious way in which group concepts, like social norms, could be subjected to psychological analysis.

GROUP INFLUENCES ON ATTITUDES

In the late 1930's Theodore Newcomb conducted a study which further substantiated group influences on normative attitudes. He pursued his research among students in the real-life environment at Bennington College, a small women's college with a heavy emphasis on the humanities. Bennington was among those colleges in the forefront of a liberal political trend, and, because so many of its students came from politically conservative homes, Newcomb sought to assess the effects of Bennington's campus community on their attitudes. With attitude measures taken at the beginning of college, Newcomb studied these students over a four-year period, while simultaneously obtaining similar data from students at other colleges for use as a comparison. He found that there were significant shifts toward more liberal political views over the four years at Bennington. Employing sociometric techniques, he found that social acceptance within the campus community was linked with approved attitudes. Of particular interest was the conflict this posed for some students between parental attitudes and those of the college-group. The long-range consequences of this for these women have been interestingly revealed in a recent follow-up study (Newcomb, 1963).

LEWINIAN "FIELD THEORY"

Perhaps the single most important theoretical contribution in the more immediate history of social psychology comes from the thinking of Kurt Lewin. It was Lewin in the 1930's who established a whole new school of social-psychological thought embedded in his concept of the "psychological field."

Lewin held that social situations, including conditions in a group, represented themselves in individual psychological states. Interaction theory, broadly speaking, had encompassed *past* social interaction as it produced symbolic relationships. Lewin's "field theory," on the other hand, was more concerned as a starting point with the individual's *present* psychological states, particularly perceptions of the moment, as they affected his responses. He was, in short, less interested in how these states came about. While behaviorism had largely disposed of any necessity for the attitude concept, attitudes were vital in Lewin's theory as "perceptual sets." Thus the content of mind was supremely relevant in Lewin's approach. He said: "Every psychological event depends upon the state of the person and at the same time on the environment, although their relative importance is different in different cases" (1936, p. 12).

An exemplification of Lewin's work is provided in the influential experiment he did with Lippitt and White (1939) on social "climates." Briefly, in a natural setting they created a number of boys' clubs, involving ten- and eleven-year-olds, which met periodically over a several week period. Adult leaders were experimentally introduced in these groups to create climates of "authoritarian," "democratic," and "laissez-faire" leadership by their behavior. Using techniques of observation and sociometry, they studied the effects on the groups produced by these styles of leadership. The results of this experiment indicated clear differences in the effects of the psychological climate induced by these styles. Authoritarian leadership, for example, produced passive acceptance of the leader, but it was accompanied by a great deal of aggressiveness toward the other group members, especially in the absence of the leader. In general, a major consequence of authoritarian leadership was to place a tight lid on spontaneous reactions among the boys, such as "horseplay."

An interesting illustration of the release of this kind of activity as a result of shifts in leadership style, is shown in Figure 2.3. The data in this figure reveal the average amount of horseplay among the boys during the first six days, under one kind of leadership style, and then for a transition day and the last six days, all under a different style. On the whole, horseplay in the initial period is lowest under authoritarian leadership and highest under laissez-faire leadership, but this "lowness" is purchased at a price. When the lid is off, a dramatic upsurge in activity occurs. Going from a climate that is autocratic to one that is either democratic or laissez-faire produces this effect, though it is highest and stays highest in the autocratic to laissez-faire change. This research demonstrates Lewin's point that individual and group behavior depend upon the properties of the situation and the "field" conditions

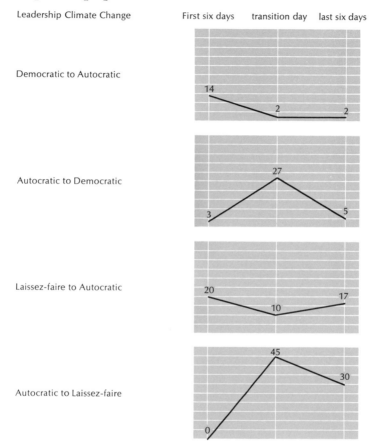

Leadership Climate Change   First six days   transition day   last six days

Democratic to Autocratic

Autocratic to Democratic

Laissez-faire to Autocratic

Autocratic to Laissez-faire

Figure 2.3: Index of average amount of "horseplay" observed in groups changing from one leadership climate to another. (Based on data from Lippitt and White, 1947.)

they produce. The results also neatly reveal how past experience conditions expectations and actions in new situations—as seen in the effects of shifts in leadership.

The broader impact of Lewin's work was especially felt in opening the potentialities for experimentation on small-scale "social systems" in the laboratory. Its consequences were of immeasurable importance to the coming of age of social psychology. One important outgrowth was the development of research on "group dynamics." Lewin felt it was entirely within reason to study the properties of groups; an important feature of group dynamics therefore was the groundwork it provided for the introduction of methods for inducing group-based effects upon individuals. Experimentation today in social psychology derives a good deal from Lewin's work, though a concern with elements of interaction is increasingly in evidence in such research as well.

Current trends in social psychology

Each of the traditions we have been considering has had an important though varying impact on the current field of social psychology. There have been continuing advances in both the theoretical conceptions begun in social philosophy and the research approaches growing out of social empiricism. Today there are many trends in social psychology, at the level of social analysis, which allow for the testing and refining of hypotheses concerned with the underpinnings of social influence.

One trend of continuing consequence is what Klineberg (1954) has called the "interpenetration of general psychology and social psychology" in terms of an examination of the manner in which social factors enter into the psychological processes of motivation, perception, and learning, and correspondingly, how older concepts from social psychology such as imitation and suggestion can be understood as outgrowths of these processes (p. 14).

The use of experimental procedures in highly controlled "laboratory" settings is another trend which has continued. Influence phenomena represented by such terms as conformity and leadership have been increasingly subjected to study under these conditions. This has provided further insight into an understanding of such phenomena in terms of social motivation and the learning which results from social interaction.

In a related way, there has been an increasing trend toward the study of aspects of this social learning process that bear upon "socialization" in childhood. How the youngster comes to have his psychological attributes shaped by his social milieu is a central focus of this work; this also has important implications for features of personality development. Such work has been extended as well to cross-cultural studies emphasizing the diversity of social demands as well as their commonality.

The analysis of cognitive processes, including perceptual and attitudinal correlates of behavior, occupies a considerable amount of attention in the contemporary scene. It is exemplified by continuing work on the formation and interrelationship of attitudes, and the influence effects of mass communications in terms of attitude change. Studies of the psychological features of language, represented in work on "psycholinguistics," also have a place in this trend.

Another feature of note has been the continuing interest in applications of social-psychological knowledge to social problems. Much research is being done in the fields of prejudice, morale, inter-group and international relations to broaden the base of understanding. Research designed to yield "simulations" of the latter two phenomena in particular has been an especially important development in recent years.

Social psychology therefore stands today as a distinctively empirical field of study, relying on facts and objective methods for obtaining them.

SUMMARY

There have been three distinct stages in achieving knowledge about social behavior. Each leads to the next and all are embodied somehow in contemporary study. They are: *social philosophy*, dating from antiquity and characterized by speculation without factual verification; *social empiricism*, originating in the nineteenth century and involving the gathering of facts largely of a descriptive form; and *social analysis*, a twentieth-century development aimed at understanding the relationships underlying social phenomena.

Social philosophy was concerned for a long time with the issue of what is "human nature" and whether its characteristics were "good" or "bad." As posed, these questions were difficult to resolve since the evidence was conflicting and support could be mustered for either view of Man. Moreover, philosophical viewpoints tended to offer a static conception of human conduct with instincts such as power, imitation, and pleasure each invoked as the single, all-embracing explanation of behavior. These instinctual views proved faulty on several grounds, but especially because of their disregard of the dynamic quality of human learning within the experiences provided by the social environment. The failings in this kind of excessive generality apply as well to the contentions of Social Darwinism, which emphasizes conflict and competition as implicit features of life, and to Freud's assertions regarding "innate aggressiveness" and the "death instinct." Other unsupported conjectures in the more immediate background of social psychology were those regarding imitation and the "group mind" advanced by Gustave LeBon and Gabriel Tarde.

Social empiricism came about in part as a response to the Darwinian era and its focus on the evolution of Man and his qualities. Galton, with his work on genetic transmission, and Binet, who developed the first standardized test of human intelligence, were in the vanguard of this movement. Others who provided a foundation for empirical study of the qualities and conditions of human life were the sociologists Comte and Durkheim and the cultural anthropologists Tylor, Malinowski, and Boas.

Social analysis, as a way of probing beneath the surface of description alone, is a distinctive feature of the twentieth-century "behavioral sciences." These may be considered to be psychology, sociology, cultural anthropology, and to some extent political science and economics. While these fields differ in their level of analysis, each may employ a social psychological framework of analysis within or across disciplines.

Modern social psychology grows out of traditions which are founded in psychology and sociology, the first emphasizing attributes of the individual and the other, qualities of the social environment. The experimental emphasis of John Watson and his behavioristic movement in psychology had a profound effect on the development of experimentation in social psychology. The measurement of attitudes, the development of concepts regarding social interaction, and the study of groups through techniques of sociometry and by experimentation were other important historical landmarks. Lewin's Field Theory, which underscored the individual's perception of his world, was an especially significant departure for much current research. Today, social psychology stands as an empirical field encompassing studies of group processes and learning through interaction, the socialization of the young including social effects on personality, attitudinal and perceptual elements in language and communication, attitude change and mass communications, and inter-group as well as international relations, among other problems.

SUGGESTED READINGS

From E. P. Hollander and R. G. Hunt. (Eds.) *Current perspectives in social psychology.* (2nd Edition.) New York: Oxford University Press, 1967:

5. David C. McClelland: *The achievement motive*
6. Frank A. Beach: *The descent of instinct*
7. Robert W. White: *Motivation reconsidered: the concept of competence*

SELECTED REFERENCES

Berelson, B. R. & Steiner, G. *Human behavior: An inventory of scientific findings.* New York: Harcourt, Brace & World, 1964.
*Heilbroner, R. L. *The worldly philosophers.* (Rev. ed.) New York: Simon & Schuster, 1961.
*Kardiner, A. & Preble, E. *They studied man.* New York: New American Library, Mentor Book, 1963.
Rohrer, J. & Sherif, M. (Eds.) *Social psychology at the crossroads.* New York: Harper-Row, 1951.

3

Theory and method in social psychology

To grasp why something is as it is requires a theory. To determine whether that idea has merit requires verification by some objective procedure. The heart of any scientific activity therefore rests in the important relationship between theories and the methods used to obtain appropriate evidence for their verification.

Opinions do not help to settle questions of fact, nor do they help us to understand the "why" of events. Furthermore, people will sometimes disagree about what constitutes fact. An inevitable problem surrounds what set of facts, from what source, will be acceptable as *evidence*. A cardinal task in science accordingly is to provide objective evidence through established methods of research. In this chapter we will be considering ideas which guide research—theories—and the methods used in social psychology to test them.

The essence of theory

Theories are quite purposeful and practical. For one thing, they direct our thinking by suggesting relationships and explanations. For another, they lead to effective technology by suggesting what results should follow from some process. Furthermore, in *testing the hypotheses* growing out of a theory, we are able to refine it through the study of research findings, thus achieving a theory which is more explanatory.

54

Basically, a theory consists of one or more functional statements or propositions that treat the relationship of variables so as to account for a phenomenon or set of phenomena. The implicit selection of some variables as relevant to these phenomena, and the exclusion of others, also points up the usefulness of theory in refining some distinctions and eliminating others. For example, in the social psychology of leadership it has become apparent that a distinction is required between competence in handling a group task, on the one hand, and popularity on the other. In thus making a new distinction, a theory can yield further understanding of a social process. This refinement, however, calls for an additional procedure for measurement which necessarily poses a methodological requirement.

As we shall see, a simple analogy can serve as a theory, just as a complex mathematical formulation can. A theory may also vary in its degree of comprehensiveness in representing the phenomenon with which it deals. Thus, it may be too inclusive, insofar as it includes unnecessary details, as in the outmoded phlogiston theory of combustion. Or it may be incomplete in the sense of leaving out variables of relevance. One case of this latter failure to account for social behavior was the long absence of concern for the degree of an individual's motivation to identify personally with a group; this is now rectified by the more recent conception of reference-group affiliation. The measurement of this variable has aided considerably our understanding of otherwise confusing findings regarding the effects of group membership.

While not usually thought of as theories, proverbs growing out of simple "folk wisdom" provide us with statements of a functional sort which can be used to illustrate the qualities of theory. For example, note the proposition in "out of sight, out of mind" and in its opposite number, "absence makes the heart grow fonder." Both of these proverbs make assertions about personal contact as a variable affecting interpersonal attraction. In the first case, the assertion is essentially that as contact decreases, individuals develop weaker attraction; the other is essentially an opposite proposition. As with many other pairs of proverbs one could cite, these are in direct conflict. Moreover, neither statement by itself is complete in accounting for outcomes. To construct a more adequate theory explaining the phenomenon requires the introduction of still other variables, including some about the relevant relationship and attributes of the individuals involved and the alternatives available to them. This essential inadequacy of proverbs points up the larger problem of any theory which suffers from incompleteness.

Since it is also possible for a theory to be loaded with excess baggage, unneeded for an adequate explanation, there is value attached to simplicity of explanation. This is what is referred to as "parsimonious" when discussing a theory's merit. Considering the complexities of social behavior, however, the too ready tendency toward simple analogy can be a treacherous pitfall. Analogies by themselves, however parsimonious, often prove as misleading as proverbs. Society is *not* one enormous "organism"; nor is a government a "ship of state," in the literal sense of a captain and crew; and in actuality increased supply does not push up consumption like a "hydraulic pump."

Since theories make assertions about the relationship between certain variables only, they often lead, as we have said, to a selective emphasis. Though selectivity can be a limitation when, for example, we overlook some important factor, it is indispensable in guiding research and the interpretation of evidence. There are several such emphases in theories of social behavior to which we now turn our attention.

Some theoretical distinctions in social psychology

Generally speaking, theories of social behavior may emphasize the *characteristics of a person growing out of his past experience* or the *characteristics of his immediate social situation*. The first emphasis is clearly in keeping with a psychological tradition, while the second is somewhat more indicative of a sociological one. We have already noted how each emphasis contributed to early formulations of social psychology. Apart from their origins, though, each is useful in giving direction to research; nevertheless, we should be aware that at the extreme either one is an oversimplification. Their main characteristics can be briefly summed up as follows:

> Research emphasizing the *individual* views social behavior as being intimately tied to such personal characteristics as achievement motivation, self-esteem, rigidity, or authoritarianism, to name just a few. These are essentially *qualities of personality* which vary from person to person. *They are measured*

to study the typical responses of a person across various social situations and relationships.

Research emphasizing the *situation* looks upon individuals as being influenced by pressures emanating from the demands of the present social structure including the expectations of others. A good deal of research on conformity exemplifies this view of social behavior as being readily altered by *operative factors* in a situation illustrated by a group's cohesiveness or its social structure. *These situational factors are measured to study their effect in producing typical responses across persons in the same situation.*

Despite the tendency of these two emphases to produce distinctive research, it is quite possible to embody both within a given study. Today, there are clear evidences of precisely this closure of approach. A particularly apt illustration is to be seen in work relating the individual's perception of his world to behavior. While Lewin conceived of the "psychological field" with particular regard to the perception of the present situation, others have looked at it in the more historic sense of how the individual *comes* to see his situation as he does. But in either case, subjective perception appears to provide one key to social behavior. Its implications are conveniently summed up in W. I. Thomas's classic dictum that "situations defined as real are real in their consequences." This means that since people "define" a situation, their perception of it represents a source of "reality" on which to base action. Elements of a person's situation thus take on significance for him in line with his past experience as well as his anticipated gains. Hence, both personality characteristics and properties of the situation are mutually involved in social behavior.

Human behavior is after all highly dependent upon learning from interaction with others. Therefore, people come to any situation with a history of past interactions in other situations. This past contributes to those personal characteristics of behavior which make each person unique. Accordingly, past experience affects the present through the process of *historicity*.

Consider this as an example. The situational emphasis, illustrated in Sherif's study (1935), looks upon conformity as a feature of the uncertainty or ambiguity of stimuli presented to individuals. It is a common finding that an ambiguous social situation increases reliance on the judgments of others because individuals are less sure of their own perceptions. This effect appears to be founded in a need to know "social reality," i.e. reality as other individuals see it or corroborate it. Though this need is supposed to be instigated by a property of the situation, there are nevertheless persisting individual differences, such as "intolerance of ambiguity," which become relevant too. The reason for this difference between individuals would reside within the person and be a consequence of his past experience.

There are of course situations that lead to quite uniform effects upon many individuals, despite obvious variations in their past history. One example would be a condition of intense ambiguity where there is also great importance attached to knowing the facts or verifying an outcome. An illustration of this occurs frequently where a military detachment is awaiting orders for overseas assignment. The combination of an uncertain situation with very high motivation to obtain information is exactly what has been found to foster the production and spread of rumors (Allport & Postman, 1943). Even here, however, there could be individual differences in susceptibility to rumors, depending upon past experience and personal capacities.

Two other theoretical distinctions of a bi-polar variety persist as emphases in social psychology. One contrasts so-called "behavioral" theories with those which are "cognitive." The other provides alternatives that can be summed up in the descriptive terms "conscious" and "unconscious." We can treat these briefly to suggest the kind of variables with which they tend to deal.

A behavioral theory, as the term implies, is concerned with behaviors, usually alterations in behavior which can be systematically shown to vary with environmental stimuli. In the strictest sense, such theories would not concern themselves with what occurs within the individual in eliciting behavior. Some concepts of learning, which can be adapted to social behavior, such as the "reinforcement" views of Skinner, fall within this category. The term cognitive conveys the idea of "knowing." A cognitive theory therefore would be concerned with the inner experiences of the individual in inducing action. Lewin's Field Theory, which we have already encountered in terms of the "psychological field" concept, is a theory of this kind. It emphasizes in particular the individual's perception of events he experiences. Thus, any theory which involves attitudes as relevant variables is cognitive. This does not mean that a cognitive emphasis disregards behavior but rather that it looks upon cognitive factors as "mediators" of behavior, i.e. variables which intervene between the stimulus and response.

To say that a theory emphasizes consciousness means that it is more concerned with the individual's awareness of the experiences on which he acts. An example of this is to be seen in Festinger's Theory of Cognitive Dissonance. Here, the individual is viewed as perceiving and avoiding conflicts between his store of cognitive elements—attitudes, motives, actions, and new facts. Alternatively, theories of the unconscious owe their existence almost entirely to the concepts of Freud and his followers in the importance they attach to unrecognized motives affecting behavior. Several theories regarding the development and functioning of attitudes view them as sources for affecting behavior through unconscious processes of this kind.

There are *not*, of course, six kinds of theories in social psychology as these three bi-polarities might suggest. The kinds of emphases we have been discussing overlap, and most theoretical views we will be encountering are a mixture of these. This can be exemplified in a number of ways. Theories emphasizing the situation are frequently behavioral and neutral on the consciousness-unconsciousness dimension; and theories emphasizing cognition usually convey as well an implicit concern with the dispositions of the individual, whether at a conscious or unconscious level. Thus, studies of the effects of culture on individual psychological states, such as perception, employ measures to get at conscious as well as unconscious factors, for example, through various kinds of standard psychological tests.

What is especially important is that whichever emphases produce a study of a social influence phenomenon, they dictate the relevant variables to be measured. Measurement is one of the hallmarks of scientific study as distinguished from reliance on subjective experience and opinion. The choice of variables is therefore a critical consideration in determining research methodology and the measurement it involves.

The nature of variables in social psychology

Two important characteristics of social behavior rest in its *multi-causal nature* and in its *historicity*. We have already noted that more than one variable may, and often does, produce social behavior. Also, we have said that the history of past relationships affects responses in the present. For example, the precise sequence of past events holds an important key to causality, as in the everyday query of "Who said what first?" Since the variables studied in social psychology are not easily categorized as "dependent" or "independent," their relationships are not best seen in simple stimulus-response terms. Furthermore, the fact that there are *ongoing processes* at work means that we must take account of time relationships to specify what is altered and what alters others things in turn.

A convenient way to give further body to these points is to discriminate between the several different kinds of variables that may be involved in any social psychological study. In the first place, we have *elements*, usually people or groups of people. Second, we have the *states* of these elements, as in the case of individual attitudes or group cohesiveness respectively. Third, we have the *processes* themselves, into which these elements enter, the best example of which is social interaction. And, finally, we have the *outcomes* of these processes.

Theories usually make assertions about elements and their relationships, often in terms of the states that they possess. Outcomes tend to be those phenomena of interest, like conformity and social attraction, which *depend* upon the states of elements and processes. Sometimes, though, states may themselves be outcomes of a prior process. Indeed, a state usually arises from some causal sequence which can be tied back to earlier processes whether or not there is direct concern with these processes. When we refer to cohesiveness, for example, we may be referring to it as a state possessed by a group which presently enters into some process, or as an outcome of a process, perhaps just completed. There are, then, some arbitrary distinctions concerning elements, states, processes, and outcomes, which are mainly a matter of the focus of the scholar. Therefore, it is well to bear in mind that in social psychology a term such as "conformity" may refer to something produced, or to something producing other outcomes—that is, to a *consequence* of prior processes or to a *cause* of subsequent effects, and that this difference is essentially a function of time-reference.

The research strategy of the social psychologist is inevitably shaped by the juxtaposition of variables in his guiding ideas or theory. In addition, he must make some choices in regard to how he will measure his major variables and decide on a research procedure within the diversity of empirical methods available for social psychological research. Before reviewing these, it is useful to consider several characteristics of empirical research.

Some characteristics of research in social psychology

The term research itself is many-faceted. To some it means consulting past findings in the library; to others, it may mean gathering facts selectively to make an argument, as in a debate. Empirical research, however, relies upon data obtained systematically, through observations and measurements, under natural or experimental conditions.

Studies of any kind in social psychology do not, strictly speaking, test theories directly. More properly, we say that they obtain data "empirically" to support or refute hypotheses. An hypothesis is a direct statement or indirect deduction from a theory which provides the guiding orientation for conducting a study, in terms of the treatments and measurements employed.

In general, empiricism refers to that stage of science which stresses the objective gathering of data. For social psychology today, as in many other fields of scientific activity, empirical evidence offers a basis for testing and discovering relationships. It is not an "end-point" in itself, but rather an aid to *social analysis* insofar as it contributes to understanding some phenomenon of social influence. This is especially important in developing and evaluating theory, as we have pointed out.

The essence of empiricism resides in making observations and measurements according to rules which allow *replication* by others. It also involves applying logic rather than accepting the untested assertions of past authority. In modern science certain standards are demanded for the acceptance of a piece of evidence, that is, a "finding." Some of the key considerations in establishing acceptability are these:

> objectivity of observation including measurement
> verifiability by repeated observation
> use of standard methods
> recognition and control of extraneous or chance factors
> relationship to what is already established
> soundness of logical inference.

Social psychology has benefited from the empirical methods developed in the related and older behavioral science disciplines of psychology, sociology, and anthropology. Psychology in particular has a century-long tradition of experimentation, the most controlled of empirical methods. Drawing on this tradition, social psychology has inclined toward an insistence on rigorous data-gathering and refined analysis, whether by experimentation or by studying association.

In experiments, measurement provides for a comparison between two or more treatments or, in "before-after" designs, between measurements taken in advance of and following some intervening treatment. As a means of comparison a "control" group is also instituted to which *no* treatment is applied; thus the effect of the actual treatment represented in the independent variable may be seen. In this sense, we control for the effect of extraneous factors in order to see whether the independent variable and not something else yields an effect on the dependent variable.

Another kind of research employs indices of association, such as correlation. This is the usual strategy embodied in studying the results of questionnaire surveys. Whereas experiments involve some treatment in the environment to see the effect on the dependent variable, correlational analysis involves the relating of measurements with one another —age with attitudes, education with child-rearing practices, popularity with productivity.

Both approaches allow for the testing of hypotheses, though the latter method usually allows *less* generalization about the direction of causality than the former. Still, in doing correlational analysis, it is possible to institute "controls" by studying one relationship at a time, holding others constant by statistical procedures. The difference of strategy lies in the fact that in the experiment the control is instituted by a treatment provided in the environment itself, while in computing a correlation it may be applied only within the data once collected.

In the section to follow, we will consider a variety of methods for studying social influence processes and social behavior. For each of these we will present examples from research literature. We begin with four major methods of study and then review several specialized techniques. These are by no means entirely separate from one another since any one study can involve their application in various combinations.

Major methods of study

The major methods of study are: observation, field studies, questionnaire surveys, and experimentation of two varieties, i.e. in the "field" or the "laboratory." The key features which vary in these approaches are the *naturalness of the environment for the subjects of the study* and the degree to which the experimenter is able to *exercise control over their environment* in the sense of altering some things and holding others constant. These features are related in that maximum control by the investigator tends to be found in experiments conducted under conditions created in a laboratory.

It should be made clear that there are no hard and fast lines separating these methods since they can be employed in concert with one another. Furthermore, of necessity, some become part of the others. This is most notably true regarding "observation," which we treat alone first, but in the recognition that behavior may be observed under a diversity of research conditions.

OBSERVATION

In general, observation is the oldest technique for studying behavior. By our use of the term "observation," however, we especially mean looking on in a *systematic* way for certain categories of response, and for factors which appear to be associated with those responses. In social psychology and other behavioral science fields today, research in many situations involves the method of "field observation." The term "field" refers to a *natural situation* in which people carry on normal pursuits, usually without being aware they are being studied. The investigator does not apply treatments but does seek to focus his attention on certain behaviors to ascertain their sources and their effects.

For example, in observing a group meeting interest might be directed to the response of individuals to particular kinds of statements made by other individuals, or to those kinds of statements to which an individual reacts. We will return to this shortly. As another illustration, the field investigator might be interested in observing children under different conditions. One notable exemplification of this is found in the work of

Barker and Wright (1954) who observed the different "behavior settings" in a small town in Kansas they called "Midwest." After extensive categorizing of these settings as features of the cultural milieu of the entire community, they determined what characteristic patterns of behavior occurred in each milieu. In Table 3.1 their results from the observation of children in the second grade are shown. The striking feature is not only that these same children show these different behavior patterns in different milieu day after day, but that in succeeding years other second-graders show similar patterns of behavior in these same milieu. This dramatically underscores the effect of culture in eliciting regularities of behavior.

Table 3.1: Patterns of behavior of the same children in different behavior settings (Table on p. 54, *Midwest and Its Children* by R. G. Barker and H. F. Wright. Harper & Row, 1954).

| | BEHAVIOR SETTING | | | |
	CLASSROOM, BEFORE SCHOOL	ACADEMIC ACTIVITIES	PLAYGROUND	MUSIC CLASS
Milieu	Second-grade classroom, 8.30-8.50 a.m. Monday through Friday	Scheduled periods for work; books, paper, pencils, etc.	School playground at recess; swings, teeter, balls, etc.	Scheduled period in music room; piano, music books, etc.
Behavior pattern	Unorganized activity; free locomotion; medium tempo, noise, and energy; cheerful mood; large variety of behavior	Organized activity; little change in positions; slow tempo, noise and energy; serious mood; limited variety of behavior	Unorganized or partly organized activities; fast tempo, loudness, and vitality; exuberant mood; large variety of behavior	Organized activities; variation in tempo, noise, and energy; medium cheerfulness; little variety of behavior, singing predominant

An essential feature of effective observation in the field rests in not letting the investigator's presence intrude on the activity of the people under observation. In most cases this is facilitated by remaining at a distance while noting behaviors in one or more prescribed categories. An example of this which tests an hypothesis about the common quality of conforming behavior across situations is provided in the work of Floyd Allport (1934). He gathered data on the behavior of different persons in several kinds of situations to calculate the distribution of frequencies of such responses, relative to a social expectancy. With persons observed in such situations as bringing a car to a halt at a stop sign, coming to work at a definite time, and practicing religious forms on entering a church, he found a distinctive pattern of response which he called a "J-curve." The horizontal axis in Figure 3.1 shows the degree

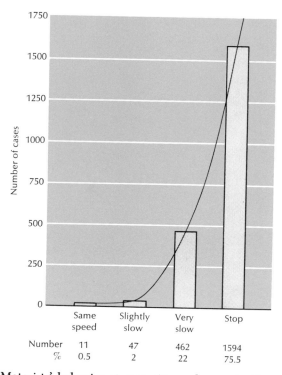

Figure 3.1: Motorists' behavior at stop sign and cross traffic corners; 2114 cases observed by M. Dickens. (Based upon data from F. H. Allport, 1934.)

of conformity with the expectancy for stopping at a stop sign, and the vertical axis the frequency with which it occurred. While it is of course true that a finding such as Allport's is evidently of a descriptive nature, its particular importance at the time was in pointing up the similarity of the curves obtained across the various situations studied. Here again, then, we see a regularity of response.

Observation is especially appropriate as a first stage in field studies. It should be emphasized once more, however, that the method of observation is almost always implicitly involved as a source of useful data even in other methods of study. Thus, research on groups—whether in the field or laboratory—often requires a measure of the qualities of social interaction. In laboratory experiments, for example, behaviors can be tallied within the categories developed by Robert F. Bales in his technique of "interaction process analysis" (1950a, b), thus permitting the test of hypotheses about the effects upon, or effects of, interaction. Figure 3.2 indicates the twelve kinds of distinctive behavior within which

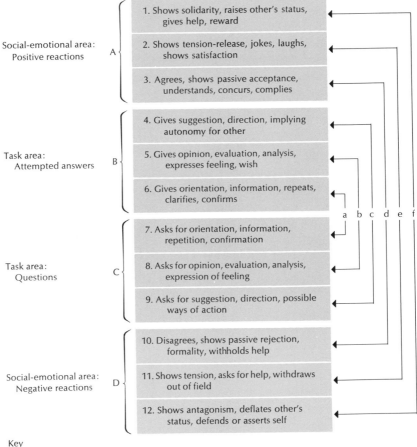

Figure 3.2: The system of categories used in observation and their relation to major frames of reference. (From Bales, 1950a.)

the interactions of the group members can be coded. Each behavior is connected with its opposite number by a line with arrows.

FIELD STUDY

A field study differs from observation alone in that it requires contact with the persons studied to obtain information from them. Thus, they are necessarily made aware of and involved in the study. In his research on the "cash posters," as an instance, George Homans (1954) was interested in testing certain conceptions about social interaction among women working as clerks in the billing department of a utility firm. He spent many weeks unobtrusively observing the pattern of social relationships in the office as the women moved about. He ascertained which workers took the initiative in seeking out and talking to which others, and this provided him with his major observational data on the attraction of persons to one another in this group. Then, as with many field studies that begin with observation, Homans interviewed these women to obtain additional data regarding their attitudes. Among other findings, his results supported the hypothesis that popularity, as measured by the number of choices received from others on a sociometric rating, was directly related to the frequency of interaction with others.

The essence of a field study then is the requirement of direct contact with individuals in a natural life setting. It is appropriate for use whenever investigations of behavior, and of attitudes, are carried out by studying people in such settings as their home or school. The Homans study illustrates the point that the investigator makes observations of behavior, but also requires direct contact with people to get information from them through an interview and sociometric ratings. His purpose is to obtain data that would otherwise be unavailable without such contact. Another device for gathering such information, usually on a wider population, is the questionnaire survey in the field.

QUESTIONNAIRE SURVEY

In a questionnaire survey, or "sample survey" as it is sometimes called, the central interest is in how a population, falling into certain descriptive classes, e.g. age, sex, level of education, birth order, responds to certain questions. There is of course also considerable interest in the relations between responses. Unlike a field study, the focus of attention is usually *not* on a particular group in a natural setting, but on a collection of respondents. It is the interrelationships of respondent attributes and responses which is being sought primarily. This is normally achieved by correlational methods. Though questionnaires may be employed in a field study, usually the field study is distinguished more by its focus on behaviors, or reports of behaviors, quite apart from questionnaire data.

Sometimes a natural event can be employed as the independent variable in a questionnaire survey, and it takes on the quality of a scientific experiment. For example, in studying attitude change as a result of a political campaign, measures can be taken before and after the event, and the effects of the campaign assessed, particularly as it influences persons with varying shades and intensities of commitment. Some studies of attitude change use a procedure called the "panel survey," which involves interviewing the same people repeatedly. For instance, as part of a study of elections, a panel of respondents might be interviewed one or more times to see how their initial position with regard to the candidates and the parties was modified by, or affected their reaction to, the campaign. Lazarsfeld and his coworkers (1948) have conducted a number of such surveys, the first in the 1940 presidential election. In that survey, they were able to demonstrate, for example, that the greater the number of cross-pressures an individual is subjected to—by conflicting political attitudes, social positions, or group affiliations—the less interest he has in the election and the later he decides his vote (see Figure 3.3). This kind of relationship has been found repeatedly since. The Bennington study by Newcomb (1943), on the effects of a college environment, was essentially a field study in a different context, though it tested a similar hypothesis regarding the consequences of conflicting affiliations.

As Figure 3.3 reveals, there is a relationship between the number of cross-pressures to which an individual is exposed and his interest in the election, seen by the relative proportions for the numbers in the columns. Fewer cross-pressures yield greater interest, proportional to that for more cross-pressures. Almost three-fourths of those in the first column knew in May how they would vote in November, while only one-fourth of those in the last column did, which demonstrates the major relationship.

Another example of a questionnaire survey is the research conducted by Albert Hastorf and Hadley Cantril (1954) following a particularly rough football game between Princeton and Dartmouth in which Dick Kazmaier, a Princeton All-American, was severely injured in his last appearance with the team in a home game. Passions were high that day and following the game there were many accusations concerning which team started the rough play on the field. In a survey conducted a week later among a sample of those in attendance, these researchers were

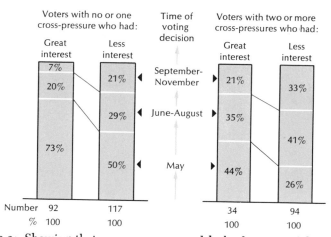

Figure 3.3: Showing that cross-pressures and lack of interest delay the time of final voting decision. Their joint effect is especially strong. Separately, they show about equal strength. (After Lazarsfeld, et al., 1948.)

able to test an implicit hypothesis regarding the relationship of school loyalty, essentially a "reference group" conception, to perceptions about a commonly observed event, the football game. They found that 86 per cent of the respondents at Princeton felt the Dartmouth team to be at fault, while 55 per cent of the Dartmouth respondents mainly felt it to be a matter of more equal blame. They had witnessed the same game.

Clearly, students at these institutions saw and interpreted the happenings on the gridiron in line with school loyalty. This underscores the profound psychological effect of group affiliation on perception. It also was further evidenced when a sample of Princeton and Dartmouth students were shown an identical movie of the game. Thus,

When Princeton students looked at the movie of the game, they saw the Dartmouth team make over twice as many infractions as their own team made. And they saw the Dartmouth team make over twice as many infractions as were seen by Dartmouth students. . . . When Dartmouth students looked at the movie of the game they saw both teams make about the same number of infractions (Hastorf & Cantril, 1954, pp. 131-132).

FIELD EXPERIMENTATION

In general, the experimental method in social psychology involves the alteration of conditions in the situation to determine the differential effect upon the responses of subjects. It may also proceed by studying the effect of the same experimental conditions upon persons who differ on some characteristic. Experiments may be done in natural-life settings, in which case we call them "field experiments," or in highly controlled, artificial settings, which we refer to by the term "laboratory experiments." We begin with the first of these.

The method called "field experimentation" is considerably more complex and difficult than would be the usual field study or questionnaire survey. Here the investigator actually arranges to create situations in a natural environment to study the consequences produced. To control for the effects of extraneous factors requires a "control group" matched on all other possible variables. Thus, some individuals might be exposed to a unique treatment to which other similar individuals are not. Illustrating this, Kurt Lewin instigated a number of studies on the effect of different social practices in producing changes in behavior, with the aim of testing hypotheses in particular about more pronounced changes occurring from commitments made in a group discussion. In one of these experiments (1947) some mothers of infants, as a control, were given individual instruction encouraging them to use orange juice, among other foods, in baby feeding. Other mothers were given the treatment of being allowed to take part in a discussion, in groups of six, to consider the advantages of different foods in a baby's diet and reach a common decision. In this experiment, groups reached decisions favoring orange juice in about 25 minutes. As will be seen in Figure 3.4, those mothers who took part in the decision, and were more publicly committed, had a significantly higher rate than the control condition for giving orange juice. Furthermore, this difference persisted after four weeks, and probably far longer.

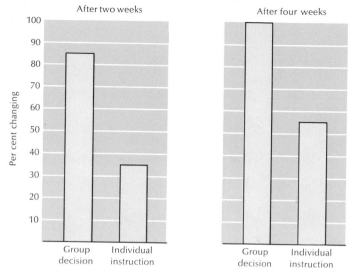

Figure 3.4: Percentage of mothers following completely group decision or individual instruction in giving orange juice. (Adapted from Lewin, 1947, after M. Radke and D. Klisurich, 1947.)

A classic illustration of field experimentation is represented in the work of Coch and French (1948) who conducted an experiment in a factory where pajamas were manufactured. The fundamental independent variable was the degree to which workers were permitted to participate in planning a needed production change. Some workers were allowed total participation, and others were allowed only indirect participation or no participation. The results showed that participation in any degree yielded significantly higher production than did no participation. The findings for the three kinds of conditions are indicated in Figure 3.5 and graphically affirm the implicit hypothesis that participation in decision-making induces attitudinal differences which affect subsequent performance.

The field experiment often takes the form of creating certain conditions which induce a "psychological set," that is, a pre-formed perception, to see its later effects. This can be done with simple written instructions given in a classroom. Thus, in one such experiment, Kelley (1950) was able to test an hypothesis about the way different sets, once created, can lead to divergent perceptions of the identical stimulus person. He gave students in a college classroom brief written descriptions

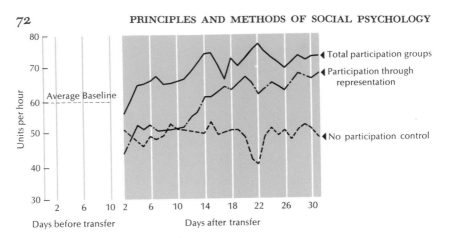

Figure 3.5: Smoothed production curves for total participation groups, and for participation through representation and no participation control groups, after transfer to new production procedure. (Adapted from Coch and French, 1948.)

of a guest lecturer prior to his actual appearance. Two kinds of descriptions were used. These were the same in every way, except that in one case the person was described as a "rather cold" person and in the other as "very warm." Students received one or the other description without knowing that different terms were being used. After hearing the same lecture, the students who had received the "set" for warmness rated the lecturer as more considerate, more informal, more sociable, and in general more favorably on other factors of personality, than did those students who had received the "set" for coldness. This finding supports the hypothesis that first impressions can be markedly affected by prior information.

LABORATORY EXPERIMENTATION

The most controlled method employed in modern-day social psychology, and the one increasing most in use, is "laboratory experimentation." It involves the introduction of conditions, in a controlled environment (hence the term "laboratory"), which will simulate certain features of a natural environment. This permits the creation of a situation with closely supervised manipulation of one or more variables at a time to observe effects produced, something that would be quite difficult to achieve in a natural setting.

A classic example of laboratory experimentation is provided in the Sherif (1935) research with the autokinetic effect (see p. 46). That work is significant in pointing up the effects on perception of the judgments of others, especially where the stimulus to be judged is highly ambiguous. An extension of Sherif's work is represented in the experimentation done by Solomon Asch (1951). In his research, a group of people, usually eight in number, are seated side by side. On a screen before them they each see a line which they are asked to match by size with one of three unequal lines. These are labeled and group members are asked to give their response aloud. Except for one person, the "critical subject," the group had actually met before and received instructions to respond unanimously with wrong judgments on certain trials. Thus, the critical subject faced a unanimous contradiction of his own perception on these trials. Asch found a distinct movement toward the majority estimates in the direction of the group's distortion of accuracy. There was, however, marked variability from one subject to another. About one-quarter of the subjects remained completely independent. Overall, 32 per cent of the judgments of critical subjects were in the pro-majority, or incorrect, direction. When a person reporting in advance of the critical subject was instructed to give a response contrary to the group's erroneous judgment, the effect was considerably altered. Under conditions of such support from even *one* other person, the critical subject gave a more accurate response indicative of what he actually saw. Asch says: "The results clearly demonstrate that a disturbance of the unanimity of the majority markedly increased the independence of the critical subjects. The frequency of pro-majority errors dropped . . . to 5.5 percent" (1951, p. 185). Laboratory experimentation of this kind supports the hypothesis that our reports of what we perceive are susceptible to the influence of others and are highly sensitive to the degree of support from others.

Leavitt (1951) conducted an experiment whose results dramatize the consequences of the group's communication structure on performance and satisfaction. He arranged different communication patterns or "nets" for groups (see Figure 3.6) which had the effect of restricting in varying degrees the channels for passing messages between members. Thus, in the circle, subjects could communicate only with those persons on either side of them; in a wheel the central person could communicate with any of the others, but they could only communicate with him, and

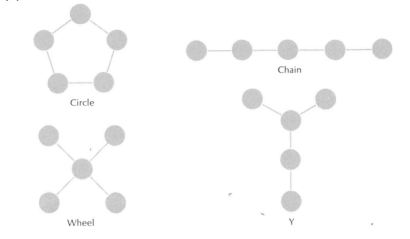

Figure 3.6: Communication nets used in the experiment by Leavitt (1951).

so on. The task was to solve a problem involving the discovery of the symbol group members shared in common on the cards given them. Leavitt found that the communication nets were significant determiners of behavior, accuracy, and satisfaction of group members. This demonstrated the extent to which a feature of the social situation can be influential in affecting such outcomes. In general, the wheel was found to be most efficient, in terms of the single fastest correct solution. However, the circle tended to be more satisfying to the group members. Other relationships found indicated that the "centrality" of a group member's position in a net had a great deal to do with his satisfaction.

One element sometimes embodied in laboratory experimentation is a "confederate" or "stimulus person," instructed to behave in a certain way so as to determine the effects of such behavior on the subjects, as in the Asch experiment already described. An experiment by Schachter (1951) illustrates the utility of this procedure. He had college students indicate in advance what kind of clubs they would like to join. Two kinds of clubs were then comprised: one kind with students who indicated moderate to extreme interest in them, and the other kind made up of students who had favored being in other clubs. These were defined as being "high cohesive" or "low cohesive" groups, respectively. In one-half of each of these two kinds of groups, members discussed material relevant or non-relevant to the group.

In every group there were three participants who served as confederates of the experimenter. In each meeting one played the role of a "deviate" who rejected the group's main viewpoint, another played the role of a "slider" who shifted toward the group's main viewpoint during the meeting, and the third, a "non-deviate," championed that main viewpoint throughout. The latter two confederates were controls to establish evidence of the differential reaction of the group to the "deviate." This permitted a test of several postulates from Festinger's influential theory of social communication (1950). Those two of particular relevance can be paraphrased briefly as follows: the force to communicate to a particular group member will increase as the discrepancy in opinion between that member and the communicator increases; and, that force will decrease to the extent that he is no longer wanted as a member of the group. One dependent variable in this study, therefore, was the amount of communication directed to each of these participants over the time of a group meeting.

In Figure 3.7 curves for this variable are given for the three confederates for the groups studied under the condition of *high* cohesiveness and *relevant* discussion. The "deviate" was found to receive the highest number of communications from the other group members with a rise and then clear drop-off, toward the end of the session. For the "slider"

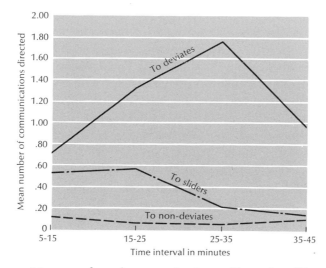

Figure 3.7: Mean number of communications addressed to "deviates" who reject group views, and to "sliders" and "non-deviates" during meeting under conditions of high cohesiveness and relevant attitudes. (Based on data from Schachter, 1951.)

this was much less so. This reflects a rejection of the deviate which was also noted in the responses to a "post-interaction" questionnaire which measured other dependent variables, i.e. nominations for a steering committee and a measure of willingness to eliminate someone from the group. These measures were mutually supportive in indicating a willingness to reject the "deviate" significantly more than the "slider" or "non-deviate" by not having him on the steering committee and indeed by dropping him entirely from group membership. This experiment confirms the interrelated hypotheses from Festinger and can be interpreted to show that group pressures toward conformity exist, especially as a function of high cohesiveness. Moreover, these pressures evidently operate to bring about the rejection of members who fail to conform to group expectancies regarding relevant attitudes.

Specialized techniques of research

The methods of study we have been considering represent the major approaches to investigations of social behavior and the factors associated with influence upon it. As we have pointed out, each may involve some features of the others. There are, in addition, a number of specialized procedures which cut across any or all of the methods. These are techniques of gathering or organizing data which provide answers to questions concerning the processes involved in influence relationships. There are essentially four of these which have a justifiable place in our consideration of the research methods of social psychology. They are: depth interviews, projective techniques, attitude scales, and content analysis. Since these are not mutually exclusive of one another, they may be and are used in combination. Thus, depth interviews are frequently supplemented by the administration of projective techniques. These may be scored in turn by content analysis procedure. Similarly, attitude scales may be administered in connection with an interview.

DEPTH INTERVIEWS

An interview is a way of studying individuals intensively. It provides for a degree of freedom in getting at information that otherwise would be unavailable in the more structured questionnaire format. Putting it another way, a questionnaire is a highly structured interview. With the more conversational approach usually permitted in an interview, a good deal of latitude is provided for the spontaneous probing of certain attitudes held by the respondent. This is especially true in depth interviewing which is designed to be penetrating and demands considerable skill on the part of the interviewer, who must retain throughout a sense of what particular kinds of information are to be obtained. With the feature of personal contact, he is also able to observe the behavior of the interviewee while responding.

One example of the contrast between a broad questionnaire survey and a depth-interview approach is found in the work on attitudes by Smith, Bruner, and White (1956). Rather than survey a large population, they devoted considerable attention to only ten persons, who were interviewed intensively over an extended period of time. The aim of the research was to understand better the relationship between political attitudes, particularly regarding the Soviet Union, and personality. Formal questioning was supplemented by tests and an opportunity was also afforded for spontaneous and penetrating discussion. Their major conclusion was that the relationship between personality and these particular attitudes did not fit a consistent pattern.

PROJECTIVE TECHNIQUES

A way of extending an interview to further probing beneath the surface of verbal expressions is provided by projective techniques, which represent one kind of personality test. The term "projective" refers to the fact that the individual respondent "projects" his impressions of relatively ambiguous and standardized stimulus materials, thus giving a view of his underlying attitudes or perceptions. Probably the best known of the projective techniques is the Rorschach Ink-Blot Test. This test involves standard inkblots, which have been used for several decades with a range of adults; these are presented one at a time to a person in order to get reactions from him which are then scored by an established system.

In social psychology, the projective techniques which tend to be most often used are those involving sentence completion, and to some extent word association and storytelling about standard pictures. The latter approach is exemplified in the so-called Thematic Apperception Test (TAT), which is used for a variety of purposes. The social psychologist's main interest in projective techniques is not so much personality as such, but the person's psychological field, that is, his interpretation of the world and his attitudes toward its features. David McClelland and his colleagues, for example, have made extensive use of projective devices in measuring achievement motivation, usually by analyzing the content of the specific stories told in connection with TAT pictures (1953). On balance, projective tests are a useful technique for getting at what McClelland has called the "content of mind," since the person usually is not fully conscious of precisely what his responses may convey and accordingly is less guarded.

ATTITUDE SCALES

For several decades there has been a good deal of interest in attitude scaling. This method provides a way of systematically measuring one part of a person's psychological field. We shall be further considering procedures for attitude scaling in Chapter Six. Our interest here is in presenting a particular kind of attitude scale used as a measure of personality, i.e. the "attitude-trait" scale.

In general, an attitude scale is composed of a set of "items," usually statements, with which a person indicates degrees of agreement or disagreement. In the attitude-trait scale, these responses usually have to do with others in the person's social world. This is taken to be indicative of a characteristic mode of reacting to others and is exemplified in the scale of authoritarianism, called the "F Scale," developed at the University of California during the 1940's (Adorno, *et al.*, 1950). Items from that scale are designed to assess various kinds of conventional attitudes found to cohere in the "authoritarian personality." Here are some examples from that scale:

> Obedience and respect for authority are the most important virtues children should learn.
> What this country needs most, more than laws and political programs, is a few courageous, tireless, devoted leaders in whom the people can put their faith.
> There is hardly anything lower than a person who does not feel a great love, gratitude, and respect for his parents.

If people would talk less and work more everybody would be better off.

People can be divided into two distinct classes: the weak and the strong.

Human nature being what it is, there will always be war and conflict.

A sum of the responses of agreement or disagreement for about 30 of these items represents a measure of authoritarianism. Other scales of this sort, which are taken to be insightful of personality are those for dogmatism, rigidity, empathy, and so forth. What distinguishes this approach from earlier measures of personality is that previously persons were asked to describe their own behavior by agreeing or disagreeing with a set of statements such as "I find it difficult to get up in the morning." This represents the classic approach of personality inventories, such as the Bernreuter and the Minnesota Multiphasic Personality Inventory (MMPI). More recently, as a development within social psychological study oriented toward individual differences, measurement of *other-perception* through these scales is applied to assess personality features.

CONTENT ANALYSIS

The technique known as "content analysis" is a procedure that covers a variety of different tasks. Mainly, however, this technique refers to the coding and categorizing of qualitative materials so as to permit their quantification. One way of seeing the problem is to recognize that any verbal communication, e.g. a statement, a letter, a newspaper editorial, carries various elements within it which might be studied quantitatively in terms of the frequency with which they occur. One such study was conducted by Sargent (1939). He compiled a representative list of twelve terms regularly encountered in the editorials appearing in each of two major metropolitan newspapers when referring to the same events or people. Without revealing their source, he had sixty college students indicate if they liked, disliked, or were indifferent to these terms. Some illustrative pairs of terms were: "progressive" vs. "radical," "crop control" vs. "farm dictatorship," "investigator" vs. "inquisitor." He found a consistent tendency for the responses to indicate less favorability for those terms used by one of the papers; in the pairs given here that paper's terms are given last. Sargent concluded that the "loaded" terms used in this paper's editorials were reacted to in a direction consistent with the political and economic policies of the paper.

Another intriguing use of content analysis is shown by a study conducted by deCharms and Moeller (1962) on the values expressed in American children's readers. They had two people independently score every third page from representative children's readers drawn on the basis of at least four from each 20-year period beginning in 1800. These were mainly from the fourth-grade level. The aim of this content analysis procedure was to quantify several kinds of values, or imagery, including achievement motivation. This variable has been found to be a rather stable feature of personality which relates to the individual's entrepreneurial activity (McClelland, *et al.*, 1953).

This particular study was prompted by McClelland's extension of his theory to include cultural development. Through the analysis of literary materials, he found confirmation of his hypothesis that achievement motivation preceded economic and technological growth in the Athenian civilization of classic Greece (1958). In his book, *The Achieving Society* (1961), he further illustrated this pattern by citing the content of children's readers in various cultures. Accordingly, one of the key

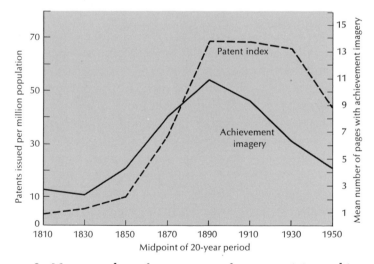

Figure 3.8: Mean number of pages out of 25 containing achievement imagery, and patent index per million population, both plotted against time. (From deCharms and Moeller, 1962.)

hypotheses that deCharms and Moeller tested in their study was that the incidence of achievement imagery found in these books would be positively related to the number of patents issued, corrected for population growth. Clear affirmation of this hypothesis is shown by the high statistically significant correspondence between the two curves plotted in Figure 3.8, one for the incidence of achievement imagery and the other for patents issued. Both reveal a peak close to the turn of the century and a steady decline since. Apart from any precise interpretation of what these curves reveal, the notable quality of this study lies in the way it demonstrates the use of content analysis to get at the psychological correlates of cultural trends.

The generalizability of findings: some conclusions

All of the methods and techniques of social psychology we have covered in this chapter are designed to provide data to evaluate theories. This is necessarily a dynamic function which involves constant re-evaluation. No finding by itself is sacrosanct since there is never absolute certainty in science; and a theory is potentially subject to alterations when new data come in.

But what is the purpose in all this if our generalizations must be limited? As we have tried to suggest by the illustrations, the essence of the dialogue between theories and findings is to broaden our understanding and increase the range of applicability of our conclusions. In short, the purpose is to improve our generalizations about processes of social influence, and the behavior to which it gives rise. This is only possible to the extent that we employ methods that provide a good test of our theories, and good theories for guiding our pursuit of new data.

SUMMARY

Theories and the methods employed to verify them are essential features of any scientific pursuit. Theories are practical too for they select and refine variables for emphasis, and provide hypotheses for testing against data.

In social psychology, theories may emphasize characteristics of the individual or of his immediate social situation. Either emphasis taken to the extreme is likely to produce an oversimplification in view of the multi-causal nature of social influence and the behaviors to which it gives rise. Increasingly, both emphases are accounted for in research on these processes. An especially important point of closure between them resides in the concept of the "psychological field" which gives attention to the way the individual is "set" to define situations in which he finds himself.

Another pair of theoretical distinctions in social psychology, which determine the variables studied in research, are "behavioral" vs. "cognitive" theories and those theories embodying "conscious" vs. "unconscious" determinants of behavior. These distinctions cut across individual and situational orientations to produce a variety of combinations. Accordingly most theoretical views providing research on social influence are a combination of these leading to the measurement of some variables and the exclusion of others.

Variables in social psychology are not easily categorized as "dependent" or "independent" in any persisting sense. The element of time-relationship must be taken into account in determining whether a variable is altered by, or alters, other variables, or combines both processes in sequence. The several kinds of variables studied in social psychology may be *elements,* such as people or groups; *states,* such as attitudes; *processes,* such as social interaction; or *outcomes* of these processes, represented in social phenomena. The treatment of a variable as one or another of these depends upon the aim of the researcher.

We obtain data "empirically" in social psychology to test hypotheses which may be direct statements from a theory or deductions from it. Empiricism refers to gathering data objectively and according to rules that allow for replication by others. Two distinctive empirical methods are experimentation, which involves the introduction of an experimental treatment matched with a control, and studies of association through a procedure employing some mode of correlational analysis.

The four major methods of study in social psychology are: *observation, field studies, questionnaire surveys,* and *experimentation* in the *"field"* or the *"laboratory."* These methods are not exclusive of one another and observation, in particular, is frequently employed as part of the others. Reference to research in the field means carrying on a study in a natural situation such as an office, home, or school; research in the laboratory refers to conducting a study in a highly controlled, artificial situation.

Observation usually takes the form of looking on systematically for behavior falling into various categories. A field study may employ observation but also requires *contact* with the persons being studied to gather data from them. A questionnaire survey may also be conducted in the field, but with a greater emphasis on studying a population in terms of the relationship between certain descriptive categories, such as the age, sex, and education of respondents and their responses to certain questions, usually of an attitudinal nature. A natural event may also be exploited to study its effect on persons with different attributes, as in a survey of political attitudes during an election campaign.

Field experimentation is very demanding in that it involves the creation of situations, in what is otherwise a natural environment, to measure their consequences in contrast to an untreated control. Laboratory experimentation permits the selective manipulation of one or a few variables under artificially arranged conditions which are highly controlled by the experimenter.

In addition to these major methods of research in social psychology, there are a number of specialized techniques which may be used separately, or in concert with them, to obtain relevant data. These are *depth interviews, projective techniques, attitude scales,* and *content analysis.* Depth interviews study individuals intensively and usually go beyond the scope of a questionnaire alone. Projective techniques also are utilized to get beneath the surface of verbal expression to a view of the person's unconscious processes. Attitude scales provide an avenue for the systematic measurement of one or more dimensions of the person's outlook on the world, his "psychological field"; the "attitude-trait" scale is especially geared to measuring attitudes toward others. Content analysis in the main refers to the coding and categorizing of qualitative material, usually in verbal form, in terms of measuring certain variables that may lie within it.

Findings in science never hold absolute certainty, nor are theories forever fixed. The purpose of research in social psychology is to verify theories and to refine them so as to increase the understanding of social influence and the range of generalizability of conclusions about it.

SUGGESTED READINGS

From E. P. Hollander and R. G. Hunt. (Eds.) *Current perspectives in social psychology.* (2nd Edition.) New York: Oxford University Press, 1967:

16. Gordon W. Allport: *The open system in personality theory*
42. Leon Festinger: *Informal social communication*

SELECTED REFERENCES

Deutsch, M. & Krauss, R. M. *Theories in social psychology.* New York: Basic Books, 1965.

Festinger, L. & Katz, D. (Eds.) *Research methods in the behavioral sciences.* New York: Dryden, 1953.

Hyman, H. H. *Survey design and analysis.* Glencoe, Ill.: Free Press, 1955.

*Lazarsfeld, P. F. & Rosenberg, M. (Eds.) *The language of social research.* Glencoe, Ill.: Free Press, 1955.

Proshansky, H. & Seidenberg, B. (Eds.) *Basic studies in social psychology.* New York: Holt, Rinehart & Winston, 1965.

Selltiz, Claire, Jahoda, Marie, Deutsch, M., & Cook, S. W. *Research methods in social relations.* (Rev. ed.) New York: Holt, Rinehart & Winston, 1959.

Steiner, I. & Fishbein, M. (Eds.) *Current studies in social psychology.* New York: Holt, Rinehart & Winston, 1965.

4

Adjustment and the psychological dynamics of social influence

Man influences and is influenced by others. Man's many distinguishing attributes—language, social organization and symbols, a sense of values and of continuity—can only be acquired from contact with other humans. This vital relationship arises from social interaction and involves the interplay of psychological processes such as motivation, perception, and learning. Our interest in this chapter will be directed toward how these processes are involved in the ever-present necessity for adjustment, especially in terms of the social forces affecting the individual.

The concept of adjustment refers to the quality of adaptive change basic to human experience over time. It involves the *present* necessities of the individual, the way these have been shaped by *past* experience, and their relationship to *future* satisfactions. Beginning with earliest life, adjustment therefore depends upon *a process of learning*, within social influence relationships.

Adjustment in broad perspective

While it may be glibly said that all human beings must adjust to their environment, this tells us little by itself. The very term adjustment can be viewed in various ways. Furthermore, every individual "adjusts," however disruptive or bad that may be in terms of socially disapproved

85

actions. Apart from the obvious fact that one had to contend with physical factors in the environment to sustain life, adjustment also grows out of the many demands of the "social environment." Individuals encounter these demands directly in social interaction, and also through the societal practices and group expectancies in their surroundings.

SOME DEFINITIONS OF ADJUSTMENT

There are three major ways of defining individual adjustment. In some sense, all of these have a place in social psychology since they involve individual psychological factors which are influenced by the social setting. Furthermore, though differing in emphasis, these views relate to the key theme of individuals achieving gratification of their motives within the framework of social demands and the broad requirement for social acceptance.

The three major ways of looking at individual adjustment are briefly as follows:

> Adjustment can be viewed in "ego-centric" terms as the satisfactions achieved by the individual through a more or less pleasing relationship with his environment. This view focuses upon *individual needs* and satisfactions in certain relationships, or transactions, with other people, within the social constraints of a culture.
>
> Adjustment can mean the process of adapting certain individual tendencies or desires—e.g. motives, attitudes, values—to social requirements. This view emphasizes a conception of *society as a force* requiring an individual's compliance. A good part of the concern with "mental health" stresses the *balance* needed between internal psychological states and behavior. Relatedly, adjustment can be represented as the consistency of the individual's psychological states themselves.
>
> Finally, adjustment is sometimes presented in terms of an *unfolding of the individual's potentialities* through maturation and experience. This is a view growing out of those theories of personality which emphasize the "actualization of the self." It is also encountered somewhat in the literature of existentialism.

ADJUSTMENT AS A RESPONSE TO SOCIAL INFLUENCE

Whatever the approach to adjustment, its essential quality is one of dynamism, that is, the prospect for change. From an external viewpoint, adjustment occurs whenever the individual encounters new experiences that require a response. But there are also internal motivations of the individual, which arising from past learning may operate to move the individual toward the achievement of social goals in the environment such as status, recognition, or power. But even those internal motives construed to be physiologically based, such as hunger, are fulfilled in socially prescribed ways: what we eat, when we eat, and how we eat are learned in the context of a society and its pattern of culture.

Indeed, the first and most pervasive of the social influences of early life is the highly selective quality of the experiences a society provides for us. Asch (1959) puts it in these terms:

> Each social order confronts its members with a selected portion of physical and social data. The most decisive feature of this selectivity is that it presents conditions lacking in perceptual alternatives. There is no alternative to the language of one's group, to the kinship relations it practices, to the diet that nourishes it, to the art it supports. The field of the individual is, especially in a relatively closed society, in large measure circumscribed by what is included in the given cultural setting (p. 380).

The group-based quality of human society is an inescapable fact of life. Social relationships pervade human experience and carry demands in the form of the expectations of others. These are especially important where those others are significant to an individual's identities. The flow of social interaction progresses within the context of group norms and role demands. In psychological terms, the perception an individual holds of what others expect of him is a vital determinant of his social behavior; and the degree to which an individual perceives others as rewarding him enhances his motivation to be identified with them; this motivation also serves to heighten the individual's perception of expectancies.

There are then purposive, motivational features of ongoing experience which are future-oriented in terms of goals to be achieved or desires to be fulfilled. These play an important part in understanding the alterations of behavior occasioned by social interaction. They are intimately involved in the demands made for adjustment, as we shall observe in further detail shortly. While humans may seek the familiar and the comfortable ways of the past, these habitual patterns are modifiable through new experience and learning in contact with others.

ADJUSTMENT AS A RESPONSE TO INTERNALIZED FRUSTRATION AND CONFLICT

Because individual motives cannot always be satisfied, we often find ourselves in a state of "frustration." This factor accounts for many theories of adjustment based in the ego-centric definition offered as the first above. Furthermore, the satisfaction of one motive is sometimes inconsistent with the satisfaction of another equally impelling motive; this leads to a state of internal "conflict." In many contemporary views, frustration and conflict are conditions which represent the essential psychological bases for adjustment. They can lead to *expressive* behavior, as a relief from the tension produced by frustration, or to behaviors which can be *instrumental* in achieving the goal.

Several kinds of "mechanisms" or "techniques" of adjustment have been delineated which are responsive to frustration and conflict, and these deserve a brief review. Though we may generally react so as to indulge some of these more than others, all of us employ these techniques at some time in dealing with frustration. These are shown graphically in Figure 4.1 where the individual is seen to be aroused to move toward a goal which is blocked by a barrier that could be of a literal physical nature. More significantly however it might be of a social-psychological nature, as exemplified by a conflict of values represented in wanting to do something of questionable morality.

One obvious way of dealing with the barrier is to find an alternative goal, which can be called *compromise.* Should you go to the cafeteria bent on having apple pie, you might settle for cherry or peach pie if apple is no longer available. Another technique of adjustment is *withdrawal,* in which case you would "deny" the desire and, in our food instance here, accept no alternative goal at all. Two other techniques of adjustment which appear to resemble each other, but which are quite different, are *direct aggression* and *displaced aggression.* Neither is likely to be productive of securing the goal since both are essentially expressive behavior that has little instrumental value.

Direct aggression is usually thought of as an assault on the barrier, or what appears to be the barrier. The clearest exemplification of this is found where the individual strikes out, verbally or otherwise, toward the evident source of frustration. Thus, the countergirl who announces that the apple pie is all gone might be the object of a sarcastic remark, which does little to achieve the goal.

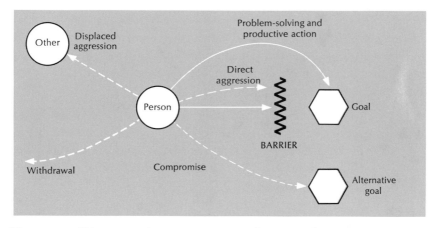

Figure 4.1: Diagrammatic representation of major adjustive responses to frustration.

Displaced aggression is seen in the classic instance of kicking the dog, that is, a hostile reaction toward a bystander or other innocent party as a way of dealing with frustration. Interpersonal relationships are of course affected by such displaced aggression as indeed are inter-group and international relations as well.

The adjustive technique of surmounting the barrier through *problem-solving* and *productive action* is usually thought of as the highest order of these techniques. It illustrates instrumental behavior, which can also occur through a process of thought. This ability to indulge in higher level symbolic activity through thought represents Man's great potential for mastery over his environment and the forces of circumstance. What is more, human adjustment has a future-oriented quality which transcends the present and implicates complex relationships between motivation, perception, and learning. We will attend to some features of these now.

The psychological underpinning of social behavior

Man as we observe him is not in a *natural* state. Human behaviors are constituted within and conditioned by the envelope of influence relationships in a society. That we are directly affected by this process, though the specific content of experience may vary, is due to social interaction. As infants we depend upon other humans for survival and are influenced by them. We are all capable of thus becoming initiated into human society if, as Newcomb (1950, p. 50) suggests, we have these three capacities:

> A capacity for *irritability*, in the sense of being sensitive to the absence of those environmental conditions upon which survival depends. If we are not irritated by excessive heat or cold, or by hunger, we will not respond to the environment in such a way as to sustain life.
>
> A capacity for *response* when irritated. If as infants we cannot suck or swallow or breathe, we will not be able to survive.
>
> A capacity for *learning*, that is, profiting by experience. While we could survive without the capacity for learning, it is of the greatest importance to adjustment and the acquisition of distinctively human behavior.

Given the availability of these three capacities, new members of a society may take part in social interaction and, in so doing, be influenced to acquire appropriate social behaviors. The task of the social psychologist is to provide understanding of how this process proceeds. Thus we can distinguish two levels of influence: one of high dependency having to do with the *initial* shaping of approved behavior in childhood as part of the "socialization process," that is, the upbringing of the child in the ways of the culture where *no* apparent alternatives are offered; and the other of less dependence where influence operates *after* early upbringing as part of adjustment to *new* social demands where there *are* alternatives for response that can be learned.

Individuals are brought within the framework of acceptable attitudes, values, and behaviors of the society in which they live through a process involving a great deal of *implicit* learning. By this we mean the acquisition of many of these attributes in the absence of any deliberate design to learn them or to teach them. This is in contrast to *explicit* learning, where either or both of these conditions of deliberateness are present. What is even more striking, however, is that what is learned in this implicit way is readily found congenial. Few of us, for example, resist the norms of our society in matters of monogamy, private ownership, and the use of the mother tongue. This is the essence of the point quoted above from Asch (1959). It is also true, as Erich Fromm (1949) has put it, that society shapes experience in such a way that ". . . *people want to act as they have to act* and [therefore] find gratification in acting according to the requirements of culture" (p. 5).

When instinct theories were in vogue, the problem of defining the motivational attributes of humans was relatively simple. There was, however, in the instinct idea a dubious logic, which largely led to its abandonment as applied to human affairs. It was simply *not* sufficient to make assertions of a circular sort such as "people strive for social acceptance because they have an innate tendency to seek social acceptance." As we noted earlier, the concept of instinct was especially misleading because it slighted the effect of Man's profound capacity for learning, in the broadest sense of adaptation. However, with the demise of instinct as a principle governing human conduct, it quickly became evident that other explanatory schemes would be necessary. This led to several kinds of distinctions which are still important points of reference today.

The first of these essentially distinguishes between *primary motives* which are physiologically based and necessary for the maintenance of life—such as hunger, thirst, the need for oxygen—and those learned or *acquired motives* which arise as a consequence of experience in society. The other kind of distinction has to do with the nature of human motivations that make Man distinctively different from other species. As we will see, however, the concept of motivation is itself undergoing considerable revision. Before turning to that, there is some merit in considering how the sources of human behavior have been looked at by social scientists, if only for an historical perspective on the complexity of the problem.

GENERAL CLASSIFICATION OF HUMAN MOTIVATION

The rich diversity of human motivation is widely acknowledged. But because the classification of motives was for so long identified with the imputation of different instincts to account for each and every observable behavior, the pendulum swung toward behaviorism with its minimal interest in motivation as such. In contemporary social psychology, it is fair to say that the global classifications of motives affecting social behavior are viewed with growing interest particularly in terms of the clustering of *social motives*. The question of Man's basic motivations remains an open and intriguing one.

Otto Klineberg's (1954) classification for four major categories of motives draws upon extensive anthropological and biological data. His aim was to distinguish between what he refers to as the "dependable" motives, which have a definite physiological base and admit of no exceptions, and the varying degrees of less dependable motives which have no discernible physiological basis and which have been found to have a greater frequency of exceptions in groups and in individuals, across cultures. He proposes the following classification (p. 164):

> Motives which are absolutely dependable have both a physiological basis and a universal quality. These include hunger, thirst, the need for rest, sleep and elimination, and also activity and "esthetic" drives.
>
> Motives which have a physiological basis but which admit of individual exceptions. These include sex, post-maternal behavior, and possibly self-preservation.
>
> Motives which have an indirect physiological basis, occur with great frequency, but are less dependable since they have exceptions in societies and among individuals. These include aggressiveness, flight, and probably self-assertiveness.
>
> Motives which have no known physiological basis but which occur with some frequency either because of common social patterns or as a means for satisfying practical ends. These essentially undependable motives are gregariousness, the paternal motive, the pre-maternal motive, the filial motive, acquisitiveness and self-submission.

Another approach to human motivation is represented in Abraham Maslow's (1954) hierarchy of motives. His basic idea is that motives may be arrayed from the strongest and most dominant through those which are likely to be significant only when the former are satisfied. In order, his hierarchy is as follows:

Physiological needs, such as hunger, thirst, sex, physical activity.

Safety needs, including security from physical and psychological deprivation.

Belongingness and love needs covering relationships of a responsive, affectionate, and affiliative nature.

Esteem needs seen in the desire of all people for a stable and high evaluation of themselves summed up in self-respect and the esteem of others.

Actualization representing the fusion or culmination of the other needs in a desire for self-realization or fulfillment of one's total capacities.

From his work across many cultures, the anthropologist Ralph Linton has proposed three "psychic needs" which he finds ". . . to be the most general and most significant for the understanding of human behavior" (1945, p. 7). He says that their origins are not necessarily innate, but that they have great generality in terms of observed behavior. They are:

The *need for emotional response from others,* which could arise from the early dependency relationships in infancy.

The *need for security of a long-term sort,* which takes account of the ever-present fact that humans have the ability to perceive time beyond the present and into the future. Hence, humans have a need for reassurance and hope but can live with the prospect of later gratification.

The *need for novelty of experience* which comes into play when the other needs are satisfied. It finds its counterpart in boredom and the need for experimentation.

Robert White (1959) has extended this idea of a human desire for experimentation, and an avoidance of boredom, to the concept of *effectance.* He sees as characteristic of Man a seeking for competence in handling the environment. Rather than be inborn in an instinctive sense, he contends that effectance motivation is part of Man's *need for exploratory and playful activity aimed at achieving competence* in an adjustive way. He says: "Putting it picturesquely, we might say that the effectance urge represents what the neuromuscular system wants to do when it is otherwise unoccupied or is gently stimulated by the environment . . . . The motive need not be conceived as intense and powerful in the sense that hunger, pain, or fear can be . . . [though] there are plenty of instances in which children refuse to leave their absorbed play in order to eat or visit the toilet" (p. 321).

The several viewpoints regarding social motivation that we have reviewed have certain common elements. Essentially they suggest that humans require more than the fulfillment of their survival needs in order to partake of a fully human experience. Reduced to a basic residue that begins necessarily with obvious demands for physical survival, these various systems, despite their varying emphases, suggest the following commonalities:

> Man requires social relationships and identifications but also a sense of his own personal identity and fulfillment.
>
> Man requires regularity, predictability, and order in his experience, but also the opportunity for activity and for experimenting with his own capacities in meeting the environment and having new experiences.

Summing up these points, we find what appears to be a paradox. How can Man want what seem to be contradictory satisfactions? One answer of course lies in the primary consideration that they are *not contradictory but complementary*. It is also noteworthy that we have been talking about "Man" in general, not a given person. Pursuing that point a bit further, we can readily see that though any one person may embody tendencies toward all of these satisfactions, they do not all operate for him simultaneously. A time element is implicitly involved. The great virtue in Maslow's conception, for example, is that he places his motives in a hierarchy such that those at one level do not have a pronounced effect on an individual when those at a more basic level are as yet unsatisfied for him, hence Maslow's appropriate comment that ". . . Man lives by bread alone—when there is no bread."

MOTIVATION: A BRIEF REVIEW

Thus far we have been treating motives as if they somehow "pushed" individuals toward goals. However, the idea of motivation as a drive state is much too confining. In a more up-to-date vein, Cofer and Appley (1964), for example, have placed considerable weight on generalized "arousal" as a pervasive feature of action. They see such arousal as having a future-oriented quality which they term the *anticipation-invigoration mechanism* (cf. Berlyne, 1960; Dember, 1965).

A "motive" may not be a single push, or pull, but an arousal of a sequence of behavior in an anticipatory, even playful, way. Furthermore, that sequence may serve multiple purposes. As Krech and Crutchfield (1948) point out, the regular church-going behavior of people who seem largely disinterested in religion can be revealed to be ". . . a meaningful, motivated action, fulfilling present needs and goals of gregariousness, social approval, wealth display, rest, or something else" (p. 32).

The traditional idea of motivation is concerned with behavior in terms of the goals toward which it appears directed. The problem, however, is that people often do the same thing for different reasons, and these reasons are never directly observed but are usually inferred from behavior. Furthermore, the actions implied by the same motive—or state of arousal—may differ widely depending upon the other people who are influential in supporting such action. Thus, a desire for "social acceptance" can lead one person to drive fast cars in a drag race and another to produce poetry.

The special relationship between motives and the goals they imply is of singular importance. Despite the fact that many social behaviors appear to be entirely dependent upon social practice, they nonetheless rely on the reciprocal relationship of motives and goals. Customs and institutions, and the appearance of imitation and suggestion, do not reduce the importance of the individual as an aroused actor. Granting the social basis of our attitudes and prejudices, it is not correct to understand them as being simply a result of some process of social habituation. Rather they should be seen as actions or reactions which anticipate desired outcomes, even though these may be obscured to immediate view. For example, the fact that individuals dislike those disliked by other members of their community does not stem just from exposure to social attitudes. This merely describes a circumstance that can better be explained by the motivation to participate with and be identified and accepted by important others.

As we have said, motives are considerably more complex than would be suggested by the helpful but simple notion of a "push" toward a goal. The goals that are implied by motives are themselves implicated in the underlying arousal that is associated with behavior. The goal does not stand apart from the individual but is actually encompassed within his psychological field. Hence, becoming aware of a favorable goal, or outcome, has something akin to a pulling effect on the individual in terms of a forward-thrust. This necessarily varies considerably depending upon the individual's interpretation of the total situation.

Lewin treated these mechanisms by considering objects, persons, and activities to have *positive valence* for the individual if they attract him and *negative valence* if they repel him. In these terms, a main determinant of valence rests in the person's past experience with the particular stimulus in question. Hence, a hungry individual in our society is likely to have a positive valence for hot dogs but a negative valence for whale blubber; for a hungry eskimo, we should not be surprised to find these valences reversed.

The valence of goals varies depending upon the particular state of arousal of the organism. Having eaten heartily of our meal of hot dogs, we are less likely in the ensuing hours to have a high valence for the same fare. This highlights the intimate association of perception in understanding arousal with regard to motivational-perceptual processes. It also points up the necessity to view behavior as a sequence of activities involving anticipations that may or may not be met, particularly in terms of adjustment to frustration.

PERCEPTION: A BRIEF REVIEW

The process of perception is basic to the organization of the individual's psychological field. As Allport (1954) and Bruner (1957) have pointed out, perception begins as an act of *categorization*. We define "reality" in terms of the categories into which we place experience. In the absence of appropriate categories, we may use old ones to account for new experience or develop new categories. Perception, therefore, relies heavily upon past experience. However, perception is also *selective* in its processing of new experience, depending upon the motives currently acting upon us and the goals that we are accordingly in search of at a particular time.

The categorical quality of perception is illustrated when primitive tribesmen see an airplane in flight for the first time. For them, the best category growing out of past experience would be "bird," and it is often the case that the airplane is first categorized by them under the label of "big bird." If they also have reason to be fearful, which implies present motivation to avoid harm, they might further perceive the bird in the more selective sense of a "big *angry* bird." In sum, perception employs categorization in the purposive sense of finding meaning. It is therefore *aimed at interpretation.*

In psychology, perception is said to depend upon sensation, and a distinction is usually made between those terms. Essentially, sensation is the awareness of a stimulus—e.g. hearing a loud noise—while perception is the interpretation of that stimulus as a result of further processing by the individual. The loud noise could be disregarded. Or, if perceived under essentially tranquil conditions, it might be interpreted as a car backfiring; and, under tense conditions of high threat, it might be interpreted as a bomb exploding.

The intimate commerce between perception and motivation actually operates reciprocally. It is for this reason that we have spoken of motivational-perceptual processes underlying adjustment. Individuals are likely to perceive events as a function of the anticipated goals of the moment, but the reverse is also true: *they are likely to be aroused by what they freshly perceive.*

The phenomenon of motivational effects on perception has been documented by a considerable volume of research over the past decades. Levine, Chein, and Murphy (1942), for example, found in an experiment that hungry persons who had not eaten for many hours tended to perceive many more "food items" on an ambiguous ground-glass screen than did non-hungry persons.

Motivational states can also directly affect perception, as Bruner and Goodman (1947) found in a classic experiment. They asked ten-year-old children to try to match the actual size of several different coins by turning a knob to alter the magnitude of a disc of light. Cardboard discs were used as a control. On the average, perceptions of the size of real coins were found to be overestimates. However, as is shown in Figure 4.2, children from poorer families differed significantly from children from wealthier families in overestimating size, especially of the quarter and half-dollar. The greater motivation associated with the value of money for the poorer children was the basis for explaining this perceptual discrepancy. Some questions have been raised about the generalizability of these results in light of nonconfirming studies (e.g.

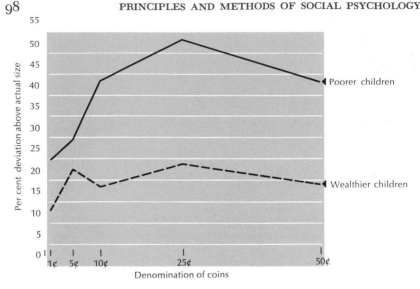

Figure 4.2: Size estimations of coins made by poorer and wealthier ten-year-olds. (From Bruner and Goodman, 1947.)

Carter and Schooler, 1949). However, the phenomenon of perceptual distortion has often been demonstrated to apply to valued stimulus materials of different kinds such as tokens which could be exchanged for candy (Lambert, Solomon, and Watson, 1949). Tajfel (1957) has pointed out that contradictory findings can be explained largely in terms of the *relevance* of size to value. Thus, where size is not important as a feature of value, then the phenomenon is usually not found.

Everyday experience reveals the selective effect of motivation on perception each time we are tuned to some qualities or things and neglect to notice others that are also present. The effect of perception on motivation is another readily observable phenomenon seen when individuals encounter experiences which are novel for them—such as trying a new food—and thus develop a "taste" which takes on the properties of a motive. This restructuring effect of new information is also humorously revealed in the heavy smoker's statement: "I've been reading so much lately about the evils of smoking that I've decided to give up reading."

Changes in our psychological field resulting from the input of new information are a source of influence of considerable importance. There are, however, underlying reasons for the tendency to resist such re-structuring, as we shall see.

Perception "sets" the individual to expect to encounter the world in a characteristic way. One reason that the statement just quoted is funny is that it prepares the listener for one thing and confronts him with another. This is true of a good deal of humor, which often operates by playfully disturbing a "set."

A fundamental principle of perception which grows out of the phenomenon of set is that individuals *tend to perceive experiences in the way they expect to perceive them.* This is sometimes summed up in the principle of perceptual *constancy,* that is, the tendency to perceive things in the same way as before. The importance of this point in social psychology rests in the significant association between expectation and outcome. Recall, too, the concept of "definition of the situation" in terms of the way this leads to anticipations in advance of experience. Since people frequently act in accordance with their expectation or anticipation of what will occur, they effectively increase the prospect that it will occur. This is the essence of the "self-fulfilling prophecy" concept mentioned in Chapter One.

The specific content of our perception, in the sense of our categories for defining experience, and the sets we may be operating under, as well as the motives instigating them, are referred to as "functional" features of perception. It is this in particular that we have been emphasizing to this point. There are also "structural" features of perception which have great generalizability since they arise from the nature of physical stimuli as they relate to the neurological characteristics of humans.

One such structural principle is that of *wholeness,* a tendency to see stimuli as fitting together. Related to this is the principle of *closure,* referring to the adding in of absent elements so as to achieve wholeness. Another ramification of this is the *imputation of causality* when stimuli are encountered in certain proximal or sequential relationships. Thus, individuals tend to perceive events which occur in sequence to be related causally. If a given event is followed by an observed outcome, that event takes on the quality of a "causal factor." This is the basis for the notion of luck and many other magical beliefs seen in the use of such "charms" as a rabbit's foot.

An additional quality of structural perception is the principle of

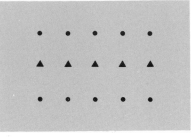

Figure 4.3: An illustration of "grouping" in perception.

grouping. Grouping is illustrated whenever things which have a common attribute are perceived as related. In Figure 4.3, for example, we are likely to see three lines rather than a rectangle or isolated dots and triangles.

The Gestalt psychologists have devoted a great deal of attention to the way in which perception is affected by patterned relationships; indeed, the German word *"Gestalt"* means a pattern or configuration. An essential quality of any pattern resides in a *contrast* effect between a figure and its background. A "figure-ground" relationship refers to which part of the pattern stands out as a figure and which serves as background. This is essentially a matter of "imbeddedness," pointing up the consideration that a stimulus is perceived within the context in which it is placed. When a shade of gray is viewed against a black background, it is seen as lighter than when it is seen against a white background. Many of these points regarding object perception apply in important ways to the perception of persons, as we will consider in detail in Chapter Seven.

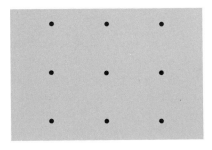

Figure 4.4: An illustration of "wholeness" in perception.

Structural properties of perception are by no means separable from the functional features arising from past experience and present motivational states. Patterns may be learned, as is revealed when we acquire the sense of "squareness," shown, for example, in Figure 4.4. The nine dots are not seen separately but are perceived to form together a dominant pattern. Hence, motivational-perceptual processes depend to a considerable degree on learning as a feature of adjustment.

Adjustment and learning

Learning is the major process of study in psychology. There is good reason for this emphasis in view of Man's great capacity to adapt his behavior. Basically, learning refers to *actual* or *potential* alterations of behavior which may be more or less permanent. This definition takes account of the fact that the effects of learning need not be observed directly to be ready for later elicitation, and that they need not take hold in a lasting sense. Thus, the psychologist is interested in responses, but he also takes account of the internal restructuring of the psychological field, which is closer to what occurs when, in the conventional sense of that term, we "learn" in school.

The study of learning in terms of observable responses has been approached in two distinctive ways: the *conditioning of involuntary reflexes,* and *instrumental conditioning.* Both approaches have yielded concepts which are useful in social psychology. In the first case, learning is studied in terms of involuntary acts which grow out of the association of a new stimulus with a response such as salivation, eye-blinking, or any other reflexive act. In the other case, learning is studied in terms of voluntary or "emitted" behaviors which can have instrumental value in achieving a goal. The former approach, often referred to as "classical conditioning," is identified most with the work of Ivan Pavlov; the latter, sometimes called "operant learning," is associated most with the work of B. F. Skinner. These approaches are not as different as would appear since they each rely on associative learning under motivating conditions. Furthermore, neither depends upon conscious processes for elicitation.

Both approaches to learning look upon motivation as an energizer of action or reaction. Perception is also involved in both in terms of the cues which elicit behavior in line with the satisfaction of motives. The fundamental principle which underlies any learning and which therefore applies to both approaches can be summed up briefly: whenever an action or reaction satisfies a motive, this increases the probability of that action or reaction occurring subsequently when the motive is again aroused.

In any learning, adaptive behavior is not literally created so much as its probability is increased. Skinner says that he "reinforces" an already emitted behavior and by an appropriate sequence of "reinforcement" increases its probability of emission. But reinforcement need not be thought of only as something outside the person, such as an attractive goal-object. For example, Mowrer (1960) has contended that it can be conceived as a positive feeling—of anticipation or hope—experienced internally by the individual. Mowrer's current theory of learning is built on the emotional states of hope and fear as counterparts to what Skinner calls positive and negative reinforcement.

Adjustment can be looked upon as a progressive process of learning, mainly of appropriate instrumental acts, but also of motivational-perceptual processes which guide integrated response sequences. Two important and interrelated features of learning that affect these sequences are summed up by the terms "generalization" and "discrimination." Given positive outcomes, responses become *generalized* to other similar stimulus patterns; and, alternatively, selective perception can occur between stimulus patterns so as to yield a *discriminated* response depending on their different qualities.

It is generally found that learning not only is instigated by motivation but that it also persists where motives continue to be served. This need not be on a completely constant basis, however. Reinforcers have been found to be especially necessary at the *start* of learning to produce appropriate and consistent responses. Furthermore, their absence after learning leads to comparatively rapid "extinction" of responses. Yet, responses do persist in the absence of reinforcers if learning has taken place with a schedule of *partial* rather than *continuous* reinforcement. In Figure 4.5, cumulative response curves are given for these two conditions of learning seen in the extinction phase. One striking finding is that the most persisting learned responses are usually those associated with a kind of partial schedule—the condition of "variable reinforcement" in which the respondent does not know on which response-trials

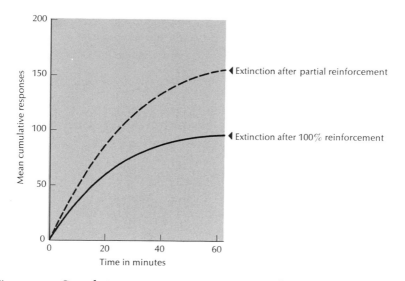

Figure 4.5: Cumulative response curves over time illustrating extinction effects following partial reinforcement and constant reinforcement. Responses have ceased when the curves become horizontal. (From *Introduction to Psychology* by C. T. Morgan. Copyright © 1961 by McGraw-Hill Inc. Used by permission of McGraw-Hill Book Company.)

he will be reinforced. This is said to account for the appeal of gambling with its unpredictable, hence variable, pay-off sequence.

The implications from studies of learning can now be briefly summarized. Whether learning is construed within the framework of classical conditioning or instrumental conditioning, motivational-perceptual processes are involved, including generalization and discrimination of stimulus patterns, as a basis for response. Associations are thereby developed which increase the probability of a similar response being occasioned again under comparable circumstances. The individual may experience a "good" feeling when his actual or implied response is the same as that he gave before under pleasant-feeling circumstances. The tenacity of a response is affected by the initial conditions of learning. Thus, extinction of a response is less likely if "partial" reinforcement was provided rather than "continuous" reinforcement, though continuous reinforcement is useful in the initial sequence of learning. Learning does not necessarily involve conscious processes but can affect thought in the sense of reconstituting the psychological field.

One further point concerning adjustment and learning is represented in Helson's (1959) concept of *adaptation level*. Psychologically defined, it is the stimulus value (e.g. coldness, heaviness) which is neutral and with regard to which stimuli above it or below it are judged. Essentially, our judgments of stimuli grow out of past experience and a process of learning. In social judgments our adaptation often takes the form of perceiving ourselves as the person in the center. Someone says he is "liberal" about government spending. He then considers anyone who is more liberal to be a "spendthrift" and anyone who is less liberal to be a "tightwad." Similarly, he may say that he is "friendly," but that you are "familiar" and I am "aloof."

In social psychology, the concept of adaptation level is particularly important for understanding reactions to new information. As a general rule, communications are judged within the scale of the attitudes currently held by the individual recipient. Thus, the communicator who appears to advocate a moderate position on an issue such as civil rights would be perceived as a "raving radical" by a recipient positioned more negatively on this issue, and as a "go slow conservative" by a recipient positioned more affirmatively on it. This phenomenon is considered further in Chapter Six in connection with attitude change.

Learning and social influence

A convenient way to approach social influence is to see it in terms of learning. As it is presently understood, learning is a process of adaptation occasioned by new experience. It therefore directly involves the input of information to the individual as a basis for his response. Whenever one person or some persons collectively provide information to another person, the elements of an influence relationship are produced. While all learning is *not* indicative of social influence, all influence relationships have the essential features of learning in these terms.

In recent years a good deal of research has been done leading to the conclusion that individuals are affected, often unknowingly, by the reinforcement others provide. For example, in summarizing the results of thirty-one studies of this phenomenon, Krasner (1958) reports that there is considerable regularity in the effect of verbal and non-verbal acts of one person on the behavior of another. These reinforcements

may be such things as saying "good" or nodding affirmatively. Verplanck (1955) conducted an experiment which illustrates this effect
quite conclusively. He had experimenters systematically agree to opinions offered unknowingly by other people in conversation. His results
are shown in Figure 4.6 in the form of cumulative response curves. The

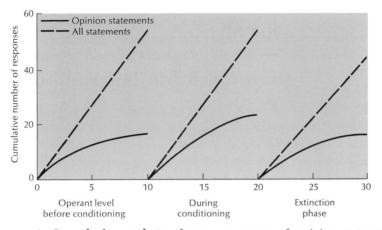

Figure 4.6: Smoothed cumulative frequency curves of opinion statements
and of all statements for ten-minute segments of the experiment. (From
Verplanck, 1955.)

first two portions reveal a marked and significant increase in the proportion of statements of opinion after conditioning, and before extinction. No significant increase was observed in the total amount of speaking, just the proportion of opinion statements. Bachrach, Candland,
and Gibson (1961) have demonstrated a comparable effect using a
group of others to reinforce the verbal responses of individuals by such
positive reinforcers as saying "Yes," "Good," or "Mmm," and such negative ones as saying "No" and giving horizontal head motions.

The influence effects of reinforcement have also been studied with
regard to leadership. Thus, in a laboratory experiment conducted by
Pepinsky, Hemphill, and Shevitz (1958), it was found that those subjects who had been low on leader activity could be encouraged, without awareness, to increase that kind of behavior by the group's support
of their statements; on the other hand, those who had been high on
leader activity were affected in the opposite way by the group's evident
discouragement of their statements.

Experimentation with the phenomenon of conformity has also re-

vealed the consequences of reinforcement by others upon an individual's willingness to accept the erroneous judgment of the group, as in
the Asch experiment described in the last chapter. One tack in such
work is to have the experimenter reinforce the "independence" of the
subject by introducing the experimental treatment of telling him in advance that he is more accurate or correct than his coworkers. This characterizes one aspect of the work of Kelman (1950), Mausner (1954a),
and Luchins and Luchins (1961). Another tack that such research may
take is to have the group serve as a source of reinforcement of one's
sense of accuracy, in advance of presenting erroneous group judgments.
This is illustrated in an experiment by Hollander, Julian, and Haaland
(1965) where "dependence" upon the group was variously contrived
by having true subjects report first among five group members in a
situation requiring the judgment about a simple unambiguous task
over twenty trials. Some subjects found everyone agreeing with them
on all twenty trials, some on fourteen randomized trials, and others on
ten randomized trials. A control condition provided no feedback of
others' judgments. Then, in all conditions, the true subjects were placed
in the *last* response position for the twenty additional trials. This time
all of the other group members appeared to be giving totally erroneous
responses, and *in advance* of the subject. Conformity was measured by
trials on which subjects gave this same incorrect response.

As is seen in Figure 4.7, those subjects who had the prior experience
of agreement from others on all twenty earlier trials (100 per cent condition) gave the highest initial conformity, in the first block of the five
later trials, with also a great drop-off in time associated with extinction.
Support in the form of partial reinforcement (70 per cent and 50 per
cent conditions) yielded lower initial conformity to the group's erroneous judgments but greater persistence of response.

This kind of research provides a link between social influence and
learning as a function of new experiences which can have observable
sequential effects. Summarizing this point, it seems apparent that what
is learned in any influence situation is a greater or lesser dependence
upon the agent or source of influence as a basis for judgment and related action. There is considerable virtue, therefore, in looking at social
influence in terms of a sequential learning process.

It is also worth noting again that partial reinforcement tends to produce a more persisting response. In their review of thirty-five studies

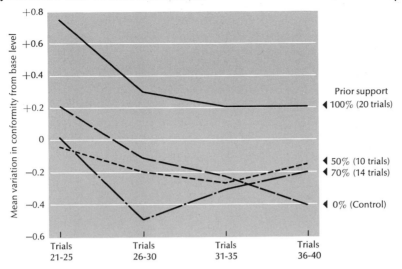

Figure 4.7: Subsequent conformity responses by blocks of five trials each for subjects exposed to different levels of prior group support in the first twenty trials. Scores are given as average difference from base level, combining sexes. (Based on data from Hollander, Julian, and Haaland, 1965.)

covering subjects in a wide variety of training situations, Jenkins and Stanley (1950) conclude that "the most striking effects of partial reinforcement are apparent in response strength as measured by resistance to extinction" (p. 231). This has particular importance to social psychology in view of the discontinuous quality of reinforcement provided in social interaction. In the upbringing of a child, for example, it is rarely possible to provide constant reinforcement. This may make the learning of appropriate behaviors slower, but it has the effect of heightening the persistence of that behavior when reinforcement is no longer provided regularly, or not at all, as in conditions of extinction.

Social influence process: some conclusions

Throughout this chapter we have emphasized the continuing thread of Man's capacity for learning. While individuals adjust in terms of the experiences of the past, they also encounter new experience and the demands it makes for adjustment. Accordingly, the exposure to change and to novel experience or information is a central feature of social influence. In that regard, an influence relationship can be thought of as inducing a process which functions to change behavior and associated attitudes by an informational input. That humans are also capable of a high level of information-processing, in the form of thought, underscores this point.

Viewed now at a general level, all influence events appear to involve three essential elements which are not fixed but quite alterable in time. Though these may be variously labeled and can be treated at different levels of abstraction, they fundamentally come down to:

> An *influence source* which, at a given moment, might be another person, a friend, a father, a leader; a group of others; or a communicator, such as a public figure appearing on TV. Influence sources can be perceived by the recipients of their communications to have attributes arising from actual interaction with them, or from what has been learned from other sources about them.
>
> A *communication* or *message,* that can be in the form of behavior, in terms of actions seen to have certain properties, or in the usual form of a verbal message.
>
> A *recipient of the communication,* the target of influence at the moment, possessing personal motivations and associated perceptions, which include group identifications and attitudes guiding response.

Influence patterns may differ across many situations, but the three essential elements we have noted can always be found. In the case of face-to-face interaction, both persons have the characteristics of influence source and recipient insofar as they have a reciprocating effect upon one another. Generally speaking, in conformity the group is the influence source. In leadership, the influence source is a person and the "recipients" of the communication are the followers in the group. Direct interaction is not, however, a requisite for influence to occur. The perception of negative or positive attributes of the source can also be learned indirectly through a kind of "implied interaction."

One central question raised earlier concerns the psychological meaning of group affiliation. In other terms drawn from our considerations in this chapter, we may now ask what motivation leads to the acceptance of social influence assertions. We have already suggested that the individual is dependent upon others in several ways, including his identification with them, a reliance on them for approval, and also for assistance in defining reality. As major motivational themes, then, we can now place these for convenience under the headings of social identity, social support, and social reality:

> *Social identity* refers to the attachment a person feels toward others, individually or collectively, which gives him a sense of having a place in society. It is related to the idea of having status, both as a literal position and as a standing in the eyes of relevant others. Accordingly, social identity provides a significant social anchorage for the person in terms of "belonging."

> *Social support* refers to the favorable response a person secures from others which sustains his behavioral sequences. In this sense, support may be thought of as arising from signs of recognition and approval in terms of the "social reinforcement" received for valued actions and attitudes.

> *Social reality* refers to the shared outlook which a person acquires from others. It provides him with a way of viewing the world that helps to simplify complexity and clarify ambiguity.

These motives, although not entirely separable, do suggest a clustering of sources of arousal that affect the individual's reactions to influence. Where there is a continuing relationship between an individual and one or more others, it is quite likely that at least one of these motives is aroused and served by that relationship.

The implication of these points is that there are several bases for affiliations and social relationships which have influence effects. We shall return to these points in various ways. With this general background in mind, we can now turn to a concern with attitudes in the next two chapters, beginning with their composition and acquisition.

SUMMARY

Man's distinctive characteristics depend upon learning from contact with other humans. Social interaction is a vital feature of social adjustment, in terms of the relationships the individual has with the other people in his environment. Adjustment can be viewed as comprising a sequence of processes which interrelate to produce integrated behavior. These processes are motivation, perception, and learning. Studies of these processes in individual psychology have been useful in helping to understand social influence.

Adjustment can be viewed in at least three ways: first, in the *egocentric* terms of the satisfactions obtained by the individual from the environment; second, in terms of *social forces* requiring compliance and the striking of a *balance* between these and individual psychological states; third, as an *unfolding* of individual potentialities. All of these views implicitly convey the idea of change and dynamism, but also of habituation.

Adjustment to society is a pervasive requirement of life. For the most part, however, individuals readily accept the selective quality of experience and related demands of society. Because an individual's motives cannot always be satisfied, a state of *frustration* occurs which represents an essential psychological basis for adjustment. Adjustive techniques include compromise, withdrawal, direct aggression, displaced aggression, problem-solving and productive action.

Motivation instigates behavior sequences aimed at goal-achievement. In psychology, a distinction is usually made between *primary motives*, such as the "hunger drive," which are physiologically based and necessary for the maintenance of life, and *acquired motives*, which are learned, e.g. achievement of social acceptance. Both imply goals which are incorporated in the psychological field. Moreover, the primary motives are subject to social influence, insofar as their satisfaction is regulated by society.

Attempts to codify Man's basic motivation have produced various systems. These point to the complementary quality of Man's requirement for: social relationships as well as personal identity; regularity and predictability but also new experience.

For the individual to adjust, he must modify his responses as well as reconstitute his psychological field. This involves motivational-perceptual processes which operate together to affect learning, through such mechanisms as "discrimination" and "generalization" of response to stimuli.

Perception is a process of categorization that is selective as a function of past experience, present motives, and anticipated future gains. It also directs the interpretation of stimulus patterns toward constancy and wholeness, in terms of the context in which they are imbedded. For social psychology, a key feature of perception is the phenomenon of "set" which leads individuals to perceive stimuli the way they expect to perceive them.

The study of learning of responses has been approached in terms of *classical conditioning* and *operant learning.* Both have yielded useful concepts for the understanding of social behavior. In either case learning depends upon motivation as an energizer of action or reaction. Where a motive is satisfied, this tends to increase the probability of the same response when the motive is again aroused. Where satisfaction of the motive is no longer provided, learning under conditions of constant reinforcement is not as effective in producing later consistency of response as is partial reinforcement. Perception is also affected by the process of learning, in the sense of restructuring the psychological field. Thus, *adaptation level,* which refers mainly to perceptions of the intensity of stimuli, grows out of what an individual has become used to from past experience.

Social influence can be looked upon as a phenomenon involving learning through the input of new experience. Experimentation has revealed that individuals are affected by the "reinforcement" others provide through verbal and non-verbal acts. This has been shown to affect statements of opinion, leadership, and conformity.

Any influence relationship induces a process which functions to change behavior and related attitudes. It usually involves three essential elements which may be altered over time, as in social interaction. These are: an *influence source,* a *communication* or *message,* and a *recipient of the communication.* The acceptance of influence rests in a *dependence* relationship with the source. Three affiliation motives which can produce this relationship are the needs for *social identity, social support,* and *social reality.*

SUGGESTED READINGS

From E. P. Hollander and R. G. Hunt. (Eds.) *Current perspectives in social psychology.* (2nd Edition.) New York: Oxford University Press, 1967:

8. Hadley Cantril: *The human design*
Introduction to Section II: *Culture, learning, and group identification*

9. Tamotsu Shibutani: *Reference groups as perspectives*
10. John W. Gardner: *Individuality, commitment, and meaning*

SELECTED REFERENCES

Bandura, A. & Walters, R. H. *Social learning and personality development.* New York: Holt, Rinehart & Winston, 1963.

Cofer, C. N. & Appley, M. H. *Motivation: Theory and research.* New York: Wiley, 1964.

Crowne, D. P. & Marlowe, D. *The approval motive: Studies in evaluative dependence.* New York: Wiley, 1964.

*Lazarus, R. S. *Personality and adjustment.* Englewood Cliffs, N. J.: Prentice-Hall, 1963.

Schachter, S. *The psychology of affiliation.* Stanford, Calif.: Stanford Univer. Press, 1959.

5

The composition and acquisition
of attitudes

The myriad effects of attitudes are evident all around us. For attitudes carry expectancies about our own behavior and the behavior of others, and they touch on all aspects of social life. Our tastes, manners, and morals reflect our attitudes and, relatedly, the social values which underlie them. How an individual views his world and acts toward it can be understood in great measure through the attitudes that make up his psychological field.

Attitudes, as well as values, are acquired as a result of being introduced into the ways of a society. In the broadest sense, therefore, attitudes can be considered to be the psychological representations of the influence of society and culture in the individual. They are very largely inseparable from the social context which produces, sustains, and elicits them under appropriate circumstances. Yet, attitudes retain the flavor of unique individual experiences as well. They are learned and tend to persist as a consequence of past social interaction. These experiences are conveniently summed up by the individual's present attitudes which, in turn, have directive effects on his ongoing, future-oriented activity.

The study of attitudes and values has occupied a major share of attention in social psychology for several decades. This is understandable, since they are the result of social influence and help to account for individual differences in reactions to similar circumstances. Though in some way attitudes bear on each of the topics covered in the chapters here, this chapter and the next will be directed especially to presenting the various characterizations of attitudes, their acquisition, measurement, and processes affecting their change.

The general nature of attitudes and values

Both attitudes and values have properties which define what is *expected* and what is *desired*. They can both therefore be thought of as motivational-perceptual states which direct action. Despite this common quality, it has been traditional to treat attitudes and values as distinctive. The major reason for this is as much a matter of stress as of function. For one thing, individuals hold many more attitudes than values. As Rokeach (1966) has put it:

> A grown person probably has tens of thousands of beliefs, hundreds of attitudes, but only dozens of values. A *value system* is an hierarchical organization—a rank ordering—of ideals or values in terms of importance. To one person truth, beauty, and freedom may be at the top of the list, and thrift, order, and cleanliness at the bottom: to another person, the order may be reversed (p. 10).

Another distinction between attitudes and values has to do with their cultural linkage. A culture is seen to have certain values, rather than attitudes. Individuals are therefore sustained in their values by their cultural surroundings. As we pointed out in connection with the work of McClelland on the "achieving society" (1961) in Chapter Three (p. 80), achievement motivation may be a cultural value. In simple terms, it represents the culture's emphasis on achievement as a significant social goal. The greater stability of values is usually accounted for in part, therefore, by their existence as guiding influences within the culture. The learning of values which goes on in socialization is probably not, however, distinctive from the acquisition of attitudes. What is more, a person's "value system," in the sense of an ordering of values, is in fact usually determined from a measure of attitudes. Accordingly, in what follows, our primary emphasis will be upon attitudes with a recognition that they are intertwined with values.

SOME POINTS OF DEFINITION

An *attitude* may be defined as a learned and relatively enduring organization of beliefs about an object or situation disposing a person toward some preferred response (Rokeach, 1966). The term "enduring" emphasizes the perceptual constancy of attitudes as *sets*. In this regard, Asch among others considers that attitudes are "enduring sets formed by past experience" (1952, p. 585). The term "organization of beliefs" stresses the consideration that attitudes do not simply stand alone so much as they *cluster* together. The reference to "response" reveals the *motivational* force attitudes exert on action. People typically hold attitudes toward a wide range of social entities including, for example, the institutions and organizations of society, racial and religious minorities, and political and social issues. Thus, to take one illustration, they believe an interrelated cluster of things about political affairs, may accordingly reject other views, and are disposed toward certain behaviors, as exemplified in voting, writing letters to congressmen, or their political activities.

Values may be considered to be the core component of a clustering of attitudes which direct behavior on a long-range basis toward some goals in preference to others. In a motivational sense, therefore, values have a more central quality. Furthermore, they have been found to be less subject to the effects of a situational change. Within a culture, a fair degree of congruence is usually found in the ordering of values. In one illustration of this, Morris (1956) had a sample of American college students rate thirteen "ways of life"—"preserve the best that man has attained," "cultivate independence of persons and things," and so on— and then analyzed these for major factors. In order, five factors emerged which may be paraphrased as follows:

> Participation and involvement with others
> Activity rather than receptivity
> Enjoyment in progress and achievement
> Socal restraint and self-control
> Self-indulgency.

More than five factors would undoubtedly better describe a person's total value system. However, when Morris compared the relative "loadings" of these factors with those secured in other cultures, he found several differences despite this shortcoming. In India and Norway, for example, the highest loading among these value factors was found to be "social restraint and self-control." Furthermore, "self-indulgency" which had been rated lowest but nonetheless positively among American students, was rated negatively in India, Norway, China, and Japan.

There is, of course, a considerable question about the breadth and stability of these values across a total society. This is a point to which we return in Chapter Eleven, in connection with sub-cultural variations. Nonetheless, a degree of consistency is frequently found in the value systems of members of the same society who have been exposed to a dominant cultural pattern. Osgood, Ware, and Morris (1961), for example, found a considerable parallel between the values from Morris's study using rankings and those obtained from a "semantic differential" procedure (see p. 261) used with another group of American college students at a later time. Bearing in mind that there may still be a fair degree of individual difference in values, we now will consider the broader influences of cultural factors in attitudes and values.

CULTURAL FACTORS IN ATTITUDES AND VALUES

Taking on the appropriate attitudes toward other people, toward groups, toward food and other objects in the environment is basic to being human. Attitudes about culturally significant objects carry an implicit valence in a positive or negative sense. Foods serve as one apt illustration. Among the earliest experiences in any culture are those which have to do with approved or disapproved foods, as well as the scheduling of meals.

In American society, for example, the culture dictates a breakfast which typically could consist of fruit juice, cereal or eggs. Other societies have cultural patterns emphasizing a breakfast of rice, or yoghurt, or kippers. We eat three meals a day and accept that pattern much as the air we breathe. We also expect to eat them "on time," which in itself is culturally relative. Thus, it comes as a jolt to find a different pattern when, for instance, Americans traveling in Spain discover that restaurants customarily open in the vicinity of 9 p.m. for the evening meal. Even the sense of time, and the significance attached to it, is dependent upon the learned patterns of a culture, as the work of such anthropologists as Hallowell (1937) and Hall (1959) reveals (see Chapter Eight, p. 231).

The characteristic values of a culture have a quite pervasive effect as key points of reference for individual judgments. As a case in point, in our society we are inclined to value height. In other societies our own culturally based view of the merit of tallness may be eyed differently, especially if people tend to be considerably shorter. A story illustrating this comes from an American visitor to Hong Kong who was ordering a suit from a tailor there. The visitor, ranging a bit over six feet in height, was asked by the tailor whether he would prefer a two- or three-button model. The man disclaimed a preference so the tailor apologetically urged him to take a two-button suit, explaining "It will make you look shorter."

What any society dictates by way of cultural patterns materially influences its members' expectations about events and things in the environment. When people encounter contradictions of their expectations, especially when the issue has immediate importance to them, as in the matter of eating, they are likely to experience some distress. This quality of shaping experience makes attitudes and values very consequential as systems affecting human life. In speaking of this effect, Ralph Linton (1945) says:

> Behavior which is not in accord with the individual's system elicits responses of fear, anger, or, at the very least, disapproval. . . . Thus an individual who performs an act contrary to one of his own value-attitude systems will experience considerable emotional disturbance both before and after (p. 112).

ATTITUDES AND VALUES AS MOTIVATIONAL-PERCEPTUAL STATES

In the last chapter we spoke of learning in terms of motivational-perceptual processes. Attitudes and values can be thought of and will be dealt with here as motivational-perceptual *states* (cf. F. H. Allport, 1955). An individual's attitudes set him to respond through the perceptual quality of selecting, categorizing, and interpreting experience in line with expectation; an individual's values are associated with the central tendency of a cluster of his attitudes in a long-range motivational sense. Attitudes and values are both learned in terms of a restructuring of the psychological field. This process is a dynamic one insofar as attitudes and values are subject to change through the acquisition of new information. However, attitudes appear to be more susceptible to apparent change while the basic value underlying them may persist.

As we have already observed, attitudes and values are important in social psychology because they sum up the past experience of the individual in terms of *directive* motivational-perceptual states, growing out of learning. It is also possible that learning in turn will bring about a restructuring of these states. Thus, a directive motivational-perceptual state can be thought of as an outcome of a process of learning which fashions further learning. This process therefore has consequences not only in terms of observable behaviors but also with respect to potentials for the individual's action.

THE RELATIONSHIP OF ATTITUDES AND VALUES

Though there is a commonality between attitudes and values, they are not necessarily in harmony. Indeed, a given value can lead to different and even opposite attitudes in the same person. For example, the need for achievement may yield a belief in one's right to individual betterment through competition, as well as a belief in the necessity to work with others co-operatively. In addition, a given attitude held by one person can arise from a different value than that underlying the same attitude held by someone else. One person might believe in helping the poor out of a sense of social obligation for the improvement of society, while another might believe the same thing out of a sense of superiority. Furthermore, the quality and texture of their actions toward the poor would vary accordingly.

A schematic representation of the probable relationship between an individual's attitudes and values is shown in Figure 5.1. As indicated there, the same value may give rise to conflicting attitudes, as might be

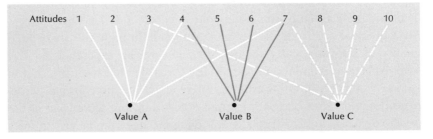

Figure 5.1: Diagram showing schematic relationship between three values with varying clusters of attitudes. Note that each value has several attitudes organized about it to indicate what is merely a sampling of those attitudes.

the case for attitudes 8 and 10, for example. Different values may sustain one attitude, though with variable intensity, as noted for 3 (A and C), 4 (A and B), 7 (A, B, and C) as instances.

Even given the refined measuring techniques presently available, it is difficult to separate attitudes and values entirely since there are so many points of interrelation between them. One thing appears to be generally agreed; attitudes are inclined to be more susceptible to change—at least in their outward expression—as a consequence of real or contrived circumstances. In this connection, Hovland (1959) points out that experimentation on attitude change routinely shows a more pronounced effect in shifting attitudes than is evidenced from questionnaire surveys. He also indicates that this is probably due in part to the fact that experiments often deal with attitudes which are more trivial to individuals than those studied in surveys. Thus, political attitudes can be highly significant as a feature of the individual's value system and hence be less subject to change.

The systematic measurement of values has usually been based on a limited number of values which may represent the central core for many attitudes. Allport, Vernon, and Lindzey (1951), for example, have developed a widely used, standardized scale for measuring the relative importance individuals attach to six values:

> *Theoretical:* being oriented toward a quest for truth through empiricism, criticism, or rationality.
> *Practical:* stressing utility and adherence to prevailing economic views.
> *Aesthetic:* giving prominence to form, harmony, and symmetry as sources of enjoyment.
> *Social:* emphasizing humanistic orientations such as altruism and philanthropy.
> *Power:* weighting personal power and influence, including those aspects of politics.
> *Religious:* seeking transcendent or mystical experiences through which to understand the unity and meaning of life.

An individual's value system is established by means of a "profile" derived from his indicated preference among alternatives on many items in the scale. Employing this measure, Allport, Vernon, and Lindzey have demonstrated that a group of medical students was high on the theoretical scale but low on the religious scale; the opposite was the case for theology students. Generally speaking, vocational preferences have been found to be part of a clustering of attitudes, related to basic value systems, and not the result of a single attitude toward a given field.

The entrenched nature of values has recently been studied by an experimental procedure employing a variant of Asch's group pressure situation (Vaughan and Mangan, 1963). In this work, the subjects had previously expressed preferences for various values on the Allport-Vernon-Lindzey scale. They were then exposed to a task involving accurate recognition of statements quickly flashed on a screen before them. The three other apparent subjects were instructed to report incorrect recognitions of these sentences in each instance opposite to the true subject's values. Thus, one actual sentence, involving a highly practical (economic) value was: "Production efficiency is a matter of *vital* concern." It was incorrectly rendered as: "Production efficiency is a matter of *minor* concern." The results indicated that the rest of the group's recognitions were strongly resisted when the actual sentence held a meaning of high value for the subjects. On the other hand, where it did not, the subjects showed little resistance at all.

The structure and functions of attitudes

In the early study of attitudes, it was quite common to rely largely on the description of an individual's attitudes, their direction in terms of valence, and the belief systems that they constituted. More recently, attitudes have been viewed with considerably greater stress on what can be called their *structural relationships* and *functional features*. The first of these newer emphases has been called "cognitive interaction," which conveys the idea of a relationship between attitudes within the psychological field. It also encompasses the processes by which new experiences become absorbed as added information. Within this approach a great deal of contemporary research has been directed toward attitudinal consistency and congruity, about which we shall say more shortly. The second emphasis, on functional features, concerns especially the motivations which attitudes serve.

COMPONENTS AND ASPECTS OF ATTITUDES

There are a great many ways to approach the organization of attitudes, but for convenience, we can consider them with reference to three major components and three aspects of study. Regarding the components, Katz (1960) observes that attitudes have been treated with respect to a *cognitive component,* which refers to belief-disbelief, an *affective component,* which deals with like-dislike, and an *action component,* which embodies a readiness to respond. The relationship of these components continues to be a lively interest in contemporary social psychology (e.g. Rosenberg, 1956, 1960a, b; Campbell, 1963; Festinger, 1964a). Thus, believing or not believing something, and liking one or the other alternative, are by no means simple distinctions to make. As Rokeach (1966) has pointed out, a firmly entrenched belief, especially when challenged, is usually found to have considerable positive affect. There may be little apparent liking—in the sense of positive valence— associated with one's belief that the earth is round, yet a contradiction of it would generate strong feeling. This point bears on consistency which will be considered below.

The three major aspects in the study of attitudes are: the *relationships* of their components, especially in terms of cognitive interaction and individual adjustment; their *source,* that is, the patterns by which attitudes are acquired through learning; and attitude *change,* with reference to the influences on the individual which result in the incorporation of new experience and the modification of attitudes. In this chapter and the next we shall be dealing with each of these and also with measurement which is important in their study. Moreover, since they are highly interrelated, a good deal that can be said about one aspect bears upon the others. The source of attitudes, for example, has direct implications for their change. Knowledge of how individuals "acquire" attitudes and "retain" attitudes can have implications for understanding why individuals "act" on some and not others.

Viewed broadly, there are several qualities of attitudes which we may now generalize as follows: they are beliefs and feelings about an object or set of objects in the social environment; they are learned; they tend to persist, though subject to the effects of experience; and they are directive states in the psychological field which affect action.

THE CONSISTENCY OF ATTITUDES

Individuals are not fully aware of their attitudes, and this in part accounts for their possible inconsistency with one another. Indeed, to a considerable degree attitudes exist at a low level of consciousness. Unless circumstances force the individual to face conflicts between them and perhaps resolve them, they may remain unnoticed.

One situational factor which can produce an observable inconsistency between expressed attitudes occurs in connection with the roles an individual must take requiring him to say one thing in one circumstance and something else in another. Depending upon the nature of his role, a person expresses attitudes within the framework of the social expectancies of others, as well as his own motivations.

It may also be the case that an individual will say one thing but do another. This variance between attitudes and actions is a further kind of inconsistency which can be tied to the variable nature of social circumstance, as we shall observe further in the next chapter. In addition, such apparent inconsistency suggests the importance of distinguishing between *private attitudes* and *public commitment*. There is reason to suppose that the relationship between these is by no means direct as Kelman (1961), among others, has observed. In short, an individual may or may not change his underlying attitude due to the force of circumstance.

Another kind of inconsistency, that between the cognitive and affective components of an attitude, has gained particular attention in the work of Milton Rosenberg. In one of his studies (1956) he found substantial evidence that these components tended to be highly correlated with one another. Thereafter he set forth the proposition that "When the affective and cognitive components of an attitude are mutually consistent, the attitude is in a stable state" (1960a, p. 322). Thus, if an individual undergoes a change of belief, his feelings about the object of the attitude should change accordingly; the reverse proposition is harder to test, but should be equally true. In another experiment (1960c), Rosenberg employed hypnosis to induce shifts in the direction of negative feelings toward foreign aid. He then found that his subjects' beliefs altered in the same negative direction to be consistent with the negative affect. Apart from the question of the stability of these changes, it is difficult to maintain a fine separation between cognitive and affective components as dependent and independent variables (Rokeach, 1966).

Undoubtedly the largest program of current work directed toward an understanding of the consistency of attitudes, and of attitudes and actions, grows out of Leon Festinger's "cognitive dissonance" theory (Festinger, 1957, 1964b). The main theme of this work is that psychological structure is made up of an organized set of cognitions. In maintaining this structure, individuals avoid dissonance and seek consonance among their cognitions, including attitudes. A dissonant relationship exists between two attitudes, or cognitive elements, when one implies the opposite of the other, e.g. "I feel rain, but there are no clouds in the sky."

A cardinal principle of dissonance theory is that people are disinclined to accept new cognitive elements—e.g. information—which violates a belief system they already hold. The idea is summed up in the half-comic, half-serious quip: "Don't bother me with the facts; my mind's made up."

Within the dissonance framework, commitment to action has been found to be a key feature in determining the stability and change of attitudes. Studies by Festinger and his associates (e.g. Festinger, 1957, 1964; Festinger and Carlsmith, 1959; Brehm and Cohen, 1962) lend support to the adaptation of attitudes to a change of behavior, or circumstance. This cognitive "shift" as a consequence of commitment—a kind of *fait accompli* effect—is nicely illustrated in *Life* magazine (June 17, 1966, p. 44) in an interview with the highly successful dress designer Mollie Parnis. She speaks of the threat and doubts that she experiences when her "reputation is at the scaffold" four times a year, and continues:

> When I look at the collection seconds before I present it to the buyers and press, I think, "God, I am mad—I should have stopped last year when I was good." I think of dozens of points that I should change, but it is too late. Yet after the collection is shown my panic disappears and my whole attitude switches. Then I won't alter anything and if anyone suggests a change, I resent it.

This statement also exemplifies the interrelated functioning of the cognitive and affective components of attitudes. With the presentation of her collection an acknowledged fact, Miss Parnis experiences strong positive feelings about it which serve to resist any dissonant elements, such as suggestions for changes in the collection.

We have dealt here only with some facets of consistency concepts applicable to attitudes. In the next chapter we will consider others in connection with cognitive approaches to attitude change. At this juncture, it is useful to widen our focus to the functional features of attitudes more generally.

FUNCTIONAL FEATURES OF ATTITUDES

The functions that attitudes serve fall into several categories. In keeping with our earlier discussion, it should be borne in mind that the complexity of human motivation is such as to involve various kinds of social goals which may be served at one time. Thus, holding and expressing certain attitudes fulfill the individual's needs to achieve social identity, social reality, and social support. By believing those things which our associates believe we achieve all of these goals in some ways.

The most prominent exponent of the study of the different kinds of functions served by attitudes is Daniel Katz. His emphasis lays stress on the psychodynamic factors, especially of a motivational sort, with which attitudes are involved. In his definitive presentation of this approach (1960) he says:

> Stated simply, the functional approach is the attempt to understand the reasons people hold the attitudes they do. The reasons, however, are at the level of psychological motivations and not of the accidents of external events and circumstances. Unless we know the psychological need which is met by the holding of an attitude we are in a poor position to predict when and how it will change (p. 170).

The four kinds of functions which according to Katz form the motivational basis for attitudes are:

1. the instrumental, adjustive, or utilitarian function
2. the ego-defensive function
3. the value-expressive function
4. the knowledge function.

Essentially, the *adjustive function* refers to the favorable responses the individual achieves from his associates by evidencing acceptable attitudes. This conveys the idea of reward or goal-attainment in terms of some socially valued object. Katz and Stotland (1959) have indicated that attitudes which serve the adjustive function may be the means for reaching the desired goal or be identified with experiences that have previously led to the satisfaction of such goals. In general, then, attitudes may be rewarding because they yield social rewards, including approval from others or because they are somehow related to those rewards.

With regard to underlying processes, the *ego-defensive function* allows the individual to protect himself from acknowledging his deficiencies. The mechanism of denial, which is a form of avoidance, permits the individual to defend his self-concept. To a considerable degree, for example, attitudes of prejudice help to sustain the individual's self-concept by maintaining a sense of superiority over others, as we note further in Chapter Ten (p. 307).

Through the *value-expressive function* of attitudes, the individual achieves self-expression in terms of those values which are most cherished by him. While the ego-defensive function may mean the individual holds back self-knowledge, in the case of the value-expressive function he seeks openly to express and acknowledge his commitments. In this instance, the reward to the person may not be so much a matter of gaining social support as it is one of confirming the more positive aspects of his self-concept.

In regard to the *knowledge function,* Katz says that people seek a degree of predictability, consistency, and stability in their perception of the world. Knowledge represents the cognitive component of attitudes which gives coherence and direction to experience. This emphasis is very much in line with the trend toward an understanding of cognitive interaction and the stability of cognitive structures dealt with above.

The motivational functions which Katz presents must be understood to be interrelated rather than highly segmented, as might appear. Accordingly several motives may be simultaneously served by holding a given attitude. Consider, for example, the worker who has a set of social and political attitudes concerning management and the role of government in society. These attitudes may implicate all four functions. In utilitarian terms, they may advance the worker's lot economically through his union activity, his voting preferences, as well as gaining for him the approval of his co-workers. In terms of the ego-defensive function, the worker can continue to see himself on the side of right, and management more on the side of wrong, even when his union makes economic demands which reflect the same emphasis on economic gain which is ascribed to management in negative terms. The value-expressive function may be served by avowals of liberal social measures. These, in turn, are sustained by the social reality of his co-workers' construction of their world, which becomes a part of the knowledge he readily accepts. Incidentally, had we reversed the example and used an executive instead of a worker the same implications would hold though the content would be substantially the opposite.

Despite the fact that these functions may be interrelated, Katz nonetheless notes that arousing and changing attitudes require different kinds of appeals in terms of the primary functions served by an attitude. Thus, in changing attitudes which are mainly utilitarian, whatever their other functions, he says that it is necessary that the attitude and its associated activities be seen as no longer providing its former satisfactions. In a comparable way, arousing attitudes which have a major ego-defensive function, in order to change them, often poses threats to the individual's self-concept. In that case, the consequences may be unexpected and in the reverse of the intended direction (see Katz, Sarnoff, and McClintock, 1956).

Where attitudes have a pronounced value-expressive element, a change demands the individual's recognition that his former attitudes no longer serve to adequately express his newly acquired values of significance. Changing attitudes which serve the knowledge function is most readily achieved in a condition of high ambiguity which increases the need for cognitive clarity analogous to perceptual closure. This phenomenon often is seen in circumstances where rumors become rife. It also applies to conditions which favor the acceptance of influence in terms of conformity (see Chapter Fourteen).

In general, the functional approach to attitudes focuses primary attention on the individual and his underlying psychological states. We will consider the processes involved more fully in Chapter Ten in connection with personality. By implication, this approach is also oriented to the motivational circumstances that are implicated in the acquisition of attitudes, which we will now consider.

Acquisition of attitudes and values

The infant is born with potentialities for a wide variety of behaviors. But, as Irvin Child (1954) has noted, he is "led to develop actual behavior which is confined within a much narrower range—the range of what is customary and acceptable for him according to the standards of his group" (p. 655).

The complex process of being "led" into the ways of a society is conventionally called *socialization*. More than behavior alone, however, this process involves the acquisition of dispositions to view the world in distinctive ways and be attuned to certain satisfactions in it. A child in our culture, for example, learns that monogamy, private ownership, and cleanliness are approved. He is rewarded for behaving in accordance with these values. The child who persists in calling every adult male "Daddy" is quickly brought up short, probably by his mother. Mostly, however, attitudes are "caught" rather than literally "taught."

Socialization is therefore very much a matter of taking on appropriate attitudes and values. This begins in the family where the child encounters the first representation of the culture but broadens to continue on through life. It involves, as we shall see, several kinds of processes, all of which are subject to the effects of ongoing experience through adulthood.

Essentially, there are three major patterns by which attitudes may be acquired: through *direct contact* with the object of the attitude; through *interaction* with others holding the attitude; or through more deep-seated values arising out of *upbringing* experiences within the family. Whatever the mode by which they are learned, attitudes appear to be reinforced from childhood onward through varying group identifications.

In moving toward adulthood, new reference groups may be taken on which encourage changes in attitude. In Chapter Three (p. 47) we touched on this process in connection with Newcomb's Bennington study (1943). In the follow-up of his subjects after twenty years (Newcomb, 1963), he finds that these changes were sustained by a favorable social environment, exemplified in their selection of a spouse with similar attitudes.

Another classic study illustrating the socialization of attitudes (Sims and Patrick, 1936) measured attitudes toward the Negro among three groups of college students: Southern students in a Southern school; Northern students in a Northern school; and Northern students in a Southern school. Their data showed a considerable overlap in attitudes among the groups, reflecting a great range of individual differences in each. However, as will be seen in Figure 5.2, the Northern students on

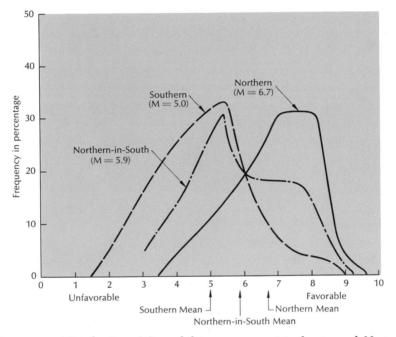

Figure 5.2: Distribution of favorability scores on attitudes toward Negroes for three samples of college students. (From Sims and Patrick, 1936.)

the average were significantly more favorable to the Negro than were the Southern students. Most importantly, the Northern students in the South were found to be in between the others on this dimension. This can be interpreted to reflect a probable shift in attitude in line with the influence exerted by the community in which these students found themselves. An alternate interpretation is that students residing in the South are exposed to comparable experiences with Negroes which yield more negative attitudes. But whether students were from the

North or South, they would be affected by the dominant cultural patterns of the community which have tended to place Negroes in inferior roles.

It is also quite common to observe such effects in the matter of accents. Younger people, in particular, are inclined to take on the distinctive speech pattern and dialect characteristics of a new region. This kind of adaptation to regional speech is another indication of social influence in keeping with a cultural pattern. Adaptation to the speech of those about us typically leads to a sense that "outsiders" are the ones who have accents. This tendency is revealed in a lighter vein by the story of the Texan who indicated disapproval of many of President Johnson's policies but said it was good at last to have a president "without an accent."

These examples are indicative of adult socialization where the individual influenced is beyond childhood and presumably less vulnerable to social pressures, if only because of alternatives available to him. We turn now to the processes of primary socialization whereby the child, especially within the context of his early contacts in the family, acquires his initial attitudes.

THE BASES AND CONTENT OF PRIMARY SOCIALIZATION

In considering the socialization of the child, two guidelines are especially important here: first, we are interested in changes which occur through learning, rather than as a function of growth and maturation; and second, we are emphasizing changes based in a social influence relationship, involving direct interaction, or other symbolic communications.

The dependent child very much requires supportive contact from adults. This is of course a matter of the critical demands for physical survival, but there are also potent psychological rewards associated with securing social identity, social support, and social reality. The family is the first group to provide these. It therefore initiates orientations which persist through the child's later relationships in society. This is exemplified by a good deal of research on the transmission of political attitudes from parents to their children. In summarizing this work, Hyman (1959) reports that attitudes toward public affairs and political party affiliation are consistently found to approximate closely those of the parents, or at least the father (p. 31). Campbell, Gurin, and Miller (1954) found from their survey among a national sample of voters that, given the same political preference by both parents, there is approximately a two-thirds probability over-all that children will hold that same party identification in adulthood (p. 99). This pattern of association is shown in Figure 5.3. It is also evident there that

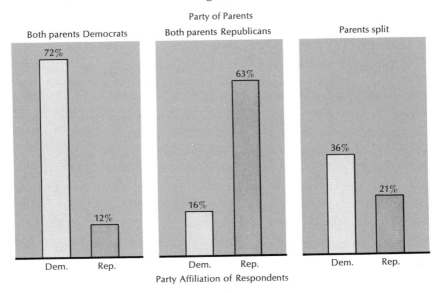

Figure 5.3: Relation of parents' party affiliation to that of offspring. Based on 1489 respondents. Those indicating no party affiliation and minor party affiliation are the absent cases which would yield a 100 per cent total for each of the three major headings. (Based on data from Campbell, Gurin, and Miller, 1954.)

the prospect exists for the primary influence of the parents to be altered by new exposures. However, that is far more likely to occur where parents are *not* identified with the same party.

The pre-eminence of the family in socialization has several bases. Not the least of these is the repeated finding that prolonged separation from the security of the home environment, and especially early in life from the mother, leads to serious psychological effects including intellectual retardation. Moreover, much that we associate with male and female behavior in a society is developed out of early identifications in the family circle (Kagan and Moss, 1961). The family also provides the youngster with his first and most significant "reference group." Indeed, one might well look upon the family as the child's first "culture," and Jules Henry (1963) has said that each family represents a unique sub-culture. There are of course many consequences of this kind of affiliation that can be seen in the later orientations and conduct of the child.

There is, in short, a great deal of significance associated with early experience if only because things which are learned first give direction to subsequent learning. Indeed, later learning may be handicapped by the necessity to "unlearn" some things before learning others. In psychological terms, this is called "pro-active inhibition" or "negative transfer." Its consequences are seen whenever the familiar or habitual must be discarded in favor of new behaviors. This phenomenon appears in general to be a main factor in resistance to change.

THE IMPACT OF SOCIAL INTERACTION

To say that attitudes and values grow out of experience does not mean that hereditary factors are excluded in the process. They obviously inter-relate with experience in various ways. Thus, a good deal of work indicates that glandular functioning, which is hereditarily based in the physiology of the individual, can affect the way the individual is reacted to by others. A child with a high activity level, for example, will necessarily collide with many more social restraints than will one with a relatively placid disposition. The former child therefore has a set of experiences which are likely to yield a quite different sequence of learning than will be the case for the latter.

Physical attributes can similarly produce differential outcomes. Whether these are valued by a society or not is of substantial significance to the way the person is reacted to by others. Kagan (1966), for instance, reports that boys who are shorter and broader than their classmates, in the early grades, are more likely to behave impulsively rather than reflectively because of anxiety in interpersonal relations. Furthermore, the distinctions society usually makes between the sexes is a primary determinant of the actions of others which may yield certain characteristic directive states in the individual. Being blind, being fat, or physically attractive—all of these in some respect affect the experience of the individual. In each instance, a physical attribute conditions social interaction.

Related to the individual's physical attributes, and the way in which these mold interaction with others, are the attitudes an individual holds toward himself. It is common to find that these attitudes, summed up in the term "self-concept," are among the most vital for the individual's relationships and adjustment. Recalling our example in Chapter One of the red-headed child who repeatedly encounters the notion that he or she has a "bad temper," we can see how beliefs about one's own selfhood can be occasioned by impressions transmitted from others, however faulty in fact. In Chapter Ten it will be further noted how crucial these self-oriented attitudes are in the functioning of an individual's personality. Attitudes of self-esteem also shape the course of social interaction. Thus, Walster (1965) found that when a girl's self-esteem was low she was more receptive to liking a person offering affection than when her self-esteem was high.

Acquiring attitudes and values is more than merely a matter of exposure to them. Other variables such as motivation must be operative to facilitate their successful acquisition. One facilitator is the identification with the parent or other model through social interaction. Another has to do with the structure of the family pattern. Clearly, then, it is a mistaken conception to think of socialization as involving a shaping of personalities in just one given mold. Because of the unique qualities of experience, socialization produces varying effects between persons. Birth order exemplifies such a factor. Thus, the work of Schachter (1959) indicates that first-born children tend to be more dependent and more easily made anxious than are later-born children. A common explanation for this finding is that parents are more likely to be concerned about their first-born and to transmit that feeling in their attentive treatment of the child.

Apart from underlying psychological states, socialization involves many kinds of learning such as learning to throw a ball. However, it is not so much behaviors which directly concern us at the moment. More to the point are the orientations conveyed to the child about his world. We turn now to a detailing of some of the features of this social influence process.

However unwittingly, adults provide models for a child's behavior. Beyond a doubt, this has a determining influence upon the development in the child of socially approved attitudes and values. Kagan and Moss (1961), for example, report that ". . . many researchers agree that one of the major signs of a strong identification was the child's adoption of the behaviors, motives, attitudes, and self-conceptions of a model" (p. 469). There are, however, numerous questions about the nature of the identification process. In another paper, Kagan (1958) defines identification as an "acquired cognitive response" which has the property of making a person react to events occurring to a model as if they were happening to him. Rather than be directly taught, it appears to rest in vicarious experience through "incidental learning."

In some ways, identification is a form of imitation. By itself, however, that label is inadequate as a basis for understanding the actual process involved. Without reviewing again the several arguments against the blanket quality of imitation as an explanation of behavior, it is useful to recall that no evidence exists for a generalized tendency toward imitation. On the other hand, it is well recognized that learning involves generalization and discrimination in terms of actions which are rewarded. Miller and Dollard (1941), for example, have dealt with imitation largely in terms of a learning framework where the learner is rewarded if he matches the behavior exhibited by the model. They refer to this as *matched-dependent* behavior, and conceive of it as being reinforced by the favorable comments of the model or some others. Much of the learning in childhood appears to be of the matched-dependent variety, where the actions and statements of parents, siblings, and peers become sources of reinforcement for the child. An extension of this view has recently been provided by Bandura and Walters (1963) in their work on personality development as a learning process.

A counterpart to the Miller-Dollard view is Mowrer's (1950) explanation of identification in terms of associations between a stimulus that is reinforced and those stimuli which are paired with it. This leads to what has been called "secondary reinforcement," which is one way of treating the process by which attitudes and values are learned. This process is illustrated graphically in Figure 5.4. As will be seen there, it is possible to view the acquisition of attitudes, values, and behaviors as generalizations to associated stimuli.

Whatever the emphasis brought to bear in accounting for identification, two things seem clear. It is a process of learning and it neces-

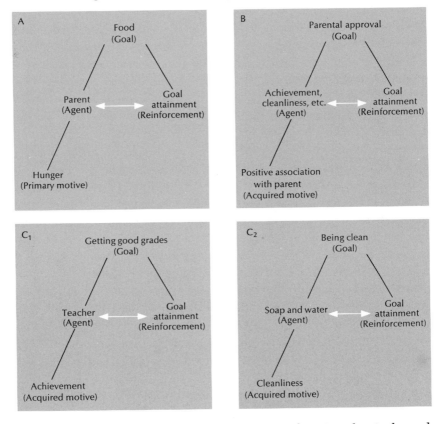

Figure 5.4: Schematic representation of associative learning of attitudes and values as acquired motives. In each case the agent intervenes between the motive and goal, thus becoming identified with the reinforcement produced by goal attainment. In A, a primary motive leads to the agent becoming valued as a goal in itself. In B, the attitudes associated with the agent are acquired under conditions of dependency. In C_1 and C_2, two examples of these values as goals in themselves are shown as indications of how the sequence proceeds.

sarily involves a relationship of dependency, however transitional. The crucial effect of the process is to inculcate attitudes and values in the child's psychological field, even without an explicit intent to do so. Among the most important outcomes of this process is the acquisition of a conscience and moral values.

Conscience means resisting temptation. Sears (1960) has conducted a series of experiments with nursery school children to study the strength of conscience. In one of these, a five-year-old child is left alone in a room filled with toys that can be played with. On the table is a bowl of candy that the child has been specifically told *not* to touch. A younger child then enters the room. He or she has been told that it is all right to take the candy. The central interest of this experiment is in how the older child handles the younger child. Some children try to distract the younger one with the toys. Others are found to threaten physical punishment. Sometimes the older one shares in taking the candy. Following observation of the child confronted with this conflict, Sears interviews the mother to get at determinants of the observed behavior. He finds that the child's ability to exercise self-control is a function of a greater or lesser degree of identification with the parents. Thus, a boy who immediately helps himself to the candy is often found to have a weak identification with his father.

In general, Sears concludes that identification results in the first place from dependency upon the parents. If they provide adequate models of moral conduct, the child is likely to incorporate this value and will learn to behave morally. This depends upon a balance of discipline and affection. Identification originally arises from a desire to keep the parents close by and approving but later takes on the properties of a personal conscience. This work reveals, as have other findings, that many children at the age of five are quite capable of having developed a conscience.

Moral values are a component of conscience. From his extensive work on thought in young children, Piaget (1932) contends that these values are not taught in a step-wise way. They are learned, he asserts, by a restructuring of the child's psychological field spontaneously, as a consequence of new experience. The research by Piaget, exemplified by the book just cited, *The Moral Judgment of the Child,* has been of redounding significance to understanding human development in terms of psychological states.

FAMILY STRUCTURE

The pattern of family relationships, especially regarding the exercise of parental power over the child, has also been found to be a significant source of attitudes and values. Where the father is a strong, punishing figure, this frequently gives rise to a persisting orientation to the world called "authoritarianism." Its dominant value is *power,* whether in terms of aggressive display or submissive yielding.

Erich Fromm was among the early delineators of the behavioral and ideological properties of authoritarianism. The rise of the Nazis in Germany prompted him to write *Escape from Freedom* (1941). This monumental work describes the ambivalent power orientation of the authoritarian person and accounts for the historic cultural patterns which produce it and sustain it.

In a related vein, Maslow (1943) soon afterwards produced a definitive paper on the authoritarian character structure. Fundamentally, said Maslow, it embodies an ideology that views the world in terms of a jungle ". . . in which every man's hand is necessarily against every other man's, in which the whole world is conceived of as dangerous, threatening, or at least challenging, and in which human beings are conceived of as primarily selfish or evil or stupid" (p. 403).

During the 1940's at the University of California, extensive interviewing was done to ascertain the personal histories of individuals who held authoritarian attitudes. This necessitated a measure of authoritarianism now called the California F Scale (Adorno, Frenkel-Brunswik, Levinson and Sanford, 1950). The essential thrust of this extensive work was that a variety of attitudes toward other people arise not from contact with the object or even another attitude, but from an authoritarian *family structure.* Among these attitudes are ethnocentrism and prejudice, categorical and conventional thought, superstition and suggestibility, and tendencies opposed to self-examination. Some items from the F Scale were presented earlier in Chapter Three (see pp. 78-79).

Another line of work on family structure as a source of attitudes is seen in research by Bronfenbrenner (1961). He has conducted classroom surveys and interviews on the distribution of power in the home, in terms of mother- or father-oriented patterns. Such patterns evidence differential effects on the attitudes and behaviors of adolescents, with the role of the father having special importance. Bronfenbrenner also finds differential effects associated with the sex of the child. Thus, leadership and responsibility are affected by interaction with the parent of the same sex. He finds highest leadership ratings are obtained by *boys* from families in which the *father* is often present and gives affection; the most independent *girls* come from homes where the *mother* is present and gives affection. In terms of distribution of power, boys tend to be the most responsible when the father is the principal agent of discipline and girls when the mother has relatively greater power. Where the parents exercise equal power in the family, children of both sexes tend to be less responsible (pp. 267-269).

The importance of this kind of research lies in specifying the structural features of learning experiences in the family which can have a long-range consequence in terms of attitudes and values. It also points up the persisting consequences of early social interaction. Before considering that topic in greater depth, we will turn in the next chapter to two topics that are of central importance in the study of attitudes—attitude measurement and attitude change.

SUMMARY

Attitudes and values are acquired as a vital part of being introduced into the ways of a society. They both may be considered to be the psychological representations of social influences retained by the individual. The concept of attitude is important in social psychology in that it conveniently sums up the *past* experience of the individual to account for present actions. As such attitudes help to explain the different responses of people to what is apparently the same situation.

An *attitude* is essentially an organization of beliefs which sets the individual toward a preferred response. A *value* can be viewed as the core of a clustering of attitudes. Both attitudes and values reside in the psychological field and define what is *expected* and *desired*. Both can be conceived of as motivational-perceptual states which direct behavior.

An individual holds many more attitudes than values. Values tend to be sustained and shared in common within a culture. Around these there may be considerable variations in individual attitudes. Attitudes and values have an important effect in *organizing experience* and *di-*

recting action. In their outward expression, attitudes generally appear to be more susceptible to change than are values. Attitudes and values are not necessarily in harmony. A given value may give rise to inconsistent attitudes.

In the study of attitudes, recent trends have inclined toward a greater stress on their *structural relationships* and *functional features.* The relationship between attitudes, in this newer emphasis, is called *cognitive interaction.*

There are three major components of attitudes, the *cognitive* component of belief-disbelief, the *affective* component of like-dislike, and the *action* component of readiness to respond. These are not sharply distinct from one another but share a common relationship. Three interrelated aspects in the study of attitudes are the *relationships* of their components, their *source,* in terms of the patterns by which they are learned, and attitude *change,* referring to the social influences affecting them, including new information.

An individual's attitudes may be inconsistent. Social pressures often produce the necessity for an individual to act in a way contrary to his attitudes. Therefore, there may be disparity between an individual's *private attitudes* and *public commitments.* It may also be the case that there is an inconsistency between the cognitive and affective components of an individual's attitudes, in terms of his beliefs and feelings. Festinger's *theory of cognitive dissonance* deals with inconsistency in terms of the individual's avoidance of open conflicts between attitudes as well as other cognitive elements. Thus, individuals are disinclined to accept new information which violates an attitude which they hold. This theory also postulates that attitudes change to accommodate changes in behavior or circumstance.

Attitudes may serve several motivational functions. Katz considers these to fall into four categories: the *instrumental,* the *ego-defensive,* the *value expressive,* and the *knowledge* functions. Arousing and changing attitudes require different appeals in terms of the primary function an attitude serves. Rather than be entirely distinct from one another, these functions are interrelated in various combinations.

The acquisition of attitudes and values is part of the process of being led into the ways of the society called *socialization.* Attitudes are acquired in three ways: *direct contact* with the object, *interaction* with those holding the attitude, and *upbringing* experiences within the family's structure. Attitudes are held in line with reference-group affiliations and may change as new reference groups are taken on. The early socialization of the child, called *primary socialization,* mainly occurs in the family. The dependence of the child on the family, especially at a time when few alternatives are available to him, leads to a persisting impact on attitudes and values, including political ideology. In general, the acquisition of attitudes and values is heavily affected by a process of learning through social interaction. This process may shape the child's crucial development of attitudes toward himself in terms of his *self-concept.* Physical attributes can be significant in determining the character of this interaction.

An important consequence of childhood experience is *identification* with parents as models for action. It has an effect, too, upon the development of a conscience and of moral values. Identification is determined by dependence upon the parents in the context of a balance of discipline and affection. *Family structure* is another feature of early life which may lead to a persisting set of attitudes, such as authoritarianism, which carries over into later life.

SUGGESTED READINGS

From E. P. Hollander and R. G. Hunt. (Eds.) *Current perspectives in social psychology.* (2nd Edition.) New York: Oxford University Press, 1967:

Introduction to Section VI: *Attitudes and cognition*
35. Daniel Katz: *The functional approach to the study of attitudes*
36. Leon Festinger: *An introduction to the theory of dissonance*
37. Charles E. Osgood: *Cognitive dynamics in the conduct of human affairs*

SELECTED REFERENCES

*Adorno, T. W., Frenkel-Brunswik, Else, Levinson, D. J., & Sanford, R. N. *The authoritarian personality.* New York: Harper, 1950.
*Campbell, A., Converse, P. E., Miller, W. E., & Stokes, D. E. *The American voter.* New York: Wiley, 1960.
Hyman, H. H. *Political socialization: A study in the psychology of political behavior.* Glencoe, Ill.: Free Press, 1959.
Sears, R. R., Maccoby, Eleanor, & Levin, H. *Patterns of child-rearing.* Evanton, Ill.: Row, Peterson, 1957.
*Smith, M. B., Bruner, J. S., & White, R. W. *Opinions and personality.* New York: Wiley, 1956.

6

The measurement of attitudes and the dynamics of attitude change

Attitudes play a major part in both capturing and shaping experience. As we observed in the last chapter, they have accordingly been a major focal point for study. The measurement of attitudes, and the factors affecting their change, are two interrelated and challenging aspects of study that are at the heart of this effort. We will consider these aspects in this chapter, as well as the relationship of attitudes and actions.

Problems and procedures in the measurement of attitudes

There are several problems involved in the measurement of attitudes, perhaps the most important of which is to define a cluster in "attitudinal space" and obtain an index of how individuals differ within it. Associated with this is the necessity to assess those attitudes that are related meaningfully to behavior. There are also technical questions in attitude measurement which concern, for example, the way that measurement procedures themselves may affect the responses of individuals.

Regarding the first issue, the very term "attitude" is multi-faceted in its meaning. In breadth, it may cover many attitudes or a very narrow issue. Thus, a person may be generally favorable to "desegregation," but within that complex can be opposed to bussing white children to predominantly Negro schools. In terms of action, that person might take

140

part in civil rights activities, perhaps through financial contributions to appropriate organizations, and yet argue against bussing on other grounds. As we shall point out, this is not necessarily an inconsistency but a matter of the "situational hurdles" that the action component of an attitude can surmount (Campbell, 1963).

Another consideration is the *centrality* or *peripherality* of an attitude. In his analysis of attitudes, Rokeach (1963) indicates that they exist on a continuum from "primitive beliefs," which are very central to a person's psychological field, through to "peripheral beliefs," which are relatively inconsequential. In studying attitudes, therefore, some attention is required to place a given attitude in the totality of an individual's attitudinal space. Highly central attitudes are likely to be more stable and considerably more important as bases for action than are peripheral attitudes. One implication of this, as we shall see, is that appeals which are effective in changing some attitudes may be less effective in changing others that are more firmly entrenched in personality—for example, in terms of the ego-defensive function.

THE TRADITIONAL APPROACHES TO ATTITUDE MEASUREMENT

Attitudes have usually been measured through attitude scales, questionnaires, interviews, projective tests, and observations of behavior. These have been treated previously in Chapter Three. Our aim here is to focus major attention on some of the dimensions and problems which underlie traditional attitude measurement, especially through attitude scales.

The preoccupation with a single issue rather than with the clustering of attitudes, has been a major feature in the tradition of attitude measurement. This tradition has mainly emphasized dimensions dealing with single issues in terms of the direction, degree, and intensity of an attitude toward a given object. These components are incorporated in questionnaire studies and interviews, as well as in attitude scales. Thus, individuals may be asked *how* (pro or con) they "feel about" something, and then "how strongly" they feel.

The *direction* of an attitude is essentially the cognitive component of belief-disbelief, often stated in terms of agree-disagree. The *degree* of agreement or disagreement extends this concern to how much plus or minus valence is associated with the attitude. The *intensity* of an attitude is essentially the same as degree since it, too, measures the affective component, usually in terms of "strength of feeling." Indeed, when degree and intensity were plotted against one another, it became apparent that they were highly interrelated; holding a more extreme position was accompanied by more intensity of feeling. Cantril (1946) pointed to this relationship two decades ago and, as is shown in Figure 6.1, Such-

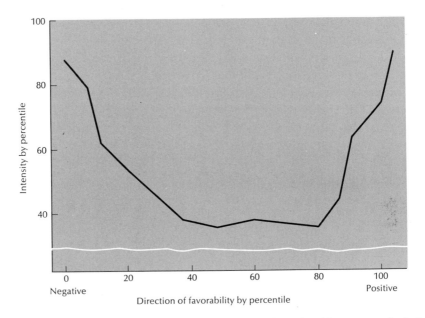

Figure 6.1: Relationship of direction of attitudes of soldiers toward their jobs and the intensity of those attitudes. (From Suchman, 1949.)

man (1949) reported it from his work among soldiers. The figure shows that attitudes of a highly negative or positive valence are held with greater intensity. Thus, both degree and intensity appear to measure the affective component of an attitude, while direction is more an indication of the cognitive component. Based upon our earlier discussion of the consistency of these components, it is understandable that they are found to be highly related.

ATTITUDE SCALES

The most widespread approach to measuring attitudes has been the attitude scale. In general, such scales consist of a number of statements with which a person may agree or disagree along a dimension with several points, usually ranging from "highly agree" to "highly disagree." In this way both the direction and the degree are indicated by the response to each statement or "item." Typically these items all relate to some common social entity, person, issue, or activity. Responses are then summed to provide a score indicating the person's overall attitude.

The development of an attitude scale requires the selection of a number of statements that will discriminate between people having different attitudinal positions. Thus, to be adequate, an attitude scale should represent a range of different positions that an individual might hold and it should avoid confounding two distinct issues in one item. This problem is illustrated in "double-barreled" items, such as: "If social class distinctions are to be reduced, the graduated income tax should be eliminated." A person might agree with the first part and disagree with the second, or the reverse. In either case, two separable issues are confounded with one another.

One of the earliest attitude scales was that developed by Thurstone with Chave (1929). They had people judge items, not in terms of their own attitude, but regarding their judgment of the position the statement represented on a scale of favorability or unfavorability toward the object of the attitude. Where there is high agreement about the position of the item among the judges, the item is considered to have a scale score for that position. Thus, the score for an item is determined by the agreement of judges prior to the actual use of the scale. When respondents agree with items later, they receive these scores toward their total. Thurstone adapted this procedure from psychophysics and it is called the method of "equal appearing intervals."

Thurstone's major contribution was in approaching the measurement of attitudes on an affective dimension. His scaling method itself, however, is no longer in wide use. Apart from the relative ease of other methods, research by Hovland and Sherif (1952) raised some serious questions about the basis for its procedures. They found that individuals tend to judge items with reference to their own position as an anchor point. Though Upshaw (1965) has challenged the inference from these findings, and offered support for Thurstone's methodology, contrary evidence continues to be reported. Waly and Cook (1965) have established that ratings of the "plausibility" of statements about a social issue—segregation—are affected substantially by whether or not the rater agrees or disagrees with the statement.

Undoubtedly the most common attitude scale in use grows out of the work of Likert (1932). It is sometimes referred to as a summated scale and is simple to construct. In this case, prior judgments of the items are not obtained, but statements are collected which represent apparently positive or negative views of the attitudinal object. The California F Scale, discussed here and in Chapter Three (p. 78), is built on the Likert procedure. The subject indicates his degree of agreement or disagreement with each item, usually on a scale ranging from one to five or one to seven. Then, a score is obtained by summing the values for each of these separate responses.

Another basic approach to scaling a person's position on an issue was developed by Bogardus (1925). His social distance scale, which we discussed in Chapter Two (p. 43), measures attitudes toward various ethnic groups, including nationalities, by a series of statements ranging from the most favorable to the least favorable, i.e. greatest social distance. Subjects are asked to indicate for each of these groups how willing they would be to admit them to the following relationships:

1. to close kinship by marriage
2. to my club as personal chums
3. to my street as neighbors
4. to employment in my occupation
5. to citizenship in my country
6. as visitors in my country.

The important feature of this scale is that it is constructed so that accepting the first alternative should imply the acceptance of all the others. Thus, if an individual says yes to the first statement, he should accept the subsequent statements in the series as well.

A modern counterpart of this scale, which positions people in terms of favorability or unfavorability toward some attitudinal object, is the Guttman Scale (1950). Rather than beginning with a set of items graduated in an obvious way, Guttman seeks the underlying order within a series of questions that can be responded to by a simple "yes" or "no." He calls his procedure "cumulative scaling." It often involves the mathematical treatment of a matrix of responses and has been applied particularly to data obtained from questionnaire surveys. In simplest form, a cumulative scale would be illustrated by a set of questions about age, as follows:

1. I am 31 years of age or older
2. I am 26 years of age or older
3. I am 21 years of age or older
4. I am 16 years of age or older.

A person responding "yes" to question 1 would have to respond "yes" to the subsequent items. Hence a "yes" on 1 implies all of the others. A "no" to question 1, but a "yes" on question 2 would imply "yes" to 3 and 4. A "no" to all four questions would place a person below 16 years of age. Notice that age is a perfectly linear dimension and that it is easily graduated. This is much less the case with attitudes.

Because an attitude scale is essentially a one-dimensional measure, it cannot readily represent the complexity of attitudinal systems. To get around this limitation requires the use of multi-dimensional ratings or the application of factor analysis to responses given over several scales. One recent approach to such multi-dimensional scaling is represented in the *semantic differential* (Osgood, Suci, and Tannenbaum, 1957) which is discussed further in Chapter Nine (p. 261). In this procedure, an attitudinal object is presented to the subject for rating along many dimensions, e.g. "good-bad," "strong-weak," "active-passive." From these ratings, with several dimensions for each, the three major factors of *evaluation, potency,* and *activity* can be extracted. An individuals "attitude" toward the object can then be represented as a point in attitudinal space where his ratings for these factors coincide. Thus, "government" might be rated by a person as favorable on the evaluative factor, very powerful in terms of potency, but relatively inactive. In general, evaluation along a negative to positive scale appears to account for the greatest part of the cognitive interaction of attitudes and associated behavior.

RELIABILITY AND VALIDITY

As with all psychological measures, attitude measurement in any form involves considerations of adequacy in terms of both *reliability* and *validity*. These issues have to do respectively with the degree to which a measure is consistent, and whether it measures what it is supposed to measure. Further problems arise, too, in avoiding bias from the framing of the question, the sequencing of items within the format of the attitude scale or questionnaire, and the effect of the interviewer.

Up to a point, the reliability of an attitude measure is increased by repeated readings. A one-item attitude scale would be a highly wavering measure at best since it alone could yield wide inconsistencies. Therefore, many items are used in constructing scales and questionnaires. Ideally these items should be correlated positively with one another in terms of the internal consistency of measurement. For example, in the semantic differential procedure just noted, several dimensions make up each of the factors thus increasing their reliability of these factors.

The problem of gauging reliability over time is complicated by the practical consideration that when an attitude measure is repeated for the same subjects, they may remember their earlier responses and strive to be consistent. On the other hand, it is recognized that since attitudes change, their measurement over time can never be totally reliable. In a longitudinal study by E. L. Kelly (1955), he retested married couples with several attitude scales and other psychological measures that he had administered to them as engaged couples sixteen to eighteen years before. He found that attitudes had the lowest repeat reliability, that is, had changed the most over the years. The measures of values and of vocational interests had the highest consistency.

The extent to which a measure is valid necessarily depends in part on its reliability. In these terms, the internal consistency of an attitude measure usually is a sufficient basis for permitting adequate validity. However, there is a larger question of validity which concerns the relationship of what a person says at one time to how he acts at another. The next section considers this behavioral aspect of the validity of attitude measurement.

Attitudes and situational hurdles to action

Broadly speaking, expressed attitudes bear a rather consistent relationship to behavior. But again this depends upon the kind of attitudes and the kind of circumstances that prevail for action. There is, for example, sufficient correspondence between political attitudes revealed in a preelection survey, and the actual outcome of an election, to permit relatively accurate forecasting. Where there are misreadings from such surveys, they can be accounted for by faulty sampling procedures or by a large bloc of "don't know" respondents who could move either way. In our national elections, in particular, outcomes often hinge on a few percentage points, making advance predictions a delicate task indeed.

When attempts have been made to study the correspondence of attitudes and behavior in concrete situations, the results have often revealed apparent inconsistencies. An early investigation in this vein by LaPiere (1934) found that the observed behavior of persons in a face-to-face situation was not in line with their expressed attitudes. In this study, LaPiere was accompanied on a trip by a young Chinese couple. Together as companions they visited many hotels and restaurants and were regularly given service that reflected no negative attitude toward Orientals. Yet, when LaPiere sent questionnaires to these same establishments several months afterward, he found that the vast preponderance of their replies indicated that they would not accept Orientals as their guests. A comparable study by Kutner, Wilkins, and Yarrow (1952) found that many restaurant owners who failed to answer a request for reservations for a group including some Negroes did serve a group composed of two white women and one Negro woman when they actually appeared in person.

The substance of these findings is that people in a situation involving face-to-face contact are likely to respond differently from the manner indicated by their answer to a letter or a questionnaire or, in the case of the latter study, by the absence of a response to a request. One resolution of this apparent anomaly is offered in Rokeach's (1966) contention that behavior is always a function of at least two attitudes, that is, an attitude toward the object and an attitude toward the situation. Regarding the two studies we have just noted, he says that one reasonable explanation of their apparent inconsistencies is that:

> . . . the investigators did not obtain all the relevant attitudinal information needed to make accurate predictions. The subjects not only had attitudes toward Chinese and Negroes, but being managers of an ongoing business, also had attitudes about how to properly conduct such a business. The investigator's methods, however, are typically focused on obtaining data relevant to attitude-toward-object and are generally insensitive toward attitude-toward-situation (p. 12).

Experiments also have been conducted on the relationship of attitudes and overt activity. In one of these, DeFleur and Westie (1958) requested white girl students to permit themselves to be photographed sitting with a Negro male. The subjects were free not to permit the photograph to be taken at all, or, if they signed an authorization, to allow the photograph to be used in various ways ranging from display in the laboratory to use in a national campaign for integration. It was found that about a third of the subjects behaved differently from their expressed attitudes—mostly in a less tolerant direction—when it actually came to signing a document indicating their willingness to be photographed with the Negro. Linn (1965) conducted a similar experiment and found that fully half of the subjects did not conform to their verbalized attitude regarding the criterion of being photographed, but that these differences operated in both directions. Some subjects who had expressed a generally intolerant attitude were willing to be photographed, and some who had expressed a tolerant attitude were unwilling to be photographed when confronted with the necessity to sign an authorization.

Campbell (1963) has also emphasized the necessity to consider different situations in explaining what is an apparent inconsistency between attitudes and behavior, or between one behavior and another. In Campbell's view, there are *situational hurdles,* which present higher levels of difficulty for an adequate response. Thus, the restaurant manager may not be inconsistent when he actually accommodates people but says in a mail questionnaire that he would be unwilling to serve them. The face-to-face situation, as we have already observed in Rokeach's comment above, presents a circumstance which is of a different order. Indeed, Campbell indicates that to be truly inconsistent would mean to *agree* to accept people on a questionnaire, and then *refuse* to serve them when they actually appear (p. 160).

The implication of Campbell's "hurdle" approach is made still more concrete in his discussion of the work of Minard (1952) who conducted research on ethnic relations in a West Virginia coal-mining community. His data indicated that the pattern of integration was different in town and in the mines. The mines were integrated but the town substantially was not. Thus, 20 per cent of the miners had favorable attitudes toward Negroes and acted in accordance with their attitudes both in the mine and in town, while 20 per cent had negative attitudes toward Negroes and acted accordingly all the time. Minard found that the great majority, or 60 per cent, altered their behavior toward Negroes from the mine setting to the town setting, treating them more as equals in one and inferiors in the other. Campbell says that the miners' behavior and attitudes are consistent with respect to the higher hurdle in going from one situation to the other. Indeed, these two situations represent a Guttman-type cumulative scale.

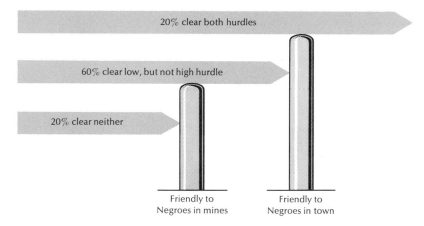

20% clear both hurdles

60% clear low, but not high hurdle

20% clear neither

Friendly to
Negroes in mines

Friendly to
Negroes in town

Figure 6.2: Relationship of situational hurdles to attitudes, from Minard's study (1952) of coal miners. (Adapted from Campbell, in *Psychology: A Study of a Science*, v. 6, edited by S. Koch. Copyright © 1963 by McGraw-Hill Inc. Used by permission of McGraw-Hill Book Company.)

As will be seen in Figure 6.2 there are no instances of miners who say they are friendly in town but not in the mine. This means that there are none who are truly inconsistent. Twenty per cent clear both hurdles; another 20 per cent fail to clear either of the hurdles. It should be plain therefore that the validity of attitude measurement in terms of action rests in some degree on the kind of situation, and attendant social pressures, which are likely to encourage the expression of an attitude. Insofar as attitudes predispose behavior, they do so in relationship to the immediate situation.

Processes of attitude change

A major theme of the previous section is that underlying attitudes predispose behavior in terms of a situation which serves as a frame for that behavior. Relatedly the very expression of attitudes depends upon the social setting. Thus, apparent changes of attitude occur by shifts that an individual perceives in his situation, in terms of what will be appropriate or approved. These may or may not reflect underlying changes. Kelman (1961) distinguishes between *compliance,* which merely reveals an overt expression of an attitude as a social convenience, and two other processes, *identification* and *internalization.* The former involves greater changes in the person's psychological field on the basis of modeling, while the latter presents a basic change in a value.

In general, when an individual acquires new information his attitudes may be altered by a reorganization of his psychological field. The potential of new experience is always in the direction of such change. Yet, the structure of attitudes tends toward stability. As we have repeatedly noted, an individual's attitudes are usually anchored in one or more groups to which he belongs or, in any case, accepts as a standard. To the extent that he is motivated to be identified with a group, his attitudes are unlikely to change if they derive support from that group (Kelley, 1955). This bolstering effect is a major source of resistance to change. On the other hand, as illustrated by Lewin's work earlier (p. 70), a group can also serve as a vehicle for producing change.

In considering the dynamics of attitude change, the significance of two kinds of factors accordingly must be recognized. The first of these is the processing of new information through cognitive interaction; the second is the impelling quality of social identifications in maintaining an attitudinal structure. Both are involved in persuasive communication.

PERSUASIVE COMMUNICATION

The attempt to influence people to change their attitudes and related behavior is widely practiced through persuasive communication. The advertiser who seeks to have people use his toothpaste, the politician who wishes to have their vote, as well as the numerous social and civic agencies that desire to affect social change, are all engaging in persuasive communication. Implicit in these activities is the intent to exert social influence.

As Bauer (1964) points out, much of the early work on attitude change was based on an asymmetric model of the influence process. Communication was viewed as a one-way influence process, usually for exploitative purposes, and the recipients of the communication were considered to accept passively messages directed to them. A noteworthy break with the tradition came from the work of Katz and Lazarsfeld (1955), who found that individuals were not as directly affected by communications from the mass media, so much as they were influenced by a process of transmission through their relevant reference groups. Katz and Lazarsfeld referred to this as the "two-step flow" of communication, meaning a flow from the mass media, through opinion leadership in relevant groups, to the individual. Thus, they emphasized the necessity to view the individual in terms of his total social involvements, including especially reference group affiliations.

Increasingly, the recipient of the communication has been studied in terms of his active selection and processing of the messages which come to him. In this regard, both the relevance of these communications, as well as their source, have been given greater attention. This particular approach has come to be called the "transactional" view of communication (Bauer, 1964). Two major themes pervade this view. One is that the recipient of the communication is not passive but may be actively resistant to it. The second is the idea that acceptance of the communication as a basis for change involves a transaction between the communicator and the recipient, producing influence effects where there is an equitable exchange. As Bauer (1964) puts it:

> The process of social communication and of the flow of influence in general must be regarded as a transaction . . . in the sense of an exchange of values between two or more parties; each gives in order to get. The argument for using the transactional model . . . is that it opens the door more fully to exploring the intention and behavior of members of the audience and encourages inquiry into the influence of the audience on the communicator by specifically treating the process as a two-way passage (p. 327).

Persuasive communications, especially from the mass media, are therefore limited in their effect partly due to selective perception by the audience. There is a strong tendency to accommodate new information within already existing attitudinal systems, and as Klapper (1960) observes, ". . . persuasive mass communication functions far more frequently as an agent of reinforcement than as an agent of change. Within a given audience exposed to particular communications, reinforcement, or at least constancy of opinion, is typically found to be the dominant effect" (p. 15).

The transactional model of persuasive communication follows the format already discussed (p. 108) regarding social influence processes in general. There we dealt with three elements in influence processes—an influence source, a communication or message, and a recipient of the communication. In the case of attitude change, the influence source is most usually called a communicator, and the recipient the audience.

Figure 6.3 presents diagrammatic representations of three prominent models of communication and attitude change. The first of these is the traditional advertising-propaganda model with its one-directional quality. The communicator actively seeks to manipulate the recipient by the content of the communication, in terms of its appeal and the information it presents. By contrast, the audience is seen in relatively inactive terms, except for salient motives on which the communicator plays. The second kind of model, represented in the Katz and Lazarsfeld (1955) "two-step flow" concept, gives somewhat more emphasis to the social characteristics of the audience, in terms of reference-group affiliations acting as a filter for the message. Finally, the transactional model gives greater weight to the interaction of the motives and social identities of communicator and recipient. Here the audience is considered to perceive these qualities of the communicator as a critical feature in accepting his influence.

Cognitive consistency, which we considered earlier as a feature of attitudinal structure, is a state of the recipient which has great relevance to the transactional idea of an exchange. The implicit question is what the communicator offers the audience which justifies an alteration in an already formed attitudinal structure and one which is likely to be sustained by important social identities. Rosenberg and Abelson (1960), for example, contend that persuasive communications will generate attitude change to the extent that they are seen by the recipient as helpful in resolving cognitive imbalances, particularly in the affective and cognitive components. There may also be a benefit received in terms of new knowledge. However, it is important to stress the general point that the cognitive component of an attitude, regarding what an individual believes, is knowledge for him even if it is not objectively verifiable. Indeed, the absence of correct information is no

A. Traditional advertising-propaganda model

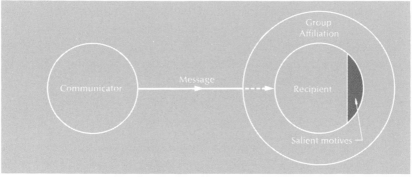

B. Two-step flow of communication model

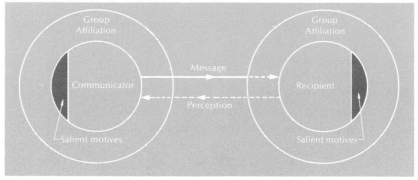

C. Transactional model of communication

Figure 6.3: Three models of persuasive communication. In *A* the expectation is that the recipient acts on the message when his salient motives are aroused. In *B* the message is initially screened by the recipient's group affiliation before it affects the salient motives. In *C* the message is interpreted by the recipient within the context of his own group affiliations and motives and his perception of those of the communicator.

barrier to the individual's persistence in holding an intense attitude, in the affective sense. In the case of an attitude which serves an ego-defensive function, new knowledge may therefore be resisted tenaciously. In a study by Katz, Sarnoff, and McClintock (1956), for example, it was found that a factual appeal to those holding negative attitudes toward Negroes had little appreciable effect. As these investigators point out, such appeals assume that the recipient is interested in more accurate, complete information, but this assumption is questionable. They found that a somewhat more effective approach, among those persons who were not too high on ego-defensiveness, was to present case material about the personality dynamics of prejudice.

Since cognitive interaction has broad implications for attitude change, we will now examine it in greater detail beginning with a review of its essential features.

ESSENTIAL PRINCIPLES OF COGNITIVE INTERACTION

While there are differences in the various theories of cognitive interaction, they all rely on certain essential points of convergence. These principles, summarized by Osgood (1960), may be paraphrased as follows:

1. Modification of cognitive structures, i.e. attitude change, results from the psychological stress produced by cognitive inconsistency.
2. The interaction of cognitive elements depends upon their being brought into some kind of confrontation with one another. In this regard, Osgood points out that the psychological awareness of inconsistency or incongruity does not so much follow the rules of logic as it follows the rules of what is called "psycho-logic" (Abelson and Rosenberg, 1958).
3. The magnitude of stress toward attitude change increases with the degree of cognitive inconsistency. Thus, in Festinger's theory, the magnitude of dissonance is the motivational factor producing changes of attitude or of behavior.
4. The dynamics of cognitive interaction under stress operate to reduce total cognitive inconsistency. This idea, that disturbances in a system set in motion processes to restore balance in that system, grows out of the work of Cannon in

connection with his study of the physiology of emotion (1932). It is now well known as the principle of "homeostasis." It also has roots in Freud's concept of repression which operates to force out of consciousness elements of experience that threaten the ego.

COGNITIVE APPROACHES TO ATTITUDE CHANGE

The earliest formulation of the consistency idea, in terms of attitude change, came from Heider's (1946, 1958) *balance theory*. He considered attitudes toward objects, as well as persons, to have positive or negative valences, which might or might not coincide with one another. Hence, there would be balance or imbalance in the attitudinal system. Heider contended that there is always movement toward a balanced state, that is, "a situation in which the relations among the entities fit together harmoniously; there is no stress toward change" (1958, p. 201). Therefore, the basic concept of balance is that a tendency exists for individuals to resolve attitudes which are not similarly signed.

Heider was essentially concerned with situations in which there were two persons, a Perceiver and an Other, each of whom may have an attitude toward a given object X. If P likes O, the assumption is that the latter's attitude should be the same as his own. Two friends, for example, might share a common positive attitude toward a presidential candidate. Thus, a balanced state would be P positive toward O, P positive toward X, and O seen as positive toward X as well. If they differed on that issue, then an imbalanced state would exist. In that event, they might try to persuade each other or else avoid the topic until the election was over, in order to retain actual or apparent balance.

In Heider's P-O-X model, then, balance occurs when there are no negative signs, or two negative signs, in the relation between P, O, and X. The assumption that an unbalanced relation produces tension and generates forces to restore balance has direct implications for social interaction, and these are discussed more fully in the next chapter (see p. 195). An extension of Heider's work by Newcomb (1953) takes account of the two-way relation between people. Newcomb postulates a "strain toward symmetry" which causes two people, A and B, who like each other, to be similarly oriented toward an object X. Thus, inter-

personal attraction is facilitated by the perception that a relevant attitude is shared in common, a basic point in the next chapter as well.

Also related to the Heider balance concept is the *congruity theory*
put forth by Osgood and Tannenbaum (1955). They deal with two
cognitive elements which are paired with one another in terms of a
positive or negative relationship. The major feature of this approach is
that it allows for more exact prediction of the direction and degree of
attitude change. Thus, Osgood and Tannenbaum assert the proposition
that the more extreme the valence of an attitude, the less probably it
will change when paired with something of opposite valence. Suppose
we like a public figure at the highest scale value of $+3$ and then learn
that he is in favor of a policy which we dislike at the relatively moderate
level of -1. The prediction then is that our attitude toward the policy
will be considerably more likely to "give" in a more favorable direction,
rather than our attitude toward the political figure shifting in an unfavorable direction. Another procedure for determining the degree of
change, in terms of "belief congruence," has also been proposed recently
by Rokeach and Rothman (1965).

One important implication of such congruity relationships is that a
communication source with a high positive valence can be more persuasive in advocating a less favored course of action. Alternatively,
when a communication source that is viewed very negatively urges a
policy which is relatively favored, the policy may itself be seen in
more negative terms. Osgood (1960) gives the example of a Soviet
representative making proposals for world disarmament, and says, "A
large segment of the American press editorializes about the deceptive
nature of these proposals. . . . It is cognitively inconsistent for us to
think of people we dislike and distrust making honest, conciliatory
moves . . ." (p. 341).

Abelson and Rosenberg (1958) have coined the term "psycho-logic"
to indicate the contrast between actual processes of cognitive interaction and true logic. Among their *rules of psycho-logic*, they give the
following: 1) A likes B and B likes C implies that A likes C; 2) A likes
B and B dislikes C implies that A dislikes C; 3) A dislikes B and B
dislikes C implies that A likes C. These rules are evidently quite valid
under many circumstances, though they are not logical.

The most prominent theory for dealing with the effects of communication on attitude change is the dissonance model developed by Fes-

tinger (1957, 1964b). Essentially, this theory contends that individuals are motivated to seek consonance of their attitudes. Thus, attitude change operates in terms of movement toward such consonance and away from dissonance. When individuals experience dissonance, they also actively avoid situations which would increase that dissonance. Festinger (1957) gives the example of a survey conducted on smoking habits and attitudes. It was found that 29 per cent of non-smokers, 20 per cent of light smokers, but only 7 per cent of heavy smokers believed that a relationship had been established between smoking and lung cancer (p. 155). To continue smoking in the face of the belief that it is dangerous increases dissonance.

Action which is contradictory to a person's attitudes has been studied in a number of experiments generated by the dissonance theory. In a study by Festinger and Carlsmith (1959), they induced subjects who had just taken part in a very boring task to tell another person that the task was quite interesting in order to help the experimenter get subjects to participate in the study. They found that subjects given $20 for providing this false information changed their attitudes less, in the direction of believing that they liked the task, than subjects given only $1. Their results are diagrammed in Figure 6.4.

Festinger explains the results of this experiment in terms of dissonance created by "insufficient rewards" (1961). Subjects who received only $1 found it necessary to rationalize a falsehood for such a

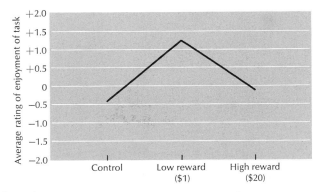

Figure 6.4: Average ratings given in response to the question on enjoyment of the tasks following compliance by two experimental groups. Control group represents no compliance and no monetary reward. (Based on data from Festinger and Carlsmith, 1959.)

small sum by believing that they had really liked this dull task. On the other hand, those who received the high reward of $20 experienced very little dissonance in telling others that this was an interesting task since they had received enough money to amply justify their actions to themselves without changing attitudes. In a recent experiment with Belgian university students, Nuttin (1966) repeated the Festinger and Carlsmith study but added a condition of "consonant compliance" where these students were to report that the task was boring and dull. Here again, the low reward led to a significant attitude change. The results for the "dissonant compliance" condition were in the same direction as those in the Festinger and Carlsmith experiment, but were not statistically significant.

In a related study, Brehm and Cohen (1962, pp. 74-78) assigned students to conditions differing as to financial inducement in terms of four levels, i.e. 50¢, $1, $5, or $10 for writing an essay which was against their own attitudinal position. They found that the lower the financial reward, the greater the reported opinion change toward the position of the essay. Similarly, Lependorf (1964) has reported, from an experiment with children, that there was less change of attitude with a 50¢ reward than with a 5¢ reward. Chapanis and Chapanis (1964) have argued in the case of the Festinger and Carlsmith study that subjects given $20 had their suspicion aroused, and thus did not change their attitudes. However, this criticism should not hold for the smaller sums in the latter experiments.

Festinger (1957) adopts the general view that the less inducement or force used to induce overt compliance, the greater will be the underlying opinion change toward that position. This is demonstrated in another experiment conducted by Freedman (1965). Boys in the 2nd through 4th grades were told *not* to play with a very desirable toy, while the experimenter was out of the room. In the condition of mild threat, the child was only told: "Do not play with the robot. It is wrong to play with the robot." In the high threat condition, this statement was used with this addition: "If you play with the robot, I'll be *very angry*." Those children who had not played with the toy were placed in the same situation several weeks later, with no threat. Freedman found that those who had resisted temptation under mild threat were less likely to play with the toy in this second session than those who had resisted under severe threat. Thus, Festinger's concept of the stronger effects of a less forceful persuasive communication was confirmed for subsequent behavior.

Though the evidence is distinctly intriguing, there remains some controversy about the greater effect on attitude change of smaller inducements. Janis and Gilmore (1965) conducted an experiment in which college students were paid $1 or $20 to present good arguments in favor of adding a year of physics and a year of mathematics to the college curriculum. As a "high incentive," some were told that this enterprise was being conducted under "public welfare" auspices on behalf of a number of leading universities in the United States. For the "low incentive" condition, others were told that the information was being gathered for a new publishing company that was trying to build up its market for science textbooks. Their results showed that subsequent attitudes changed most favorably for subjects receiving the greater monetary reward, rather than the lesser reward, and significantly so under the "high incentive" condition.

Rosenberg (1965) has argued that the degree of reward for advocating a position opposite to one's own is also contaminated by the presence of *evaluation apprehension* in the experimental setting. By this he means that the subjects, apprehensive from a desire to present themselves favorably to a critical experimenter, may resist appearing to be easily swayed by inordinately high monetary rewards. In a replication of the essay-writing experiment by Brehm and Cohen (1962, pp. 74-78) noted above, Rosenberg had the experimenter who determined the subjects' final attitudes dissociated from the experimenter who presented the essay-writing task. Using this procedure, he found that the greatest amount of change occurred for the subjects paid the largest sum of money. These nonconfirming findings clearly point to the prospect that this particular prediction from dissonance theory, regarding the effects of small inducements, may be limited to only certain conditions.

THE COMMUNICATOR AND THE CONTENT OF THE COMMUNICATION

Much of the research on the role of the communicator as a source of influence has centered on his *credibility*. This general characteristic embodies several features which the recipient may perceive which gives the source validity, including expertise and trustworthiness. There are also such factors as background, appearance, and other identifiable features of the person which might determine his acceptability. Part of the content of his communication, therefore, is the impression he conveys to the audience in terms of these characteristics.

In an experiment by Hovland and Weiss (1951), college students were given material to read presented as articles drawn from newspapers and magazines. These dealt with various technical topics including the feasibility of an atomic submarine, the use of antihistamine drugs, and so forth. In half of the communications, attribution was made to sources considered to be trustworthy, and in the other half to sources considered to be untrustworthy. As might be expected, immediately after the messages had been read, the material attributed to trustworthy sources generated significantly greater amounts of attitude change than that attributed to untrustworthy sources. Furthermore, regardless of which situation they had been in, subjects had acquired about the same level of information. Four weeks later, subjects were tested again for longer-range attitude change. Now it was found that attitudes originally influenced by the trustworthy source showed a decrease in the amount of agreement with the message, while those influenced by the untrustworthy source showed an increase in the amount of agreement with the message. Hovland and Weiss dubbed this the "sleeper effect" and concluded that it might have arisen as a result of the subjects' recalling the content of a communication but forgetting its source after a time.

In another experiment, Weiss (1957) tested the hypothesis that a communicator who agrees with the views of an audience on a given issue of importance will be more effective in changing attitudes on another issue, though unrelated. His results indicated that this effect did occur and suggests that in it there is an element of increased trustworthiness as well as a sense that the communicator shares some important characteristics with the members of his audience. In this respect, an experiment by Zimbardo (1960) indicates that if the communicator is the best friend of the recipient the greatest attitude change occurs, even if the communication is highly discrepant.

In general, the work of Hovland and his associates (Hovland, Janis, and Kelley, 1953) demonstrates the force exerted by the communicator in determining the effectiveness of the content of his message. Two of the specific kinds of things that they have investigated are the *order of presentation* of material and the presentation of *one or both sides* of an issue. From many studies by the Yale group, it appears that the order, in terms of the primacy or recency of a message, is complexly related to attitude change (Hovland, 1957).

Primacy refers to the advantage of the initial position presented, and recency to the advantage of the last position presented. In Cohen's (1964) coverage of research dealing with the communicator's message, he points out that research on primacy-recency yields highly differential results as a consequence of other factors such as awareness of intent to influence, complexity of the message, and the attempt to measure the communicator's effects.

Overall, the primacy effect operates best to reinforce an attitude already held. However, it can be reduced by a long delay between the first and second presentations. Miller and Campbell (1959) suggest that because of a high degree of forgetting, time differentials may be decisive in determining the effects of persuasive communications. In short, primacy may lose its impact if there is a sufficient delay before hearing an alternative viewpoint.

If, after hearing one side of an issue, the audience is obliged to take a public stand before hearing the alternative view, there is a strong primacy effect. Hovland, Campbell, and Brock (1957) presented one side of a controversial issue to a group of students and then asked them to write their opinion on it for publication in a magazine read by their peers. Other students, in a control group, heard the same presentation but wrote out their opinions anonymously, with no mention of any publication. Without prior announcement, both groups then heard the other side, and their attitudes were again measured. The results revealed that public expression tended to make subjects more resistant to influence by the second presentation, than were those giving less public, anonymous expression.

On the whole, the findings regarding primacy indicate that it is affected by a number of other factors. This is equally true with regard to the presentation of one side vs. both sides of an argument. Presenting just one side is more effective in reinforcing an audience's attitude already in the desired direction, while presenting both sides is more effective with an audience whose attitudes are not in that direction

(Hovland, Lumsdaine, and Sheffield, 1949). Motivational factors are also involved. Thus, order of presentation is a more important determiner of attitude change for subjects with a low degree of interest than for those with high interest (Cohen, Stotland, and Wolfe, 1955). McGuire (1957) found that when communications highly consonant with audience attitudes were presented first by a communicator, followed by those that were not consonant, more attitude change resulted than when the order was reversed.

Appeals which arouse fear motivation have been found variously to affect attitude change. In a study by Janis and Feshbach (1953), college students were divided into three experimental groups and given communications, varying in intensity, concerning the importance of dental hygiene. Data were gathered before and after on the students' dental practices. Those who had received the most fear-arousing communication, involving the presentation of pictures of diseased gums, changed least toward the recommended preventative practices for dental care. Those who had received the more moderate messages changed significantly more in the intended direction. Janis and Feshbach concluded that a result of fear arousal was to reduce compliance by the inhibiting effects of anxiety.

Similar results were also obtained by Janis and Terwilliger (1962) using appeals to smokers, ranging from high to low threat, concerning the health hazards of smoking. Alternatively, Leventhal and Niles (1964) found that smokers who reported more fear on the issue of smoking and cancer showed greater agreement with the recommendations of a persuasive communication. Berkowitz and Cottingham (1960) found that a higher fear appeal produced greater attitude change than a lower fear appeal on the issue of the safety features of auto seat belts.

McGuire (1966, p. 485) reconciles these apparently disparate findings by emphasizing the necessity to take account of the recipient's initial concern with an issue as a determinant of the effect of a fear appeal. His essential point is that given a high initial concern, a fear-arousing communication may overwhelm the recipient with anxiety and accordingly reduce the effectiveness of the communication. Optimally, the high fear arousal would be most effective with those people having a low level of initial concern. McGuire observes that studies by Niles (1964) and Millman (1965) do support this interpretation.

RESISTANCE TO PERSUASION

Hovland, Janis, and Kelley (1953) advanced the hypothesis that "when a person is perceived as having a definite *intention* to persuade others, the likelihood is increased that he will be perceived as having something to gain and, hence, as less worthy of trust" (p. 23). The idea that communicators have "an axe to grind" is a commonplace. Yet, resistance to persuasion has been found to depend upon other factors. Walster and Festinger (1962) conducted an experiment which lent general support to the resistance hypothesis. An appeal from communicators who were allegedly unaware of being "overheard" by an audience had a greater effect than when they made a "direct" appeal to a comparable audience, provided the audience had strong feelings on the issue initially. In another study involving the "incidental" character of the communication, Festinger and Maccoby (1964) obtained comparable findings.

Various studies (McGuire and Papageorgis, 1962; McGuire, 1964; McGuire and Millman, 1965; Freedman and Sears, 1965) indicate that the forewarning of a desire to persuade tends to bolster the audience's defenses by a rehearsal of their supportive arguments. There are, however, individual factors, such as self-esteem, also involved. In general, resistance to persuasion is associated with high self-esteem (Hovland and Janis, 1959, p. 230), a point to which we give greater attention in Chapter Ten in regard to the functioning of personality.

It is not enough to say, however, that open attempts to influence are rejected. Thus, Mills and Aronson (1965) found that an overt, frankly stated desire to influence can enhance persuasiveness, if the communicator is "attractive" to the audience. Similarly, Mills (1966) reports that a communicator who indicates a liking for the audience, as part of a persuasive appeal, is more effective in gaining agreement from that audience than one who does not indicate a liking. In terms of our earlier discussion of the transactional model, actions of the communicator which establish a favorable perception of him by the audience materially increase his prospect for both overcoming resistance to persuasion and becoming influential. Zimbardo's finding (1960), considered above, indicates that close friends are acceptable communication sources, even when their communications are discrepant. This appears to be a function of trust, especially regarding the perception of the motives of the communicator (see Allyn and Festinger, 1961).

ASSIMILATION AND CONTRAST EFFECTS

Our last concern here will be with the way in which the recipient of the communication perceives it in terms of his own position. The importance of this consideration is evident through much of the material that we have been surveying. In the final analysis, it is the individual who categorizes and interprets the message in light of his past experience.

For a long time, attitude studies operated with the assumption that the position advocated by a communication would be seen in about the same way by different people. This was the basis for the judging procedure in Thurstone's development of the equal-appearing intervals attitude scale. However, as we noted above, Hovland and Sherif (1952) found that there were variable judgments associated with attitudes, because individuals use their own position in evaluating other positions in terms of assimilation or contrast. In this context, *assimilation* means the acceptance of material from a communication source as tolerable within one's own view of things. *Contrast* means a rejection of such material as beyond that range. Exemplifying this, Hovland, Janis, and Kelley (1953) indicate that individuals who are in favor of the position advocated will consider a communication to be fair and unbiased; those who are opposed will see it as unfair and propagandistic.

Subsequent work by Hovland, Harvey, and Sherif (1957) demonstrated that individuals who hold extreme positions tend to see other positions in sharp contrast with their own. In this experiment the issue of the desirability of a prohibition on drinking was studied in two states, Oklahoma and Texas, where the so-called "wet-dry" issue is hotly contested. Three kinds of communications were directed at subjects through a taped presentation. One was strongly "wet," one strongly "dry," and one "moderately wet." Figure 6.5 shows the results in terms of the three kinds of communications and the recipients' positions ranging from A (very dry) through H (very wet). As is seen there, the degree of distance between the recipient and the communication greatly influences the acceptance of the communication.

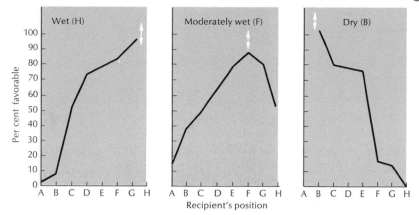

Figure 6.5: Percentage of favorable evaluations ("fair," "unbiased," etc.) of wet (H), moderately wet (F), and dry (B) communications for subjects holding various positions on prohibition. Recipients' positions range from A (very dry) to H (very wet). Position of communications indicated by arrow. (From Hovland, Harvey, and Sherif, 1957.)

This research illustrates the judgmental quality of an attitude. In their book *Social Judgment,* Sherif and Hovland (1961) extend this view as follows:

> . . . an attitude toward an object, person, group, or social issue is not directly observable but is inferred from a persistent and *charac-teristic* mode of reaction to that stimulus or stimulus class. This characteristic mode of reaction signifies differential treatment of the object of attitude. It is inferred that the object of attitude is placed in a category or class favorable or unfavorable in some degree, high or low in some degree, acceptable or unacceptable in some degree in the individual's scheme of things. In short one essential aspect of the attitudinal reaction is a categorization process, whether or not the individual is aware that he is passing a judgment (p. 5).

We may say, then, that attitudes operate as categories for defining an individual's experience, rather than single points on a scale. These are inferred through a pattern of approval or disapproval of items on attitude scales, or in terms of other behaviors. Accordingly, Sherif and Hovland (1961) contend that every individual has a range of positions which constitute his latitudes of acceptance, rejection, and non-commitment for the topic area represented by an attitude. The *latitude of acceptance* is represented by the person's own position on a topic as well as those positions which are most acceptable to him; the *latitude of rejection* constitutes the positions that the individual would find most objectionable to his own; the *latitude of non-commitment* is indicated by the "don't know" and "no opinion" categories in questionnaire surveys, which usually reveal issues respondents view with disinterest.

The idea of latitudes is especially important for its emphasis on the individual's construction of his world, within a set of ranges rather than in terms of a fixed scale point. This approach has recently been elaborated by Sherif, Sherif, and Nebergall in their book, *Attitude and Attitude Change: The Social Judgment-Involvement Approach* (1965). If a communication is extremely discrepant from an individual's own position, they find that it produces resistance to the advocated change, and even a boomerang effect, particularly if the individual is highly involved in the issue. Sherif, Sherif, and Nebergall have demonstrated that, as the individual's involvement increases, the latitude of non-commitment becomes absorbed within the latitude of rejection. The latitude of acceptance is not directly affected so much as is the rejection of almost any other viewpoints.

A readiness to accept influence toward attitude change is therefore likely to be greatest where the communication is not extremely discrepant and the issue is not vitally important to the individual. This effect is shown in Figure 6.6 from research by Freedman (1964). As predicted, with low involvement, attitude change is directly related to the degree the communication is discrepant from the individual's own position. Under high involvement, however, the greatest change occurs with a moderately discrepant communication, and a sharp drop-off in effect occurs for a highly discrepant communication.

In the Zimbardo study (1960) he obtained a different finding. There greater involvement on the part of the individual produced greater dissonance and hence more attitude change from a discrepant communication. This may be a function of how the range of discrepancy is defined. A further consideration, quite obviously, is the credibility of the communicator. Zimbardo used a close friend as the communicator. Relatedly, Aronson, Turner, and Carlsmith (1963) have found that with greater prestige the communicator's message was harder to reject even if it was highly discrepant. Once again, therefore, the perception by the recipient of the characteristics of the *complex* represented by the communicator *and* his message is vitally important.

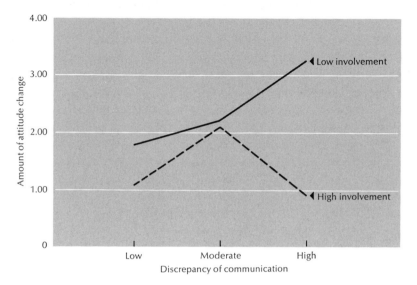

Figure 6.6: Mean amount of attitude change from initial to final response for two levels of involvement and three levels of communication discrepancy. (From Freedman, 1964.)

Social influence and attitudes: a final word

In this chapter we have considered the ways in which attitudes developing out of influence relationships are altered in the course of ongoing interaction and the input of new experience. Our emphasis, in terms of attitude change, has been on a transactional model of communication. This model has ramifications which apply to a broad sphere of social relationships. Moreover concepts of balance and dissonance, of interpersonal perception and social exchange, have wide relevance.

The effects of direct interaction on attitude change are attended to further in the next chapter. It should be apparent that interpersonal contact produces such effects in a wide-range of life situations. In the case of prejudice, for example, extensive literature sustains the proposition that such contact, particularly on an equal status basis, undermines the attitudes which nourish prejudice and its manifestations (see Allport, 1958).

Another thing that should be said is that profound experiences may have a dramatic effect on attitude change. When an individual is confronted with a major change in his life habits, or in his awareness about an issue central to his existence, changes in attitude may be very rapid indeed, and their effects quite perceptible. One provocative illustration of this comes from recent research on "role-playing" as a device in changing smoking habits.

In this study by Janis and Mann (1965), fourteen women who were known to be smokers were asked to play the role of patient as part of an experiment. Each was received in what appeared to be a physician's office and heard an experimenter, acting the role of the physician, telling her that he had some "bad news." The news consisted of the fact that a supposed X-ray examination had revealed that they had lung cancer and therefore, allegedly, they would be obliged immediately to undergo surgery. They could ask questions, and they did. From this relatively spontaneous interchange, they learned that the surgery would be painful, that there was some risk of its not being successful, that they would find it necessary to be in a state of recuperation for many weeks, and so on.

The role-playing group showed markedly greater changes in attitudes and subsequent behavior than did a control group of twelve subjects who had received similar information by listening to a tape-recording of one of these interview sessions. A follow-up after two weeks indicated that the realistic quality of the experimental situation had aroused sufficient concern to produce a marked decrease in smoking. While it would be a mistake to generalize this effect to any and all situations of threat, it suggests how a set of potent factors may profoundly alter attitudes and their associated behaviors. The factors in this particular situation were its real-life immediacy, the importance of the issue to the individuals involved, and the presumptive "credibility" of the experimenter as a prestige source (see also Elms, 1966).

Since we noted earlier that extreme fear arousal can operate to immobilize people, it should be added that a clear alternative for action should be readily perceived by the subjects if a desired effect is to be produced. An apt illustration of this is seen in Cohen's research (1957) which supported the generalization that attitude change is more likely to occur if information relevant to motive satisfaction is presented *after* these motives have been aroused, rather than before. Given the high salience of the motivation induced in the kind of role-playing situation just described, it should follow that especially those subjects, who beforehand had been relatively unconcerned, were sufficiently aroused to take action. Others, who did not change as dramatically, may have been overwhelmed by this fear-inducing experience.

In subsequent chapters we will consider a number of relationships which draw upon concepts examined here. We will observe that leadership and conformity, as examples, have common elements paralleling those we considered with regard to communication and attitude change as a process of influence. Thus, leaders are communication sources who transmit messages and are perceived and reacted to as such. In the instance of conformity, the communication source may be a broader social entity, in the form of a group, and its messages may be represented in the normative practices which it encourages. All of these partake of the characteristics and processes embedded in influence relationships.

SUMMARY

There are numerous problems associated with the measurement of attitudes, including the very breadth of the concept attitude itself. Attitudes may also vary with regard to their *centrality* or *peripherality* within the person's psychological field. The most widespread approach to measuring attitudes continues to be the *attitude scale*. In general, such scales consist of a number of statements with which a person may agree or disagree on a dimension with several points often ranging from "highly agree" to "highly disagree." Through this procedure the cognitive component of an attitude is measured by its *direction*, and its affective component by the *degree* of agreement or disagreement as well as by *intensity* of feeling. A score revealing the person's overall attitude can be obtained by summing the responses made to the scale items. A more recent procedure, involving a number of scales, is represented today in the technique called the *semantic differential* which constitutes a multi-dimensional scale. It measures the three major factors of *evaluation, potency,* and *activity.*

Attitude measurement involves considerations of accuracy with regard to *reliability* and *validity*. These issues have to do respectively with the consistency of measurement and the degree to which a measurement actually assesses what it is supposed to measure. Reliability is usually gauged by the internal consistency of an attitude scale as well as by its "repeat reliability" when administered more than once over time. Validity is sometimes determined by checking the relationship between attitudes and behavior.

The validity of attitudes when checked against behaviors in a given situation often appears low. However, this occurs as a result of situational factors which may elicit or inhibit behaviors. These factors can be considered *situational hurdles* which intervene between attitudes and action.

Two kinds of factors are involved in the dynamics of attitude change. One is the *processing* of new information through cognitive interaction, and the other is the function of *social identifications* in maintaining attitudes. The effect of persuasive communication in changing attitudes has been studied as an influence process in terms of the *communicator,* the content of the *message,* and the characteristics of the *recipient.* The *transactional model* of persuasive communication takes account of these elements and the process of exchange which occurs between the communicator and the recipient leading the latter to alter his attitudes. Cognitive consistency dictates that an individual may reject or selectively perceive new information to retain his attitudinal structure. The consistency approach to attitude change gives considerable attention to *dissonance, cognitive balance,* and *congruity.* These approaches all rely on the idea that disturbances in a system of attitudes induce processes to restore balance or consistency in that system. Research on cognitive dissonance has emphasized the effect on attitudes of actions which are contradictory to them.

The effectiveness of a communicator in changing attitudes depends upon his credibility to the recipient as well as upon his message. He may also strive to present the content of his message in such a way as to make it more acceptable with respect to the already prevailing attitudes and group affiliations of the recipient. The effects of *primacy* and *recency* of information are complexly related to attitude change. Primacy, in terms of the advantage of the initial position presented, appears to operate best to reinforce an already held attitude. The *balance of presentation* is also important. Presenting just one side is more effective in reinforcing an audience's already held attitude, and presenting both sides is more effective with an audience whose attitudes are not already in the direction of the communication. Fear-arousing appeals have been found variously to affect attitude change; those who are already concerned appear to be made more anxious by such appeals. Resistance to persuasion is complexly related to the perception of the communicator, and the personality of the recipient, in terms of factors such as self-esteem.

Attitudes have a judgmental quality which operates in terms of *contrast* and *assimilation* effects. Contrast occurs when the recipient perceives the communication as discrepant from his own *latitude of acceptance* and places it within his *latitude of rejection*. Individuals are more likely to reject a discrepant communication if they are highly involved in an issue, since such involvement increases their latitude of rejection. However, even a highly discrepant communication from a communication source which is very positively favored will be assimilated as a basis for attitude change. Intense experiences which change attitudes often involve a combination of factors which operate in common to arouse the recipient.

SUGGESTED READINGS

From E. P. Hollander and R. G. Hunt. (Eds.) *Current perspectives in social psychology.* (2nd Edition.) New York: Oxford University Press, 1967:

38. Milton Rokeach: *The organization and modification of beliefs*
39. Theodore M. Newcomb: *Persistence and regression of changed attitudes: long-range studies*
40. Muzafer Sherif and Carl I. Hovland: *Judgmental processes and problems of attitude*
41. Raymond A. Bauer: *The obstinate audience: the influence process from the point of view of social communication*
54. Elihu Katz: *The two-step flow of communication: an up-to-date report on an hypothesis*

SELECTED REFERENCES

Brehm, J. W., & Cohen, A. R. *Explorations in cognitive dissonance.* New York: Wiley, 1962.

Cohen, A. R. *Attitude change and social influence.* New York: Basic Books, 1964.

Edwards, A. L. *Techniques of attitude scale construction.* New York: Appleton-Century-Crofts. 1957.

Festinger, L. *A theory of cognitive dissonance.* Evanston, Ill.: Row, Peterson, 1957.

Festinger, L. (Ed.) *Conflict, decision, and dissonance.* Stanford, Calif.: Stanford Univer. Press, 1964.

*Hovland, C. I. & Janis, I. L. (Eds.) *Personality and persuasibility.* New Haven: Yale Univer. Press, 1959.

*Hovland, C. I. & Rosenberg, M. J. (Eds.) *Attitude organization and change.* New Haven: Yale Univer. Press, 1960.

Rokeach, M. *The open and closed mind.* New York: Basic Books, 1960.

Sherif, Carolyn W., Sherif, M., & Nebergall, R. E. *Attitude and attitude change: The social judgment-involvement approach.* Philadelphia: Saunders, 1965.

*Sherif, M. & Hovland, C. I. *Social judgment.* New Haven: Yale Univer. Press, 1961.

7

Social interaction, interpersonal perception, and social exchange

Social interaction is a pervasive feature of life. Much of the substance of our experience is shaped by social relationships involving interaction. All of our individual characteristics, concerns, and aspirations are somehow affected by it. It is no wonder then that the study of social interaction occupies a central place in social psychology.

Regarding the importance of interaction, Hare, Borgatta, and Bales (1955) have said that ". . . our very ability to experience, to decide, and to control our own behavior through our decisions is dependent in many subtle and involuntary ways on our relationship and interaction with our fellows" (p. 192). By understanding processes of interaction, therefore, we can clarify many broader features of social influence including cultural, organizational, and group effects upon the individual.

Some features of interaction

Social interaction refers essentially to a *reciprocal relationship* between two or more individuals whose behavior is *mutually dependent*. It may also be thought of as a communication process that leads to influence upon the actions and outlooks of individuals.

The widespread nature of interaction exists not only among humans but also in related species. In the monkey family, for example, inter-

173

action serves as communicative behavior which signalizes certain relationships. From his extensive studies of primate societies, Carpenter (1963) observes:

> When two primates approach each other, the quality of the conditioned social interaction is indicated by each to the other, by the pattern and rate of behavior and by *mutual recognition* of species and individual characteristics. For example, two gibbons of the same group, when coming together after even a short period of separation, express friendly predispositions by a stereotyped pattern involving facial expression, a momentary embrace and a special little cry (p. 49).

Broadly speaking, social interaction encompasses what Schutz (1958) calls an interpersonal situation, that is, one in which two or more persons interact for some purpose. Such interpersonal situations need not, however, involve actual face-to-face relationships. An individual's actions may be determined by the expectation of others who are not physically present at the moment. Thus, family members separated by many miles still retain a forceful interpersonal relationship.

Interaction can and more often does involve face-to-face contact between people; but it also takes in something we have previously called "implicit" interaction. In this case, our actions are still affected by the awareness of the expectancies of relevant others.

Interactions may also be of a long-term or short-term variety. These have a different quality, and hold distinctive expectancies, as we can easily recall from experiences with those people about whom we know very little that we may encounter when traveling. A striking Alfred Hitchcock film, *Strangers on a Train*, was built on just such a dramatic premise. Ambiguous short-term interactions of this kind have some unique properties, including what often appears to be a greater degree of self-revelation.

Face-to-face interaction of a more enduring sort has several features which can be studied in psychological terms. One is the *interdependence of behavior* between the interacting parties; this involves the way in which one person's behavior serves as the stimulus for the other's behavior. A second feature is the mutual *expectancy of behavior,* in the sense of interpersonal perceptions of one another. Underpinning these is the third feature of an implicit *evaluation* in terms of the value attached to others, their actions and motives, as well as the satisfactions they provide. Before considering these further, it is useful to review the essential nature of interaction.

Bases for social interaction

The widespread need for social interaction can be accounted for in several ways. In the first place, it serves the function of inculcating those general characteristics shared with others within one's own society. In more specific terms, as we have noted earlier, it affects the development of the individual's distinctive personality (e.g. Sears, 1951a; Secord and Backman, 1961). A repeated finding, for example, is to the general effect that the self-concept of the individual depends upon interactions with others. As Cottrell (1950) has noted, a vital interest in social psychology concerns the way in which types of interaction act to pattern the self-concept. This patterning appears to follow the line that the expectations of important others, especially in childhood, act to condition the individual's own view of himself.

There are grounds, too, for believing that social interaction reduces the effect of stress. Bovard (1959) and Zajonc (1965) have reviewed studies which indicate that the presence of members of the same species provides an arousal effect for individuals. Schachter's research (1959) yields the finding that under stressful conditions of fear or hunger college students show an increasing desire to have contact with others. Earlier findings have sustained a similar conclusion. Thus, Titmuss (1950) found in London during World War II bombing that children, separated from the close interactions of their family and evacuated from the city, experienced more stress than those who endured the bombings with their family. Other wartime research has indicated the importance of social interactions among soldiers in resisting the stress of battle (e.g. Mandelbaum, 1952; Marshall, 1951). Social interaction, therefore, has a vital preservative role for the individual, as its effects are felt through certain physiological mechanisms.

The structure of interaction

The particular kind of situation in which interaction occurs is of considerable importance in determining certain features of the behavior that the individuals present to one another. This is referred to as the *structure of interaction*. Two people might be involved in a situation structured as a competition for a mutually desired goal that only one may obtain: consider the plight of two close friends who are attracted to the same girl as one instance. Alternatively, people may be involved in a co-operative enterprise where the goal is only available if the individuals assist one another in its achievement, as in the case of the cast in a dramatic production. Other kinds of relationships which grow out of the structure of the situation include dominance, as represented in the exertion of power, and conflict of interests. Strikes exemplify this latter phenomenon at the extreme. In his field study, entitled *Wildcat Strike*, Gouldner (1954) reports a graphic illustration of conflict's effect on the perception of motivation:

> The great majority of workers viewed their strike as a justified and legitimate action. Workers usually defined the strike in ethical terms, holding it to be morally justified. As many of them said, "We're out to get our rights." The strike was not interpreted by them, as management was inclined to define it, in the amoral concepts of power. Their hostility toward the "swearing" supervisor, and against supervisors who overstepped their bounds, expressed *moral* indignation (p. 59).

FORMAL AND INFORMAL INTERACTION

In the most general terms, interaction may be divided into two large categories of structure. First, interaction proceeds with reference to a *formal* structure in terms of patterned relationships which society requires; second, it operates within an *informal* structure generated and sustained by individual perceptions and motivations. What is called the formal level of interaction is exemplified mainly in social roles, while the informal level consists of such factors as interpersonal attraction, loyalty, and a sense of equity. The biggest differentiation between formal and informal interaction rests in the consideration that the latter depends more upon individual *dispositions* and *satisfactions*. It should also be noted that interactions in a formal setting can take on the quality of informal interaction. If sustained, such a relationship would then be highly dependent upon personal inclinations. The formalized ritual of a wedding ceremony might lead the best man and a bridesmaid, unacquainted before, to develop a sustained interest in one another.

The essence of formal social interaction is its highly *prescribed* character. This is usually embodied in the concept of *role*. In any given society mothers, for example, are expected to interact with their children in distinctive ways which conform broadly to the role which we refer to as "mother." Therefore, *role behavior* may be defined essentially as the expected behaviors for an individual in terms of a position he occupies. In effect, it describes the suitability of behavior prescribed for a social position, or status. Linton (1945) presents a definitive statement of this relationship in these terms:

> The place in a particular system which a certain individual occupies at a particular time will be referred to as his *status* with respect to that system. . . . The second term, *role* will be used to designate the sum total of the cultural patterns associated with a particular status. It thus includes the attitudes, values and behavior ascribed by the society to any and all persons occupying this status. . . . Every status is linked with a particular role, but the two things are by no means the same from the point of view of the individual. His statuses are ascribed to him on the basis of his age and sex, his birth or marriage into a particular family unit, and so forth. His roles are learned on the basis of his statuses, either current or anticipated (pp. 76-77).

Formal features of interaction are more usually learned without explicit intent. Newcomb (1950) has pointed out that this proceeds via "reciprocal role relationships." The child, for example, interacts with his parents and thereby acquires a sense of the appropriate behavior for a parent, just as the pupil in school learns and often can readily imitate the behavior expected of the teacher. Berne (1964) contends that all adults retain the vestiges of the role of child and of a same-sex parent. These roles come into play, often unwittingly, in interaction. It is not unlikely to find as most parents do, that at times they are behaving toward their children as their own parents behaved toward them, and often with a sense of distaste and no better response from the children.

Interaction of a formal variety is highly vulnerable to the effects of varying settings. Jeanne Watson (1958) has distinguished three of these as the *familial, sociable,* and *work* settings. Each distinctively directs interaction in a patterned way. Thus, a familial setting is one in which the individual is accepted by the others and can be at ease in the sense of not having to "prove" himself. A work setting is much more focused on a task; the individual's value may therefore be judged according to his contribution to the achievement of group goals. A sociable setting is one in which individuals can satisfy their inclinations for social relationships, but nonetheless must display themselves favorably. Accordingly, each setting occasions particular patterns of interaction.

An essential ingredient of interaction is the challenge it presents to understanding the outlook of the other individual involved. This is particularly so in informal interaction. In formal interaction relationships run off without the penetrating kind of perception of the other individual's motives or attitudes or values that we encounter, for example, in friendship. However even in formal interaction, we are alert to the behavior and intent of the other person.

In this regard George Kelly has highlighted the necessity to view social interaction as involving "interpersonal understandings" which arise from each person's effective construing of the other person's outlook. He gives a compelling example of one kind of formal interaction—largely dictated by traffic laws—which we encounter in driving down a highway. He says:

> . . . we stake our lives hundreds of times a day on our accuracy in predicting what the drivers of the oncoming cars will do. The orderly, extremely complex, and precise weaving of traffic is really an amazing example of people predicting each other's behavior through subsuming each other's perception of a situation. Yet actually each of us knows very little about the higher motives and the complex aspirations of the oncoming drivers, upon whose behavior our own lives depend. It is enough, for the purpose of avoiding collisions, that we understand or subsume only certain specific aspects of their construction systems (1963, p. 95).

INTERDEPENDENCE, CO-OPERATION, AND COMPETITION

In classifying social interaction, one element of significance appears to be the degree to which the parties are functionally interdependent. Interdependence often refers to the degree to which individuals require one another to achieve rewards which would be unavailable to them otherwise. This is co-operative interdependence. Another kind of interdependence occurs in competition where the goal may be available only to one person, as in a single's game of tennis. This is an oversimplification however, since there are many competitive situations where both parties can gain by interdependent actions. Such situations have been called "non-zero-sum" games—meaning that the winnings by one side need not be balanced by losses from the other. Diplomacy is an interdependent relationship that involves competitive but also co-operative elements.

Several factors appear to be important in an interdependent relationship. One of these is the availability of joint rewards. Another is the establishment of trust and the related matter of communication.

Deutsch (1949a; 1949b) has contributed a number of productive concepts and findings useful to an understanding of co-operation. Among these is the proposition that co-operation increases as persons recognize their mutual interdependence and trust one another. He has done extensive experimentation on these phenomena often employing a choice matrix that is called the "prisoner's dilemma." This is shown in Figure 7.1. In it the values received by Person I always precede those

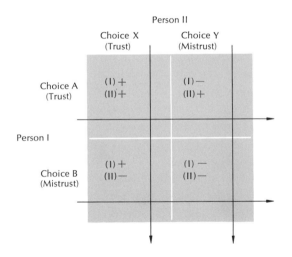

Figure 7.1: Illustration of "Prisoner's Dilemma" matrix. Outcomes for Persons I and II are determined by the cells in which their choices intersect.

received by Person II in any cell. On any trial the task requires a simple A or B choice by Person I, and an independently arrived-at choice of X or Y by Person II. Only after both have made their choices is the outcome revealed. The task is therefore competitive but it also makes demands of a co-operative nature, if the participants are not to hurt one another.

The name of the matrix comes from the analogue to a situation where two persons are apprehended for a crime and are questioned separately by the police without an opportunity for discussion between them. Both are told that if they give evidence to convict the other person they will receive a lighter sentence themselves. Looking at the matrix, we see the choices of A or B for Person I and X or Y for Person II. Assuming A and X to be the choices *not* to give evidence, it will be seen that both persons stand to gain. If I chooses Y to give evidence to spare himself, while II choses B to do the same, both lose since they have implicated each other to the authorities. If they trust one another, however, they will respond A and X respectively and both gain. If they distrust one another, they will respond B and Y and both lose. Where either one is trusting and the other is not the trusting one stands to lose.

Using this kind of matrix with money gains or losses in the cells, Loomis (1959) conducted an experiment in what appeared to be a two-person situation. Among his interests was the effect of perceived trust and of varying degrees of communication in producing a more trusting response. The task presented to the participants was to earn as much money as they could by judicious choices in the matrix. No special point was made in the instructions regarding co-operation or competition. Subjects gave their choices in separate cubicles and received back results contrived by the experimenter. Apparent communications from the "partner" were also arranged in terms of five levels from the least information about how to make mutually beneficial choices to the greatest information. These communication levels were labeled from I through V. In advance of each trial each subject was also asked to report his anticipation of his partner's choice thus revealing his perceived trust.

Loomis found that 87 per cent of the subjects who perceived trust were trustworthy themselves. Furthermore, the amount of communication permitted produced a direct relationship with perceived trust. As will be seen in Figure 7.2, proceeding from level I to level V in communication greater degrees of trust are evidenced.

Azrin and Lindsley (1956) have shown how co-operative behavior can be induced and reinforced in pairs of children merely asked to play a "game." They faced one another across a table with a glass partition between them. Before them each found a metal stylus and a metal plate with three holes. The children received instructions which said they could play the game any way they wanted to by placing the styli in the holes. They were then told: "While you are in this room some of these [jelly beans] will drop into this cup. You can eat them here if you want to or you can take them home with you." The children were then left alone.

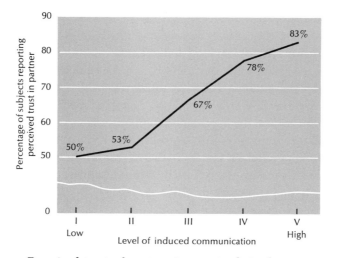

Figure 7.2: Perceived trust of partner in matrix choice by increasing levels of communication induced experimentally. (Based on data from Loomis, 1959.)

The apparatus was so wired that, if the styli were placed in opposite holes within .04 seconds of each other, a red light flashed on the table and a single jelly bean fell into a cup that was accessible to both children. This was considered to be a co-operative response and the candy served as the reinforcement.

All pairs learned to co-operate within ten minutes. Azrin and Lindsley report further:

> Observation through a one-way vision screen disclosed that leader-follower relationships were developed and maintained in most cases. Almost immediately eight teams divided the candy in some manner. Witn two teams, one member at first took all the candy until the other member refused to cooperate. When verbal agreement was

reached in these two teams, the members then cooperated and divided the candy (p. 101).

The perceived equitability of rewards is therefore quite relevant in interdependent relationships. An experiment conducted by Miller and Hamblin (1963) illustrates this point. They created conditions of high interdependence and low interdependence among students formed into three-person groups. Their task was to choose accurately which of a variety of numbers had been selected by the experimenter. On any one trial the problem was considered solved only when *each* group member knew the answer. Across the interdependence conditions, they arranged differential rewarding such that members of one-third of the groups in each of these conditions received equal rewards, one-third received rewards based on their order of completion (the medium reward condition), and the last third provided high reward to just *one* subject who solved the problem first in a group. For each group productivity scores were computed based upon the average time to complete the task. Figure 7.3 presents the results of this experiment. The major guid-

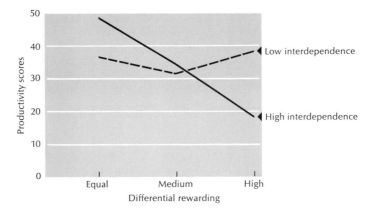

Figure 7.3: Mean productivity scores for differential rewarding under conditions of high and low interdependence. (Based on data from Miller and Hamblin, 1963.)

ing hypothesis, that high interdependence would have a significant inverse relationship to productivity as a result of the differential rewards, was confirmed. Equal rewarding yielded the greatest productivity where interdependence was high. With low interdependence no systematic effect on productivity was found. It is clear, then, that interdependence is a major determinant of whether equitable rewards are related to productivity in groups.

In general, where members of a group earn a common score based on the group's performance, there tends to be a greater degree of co-operation. In one earlier demonstration of this, Mintz (1951) used a situation in which several individuals had to pull cones out of a large glass jar with a narrow neck. When rewards were provided to each individual on the basis of his own time score, traffic jams usually developed at the neck so that participants had greater difficulty getting their cones out. Where group scores were provided, the groups developed a strategy for taking turns in withdrawing the cones. This result is in keeping with the concept of co-operative interdependence discussed above.

Research findings have generally tended to support the positive consequences of interdependent interaction in groups (e.g. Deutsch, 1949b; Gottheil, 1955; Grossack, 1954; Hammond and Goldman, 1961; Raven and Eachus, 1963). There are, nonetheless, some ambiguities about the work on co-operation and competition which arise from varying definitions. For example, co-operation might occur in a situation where the individuals were in groups that were competing with one another for high scores. In that case, co-operation within the group might be directly affected by the needs for competition between groups. Also, Shaw (1958) has found that a higher level of motivation produced by competition may lead to a decrease in the *quality* of performance. Since performance is often measured by a simple index of quantity, this might be obscured. There is also the issue of the difference between performance and member satisfaction to be considered.

A recent experiment taking account of some of these considerations was conducted by Julian and Perry (1965). They placed students together in teams of four, each to work out a laboratory exercise in experimental psychology. Co-operative or competitive relations were varied both *between* groups and *within* groups by the instructions given. In the "pure co-operation" condition, students believed that grades would be assigned on the basis of the number of team points; each member of those teams which got 90 per cent of the possible points would get an A, 80 per cent B, and so forth. In the "group competition" condition, the instructions indicated that grades would be assigned on a curve such that each member of the team turning in the best exercise would get an A, the next best team a B, and so on. This involved individual members co-operating, but groups competing. In the "individual competition" condition, with no group competition, grades were to be assigned on an individual basis with the best paper receiving an A, the next best a B, and so forth.

The quantity of output was measured by the number of words used in specifying a research design and in presenting the exploratory material. Without awareness of the treatments groups received, quality was judged in terms of the orderliness and logic of the hypotheses and of the research design. It was found that individual and group competition both produced a high quantity and a high quality of performance. The purely co-operative condition yielded the lowest level of group performance. On the other hand, it is noteworthy that pure co-operation did yield the greatest satisfaction with their relations among the group members. A point to be borne in mind, therefore, is that performance and satisfaction are by no means the same and deserve separate study.

DOMINANCE AND POWER IN INTERACTION

In general, the dependence of one person on another is likely to increase the possibility of influence. One kind of interdependent relationship which enhances the acceptance of influence is represented in the case of dominance. In other terms, this can be referred to as a relationship involving power. Bierstedt (1950) has distinguished between influence and power mainly on the grounds of persuasiveness versus coercion. He says that "Influence does not require power, and power may dispense with influence. Influence may convert a friend, but power coerces friend and foe alike" (p. 731). At the extreme, then, the presence of usable power presents a situation of coercive dominance. Influence, as we have previously discussed it, consists of the transmission of information designed to alter the response pattern of one or more individuals who have more than one perceived alternative for response. With power at the disposal of the agent of transmission, however, there is usually no perceived alternative but to comply, at least in observable actions.

A further point concerning power is represented in the work of Thibaut and Kelley (1959). They distinguish between power of two kinds—*behavior control* and *fate control*. In the first instance, by varying his behavior, A can make it desirable for B to vary his behavior too; in the second case, A can affect B's behavior regardless of what B does. Thus, power can be looked at in terms of the degree to which the less powerful person can affect certain outcomes in his own behalf. In most relationships, however, even where usable power is of the fate control variety, its exploitation may lead to unwanted effects in the form of covert resistance and outright hostility which could jeopardize the function to be fulfilled. More often it is behavior control that is in operation, and it necessarily implies a two-way influence process.

A clear illustration of a dominance relationship, where one individual exerts behavior control over another, is found in most organizational structures. There is usually a boss, or supervisor, or manager, or president, or chairman, who holds access to certain rewards which can be bestowed by him on others, or withheld. Such things as promotions, salary increases, public praise, recommendations, and other openings to opportunity are examples of these rewards. When individuals are involved in this kind of relationship, it is commonly the case that the one of less power expends some effort to construe the relevant features of the more powerful person's psychological field so as to gain rewards by his own actions and statements. This reciprocal influence has recently been considered by Jones (1964) in terms of *ingratiation*.

In an asymmetrical power relationship of this kind, one person is heavily dependent upon the other. To offset this, says Jones, ingratiation is employed through compliments, signs of agreement, and a generally favorable presentation of oneself to the more powerful person. As the dependent person becomes more attractive, the more powerful individual may be more inclined to provide rewards rather than withholding them. The idea of ingratiation then is essentially one of strategic interaction. As we shall be pointing out later, strategies are very much a part of controlling social interaction toward favorable ends.

The effectiveness of influence, or power, requires the perception of the direction of dominance by the parties in interaction. A neat demonstration of this is found in the results of research done by Miller, Murphy, and Mirsky (1955) manipulating the dominance hierarchy in a colony of ten monkeys. Relative dominance was measured by various observations over many months when monkeys were paired with one another and competing. As is generally found in such colonies, there was a considerable amount of consistency to the dominance hierarchy. An experiment was then performed which involved conditioning members of the colony to be fearful of one low in the hierarchy. The essential hypothesis was to the effect that this would raise the placement of the "stimulus monkey" within the hierarchy.

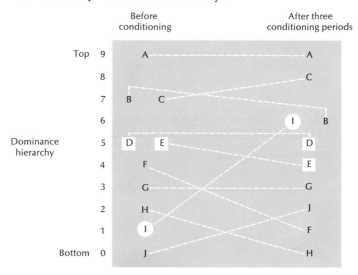

Figure 7.4: Shifts in dominance hierarchy in a colony of ten monkeys following three periods each of avoidance conditioning of Monkey *I* ("stimulus monkey," in circle) for Monkeys *D* and *E* ("conditioned monkeys," in boxes). (Adapted from Miller, Murphy, and Mirsky, 1955.)

In Figure 7.4 the actual dominance hierarchy for the ten monkeys is given before the experimental phase and then after three conditioning periods. In these, monkeys *D* and *E*, from the middle of the hierarchy, were each placed in an apparatus where they could see but not be seen by Monkey *I* who was in the adjoining compartment. In the original hierarchy, Monkey *I* was next to the bottom in dominance and was accordingly selected to be the "stimulus monkey." The procedure followed the lines of simple conditioning. As Monkey *I* became visible to the monkey being conditioned, that monkey was given an electric shock which continued until he pressed a lever which removed the "stimulus monkey" from view and terminated the shock. When Monkeys *D* and *E* had learned to press the lever in the apparatus each time

Monkey *I* was visible, each was considered to have been conditioned.

Recall that the results of this experiment were mainly of interest with regard to changes in the hierarchy of the monkey colony. In Figure 7.4 the most marked change in standing is found for Monkey *I* who went up from the ninth place to a tie for third place, after the three conditioning periods for *D* and *E*. These two "conditioned monkeys" in turn dropped to places below that of Monkey *I* whom they had been conditioned to fear. Many other shifts in the standing of monkeys in the hierarchy were also evidenced. For example, Monkey *F*, who had previously been next in dominance to *D* and *E*, fell to the ninth position, occupied before by *I*.

There are probably three kinds of perceptions at work here: first, the perception by the conditioned monkeys of the hitherto low-dominance monkey as one to be avoided for reasons of fear; then, the corresponding perception by the low-dominance monkey of the fearful reaction to his presence in the colony by the conditioned monkeys; and finally, the perception by the other members of the monkey colony of this new and different pattern of behavior being evidenced by formerly dominant monkeys toward one who was perceived to be of low dominance. The point of all this is clearly and succinctly summed up in the notion that dominance must be perceived to have its effects. When one monkey behaves as if he were less dominant than another, whether out of fear or whatever motive, this lowers his perceived standing in the hierarchy.

Another kind of situation involving dominance occurs in the interaction of husband and wife within the family. Strodtbeck has been among those interested in this feature of family interactions. In one of his experiments (1951), he asked husbands and wives to think about three families they knew well and to discuss such questions as which of the three had the happiest children, or was the most religious. Basically, Strodtbeck was interested in whether the husband or wife would be most often influential in these discussions. With white Protestant American couples he found that men and women were influential in about the same number of decisions. He compared this with results he obtained from couples coming from the Mormon and Navaho sub-cultures. Mormons generally emphasize the male role as more dominant while the Navahos emphasize the female role. With ten additional couples from each of these two sub-cultural groups, he found distinct confirmation that the most powerful partners in these discussions were in line with the sex role expectations noted. His results are shown graphically in Figure 7.5. The essential conclusion here is that a cultural pattern emphasizing certain role demands for dominance determines the direction of interaction.

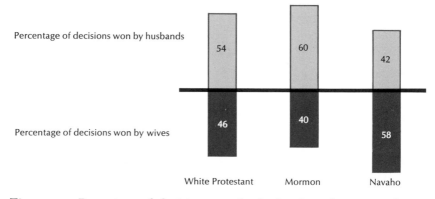

Figure 7.5: Percentage of decisions won by husbands and wives, with ten couples from each of three sub-cultural groupings. (Based on data from Strodtbeck, 1951.)

Across all couples, Strodtbeck found, too, that the most talkative member of the pair was significantly more likely to be the one whose opinions were decisive. Interestingly, such persons were also found to be willing at times to reciprocate by showing agreement with their partners. This kind of "trading" phenomenon is associated with certain features of social exchange which we will consider shortly. An additional point is that this study illustrates interaction as a communication process. The more dominant person strives to influence the other person to alter his or her attitudes. As a general rule, persons are more likely in the first place to enter into interactions with those who already share some relevant attitudes with them. But they also develop attitudes which are in line with those of another person or group they find attractive.

Communication from others, in any case, is more likely to be rewarding, and this appears to be a rather stable attribute of interaction, as Newcomb (1956) points out. It provides information about one's self and conveys "social reality." The trend toward consensus through social interaction, in terms of the development of common attitudes, produces a situation in which those with common attitudes interact more, and those who interact develop common attitudes. An example of this phenomenon is contained in the story told immediately after the upset victory of President Truman over Governor Dewey in 1948. A lady expressed surprise at the outcome saying that she couldn't understand how it could happen because *everyone she knew* had voted for Dewey.

Interpersonal attraction

A basic aspect of social interaction is the attraction-repulsion dimension of liking versus disliking. Clearly, whether or not we like someone affects the initiation as well as the continuance of social interaction. Social psychology has traditionally viewed attraction mainly as an interplay of individual dispositions which can be affected by situational factors, such as social structure and physical proximity.

Znaniecki (1965) has dealt with the particulars of attraction concretely. He says, concerning courtship, that men are supposed to initiate social interaction with women:

> Consequently, it is at first more important for a woman than for a man to appear beautiful, sexually attractive, in order to induce men to court her. But, inasmuch as she also has a choice, her response to a man's initiative will depend upon her aesthetic valuation of him. . . . After preliminary social interaction has started, other standards of personal evaluation are introduced. . . . Positive response of one to the other's attempt to initiate symbolic communication; manifestations of recognition by one of the other's self as valuable; and agreement with one's verbally expressed attitudes: all contribute to raise the personal evaluation of the other (p. 163).

Moreno (1941, 1953, 1960) emphasizes the importance of interpersonal attraction and repulsion as central features of interaction. Summing up their effects, Tagiuri (1958) says:

> No characteristic of others seems so ego-involving as their positive and negative attitudes toward us. . . . Indeed, other things being equal, when the role differentiation in a group is not too great, the category of like and dislike "packages" most of the determinants of interaction. . . . It is as if like and dislike were summaries of a great number of diverse components (p. 317).

A major approach in studying attraction is sociometry, which grows out of Moreno's work. The essence of sociometry—as the name suggests —is a group measurement for revealing graphically the attraction or repulsion bonds between persons. This provides *sociograms,* exemplified by Figure 7.6, which shows a sociometric "star," "isolate," and "clique."

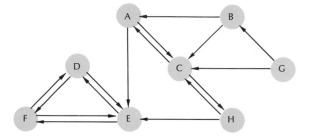

Figure 7.6: Sociogram illustrating patterns of attraction in a group of eight persons where each chooses two whom he most likes. Person *C* is a sociometric "star" chosen by four persons. Person *G* is an "isolate" who is unchosen by the others. Reciprocated choices occur where arrows are parallel in opposite directions. Persons *D, E,* and *F* are a clique who all reciprocate each other's choices.

The precise character and source of feelings of attraction are not revealed by this descriptive device alone, however. Therefore it is useful to ask additional questions in this regard. One noteworthy extension of sociometry is in so-called "relational analysis" (Tagiuri, 1952) which also takes account of a person's perception of who will choose him. Furthermore, dimensions other than liking *per se* have been extensively studied, too, by sociometric devices, as we will have occasion to consider further especially in connection with leadership.

Newcomb (1956, 1961) has delineated the bases for interpersonal attraction in terms of four criteria. Each of these is a kind of hurdle which must be surmounted in developing a friendship with another. These criteria can be broadly paraphrased as: *propinquity,* in terms of physical closeness; *similarity of individual characteristics,* including group memberships and other social identities such as educational background or social class; *common attitudes and values,* especially about matters of mutual relevance; and *personality and need compatibility.*

PROPINQUITY AND ATTRACTION

A factor which is routinely found to produce a greater prospect for attraction is propinquity. This refers to the physical closeness or contact between individuals. Its function, quite obviously, is to make possible the operation of other factors which can increase attraction. A repeated finding concerning mate selection, for example, is that individuals find mates who live close by. One of the indirect justifications for going off to college, in another locale, is to increase the range of contact with possible mates.

Homans (1950) has formulated the general proposition that, all other things being equal, the degree of liking between persons increases as a function of their interaction. However, in a later statement of his position (1961), he points out that these "other things" may be crucial. He sums up the case in these terms:

> If two men interact and at least one of them finds the activity of the other not rewarding or even positively punishing, he will sooner or later, if he is free to do so . . . decrease interaction with the other man. . . . What makes the difference is whether or not a man is free to break off interaction with another whose behavior he finds punishing. If he is not free, our proposition about the relation between interaction and liking no longer holds good. . . . When the costs of avoiding interaction are great enough, a man will go on interacting with another even though he finds the other's activity punishing. Thus the members of some families and the neighbors in some villages keep on interacting, though they fight like leopards whenever they meet (pp. 186-187).

In an extensive study of attraction, Newcomb (1961) invited 34 students transferring to the University of Michigan—17 in each of two years—to live together in a house near campus. None of the 17 men in each of the groups had known one another before. All had agreed to take part in a program of research. Over the course of a semester of living together, each of these two separate groups filled out attitude scales and value measures and also estimated the attitudes of the others in the house. The intent of the research was to determine the bases for attraction. Initial attraction was found to be highly related to propinquity, in terms of the proximity of the room assignments of these students. Later attraction grew out of greater similarity in perceived attitudes. Generally, the students increased their accuracy in perceiving the others' attitudes, but regardless of attraction.

All in all, says Newcomb, propinquity is still the most convincing primary influence on positive attraction (1956). He goes on as follows:

> Everyday illustrations readily leap to mind. Adults generally have strongest attraction toward those children, and children toward those adults, with whom they are in most immediate contact—which is to say, their own children and their own parents. And this commonly occurs, let me remind you, in spite of the fact that neither parents nor children choose each other. Or, if we are willing to accept the fact that selection of marriage partners is an index of positive attraction, then the available data are strongly in support of a theory of propinquity (p. 575).

But after propinquity other variables come into play. In his extensive writings (e.g. 1950, 1953, 1956, 1959, 1961) Newcomb has stressed the importance of *attitudinal* similarity as a determinant of interpersonal attraction. It is not merely the *actual* similarity of attitude that he considers to determine attraction, but the *perception of similarity*. There are, however, a number of complexities associated with this concept, as we shall see.

SIMILARITY AND COMPLEMENTARITY

An issue which has commanded great attention in research on attraction can be summed up in the two aphorisms: "Birds of a feather flock together" and "Opposites attract." In more technical terms, the first of these is referred to as the *similarity* hypothesis and the second as the *complementarity* hypothesis.

Though these appear to be antithetical notions, the current view is that they need not be (Levinger, 1964). As Wright (1965) has recently noted, the similarity hypothesis has greater support, but there are circumstances where complementarity of need is relevant to attraction. In matters of friendship it is usually found that those attracted to one another do tend to have similar patterns of attitudes, values, and interests (Lindzey and Borgatta, 1954). Other work has sustained the general conclusion that mutual attraction is enhanced by a similar universe of discourse which facilitates social communication. Jones and Daugherty

(1959) conducted an experiment designed to investigate how persons would perceive others in interaction as a function of their respective standing on the political and aesthetic values of the Allport-Vernon-Lindzey scale. They found that whether the similarity or complementarity hypotheses held depended on the particular value being considered as well as the particular context of interaction. In short, similarity of values may be of varying importance depending upon the kind of interaction, its locus, and its function.

The view of interaction that says people will be attracted to those who have personalities complementary to their own, has been detailed by Winch, Ktsanas, and Ktsanas (1954) in their theory of mate selection. Two studies to test the theory (Winch, 1955; Winch, Ktsanas, and Ktsanas, 1955) yielded results indicating that people with dominant needs tend to be married to people with submissive needs. In the latter study especially, they report that:

> . . . an important dimension of marital choice in the group sampled (25 university-trained married couples) is the assertive-receptive dimension. More specifically, high "assertives" tend not to marry persons who are like themselves in this respect but rather persons who are high "receptives" (p. 513).

Altrocchi (1959) has explained this by the contention that "marital partners may have developed complementary need patterns as a *result* of their process of establishing a reciprocal role relationship" (p. 306). In a study by Bowerman and Day (1956) no support was found for either the similarity or complementarity hypotheses with couples who were dating.

In evaluating the work done in this area, it seems clear that similarity is important for some kinds of relationships and complementarity for others. In most studies where similarity is found to hold as a factor yielding a mutual bond, attitudes and values are those elements which are being measured. Complementarity, on the other hand, may be more relevant to need satisfaction in an enduring interaction. As Jones and Daugherty (1959) note, however, it is necessary to analyze the most likely behavioral consequences of a particular personal attribute in different interaction settings (p. 34). For example, the need to dominate is important where social control and influence are encouraged. In such a setting, ascendant people may respond more positively to submissive people, while elsewhere the "dominator" may seek association with other dominators. Thus, the subordinate with dominance tendencies who works for a dominant superior, may comment that he dislikes working for the latter because they "are too much alike." Furthermore, Rosow (1957) says that being different on an attribute like "compulsivity" may not be a harmonious arrangement either. It seems clear, then, that depending upon the context of interaction, complementarity can be a source of either friction or harmony. Further work is required to specify what particulars of similarity or complementarity are crucial to attraction.

Interpersonal perception

In our consideration of the attractiveness of individuals to one another, an inevitable feature of concern is the perception of a person. The term "interpersonal perception" is preferred, however, when we mean the way individuals view and evaluate one another in direct interaction, and we shall use it here in that sense. As Tagiuri (1958) points out, this is a process of considerable complexity which encompasses the interrelationship of the perceiver, the person perceived, and the situation which serves as a backdrop for this perception.

Many of the principles of perception which we considered before, in Chapter Four, have applicability to interpersonal perception. Tendencies toward *perceptual constancy, wholeness, imbeddedness, closure,* and especially *causality* all play a part in this process. There are, however, two major ways in which person perception differs from object perception. First, unlike objects persons are perceived to have motives which determine their actions. Second, the person perceived is himself capable of perceiving and may accordingly react to his own perception of the perceiver.

The most noteworthy contribution to the area of interpersonal perception has grown out of the work of Heider (1944, 1946, 1958). He contends mainly that the perception of attributes of other (O) controls the way the person (P) behaves toward him as well as what he expects from him. For Heider, interpersonal perception is vitally affected by several kinds of perceptual factors, including *constancy, balance,* and *phenomenal causality*. All affect the flow of interaction.

CONSTANCY

A central function in interpersonal perception is to give constancy to P's view of O. A certain psychological economy results from constancy in that an individual is not obliged to alter his view of O each and every instant. Typically, he retains a relatively cohering, consistent view of O, but this can lead of course to a biasing effect in perceiving O's behavior. Past interaction or prior knowledge of another sort weighs heavily since primacy of experience is important. New experience may not be so quickly absorbed in altering perceptions (Ichheiser, 1949).

Other factors are associated with constancy. As in all perception, interpersonal perception involves an act of categorization. Thus, others are seen in terms of consistent attributes including affiliations and positions which may be assumed to determine their action. Quite commonly, the situational determinants of action are given little weight and P will persist in perceiving O as the master of his own actions. At the extreme, this is exemplified in the case of the "self-made man," whose success is largely seen to reside in his own initiative, aggressiveness or other attributes, without reference to the sustenance along the way from others, as well as fortuitous circumstances.

BALANCE AND IMBALANCE

Also prominent in the Heider approach to interpersonal perception is the notion of cognitive balance. What this means in terms of social influence process may be simply stated. To the extent that O is seen by P as identified with things valued by P, and having other attributes P perceives favorably, P is more likely to accept communications from O directed at changes in his behavior or attitudes. Heider (1946, 1958) has provided a convenient summary of such interrelationships in terms of concepts involving positive and negative valence which he treats in terms of *balance* and *imbalance*, as discussed in the last chapter (see p. 155).

If person P likes another person O and desires a certain object X, a balanced state results if he strives to be with the other person and to achieve the object; it is also part of balance to assume that the other person likes him too, and so forth. Imbalance would result, if for example P were to discover that O, whom he admires, does *not* like X the way he does, or that O does not like him. Heider's statements are essentially qualitative insofar as they deal with valences of either a plus or minus sort. They lead to some rather simple predictions concerning balanced and imbalanced states, as will be seen in Figure 7.7. Where all

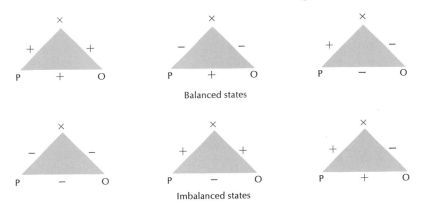

Figure 7.7: Diagrams indicating three balanced states and three imbalanced states. P is the Person; O is the Other; X is a factor they can each perceive. (After Heider, 1958.)

the signs are positive in these diagrams, a state of balance exists. If there is one negative sign or three negative signs, then there is an imbalanced state. This follows from the mathematical rule that multiplication of two minuses yields a plus.

The Heider balance approach has led to similar analyses extending these ideas by Newcomb, Osgood and Tannenbaum, and Festinger, among others. These are treated in specific detail elsewhere. An essential point here concerns the fact that social interaction can be viewed as having a basic underpinning in what can be called an evaluative or affective dimension based on positive or negative valence, both in perceiving O as well as in the common objects or persons that P and O mutually perceive.

There have been a number of attempts to study the balance concept in terms of interpersonal evaluation behavior. Deutsch and Solomon (1959), for example, conducted an experiment in a two-person situation where the object X was an attribute of P's. They hypothesized that if P and O shared the *same* evaluation of X then P would be more positive toward O than if their evaluations were different. This experiment generally supported the balance concept, though other motivational factors were found to be involved also.

Since in the Deutsch and Solomon experiment, P's evaluations of O were transmitted to the experimenter with no process of reciprocal interaction over time, Jones (1966) conducted a comparable experiment where subjects actually exchanged evaluations of one another's performance in an ongoing process. In this circumstance, he found a tendency for subjects to respond more in terms of reciprocity by exchanging social approval as a reward. Thus, a positive evaluation by O of what P perceived as his own poor performance yielded a more positive response to O by P than did a negative evaluation. Where there is continuing interaction, therefore, an exchange concept appears to fit interpersonal evaluation behavior better than a simple balance concept.

PHENOMENAL CAUSALITY

As we have already suggested, the causality of action is usually perceived to rest in O rather than in the situation in which he finds himself. However, various kinds of discriminations are made in terms of other perceived attributes of O, such as his status, as well as certain of his other characteristics.

In extending Heider's views, for example, Pepitone (1958) says that for analytic purposes, "It is useful to assume that interpersonal relations consist of valued acts, valued positively or negatively depending on whether they are tension reducing or inducing, and the context of such acts. Of particular significance in the latter category are the causal conditions which surround given acts" (p. 259). He then distinguishes these three dimensions of causality:

> *Responsibility* for the social act, in the sense of the causal agent (O).
> *Intentionality* of the agent, in regard to what he (O) seeks to achieve in motivational terms.
> *Justifiability* of the action, in the sense of what P thinks of O's action.

Thus, of the various features of person perception one that seems to be of extreme importance is the perceived cause for action. In general, it is found that persons of higher status are seen to be more the locus of cause for their own action than those of lower status. Furthermore, a benevolent action that appears to be motivated by an individual's desire rather than a social demand is usually viewed more positively. Similarly, if O is in a role obliging him to perform a disliked action toward P, then O is usually excused if, as in the case of a role, the external cause of his behavior is apparent.

Some research of interest on this point grows out of the work of de-Charms, Carpenter, and Kuperman (1965) on the "origin-pawn" variable in person perception. They had subjects read stories in which a person was being persuaded to do something. That person was seen to be more an *origin* of action when the persuasive agent was attractive than when the agent was unattractive. The epitomy of origin is a person perceived to be motivated by his own intrinsic interests.

ACCURACY OF INTERPERSONAL PERCEPTION

It is widely found that individuals assume a similarity between their own perception and the perception of others, particularly where the others are positively valued. This is related as well to the broader question of accuracy of social perception.

Steiner (1955) has found conflicting evidence regarding the relationship between accuracy of perception and the nature of interaction. In specific terms, he concludes that accuracy in perceiving the other person will have consequences in social interaction only to the degree that such accuracy is relevant. The fundamental point, however, continues to be that persons behave largely in terms of how they perceive the attributes of others. For the most part accuracy of such perception can be facilitating, though in conflict situations, for example, it may have the opposite effect. There are, however, additional methodological as well as conceptual difficulties associated with any discussion of the matter of accuracy of person perception (Cline, 1964).

Bronfenbrenner, Harding, and Gallwey (1958) have found, for example, that it is necessary to distinguish between two kinds of person perception which are not highly correlated one with the other. The first of these can be thought of as "interpersonal sensitivity" which has special regard to the ability to perceive a given individual uniquely in terms of a specific situation of interaction. This can be thought of as having features of empathy or understanding. The second kind of process they note is a "sensitivity to the generalized other" which broadly means accuracy in perceiving major trends in the social environment, including such things as the kind of music which people are more likely to prefer, food preferences, and the like.

Social psychologists must of necessity be concerned with both kinds of processes. The perception of persons, whether it comes about from the direct experience of the individual, or through the channels of communication from other individuals, has considerable relevance for understanding social interaction. But there does not yet appear to be any consistency of evidence regarding a general characteristic of "interpersonal sensitivity," in the specific sense of repeated accuracy of interpersonal perception (Shrauger and Altrocchi, 1964).

On the other hand, a fruitful line of work has emerged from research on the relationship between attributes of the perceiver and his perceptions of others' attributes. Dornbusch, Hastorf, Richardson, Muzzy, and Vreeland (1965), for example, have found that children who are more dependent tend to describe other children in terms of generosity, giving aid, or needing aid. Girls who are more aggressive describe other girls with more emphasis on aggressive behavior than do non-aggressive girls. With boys who are non-aggressive, however, they found more attribution of aggression to others than with aggressive boys. In either case, they conclude that where their respondents gave more accounts of behavior relevant to some dimension of personality, that indicated a probable adjustment problem for the child in that dimension. Sex differences in interpersonal perception are also quite commonly found in studies of accuracy (Shrauger and Altrocchi, 1964), though these are not indicative of a systematic superiority of either sex.

CREATING EFFECTS IN INTERPERSONAL PERCEPTION

Just as the perception of O by P affects the interaction between them, so it is possible for O to deliberately arrange his behavior in such a way as to affect P's perception and actions toward him. We have already touched upon this in connection with Jones's (1964) concept of "ingratiation," which involves performing acts likely to put one in a more favorable light in relationship to another person, particularly one of more power.

A wide-ranging approach to the creation of such effects is to be found in the work of Goffman (1959), who is concerned with "impression management." Goffman employs dramaturgical concepts in treating this phenomenon. Thus, persons may be thought of as being "out front" or "back stage" in their relationship with one another. A couple entertaining their guests for dinner, says Goffman, present an enactment designed to coincide with certain of the prevailing expectancies regarding host and hostess. In the kitchen together they may behave otherwise. Sometimes, he says, the individual acts in a calculating manner, to "stage" things in a way designed to produce certain specific responses from the others. At other times, however, the individual may employ such techniques without awareness.

Since P may recognize that he is being confronted with a performance designed to make an impression on him, he may carefully assess the communications from O, in terms of verbal assertions and behaviors; moreover, P may check these two channels for consistency, as when O says the dinner is marvelous but eats very little. This is in keeping with the general idea that people compare what an individual says with how he acts. In other terms, we might say that there are two major inputs to interpersonal perception, the behavioral and the verbal.

Embedded in social interaction, therefore, is the prospect for persons to structure relationships toward the end of bringing about positive outcomes. In this respect, social interaction involves what Weinstein and Deutschberger (1964) call an *interpersonal task*. They say that P attempts to organize the various factors in his interaction with O so that O is forced into a position that fits P's preferences. They refer to this process as *alter-casting*, which comes from "casting" the other individual (*alter*) in a role.

While Goffman is concerned with the way that the identity of the participants leads to a playing out of their interaction, Weinstein and Deutschberger contend that this encounter is a bargaining process in which tactics are employed to place the other individual in a position which will be more personally advantageous. The task, then, is more than one of self-presentation, it is rather the management of the interaction aimed at influencing O's definition of the situation to P's advantage. The quest for certain rewards in interaction is a matter to which we will be turning in due course.

PERCEPTIONS OF EQUITY AND JUSTICE

In many social interactions there is the possibility that one or more of the participants will perceive an inequity or injustice in the distribution of rewards. An early recognition of the potency of this factor came out of research done during World War II by Stouffer and his colleagues (1949) regarding the concept of "relative deprivation." This concept refers to the way actuality may be matched against expectation to induce an attitude of satisfaction or dissatisfaction in individuals. In the Stouffer study, the paradoxical finding was that army air corps men were less satisfied with promotion opportunities than were those in the military police. This was despite the objective reality that opportunities for promotion were vastly greater in the air corps where, at the time, 47 per cent of all enlisted men were non-commissioned officers, while the rate in the military police was 24 per cent.

The relative deprivation concept explains this by suggesting that the men compared themselves with those "in the same boat." Thus, the high promotion prospects in the air corps induced high expectations, while in the military police far lower expectations for promotion prevailed. As will be seen in Figure 7.8, comparing lower ranking men from both

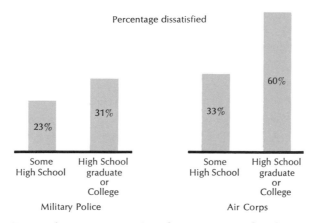

Percentage dissatisfied

23%	31%	33%	60%
Some High School	High School graduate or College	Some High School	High School graduate or College
Military Police		Air Corps	

Figure 7.8: Dissatisfaction expressed with promotion policy by privates and privates first class, with two levels of educational background, in the Military Police and Air Corps. (Based on data from Stouffer, *et al.*, 1949.)

groups, greater dissatisfaction is found among the air corps men than the military policemen, and among the better educated than the less educated. In both instances a greater discrepancy exists between expectation and actual achievement.

This finding has since been generalized as a basic comparison process related to the reference group as a standard. In an experiment involving the manipulation of relative deprivation, Spector (1956) varied the perceived probability of promotion and found that among those subjects *not* promoted, those who held high expectations for promotion were far more dissatisfied with the "system" than those with low expectations.

In general, an injustice can be thought of, therefore, as the reaction to an imbalance or disparity between what an individual perceives to be the actuality and what he believes should be the case, especially insofar as his own situation is concerned. This is the fundamental point in Homans's (1961) concept of "distributive justice," which refers to a condition where an individual's investments are balanced by his rewards. As we shall note as a generalization in connection with social exchange, a "profit" can refer to "rewards" minus "costs" incurred. A cost, briefly, can be anything that is given up or forgone in the process of interaction. Among these costs may be the investments of the individual, which would include his standing, his background of education, experience, and the like. The idea that this is merely a matter of economic gain is therefore not appropriate because of the diversity of values represented in "investments" and "rewards."

While individuals may therefore compare their rewards with another and perceive them to be smaller, they may not feel dissatisfied since there is a proportionality between the rewards received by each as against the investments of each. Thus, Patchen (1961) has found that the satisfaction with their wages of workers in an oil refinery was primarily based on the total equity they perceived in wage comparisons, rather than on the actual pay differences alone. Workers were satisfied with their wages if they felt that they were making sufficiently more money than other workers with whom they compared themselves in terms of job responsibility and seniority.

In any concept of justice versus injustice, or equity versus inequity, it must be realized, of course, that O's perception of his own investments, costs, and rewards do not always coincide with P's perceptions of them. With two persons in any interaction, therefore, it is not the actuality, nor is it the other person's perception that matters most. It is the individual's own perception of his situation which continues to have overriding significance in determining his response pattern. Accordingly, inequities may be perceived by individuals despite the fact that there is no inequity seen in the "social reality" of others.

Social exchange

As we have seen, in face-to-face interaction one person shows specific behavior in the presence of another. This in turn leads to reciprocal behavior. Each therefore can create products for the other, in the form of rewards which are reinforcing. The value of the reward will, however, depend upon the unique requirements of the participants. These rewards are also balanced by the costs of the interaction in terms of the values given in return or forgone. The general character of this process is referred to as "social exchange."

Though they are stated in terms of economic transactions, social exchange concepts embody a considerable range of different motivations and comparisons, beyond the simple notion of profit in a straight hedonistic sense. Thus, satisfactions in interaction may lie in various directions, including the challenges to one's competence in handling the environment.

Two major contributions to an understanding of social exchange come from the work of Homans (1958, 1961) and Thibaut and Kelley (1959). Both involve certain concepts associated with a rewards-costs relationship. Homans sees social exchange as the underlying factor accounting for certain features of face-to-face interaction. He contends that the rules governing social interaction apply in various settings and can be understood primarily in terms of reinforcement. Homans says that persons give off *activity*, which is essentially behavior, as well as *sentiments*, which can be thought of as indicators of attitude and feelings. The operative feature of these is that they either *reinforce* or *punish* the behavior of others in interaction.

An illustration of exchange grows out of a study by Calvin (1962). He was primarily interested in the effects of social reinforcement among college girls. He had some girls show systematic approval of others who happened to be wearing blue. Over time such approval yielded a significant increase in the wearing of blue. Of particular importance here, as a derivative result, he found that the girls who gave the approval experienced an upsurge in their own popularity. Much as Homans would predict, this demonstrated an exchange relationship in terms of giving appreciation and being liked in return.

Homans proposes that both the *quantity* and *value* of the activity or sentiment can affect the behavior of another individual. His propositions concerning the effects of activity are essentially these:

> (1) If in the past the occurrence of a particular stimulus situation has been the occasion on which a man's activity has been rewarded, then the more similar the present stimulus situation is to the past one, the more likely he is to emit the activity, or some similar activity now. . . .
>
> (2) The more often within a given period of time a man's activity rewards the activity of another, the more often the other will emit the activity. . . .
>
> (3) The more valuable to a man a unit of activity another gives him, the more often he will emit activity rewarded by the activity of the other. . . .
>
> (4) The more often a man has in the recent past received a rewarding activity from another, the less valuable any further unit of that activity becomes to him (1961, pp. 53-55).

As noted previously, Homans defines profit as total reward minus total cost. In ongoing interaction, both parties are mindful of their respective profits. If these exchange activities yield no profit, the interaction is unlikely to continue. The important consideration of the cost of any activity is defined by Homans in terms of the value of the reward that would be obtainable through alternative activity which has to be given up.

For Thibaut and Kelley, similarly, interaction should be rewarding for the parties to continue. They recognize, also, the necessity for a trading-off in terms of rewards and costs for both parties. Specifically *rewards* are defined by Thibaut and Kelley as ". . . the pleasures, satisfactions, and gratifications the person enjoys. The provision of a means whereby a drive is reduced or a need fulfilled constitutes a reward. We assume that the amount of reward provided by any such experience can be measured and that the reward values of different modalities of gratification are reducible to a single psychological scale" (1959, p. 12). Alternatively, they define *costs* as ". . . any factors that operate to inhibit or deter the performance of a sequence of behavior. The greater the deterrence to performing a given act—the greater the inhibition the individual has to overcome—the greater the cost of the act. Thus cost is high when great physical or mental effort is required, when embarrassment or anxiety accompany the action, or when there are conflicting forces or competing response tendencies of any sort" (1959, pp. 12-13).

As with the Homans idea of cost as value forgone, Thibaut and Kelley employ the concept of *comparison level.* This is a standard against which the person evaluates the attractiveness of the relationship in terms of whether he receives what he thinks he deserves relative to his costs. Associated with this concept is the *comparison level for alternatives,* which represents the reference point employed in deciding whether or not to remain in the interaction. In one sense, it can be looked at as the lowest level of reward which the individual will accept in order to continue in the relationship. In another sense, it relates to Helson's (1948) adaptation level concept of what one has come to expect.

There are some intriguing features about the association of comparison level and the comparison level for alternatives. In general, a person will be highly satisfied with his outcomes if his comparison level and the comparison level for alternatives are both exceeded by actual outcomes, and the converse holds as well.

While there are similarities between the two exchange concepts we have been considering, there are also some differences. Thibaut and Kelley, for example, are more concerned with the idea of a norm and its development. Homans tends to accept the fact that norms of conduct exist. In this respect, Gouldner's (1960) discussion of a "norm of reciprocity" is closer to the matrix notion of Thibaut and Kelley. Essentially, reciprocity represents a widespread social norm which dictates that good acts are reciprocally rewarded, as in the return of a favor, for instance.

Exchange concepts in general fit a framework which is distinctively social-psychological in that they are concerned with motivations and in varying degrees with perceptions. Blau (1964) has extended some of these ideas to tie in with Goffman's work on "impression management," and pointed up the implicit problem of social acceptance.

In Blau's view it is not enough for a person to be attracted to a group or to a relationship because of the possible rewards the group has to offer him. He must achieve acceptance and integration into the group. This in turn rests on his impressing others that he would be an asset in the group or relationship by providing rewards for them as well. This demand in new relationships is inescapable. In any such circumstance, the prospective member is therefore under pressure to exhibit qualities the other members will perceive as valuable and to minimize those aspects of himself that might prove unattractive, which is to say unrewarding.

Social exchange is thus a ubiquitous feature of social interaction, whether we wish it to be or not. It should be emphasized, however, that the rewards received are *not* to be understood as being *precisely* equal since their value is determined by the needs of the recipient. This realization goes a long way in helping to understand what might otherwise appear to be an "unfair" exchange in a continuing social interaction.

SUMMARY

Social interaction holds a central place in social psychology as an influence process. It refers, in particular, to the *reciprocal relationship* that exists between two or more individuals whose behavior is *mutually dependent*. Most of the behavior we observe is in some way affected by present or past social interactions.

Face-to-face interaction is built upon social expectancies which reside in the psychological field and have to do in large part with past experiences. Expectancies direct individuals to be set for and to evaluate certain outcomes of interdependent behavior.

The essential need for social interaction arises from several functions it fulfills: inculcation in the ways of the society, the development of personality, and the reduction of the effects of stress.

The *structure of interaction* refers to the nature of the interdependent relationship, such as co-operation or competition, dominance and conflict. Mainly, structure can be approached in two ways. In the first place, it can be viewed on a *formal* level, which has to do with regularities dictated by the society and its culture. This approach is best exemplified in the concept of *roles*, usually defined as behaviors expected of individuals in terms of the positions or *status* they occupy in a given situation. The essential quality of this emphasis is to describe the pattern of regularized social practices. Many features of social interaction are governed by such formal social demands. These are usually learned through "reciprocal role relationships," such as child with parent.

Another way of viewing social interaction is in terms of an *informal* structure. It can be looked at as an ongoing stimulus-response sequence of behavior which is sustained by various definable rewards to the parties involved. The primary interest here rests in *individual dispositions and satisfactions* in the interaction, including attraction and interpersonal perception.

In looking at the underlying process of social interaction, a basic dimension is valence, that is, liking versus disliking. This has special relevance to *interpersonal attraction* which grows out of propinquity, similarity of individual characteristics including attitudes, and personality and need compatibility. Interpersonal attraction has been found to depend a great deal upon the perception of similarity of attitudes by the persons involved. Usually, social interaction itself enhances personal attraction through a process of social communication. In general, such communication is likely to give rise to favorable rather than to unfavorable outcomes.

Interpersonal attraction depends upon a process of *interpersonal perception* which refers to the evaluations of persons through direct interaction. Principles of perception have applications to interpersonal perception, but the perception of persons differs from object perception in two major ways. First, persons are perceived to have motives determining their actions; second, the person perceived is himself a perceiver who may react to his perception of the perceiver. Heider stresses *constancy, balance,* and *phenomenal causality* in interpersonal perception. Accuracy of person perception is a factor which can also greatly affect social interaction depending upon its relevance. Such accuracy is shaped by the nature of the situation in which interaction occurs and does not appear to be a consistent interpersonal characteristic. Persons may also try to make certain impressions on others by various strategies, including the way they define the interaction situation.

Social interaction is also a transaction involving a process of *social exchange*. In general, interaction operates in terms of reciprocity, that is, the expectation that a benefit given will be returned. The nature of interaction is such that one person shows certain behaviors in the presence of another. Each therefore can do things and say things that will be rewarding for the other. The value of the reward will, however, depend upon the unique requirements of the individual participants. These rewards are also balanced by the costs of the interaction in terms of values given in return or forgone.

SUGGESTED READINGS

From E. P. Hollander and R. G. Hunt. (Eds.) *Current perspectives in social psychology.* (2nd Edition.) New York: Oxford University Press, 1967:

Introduction to Section V: *Person perception, interaction, and role*
28. Raymond G. Hunt: *Role and role conflict*
29. Ivan D. Steiner: *Interpersonal behavior as influenced by accuracy of social perception*
30. Alvin W. Gouldner: *The norm of reciprocity: a preliminary statement*
31. Hadley Cantril: *Perception and interpersonal relations*
32. Theodore M. Newcomb: *The prediction of interpersonal attraction*
33. Fritz Heider: *Perceiving the other person*
34. Erving Goffman: *The presentation of self in everyday life*
46. George C. Homans: *Social behavior as exchange*
47. John W. Thibaut and Harold H. Kelley: *On norms*

SELECTED REFERENCES

*Goffman, E. *The presentation of self in everyday life.* Garden City, N. Y.: Doubleday-Anchor, 1959.
Heider, F. *The psychology of interpersonal relations.* New York: Wiley, 1958.
Homans, G. C. *Social behavior: its elementary forms.* New York: Harcourt Brace, 1961.
Jones, E. E. *Ingratiation.* New York: Appleton-Century-Crofts, 1964.
Moreno, J. L. (Ed.) *The sociometry reader.* Glencoe, Ill.: The Free Press, 1960.
Newcomb, T. M. *The acquaintance process.* New York: Holt, Rinehart & Winston, 1961.
Thibaut, J. W., & Kelley, H. H. *The social psychology of groups.* New York: Wiley, 1959.
*Znaniecki, F. *Social relations and social roles.* San Francisco: Chandler, 1965.

8

Culture as a source of social influence

Culture is a form of nonbiological, social heritage that flows from the past, generation by generation. Mumford (1951) has captured this dominant theme in these terms: "Every human group, every human being, lives within a cultural matrix that is both immediate and remote, visible and invisible: and one of the most important statements one can make about Man's present is how much of the past or future it contains" (p. 38).

In the preceding chapters we have referred to the all-embracing influence of culture on our actions, interactions, attitudes, and values. Now we will turn attention to its own unique features. We begin with the fundamental point that in any human society individuals are bound to culture for a coherent outlook and approach toward life. These essential aspects of culture are also the very things which most differentiate segments of humanity from one another.

In highlighting this contrast in the ways of life among different societies, Linton (1945) has said: "The first man who wandered into a strange camp and found that he could not talk to the people there nor understand everything that he saw, must have had the fact of cultural difference brought home to him. Also . . . his observations must have provided him with material for numerous fireside talks. . . . The meat of any really good traveller's tale is not the strange places that it tells about but the queer people" (p. 27).

209

The basis for culture

In simplest terms, Man depends upon his culture for the development of his human qualities. Among the most important of these are *social organization for the control of the environment* and *communication across time and space*. A culture provides people with a number of ready-made answers for crucial life problems. It dictates the routine relationships and social arrangements which help to handle survival needs, the protection and education of the young, and many other necessary social functions. A culture, then, is a means for coping with the world.

A culture also is a way of viewing things as right and proper. It provides social reality. A significant part of a culture's influence resides in its pervasive psychological effects on the perceptions, including the attitudes and values, of a society's members. Through processes of communication, individuals acquire a sense of common meaning and purpose without which they would be lost. In this chapter we will have considerably more to say about this form of cultural influence in particular.

Since culture is a human product, it is subject to the evolving effects of change. In contrast to lower forms, Man's behavior is not guided mainly by instincts but can be transformed through learning processes. Thus, even within the confines of tradition, there is considerable room for individual and social adaptation.

Differences in culture originate in the geographic and historic factors unique to a society. The kind of climate and weather it experiences, its natural resources, its relationship with neighboring societies—including, for example, threat along a frontier—account for many cultural differences. These, however, are overlaid with adaptations and change that come about from circumstances including the contact between cultures. The Norman Conquest, as a case in point, brought a set of cultural patterns and the French language to England, and its influence is very much alive in the current English language. Throughout the modern world, the impact of the mass media, especially motion pictures with their vivid quality of real presence, has markedly enhanced cultural movement toward "Westernization," even in its ephemeral forms. A decade ago, during a year in Istanbul, the writer found Elvis Presley a great favorite; and a friend that year reported a high preference for cowboy garb among the teenagers seen on the street of Addis Ababa. Nevertheless, as Hall (1959, p. 33) says, "culture is more than mere custom that can be shed or changed like a suit of clothes"; these external matters of form should not be confused with content, as we shall make plain shortly.

The nature of culture

The term "culture" holds various definitions. As employed in the anthropological sense, it has a broad meaning that includes but does not refer only to those particular enrichments of life identified with literature, music, and art, as in a Molière play, a Mozart symphony, or a Mondrian painting. Rather, it encompasses a society's shared practices and products which are sustained by tradition. These could be endlessly catalogued but can be briefly exemplified by monogamy, money, manufacturing and the distinctive tools it requires.

The relationship between culture and society has also been commented upon in a variety of ways. There are several fine points that are still matters of contention. However, we can paraphrase Kroeber and Parsons (1958) and say that *culture* constitutes those meaningful symbolic systems which are transmitted over time and shape social behavior and its artifacts; *society* can be considered to be comprised of individuals who share these systems and accordingly live within a set of specific interpersonal and collective relationships. A culture, therefore, is a way of life while a society is made up of people who live by its directives. When we speak of a "member of a culture," then, we actually mean a "member of the society of culture X" (p. 583).

The anthropologist E. B. Tylor is credited with providing the first formal definition of culture almost a century ago: "that complex whole which includes knowledge, belief, art, law, morals, custom, and any other capabilities and habits acquired by man as a member of society" (1877, p. 1). This definition provides a kind of "sum total" of the different content categories which go to make up culture. As such it suffers from the weakness of omitting the important element of *integration,* in terms of the meshing of the components of culture as they exist in a so-

ciety's social institutions, status systems, and the like. This is one feature of "functionalism" which has a significant place in sociology and
will occupy our attention shortly. While Tylor's definition represented a
landmark, it therefore tended to be highly descriptive and quite open-
ended in its content.

A more contemporary view of culture is represented by Ralph Linton's definition which does place stress on integration. He defines a culture as ". . . the configuration of learned behavior and results of behavior whose component elements are shared and transmitted by the
members of a particular society" (1945, p. 32). This emphasis on transmission gives due attention to the communicative aspect of culture over
time. In this vein, culture can be viewed as a passing on of the ancestral
adjustments that have been made to the environment. Thus, culture in
effect represents the accretion of experience in contending with prevailing life conditions (e.g. Sumner and Keller, 1927). Others have seen
Man as a more active agent who creates symbols, defines experience,
and transmits meanings through culture, particularly via language (e.g.
Goldschmidt, 1959). A definition of culture as ". . . everything that is
produced by, and is capable of sustaining, shared symbolic experience"
has recently been offered by Jaeger and Selznick (1964, p. 663).

TRADITION, SYMBOLIZATION, AND INTEGRATION

These ways of conceiving culture recurringly emphasize the interrelated features of tradition, symbolization, and integration. By *tradition*
we mean especially the continuity of culture in providing directives for
routinely coping with major imperatives of life, such as birth, death,
kinship, and the passing on of worldly goods. Any culture therefore dictates a society's organization and social relationships largely along lines
which persist without awareness. This is humorously illustrated in a
dispatch from London dated September 9, 1959, which is reproduced in
full in Figure 8.1. It shows the "unwritten law" quality of tradition.

Symbolization is a vital, defining characteristic of humanity. It refers
to the importance of non-material experience, as well as to the transmission of thoughts and information without the direct presence of objects
themselves. Language is the clearest expression of symbolization, and
we shall deal with it in fuller detail in the next chapter. Because of
Man's symbolic quality, a significant part of a culture's influence rests

in its psychological effects. When we speak of symbols, therefore, we include the essential substance of attitudes and values, as well as the other components of the psychological field.

Britons Aren't Sure Why, but They Always Vote on Thursday

The New York Herald Tribune-Post-Dispatch Special Dispatch.

LONDON, Sept. 9 — A minor mystery has appeared in Britain, plaguing a few Londoners. Why is the general election, just set for Oct. 8, going to be on a Thursday?

There is no law that says it must be. Still, Oct. 8 is a Thursday, all the dates mentioned in speculation have been Thursdays and all the elections of recent years have come on a Thursday.

In an attempt to determine why a call was made to conservative headquarters, camp of the incumbents.

"There's no real reason why it should be on a Thursday, I suppose," a pleasant y o u n g lady said. "It's just by tradition that it is. Who started the tradition? Nobody here can remember when

it wasn't on a Thursday. Thursdays are election days, that's all."

At Labor party headquarters the question brought an incredulous chuckle, a moment of silence and this answer: "Well, we always have elections on Thursdays. If you really want to know, why don't you get in touch with the Home Office?"

The Home Office is in charge of elections. A spokesman, asked the question, said, "Really? It's always on Thursday? That's interesting."

As a final resort, the Encyclopedia Brittanica was consulted. It says, "Most European countries have adopted a Sunday or holiday as election day, but in Great Britain, a characteristic muddleheadeness has so far prevented its adoption."

Figure 8.1: An example of tradition as the "unwritten law." (From the *St. Louis Post-Dispatch*, September 9, 1959, p. 1.)

Integration of a culture can neither be divorced from tradition nor from symbolization since it relies on both. All human societies can be found to have social institutions—e.g. the family, government, education, and an economy—which are interdependent. Changing one has effects upon the others. This is the heart of cultural integration. Hall (1959) has captured an essential preservative feature of integration in this example:

> An American these days will not normally consider the revenge of the brothers as a price for seeing a woman without her family's permission. . . . Death of the woman and revenge on the man are within the expected range of behavior in the less Europeanized

> parts of the Arab world. . . . What we often don't know and have difficulty accepting is that such patterns fit into larger over-all patterns and that what is being guarded is not the sister's life . . . but a centrally located institution without which the society would perish or be radically altered. This institution is the family (p. 112).

Related to integration is the concept of *functionalism* which is its close counterpart. Functionalism is ordinarily traced to Durkheim and his followers in sociology. In anthropology, Malinowski is credited with having been an early proponent of this position, beginning more than forty years ago, insofar as he stressed the interdependence of the various elements of a culture.

Broadly speaking, the functionalist position asserts that every aspect of a culture, including especially the manifest actions of members of society, fulfills a function. As Kluckhohn (1949b) and Merton (1957) have suggested, though, a distinction is needed between "manifest" and "latent" functions. An example of this distinction that Kluckhohn gives is a cowboy spending an hour to catch a horse to ride only a short distance. It takes him more time to catch the animal than it does to make the trip. As Kluckhohn notes, this act—if taken literally and superficially—seems distinctly non-functional. However, he says, while it may not have a manifest function, it fulfills more than one latent function: the cowboy escapes the ridicule to which he would be exposed if another cowboy saw him walking; he also preserves his own sense of self-respect and of the fitness of things; most importantly, the basic relation between cowboy and horse is symbolized in this pattern and thus lends support to its persistence.

In the functionalist view, therefore, even apparently non-functional elements in a culture can be imputed to have latent functions. In the instance of mechanically useless items, such as buttons on sleeves of men's jackets, there exists the latent function of preserving tradition in a symbolic sense. In short, it looks and feels "right."

EXPLICIT AND IMPLICIT CULTURE

The various definitions of culture that we have been treating also suggest that culture's effects can be partitioned into two categories. The first of these may be called the *explicit* culture which deals with the behaviors and artifacts that we associate with those visible and even striking differences between cultures.

There is, however, the more profound effect on individuals which is less visible and depends upon the *implicit* culture. This effect is essentially based in the attitudes and values which govern the behavior of the members of a society, as well as in the fundamental assumptions they accept uncritically regarding life and its meaning. As we have pointed out, culture relies upon shared meanings of a symbolic nature many of which may lie below the level of conscious awareness, for example in terms of striving for goals. Thus, Kroeber and Kluckhohn (1952) say that "one group unconsciously and habitually assumes that every chain of actions has a goal and that when this goal is reached tension will be reduced or disappear. To another group, thinking based upon this assumption is by no means automatic. They see life not primarily as a series of purposive sequences but more as made up of disparate experiences which may be satisfying in and of themselves, rather than as means to ends" (p. 157).

Culture, then, can be treated with regard to the overt behaviors that people display as well as the internal experiences which constitute part of their psychological field. These are learned from other people and also shared with them. Even given the common biological qualities of Man, vast cultural differences continue to exist with respect to the way life is led and how these primary motivations are satisfied. This now leads us appropriately to a fuller consideration of the socio-psychological aspects of culture.

The significance of culture in social psychology

Cultural patterns can be considered to be a routine way of communicating certain meanings where symbols are mutually understood. Shaking hands, for example, is one of the illustrations in our own society of an action which has symbolic meaning. Objects as well convey meanings apart from their intrinsic worth, as for example the widespread use of diamond engagement rings in our society. There are, however, other symbols which are essentially discretionary in that their purpose does not have wide significance. In matters of dress, for example, cuffless trousers are not an important issue in the same way as a topless bathing suit is for women—and once was, for men. There are also apparently non-functional survivals of past practices to be seen when a man tips his hat to a lady. This is a vestige of the pattern of removing one's hat before a lady for ready identification and presumably as an assurance of no harm.

The ways of a culture include a wide range of behaviors which convey symbolic significance. This is made possible through the common features in the psychological fields of individuals. The culture, then, intrudes directly on the constructions that individuals place on their environment and in a sense intervenes by shaping expectations and behaviors. To understand a man's behavior, therefore, it is necessary to have an awareness of the symbols and their definitions that have become part of his psychological field through experience within the context of culture. That context is, in Plant's (1950) terms, an "envelope" within which we react. A significant feature of this process is that once symbols come to stand for things or social entities—a flag for a nation—it is possible for people to respond to them though the symbolized things are not immediately present. The venerable story of the Englishman dressing formally for dinner in a tropical outpost exemplifies the hold of culture in terms of its symbolic dictates.

Cultures also consist of important assumptions in the nature of beliefs about the world. Some of these have essentially a factual base, others are guided largely by evaluative components representing preferences. The belief that the earth is round is fundamental in most human cultures. But there may be vast differences in their beliefs about the nature of God, the way in which the economic practices of a society should be managed or not be managed, the kind of political or governmental structures that are needed to fulfill certain of the functions of the society, and the mode of upbringing that children should receive including education. All of these considerations go to make up the institutions of a culture, each of which is predicated on certain fundamental assumptions that persist in time. These are so taken for granted that it is all too easy, as with most things that are cultural, to accept them as almost God-given.

A pointed illustration of this kind of assumption arises in any discussion of the length and sequencing of education. Why should there be, for example, four years of high school followed by four years of college with high redundancy in the curriculum of the two? Educators from other countries, who follow different practices, find it hard to understand the merit in this. We, on the other hand, may find it difficult to accept the fact that in England five-year-olds normally enter first grade, since we know it "should" be six.

All societies provide training for their young, but the differences that exist are vitally important. These grow out of cultural values and the particular needs which exist or once existed within the society. And change comes slowly, often as a consequence of outside contact with other cultures. In education, the spurt of interest in science subjects in the United States that followed the well-publicized space achievements by the Soviet Union, beginning in 1957, illustrates this effect.

As we have previously noted, cultural patterns exist to provide for certain functions. On the other hand, we have also considered the point that the function itself may no longer be important except in its symbolic value, as in latent functions. Essentially, we can understand this distinction as one between *form* and *content*. It may be that the form persists even when it no longer fulfills the intended content of the activity. This is the essence of the distinction between the "letter of the law" and the "spirit of the law."

The formal tea has now become less a matter of content in terms of people becoming acquainted and more a ritualized event which symbolizes hospitality and a gracious intent. The military parade is another display which may not fulfill anything other than the external symbolic function of form. Thus, following the appropriate cultural form has value so long as people perceive it to be important and are troubled without it.

Psychological features of culture

From a psychological standpoint, the most basic influence effect of culture is to inculcate a perspective for viewing the world. In his discussion of reference groups, Shibutani (1955) gives expression to this in these terms:

> A perspective is an ordered view of one's world—what is taken for granted about the attributes of various objects, events, and human nature. It is an order of things remembered and expected as well as things actually perceived, an organized conception of what is

plausible and what is possible; it constitutes the matrix through which one perceives his environment. The fact that men have such ordered perspectives enables them to conceive of their ever changing world as relatively stable, orderly, and predictable (p. 564).

When we speak of a cultural perspective, then, we mean the shared content of the psychological field which defines and guides experience and action. In this section we will consider these as psychologically relevant effects upon value orientations, perceptual functioning, and social expectancies.

VALUE ORIENTATIONS

In any human society, there are values which are traditionally retained as part of explicit culture. At the individual level many of these values become incorporated as long-range, persisting motives which shape behavior. As Mumford (1951) says:

> . . . in all going cultures, Man is born into a world of established values: here every instinctual need is broadened, yet partly concealed, by a social form, as the naked body is soon covered by decorations or clothes. The production and conservation of values is one of the main concerns of human existence: all that a man does and is depends upon his taking part in this process (p. 127).

Cultural values stand, in Goldschmidt's (1959) phrase, as a "blueprint for propriety," but no more than a blue-print. There may be wide variations in the degree to which a given value is actually upheld in everyday practice. In short, some values are acted on more uniformly than others. Our society, for example, places a high value on the monogamous relationship as a uniform family pattern. From earliest experience we learn that there is one mother and one father in the family. All the influences we encounter in the society sustain the imperative quality of this as proper. Subsequently, we are oriented toward a love relationship of our own leading to monogamous marriage. As Goldschmidt (1959) puts it:

> Man must mate. But the cultured animal must select his mate according to certain rules, and the act of procreation is circumscribed by a welter of culturally established demands. We might put the

> matter this way: that even man's most basic animal drives are given a symbolic content and their fulfillment is caught up in the symbolism that is the culture of that particular people (p. 21).

As this example indicates, a prominent feature of values is that they are highly symbolic. The kind of behavior we evidence is both guided by and interpreted in light of values, such as virtue or honor. When we say, "I am a man of my word," we reveal a sense of appropriate behavior symbolizing such values.

It would be impossible for a society to retain coherence and continuity if its members did not, for the most part, share certain significant values in common. Among other benefits, this smoothes social interaction and assures individuals of social acceptance. Yet, individual differences in the adherence to values can and do occur. Furthermore, conflicts in expressed values are commonplace, especially in a complex society. In American society, for example, we place a high value on initiative and achievement. Its expression, however, is often in contradiction to other prevalent values. Thus, exponents of private enterprise are often those who would limit competition by the greater amalgamation of enterprises within an industry; higher education for all who are capable is valued, but those who have achieved it and act accordingly can be viewed with suspicion as "intellectuals"; social class distinctions are disdained, but larger and more expensive cars are sought as a conspicuous mark of social position.

Sometimes it is found that many people privately hold a value which they erroneously believe to be different from the values held by others. This is called "pluralistic ignorance" (Schanck, 1932). It is revealed in a recent study by Paul and Laulicht (1963) of attitudes toward defense and disarmament among a national sample of Canadian voters. They found that *personally* 70 per cent of their respondents favored disarmament even if it meant a loss of income; yet only 38 per cent of these respondents thought that *other* Canadians felt that way. In essence, then, the dominant value associated with disarmament actually existed but was not perceived to exist. This can lead to awkward conflicts within a society as was sharply seen following the publication of the first "Kinsey report" (1948) on the sexual behavior of American males. The interview data presented in the report raised questions about the actuality of norms regarding sexual conduct.

The fact that a society's values may be contradictory, or that individuals may give only lip service to a value, does not alter the essential point that values exist as guideposts in a cultural sense. Such discontinuities can still be reconciled within a general framework of the dominant themes of a culture. Anthropological studies frequently dwell on a culture's value-orientations as such themes. For example, the Kwakiutl Indians of the Northwest coast of North America were studied by Franz Boas over a period of many decades. Regarding these people, he said, "the importance of hereditary social rank, to be maintained by the display and lavish distribution, determines the behavior of the individual. It is the ambition of every person to obtain high social standing for himself, his family, or for the chief of his family. Wealth is a necessary basis for social eminence and the general tone of life is determined by these ideas" (1928, p. 152). The dominating value of status eminence, which is not unfamiliar to us in our own culture, was seen by Boas as an integrating principle among the Kwakiutl.

Ruth Benedict (1934), in her book *Patterns of Culture,* elaborated this approach in considering the dominant values of several cultures. She herself had done field work with the Zuñi Indians of the Southwest and discovered a distinct difference between them and the other Indian tribes of North America. In her terms, these other tribes were "Dionysian," in their emphasis on achieving psychological states of excess in personal experience and in ritual. The Zuñi, by contrast, tended to be "Apollonian" and to follow more restrained ways including an aversion to excess. Criticisms of Benedict's work (e.g. Barnouw, 1963, Ch. 3) mainly emphasize that the Zuñi were not all purely Apollonian and that other Indian tribes vary considerably in their Dionysian tendencies. Despite the absence of pure behavioral "types," there nonetheless appear to be central values which can be used to characterize a culture.

Apart from cultural influences as such, it is sometimes said that *all* people want a "decent standard of living." This is often merely a way of saying that humans value the satisfaction of their basic physical needs. But how very much this can vary in content is revealed in a new book by Hadley Cantril, *The Pattern of Human Concerns* (1965), in which he reports an intensive study of more than twenty-three thousand people in fourteen nations of the world ranging from those that are economically well-off countries on through those that are economically deprived. His main interest was in how people saw their own lives, and what they expressed as their own aspirations.

As part of his questionnaire survey procedure, conducted in each nation by trained native-speaking interviewers, Cantril devised what he calls the "Self-Anchoring Striving Scale" which is shown in its simple ladder form in Figure 8.2. Each respondent was shown this scale and

"Top" 10
        9
        8
        7
        6
        5
        4
        3
        2
        1
"Bottom" 0

Figure 8.2: Ladder used in "Self-Anchoring Striving Scale." Each respondent defines the "top" and "bottom" himself. (From Cantril, 1965, p. 22.)

asked to define the "top" and "bottom" in terms of *his own* assumptions, values, aspirations, fears, and worries. Then, regarding his *own* situation, he was asked three questions: (1) Where on the ladder do you feel you personally stand at the *present* time? (2) Where on the ladder would you say you stood *five years ago?* (3) And where do you think you will be on the ladder *five years from now?* Comparable questions were also asked regarding the respondent's view of his nation's position on the ladder, though we shall not treat them here.

As Cantril plainly points out, these ratings are entirely subjective and therefore a rating of 6 by one person does not indicate the same thing as a 6 given by another person. Nevertheless, consistent and significant differences were found between the average ratings given by people in different countries. For example, people in the three wealthiest nations represented in the study were found to rate themselves significantly higher on the present, the past, and the future than those from three of the poorest countries, as is shown in Table 8.1. However,

Table 8.1: Comparison of average personal ladder ratings and shifts across time among respondents in three wealthy and three poor countries. (Adapted from Cantril, 1965, p. 204.)

COUNTRY	PAST	PRESENT	FUTURE	SHIFT
Wealthy				
United States	5.9	6.6	7.8	1.9
West Germany	4.1	5.3	6.2	2.1
Israel	4.7	5.3	6.9	2.2
Average	4.9	5.7	7.0	2.1
Poor				
Brazil	4.1	4.6	7.3	3.2
Nigeria	2.8	4.8	7.4	4.6
India	3.4	3.7	5.1	1.7
Average	3.4	4.4	6.6	3.2
Difference in Average	1.5	1.3	0.4	—1.1

this is revealed even more through the actual words of these respondents, from India and the United States as examples:

India

I should like to have a water tap and a water supply in my house. It would also be nice to have electricity. My husband's wages must be increased if our children are to get an education and our daughter is to be married. (Forty-five-year-old housewife, family income about $80 a month) (1965, p. 205-6)

I wish for an increase in my wages because with my meager salary I cannot afford to buy decent food for my family. If the food and clothing problems were solved, then I would feel at home and be satisfied. Also if my wife were able to work the two of us could then feed the family and I am sure would have a happy life and our worries would be over. (Thirty-year-old sweeper, monthly income around $13) (p. 206)

I hope in the future I will not get any disease. Now I am coughing. I also hope I can purchase a bicycle. I hope my children will study well and that I can provide them with an education. I also would sometime like to own a fan and maybe a radio. (Forty-year-old skilled worker earning $30 a month) (p. 206)

United States

I hope that when I retire I will have enough money to travel, not necessarily in top style. We have had a nice comfortable home life raising our children and have enjoyed it. Now I'd like to do a few different things, like traveling. (Fifty-two-year-old insurance agent) (p. 221)

I would like a reasonable enough income to maintain a house, have a new car, have a boat, and send my four children to private schools. (Thirty-four-year-old laboratory technician) (p. 222)

If I had more money I could build a home, get married, move out of the city, and take a long vacation. I would like to be able to take my bride to Europe. (Twenty-six-year-old clerk) (p. 223)

It should be evident, then, that the prevailing economic circumstances of a society, such as a nation, can affect the way in which a given value is culturally defined by its members. The difference may not be so much a matter of quality as it is one of degree, but it is there.

CULTURAL EFFECTS ON PERCEPTUAL FUNCTIONING

The influence of culture on perception has long occupied a significant place in social psychology. For the most part, it is widely recognized that the unique experiences and emphases which are culturally induced become absorbed as a vital part of the individual's psychological field.

In summarizing the effect of cultural variables on perceptual responses in humans, Tajfel maintains that these variables can be grouped into three categories. The first of these is *functional salience,* which has regard to the environmental aspects of a culture which encourage certain perceptual discriminations, for example regarding edible and acceptable foods. *Familiarity* refers to the frequency of exposure that individuals may have to some human artifacts that are unfamiliar to those living in another culture. This is illustrated by the remarkable perceptual skill that children in our society reveal in readily differentiating makes and years of automobiles, even at great distance. *Systems of communication* mainly represent language as a technique of categorization and labeling to afford ready-made interpretations of the world. We shall be treating this latter feature in more detail in the chapter which follows.

Among the most interesting research on cultural effects on perception have been the studies comparing responses of people in different cultures to the same standard stimulus, sometimes a psychological illusion or a projective device, such as the Rorschach Ink-Blot Test.

An early study of cross-cultural differences in perception was conducted by Rivers (1901, 1905). He presented two well-known perceptual illusions, the Müller-Lyer and the horizontal-vertical, to Papuans in New Guinea, to Todas in India, and to a sample of English adults and schoolchildren. These illusions are shown in Figure 8.3. In the first of these, a vertical line is placed between two pairs of inwardly pointing vertices and is perceived as shorter than a line of the same size placed between outwardly pointing vertices. In the second illusion, two lines of identical size are placed in the configuration with one horizontal and the other vertical, as in a T. Usually the vertical line is perceived as the longer. Rivers found that the English subjects tended to be relatively more susceptible to the Müller-Lyer illusion than subjects of the other cultures, and less so to the horizontal-vertical illusion. There were differences, then, between the cultures but the nature of the difference depended upon the particular illusion.

Allport and Pettigrew (1957) undertook a study with the so-called rotating trapezoid devised by Ames (1951) (see Figure 8.3). To create this illusion, subjects are presented with a slowly rotating object which looks like a window but is proportioned like a trapezoid so that the

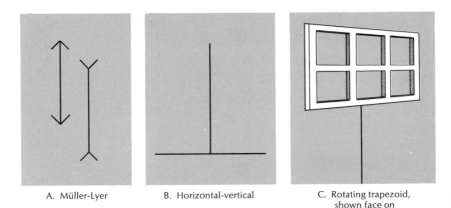

A. Müller-Lyer   B. Horizontal-vertical   C. Rotating trapezoid,
                                                            shown face on

Figure 8.3: Three perceptual illusions used in cross-cultural research.

longer edge always creates a longer image on the retina than does the shorter edge, even when the latter is closer. When viewed under optimal conditions, with one eye closed at a distance of 20 feet, the resulting perception is normally one of side-to-side movement, rather than rotation; the window seems to be swaying back and forth.

Allport and Pettigrew were interested in testing the hypothesis that familiarity with windows, and other squared-off objects which share its features, would make people more susceptible to the illusion because of the expectancies of shape they had learned. Alternatively, those living in a culture without such recurrent features should be less susceptible. They tested this hypothesis in a field study by showing the rotating trapezoid to a sample of subjects in South Africa who were Zulus in villages or in cities, and to urban South Africans of European origin. Under optimal conditions for the illusion, they did not find strikingly significant differences between the village Zulus and either urbanized Zulus or the Europeans. However, under conditions which were not optimum—such as viewing with one eye at 10 feet or with both eyes at 10 or 20 feet—they did find significant differences in the direction expected, i.e. the urban people, whether Zulus or Europeans, tended to see the illusion more frequently. One possible interpretation of these findings is that the compelling experimental condition overwhelms the effect of cultural experience which reveals itself only when the condition is less compelling. In any case, the degree of familiarity with objects of a culture appears to be a factor that does influence the individual's perception of the world.

In a series of related studies of cultural differences in geometric illusions (Segall, Campbell, and Herskovits, 1963, 1966; Campbell, 1964), subjects from more than fifteen cultures were exposed to several kinds of perceptual illusions, including the Müller-Lyer and horizontal vertical illusions already mentioned. Among the participants were subjects from the United States and from various parts of Africa. The essential idea underlying the experiments was referred to as the "carpentered world hypothesis." This hypothesis contends that where individuals live in a squared-off world of right angles, they may be more susceptible to illusions because of the corrections they normally introduce when encountering angles in perspective. In general, the results confirm this guiding hypothesis. The Western samples, for example, showed significantly greater susceptibility to the Müller-Lyer illusion than did the people from tribal areas whose housing tends to be almost entirely rounded.

Data from anthropological field studies have also provided interesting examples of the way that cultures affect visual experience from a social standpoint. In his work with the Trobriand islanders, Malinowski (1927) reports one instance of such a pattern which can run contrary to sensory evidence. In the Trobriand culture, it is considered a social indiscretion to suggest that brothers resemble one another, though both may look like their father. Once, commenting on the likeness of two brothers, Malinowski reports that "there came such a hush over the assembly, while the brother present withdrew abruptly and the company was half-embarrassed, half-offended, at this breach of custom" (p. 92). In discussing this example, Klineberg (1954) points out the difficulty in knowing whether the Trobriand islanders actually *see* the two brothers as different, despite their obvious resemblance to one another, or whether they are merely unwilling to acknowledge such a resemblance even when they do see it. He concludes that on the basis of our knowledge "the Trobrianders failed to note any resemblance because they do not want or expect to find it" (p. 205). This conclusion is sustained as well in other cultures in terms of the influence they can exert on perception in line with the phenomenon of perceptual set.

Within the general interest in psychological effects of culture, the Rorschach Test has probably been used to a greater extent than any other single psychological measure. The test consists of ten symmetrical inkblots which are always shown in the same order to the subject. He then reports what he sees in each of the blots and the examiner records his responses. In general, the test is used as a projective measure of personality. An individual response is compared with standardized norms obtained from tens of thousands of cases to provide a view of the individual's unique psycho-dynamics. Applied as an anthropological tool in the field, however, it can determine certain of the consistencies of perception for members of the same culture.

Among the many studies of the latter kind, one by Bleuler and Bleuler (1935) found, for example, that Moroccan natives responded with a significantly greater number of "details" in the inkblots than is usually found in the norms obtained from Europeans. This could be interpreted, in a psychodynamic sense, as a sign of disorder. More appropriately however, it reveals something of the salience or perceptual emphasis within the Moroccan culture. This is further clarified by another field investigation in which Cook (1942) found that young men in Samoa gave a very high percentage of responses which made use of the white space areas within the inkblots. Such responses are rather rare in the usual Rorschach norms. On further study, Cook found that 31 of the 50 young men reported white as their favorite color. Quite relevantly, in Samoan culture the color white is regarded as a symbol of purity.

DeVos (1961) examined Rorschach data obtained from two cultures where members lived by traditional as well as more Westernized ways. He found that while these Arab and Japanese subjects differed by grouping in the overall content of the Rorschach responses, there was a clear trend toward similarity in the responses of people in both groupings who had undergone Westernization. Thus, their convergence toward a common culture was revealed in the perceptual content of their Rorschach Test responses.

There are several obvious advantages in the use of the Rorschach Test in the field of cultural investigation. It does not require literacy; it is essentially culture-free since the blots do not represent anything in particular; and it can be used with people of different ages. There are, nevertheless, a number of difficulties associated with the administration of the test in the field. The procedure itself is cumbersome and particularly time-consuming where translation is required. Moreover, when it is used as a measure of cultural differences in personality, it is vulnerable in terms of the often unwitting bias in the selection of "typical" respondents, as well as in the interpretation of responses. These have questionable applicability to norms obtained from samples of Europeans or Americans.

From the accumulated evidence, quite beyond that part covered here, it is reasonable to conclude that perceptual functioning is influenced by culture. However, as H. Tajfel points out, it is not only culture as such but the broader characteristics of the physical environment which enter into the process as well. Thus, familiarity with objects, shapes, and contours cannot help but have their effect in the process of categorizing which is basic to perception.

The behavior of humans in a society follows certain organized configurations or patterns, as we have seen. These affect the experiences encountered by individuals but always within the envelope of a structured environment. Growing up within any cultural context involves exposure to examples of appropriate conduct presented recurringly from an early age. The appropriateness of some behaviors and the inappropriateness of others become incorporated in the individual's psychological field.

As we said in connection with social interaction, individuals also construe their world in ways consistent with the present situational context and in line with past experience. For the most part, this occurs through an implicit learning process that builds up "expectancies" for action, as Rotter (1954) has noted. The common expectation of regularities in conduct is the fundamental feature underlying *social norms* and *roles*.

The norms of any society can vary considerably as a consequence of different situational contexts and the meanings that they infuse into action. There are widely held forms of culturally approved behavior, however, for particular kinds of situations. Most individuals will be expected to display these. Traditionally, these fall into the broad categories of folkways and usages, conventions, and mores and taboos.

At the simplest level, *folkways* and *usages* in American society encompass such patterns of behavior as shaking hands on greeting or taking leave, or saying "hello" when answering the telephone. Violations of these norms are not punished severely, unless a special symbolic importance is attached to a given event. For example, the public refusal of a head of state of one nation to shake hands with the head of state of another nation could be a serious enough breach to create severe international repercussions. This is, however, a rare rather than a typical instance.

The norms regulating more significant aspects of social behavior are usually called *conventions*. For behavior of this kind, breaches are more severe as is the resulting punishment. Wearing clothes in public, using silverware as opposed to one's fingers when eating, and attending to bodily functions privately are examples of conventions. Violations of these are often penalized by legal as well as social sanctions.

The most significant social norms are called *mores* and *taboos*. These are usually codified in a society's laws and religious teachings and include such important injunctions of the "Thou shalt" variety as monogamy, faithfulness to one's spouse, significance of private property, and the like. Taboos represent the "Thou shalt not" injunction, seen for example in murder and incest. Mores and taboos are of course simply counterparts of the same value. Thus, the taboo against murder is another way of asserting the positive value placed on individual human life, just as respect for private property can be viewed as a directive against outright stealing, in contrast to borrowing.

The distinctions that we have made are of a more traditional variety and do not explain the "why" of norms so much as they describe various culturally determined action. From the standpoint of social psychology, there are two interrelated points concerning these norms: they range on a rough scale regarding increasing severity of the breach from folkways to mores, and represent increasing degrees of threat to organized society and the well-being of its members.

By now it should be clear that the functioning of any society depends upon a willingness of its members to comply with certain social demands in return for having others do so. In this regard, Goldschmidt (1959) says that "Social life may be seen as a bargain in which the individual subordinates himself to customary demands and receives in turn a social environment in which to operate; whether or not it is a good bargain, it is written into the commitment to social existence" (p. 64). This has applicability as well to roles.

Roles are behaviors expected of an individual in a given social position, as we pointed out in the last chapter. They are normative in the sense that they reside in shared expectancies within a culture. Practically speaking, they are particularized norms that have to do with an individual in a specified situation rather than with everyone. At a house party, for example, it is acceptable for everyone else *but* the host and hostess to say that it is getting late and is time to go home. Their roles dictate that they should *not* evidence any sign of inhospitableness, except under special circumstances, such as illness or an early morning departure on a trip.

Members of a society usually react to some aspects of a situation as *significant aspects*. In regard to roles, therefore, people abstract those features which tend to have the most important meanings just then for them, as in the instance of "hospitality." Generally speaking, what we call role behaviors are routinized ways of transmitting such meanings. Bredemeier and Stephenson (1962) have said that "Students, for example, are supposed to be 'attentive'; women are supposed to dress 'attractively'; men are supposed to be 'considerate' of their dates" (p. 14). There is, however, a range of behavior that is covered by the terms "attentive," "attractive," or "considerate." Furthermore, it is clear that these abstract qualities can be perceived differently depending upon the other person, how much we are attracted to him or her, and the attributes that he or she possesses.

Among the attributes which are significant in roles are age and sex. In any society there are cultural dictates regarding the roles associated with infants, young children, adolescents and young adults, mature adults, and old people. American society, unlike many other societies, tends to be oriented toward youth and does not generally hold those of older age in high regard merely because of their age. Most importantly for our interest here, there are roles which are only appropriate at a given age. When we say that an adult is acting "childishly" we are giving expression to one such expectancy. Age-linked roles are also bound up with sex, so much so that the term "age-sex roles" is sometimes used to describe this relationship. Little boys and girls, for example, have differential roles in regard to the kind of play in which they are expected to indulge.

As a rule, people have rather firmly fixed expectancies regarding sex roles. Illustrating this is the widespread expectancy that a nurse, and especially a secretary, should be female. Despite the fact that a high proportion of physicians in many Western societies are women, in our own society we think of this as distinctively a male role. When we speak of a "doctor" we mean a male, and females in that profession are still looked upon as an oddity—as they are in law and engineering. The best evidence indicates that women could capably fulfill these roles in greater numbers if the culture did not dictate otherwise (see Klineberg, 1954, Ch. 10).

Psychologically speaking, social norms and roles are both passed along by certain shared perceptions, or common constructions of what is appropriate. It is possible, however, for one person to perceive his role in one fashion while the person with whom he interacts perceives it in another. This is dramatically observed in cross-cultural contacts where the parties involved have different expectancies for what is correct. An instance of this comes out of the work of Hall (1959), who has studied the way in which time and space usage differs between cultures. He gives several instances of how American diplomats, unfamiliar with the ways of a foreign culture, misconstrue the behavior of their counterparts.

In one example concerning time, Hall (1959, pp. 17-18) tells of an American used to punctuality who becomes impatient and angry in a Latin American country when kept waiting what seemed an unconscionable time. Hall says: "The principal source of misunderstanding lay in the fact that in the country in question the five-minute-delay interval was not significant. Forty-five minutes, on the other hand, instead of being at the tail end of the waiting scale, was just barely at the beginning" (p. 18). Here we see one instance of how role interaction can be sharply affected by expectancies which are culturally induced. Another instance has regard to space. In American society we tend not to stand as close in conversation as people do in some other societies, including those of Latin America. Hall points out that we view the foreigner who seems to be getting too close, by our standards, as "pushy." A humorous consequence, with significant overtones, is revealed in Hall's report:

> I have observed an American backing up the entire length of a long corridor while a foreigner he considers pushy tries to catch up with him. This scene has been enacted thousands and thousands of times —one person trying to increase the distance in order to be at ease, while the other tries to decrease it for the same reason, neither one being aware of what was going on. We have here an example of the tremendous depth to which culture can condition behavior (pp. 160-161).

Another kind of problem produced by roles occurs when the individual operates with two sets of conflicting expectancies regarding his behavior. This is commonly called "role conflict" and results from being in two largely incompatible roles simultaneously. All of us experience this in milder forms when, for example, we first bring our best girlfriend home to dinner with our family, or meet our professor when out shopping with a friend. There is an awkwardness in such circumstances, if only momentarily, because of the combination of different expectancies. In some cases this awkwardness could be more severe, as exemplified by the case of a traffic court judge who found his wife brought before him charged with a violation. Another illustration in which role conflict occurs, but on a more persisting basis, is found where the son or son-in-law of its president is employed in a company. The supervisor for whom he works inevitably experiences an awkward incongruence in this relationship that he would not normally encounter in the usual supervisor-subordinate relationship.

This case not only exemplifies a situation producing role conflict for the supervisor, but also reveals an instance of "status incongruence." Homans (1961) and Sampson (1963), among others, have pointed out that there usually is the expectancy of *status congruence* in interacting roles; incongruence would mean a violation of expectancy by having someone of higher status (e.g. the company president's son) in a lower status position.

As generally conceived, status congruence means a matching of the value of a person's attributes in one dimension with his position in another. For example, in supermarkets employees who check-out purchases at the cash register are perceived to have a higher status than, and to be in charge of, employees who bundle, though they might make the same wage. The more experienced employees expect to be assigned to checking because greater seniority and experience are congruent with a higher position. However, should a more experienced worker, in a busy period, be assigned to a checker with less experience, this incongruity has been found to create tension and reduce productivity (Clark, 1958). Other kinds of background characteristics including age, sex, education, and ethnic affiliation may also enter into the perception of dimensions of status involved in this kind of matching process. The question of whether a girl should be editor of the school paper, "over boys," reveals this concern. The same kind of issue underlies the skepticism that a Negro officer could head a unit made up of white men. Notice that in these two instances status is not earned by experience, qualifications, or actions, but instead is attributed to a person by the prior expectancies of others.

In our consideration of norms and roles, we have moved back and forth between the level of culturally dictated patterns and interpersonal relations—what we called the formal and informal levels of interaction in the last chapter. This is a necessity in social psychology because a culture's influences reside in the psychological fields and related response tendencies of people. As Withey and Katz (1965) aptly observe:

> Conventional social science accepts social structure as the walls of the maze but is willing to have the psychologist study individual deviations within those walls. The social psychologist, however, is concerned with understanding the walls themselves as well as the individual deviations, because the walls of the social maze consist of the patterned behavior of people. There is no social structure apart from the interrelated habitual actions and attitudes of people (p. 65).

Adopting this metaphor, it is also clear that the social psychologist must be concerned with how these "walls" are maintained and by what processes they are changed. It is to these issues that we will now turn our attention.

Cultural transmission and social change

As a general rule, cultures tend to have continuity despite the fact that adaptation and change within a society are possible. The forces which sustain culture have considerable potency in terms of the desirability of the familiar and congenial way of life to which individuals become accustomed. This feeling is not merely an abstraction but can run deeply within the individual's sense of being. This is illustrated by interview data obtained from Turkish villagers as part of a broader study of social change in the Middle East (Lerner, 1958). Many respondents could not conceive of any other way of life than the one they knew.

In response to the question, "If you could not live in Turkey, where would you want to live?" Lerner reports that: "The standard reply of the villagers was that they would not live, could not imagine living, anywhere else." Under persistent questioning he quotes a shepherd as replying that ". . . he would rather kill himself" (pp. 24-25). Yet, four years later that very village had undergone such transformation, with the introduction of a new highway to Ankara, electric power, and radios, that these attitudes had been markedly altered.

There are compelling individual forces, then, which can act to sustain the continuity of culture, unless significant outside factors intervene. The consequences of cultural persistence can be quite dramatic. There are still societies today living by a pattern that dates to antiquity. Goldschmidt (1959) has noted as instances that "A modern photographer can catch scenes in Egyptian villages identical to ones depicted on archeological remains several millennia ago . . . Eskimo life appears to be at least a thousand years old, and some of its elements go back to the upper Paleolithic. The pigmies in Africa and in Southeast Asia have a fundamentally similar culture and some scholars believe that they date back to the third glaciation of the Pleistocene epic" (p. 143). He further points out that no contemporary societies could so closely approximate earlier societies if cultural continuity did not exist.

The transmission of culture occurs primarily through the social institutions of a society, such as the family or school, with which humans have their earliest experiences. The need for maintenance functions in childhood creates an especially important dependence relationship, which leads to the ready acceptance of such cultural influences, as we noted in Chapter Four.

This process is bolstered considerably by the potent device of language. The words we learn to label and categorize experience are of great significance in the transmission of culture. The symbolic quality of culture, which we have already commented upon, therefore assures that individuals will themselves carry a cultural imprint within their own psychological fields.

Experimental verification of the persistence and change of cultural norms comes from the work of Jacobs and Campbell (1961). In a laboratory setting, they established the basis for the transmission of an arbitrary tradition. The task consisted of judging the distance a light moved in the autokinetic situation, in line with Sherif's (1935) research. Groups were initially composed of one naïve subject and several of the experimenter's confederates who gave a pre-arranged set of judgments aloud before the naïve subject gave his. In subsequent trials the confederates were removed one at a time, and were each replaced by a naïve subject. When the confederates had all been removed, the same method of elimination was continued for the other group members in the order of their "seniority." In one control condition, subjects were alone when presented with the light and made their own independent judgments.

In Figure 8.4 results from the Jacobs and Campbell experiment are shown for an experimental group (X-4-3) made up of four people, three of whom at the outset were instructed to give an arbitrary response of 15 to 16 inches as the experimenters' confederates. For purposes of comparison, the results for the subjects in the control condition just described are also presented. In both instances, the curves show the mean

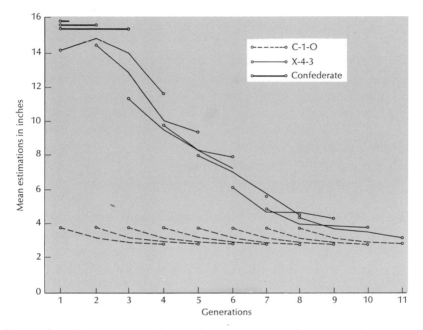

Figure 8.4: Transmission of an arbitrary perceptual norm in four-person groups (X-4-3) initially composed of a true subject and three experimenters' confederates. Control condition (C-1-o) involves subjects responding alone. All lines are plotted by a subject's mean responses for each of four consecutive generations. (From Jacobs and Campbell, 1961, p. 653.)

individual judgments for each of four "generations" during which the subject was present. A generation was composed of thirty trials, each involving one discrete judgment by each person. This figure dramatically reveals the persistence of the "tradition" for several generations, at a level significantly different from subjects who had made judgments in solitude. The importance of this research lies in its clear demonstration that cultural transmission survives the departure of specific individuals, and also that change over time does occur in the direction of a decaying of the traditional norm.

As these experimenters themselves state, this research was not capable of capturing the richness contained within a culture. Furthermore, indoctrination into their norm came from age-mates in a brief period, rather than from adults over many years. Nonetheless, they say that "the outcome may well warn us against the assumption that a purely arbitrary cultural norm could be perpetuated indefinitely without other sources of support" (p. 657).

A major psychological process at work in social change, which can lead to major effects on a culture, is the perception of new alternatives. The contrast between what is and what might be—summed up in "hope" —is a powerful spur to change. Under conditions of necessity this process becomes all the more pressing, for example, when a physical resource such as water becomes scarce, or a social calamity such as war occurs.

The availability of alternatives is facilitated by the interrelated factors of *cultural contact* and *technological innovation,* as we have previously noted. Their effects are illustrated dramatically by Margaret Mead's (1956) account of her return after 25 years to the island people of Manus near New Guinea. They had replaced their Stone Age culture with modern practices, a leap of literally thousands of years, largely because their territory was the site of a World War II base through which many Americans passed.

In Western civilization as well there have been many instances of cultural contact through travelers, such as the famed Marco Polo, population migrations, and wars. Today, through the mass media of communication and supersonic air travel, the possibility of such contact has been vastly increased. Supermarkets in Britain and France, Beatle haircuts in America, and television in Southeast Asia are only a few superficial signs of this development.

The truly big technological changes are illustrated more profoundly by the Agricultural Revolution, which Childe (1946) considers a singular landmark in human history, and by the Industrial Revolution of the last century. The Computer Revolution of this century, about which most people are still largely unaware, will have at least as much impact in rendering change. While industry brought people in droves to the cities for work, computer technology is likely to alter the entire work pattern of society and the cultural values associated with it.

Technological change may be preceded by the awareness of a need which makes the people of a society receptive to its introduction. On the other hand, once introduced it may have striking social consequences. In this respect, Kardiner (1939) reports with Linton a study of villagers in Madagascar in the Tanala tribe. An agricultural people, they relied upon the cultivation of rice which they conducted by the "dry" method. Through contacts with their neighboring tribe, the Betsileo, they borrowed the "wet" method for cultivating rice, which on the whole is more effective agriculturally. This technological innovation had marked consequences, however, on the society of the Tanala. Among other effects noted by Kardiner and Linton were the new importance attached to land-owning, particularly in the swamps, the economic significance of slaves, and the greater power vested in a royal ruler positioned over a rigid caste system.

In a similar vein, Sharp (1952) reports on a tribe of Australian aborigines whose men had made and highly prized stone axes. With the arrival of an Anglican mission, steel axes came into plentiful supply. The important symbolic significance of an ax as a valued tool belonging especially to older men was soon undercut with profound social results. Because women and even young boys could now obtain steel axes from the mission, there was a "revolutionary confusion of sex, age, and kinship roles" with many ramifications regarding interpersonal conduct.

Paul Bohannan (1959) has studied the impact of money on the Tiz tribe living in central Nigeria. The traditional Tiz society was dominated by subsistence farmers who exchanged their produce and handicrafts as a mode of trade. In due course, there was introduced an "all-purpose" money in the form of government coins, whereas in the past only "limited purpose" money existed in the form of brass rods used to facilitate particular kinds of exchange. While trade increased considerably as part of the introduction of money, there came also rather marked changes in the character of the society and its cultural values. The Tiz had been a people disdaining great wealth or its display. This value changed drastically and along with it there came a new concept of indebtedness and concommitant shifts in kinship and status relationships as well. Bohannan pointedly says: "Money is one of the shatter-ingly simplifying ideas of all time, and like any other new and compelling idea, it creates its own revolution" (p. 503).

We need not look to tribal people alone for this kind of revolution, however. In American society we had a revolution which made its first major impact about forty years ago in the widespread availability of automobiles. It, too, has contributed to significant changes in our cultural patterns. In his history of the 1920's, *Only Yesterday* (1931), Frederick Lewis Allen says that the automobile

> . . . offered an almost universally available means of escaping tem-porarily from the supervision of parents and chaperones, or from the influence of neighborhood opinions. Boys and girls thought nothing, as the Lynds pointed out in *Middletown* [1929], of jumping into a car and driving off at a moment's notice—without asking anybody's per-mission—to a dance in another town 20 miles away, where they were strangers and enjoyed a freedom impossible among their neighbors. The closed car, moreover, was in effect a room protected from the weather which could be occupied at any time of the day or night and could be moved at will into a darkened by-way or a country lane (p. 70).

The automobile has had enormous effects on our culture, not the least of which is the new value it reflects. This value is invoked when-ever we hear controversies regarding the building of additional free-ways and the tearing down of structures in their path. The great premium placed on getting people places in an automobile has con-siderably altered our landscape, physically as well as culturally (see Mumford, 1963). Similarly, airplane travel, telephones, radio and tele-vision, have brought their broader consequences to our lives.

Culture, then, is an organic thing which changes and grows. We who live by its dictates are influenced by it, very often in ways we only barely fathom. But we can also influence it and leave our mark on it by the introduction of innovations and the alteration of tradition. Most importantly for our purposes here, culture can be studied and under-stood rather than uncritically accepted.

Communication is a central feature of culture. Through processes of communication, Man succeeds in influencing others and in transmitting that influence through succeeding generations. This human propensity is uniquely represented in language, which is characteristic of all hu-man cultures and to which we now turn.

SUMMARY

A society's culture consists of the relationships and social arrangements which are passed on and institutionalized to handle routinely the characteristic problems of the society. These problems include survival needs as well as the requirements that arise from unique historical, geographic, and other environmental features such as natural resources, climate, and the characteristics of the neighboring societies. Teaching and protecting the young, implementing governmental forms, kinship systems, and the transmission of property exemplify major areas of life over which culture exerts considerable influence.

Man depends upon culture for a coherent outlook and approach toward life. The demands of culture are normally accepted as usual and proper. By providing social reality, the essential *psychological effect* of culture is to influence a society's members toward distinctive ways of thinking and acting.

The major features of *tradition, symbolization,* and *integration* characterize all cultures. Culture may also be partitioned into its *explicit* level, which refers to directly observable behavior and broad patterns of life, and its *implicit* level composed of the attitudes and values held by the members of a society.

The psychological effects of culture can be categorized under the headings of *value orientations, perceptual functioning,* and *social expectancies.* The values of a society are represented in individual actions, such as eating practices or monogamy, which have significant symbolic importance. Society depends upon widespread agreement on the cultural imperatives represented in values, although these may sometimes be in conflict. Anthropologists have characterized various cultures in terms of their dominant values. Values may be variously construed in different cultures, as exemplified by a desire for a "decent standard of living."

Perceptual functioning has been found to vary from culture to culture. This is indicative of the *functional salience, familiarity,* and *systems of communication* that different cultures emphasize in experience. Studies of susceptibility to *illusions,* and responses to the *Rorschach Ink-Blot Test* have dominated such cross-cultural research.

Cultural norms refer to those broad patterns of conduct which are expected in a society. In anthropological terms, these are often divided into: *folkways* and *usages, conventions,* and *mores* and *taboos.* These norms vary from those of least importance to those of greatest importance for the preservation of society. Some behaviors are significant for their symbolic *form* and not for their actual *content.*

In social psychological terms, norms and roles are in the nature of *social expectancies* which individuals share in their psychological fields. *Roles* refer especially to those particular expectancies regarding appropriate behavior for a person occupying a position in a given situation. One of these expectancies is for *status congruence,* which means a matching of the value of a person's attributes in one dimension with his position on another.

The persistence and *continuity of culture* arise from the attachment of individuals to the familiar and congenial patterns to which they have become accustomed. Such patterns are transmitted through significant social institutions such as the family and are strongly bolstered by language and other symbolic processes. Social change leading to a shift in a culture is likely to occur where new alternatives are perceived, and especially where necessity is widely recognized. *Cultural contact* and *technological innovation* considerably enhance the prospect for social change by making alternatives accessible.

SUGGESTED READINGS

From E. P. Hollander and R. G. Hunt. (Eds.) *Current perspectives in social psychology.* (2nd Edition.) New York: Oxford University Press, 1967:

11. George P. Murdock: *How culture changes*
12. Milton M. Gordon: *The nature of assimilation and the theory of the melting pot*
58. Warren G. Bennis: *Beyond bureaucracy*
59. Chris Argyris: *Being human and being organized*

SELECTED REFERENCES

Bredemeier, H. C., & Stephenson, R. M. *The analysis of social systems.* New York: Holt, Rinehart & Winston, 1962.
Cantril, H. *The pattern of human concerns.* New Brunswick, N. J.: Rutgers Univer. Press, 1965.

Goldschmidt, W. *Man's way.* Cleveland: World Publ. Co., 1959.

*Hall, E. T. *The silent language.* Garden City, N. Y.: Doubleday, 1959.

*Kluckhohn, C. *Mirror for man.* New York: McGraw-Hill, 1949.

Segall, M., Campbell, D. T., & Herskovits, M. *The influence of culture in visual perception.* New York: Bobbs-Merrill, 1966.

*Shapiro, H. L. (Ed.) *Man, culture & society.* New York: Oxford Univer. Press, 1956.

Williams, R. M. *American society: A sociological interpretation.* (2nd ed.) New York: Knopf, 1960.

9

Language and social communication

Language is a strikingly distinctive attribute of Man. Though animals of different species have means of communicating with one another, human relationships uniquely depend upon the subtleties of symbolic communication through words. Studies of infrahuman communication indicate that it is mainly gestural and largely predetermined by genetic factors (Scott, 1953). For example, the "bee dance" observed by von Frisch (1955) appears to be an elaborate means for signifying the location of food by patterned behavior. Humans, on the other hand, acquire spoken language and meanings associated with words, entirely through a process of learning. As Brown (1958) pointedly observes, "man does not develop language if he grows up among animals or in isolation. Language is acquired by the human being born into a linguistic community" (p. 193).

The use of language is vital in the transmission of culture and in the functioning of society. Language provides a significant symbolic vehicle by which individuals cope with their environment, including the other persons with whom they are linked in social interaction. Underscoring this function, Morris (1946) says that ". . . a very widespread opinion has arisen that society . . . is dependent upon signs, and specifically upon language signs for its existence and perpetuation" (p. 205).

While language exists in all human societies, it has a highly diversified character around the globe. Depending upon how one defines a unitary language, there are at least hundreds of major languages in the world, with several dozen in use in the Indian subcontinent alone. These are sufficiently different from one another so that it would be impossible for humans of different societies to communicate with one another through their mother tongues. The wider use of Man's crowning capacity is, therefore, severely handicapped by the diverse pattern of language over the globe. In this regard, Miller (1964) has said:

> *Every human group* that anthropologists have studied has spoken a language. The language always has a lexicon and a grammar. The lexicon is not a haphazard collection of vocalizations, but is highly organized; it always has pronouns, means for dealing with time, space, and number, words to represent true and false, the basic concepts necessary to propositional logic. The grammar has distinguishable levels of structure, some phonological some syntactic. . . . The syntax always specifies rules for grouping elements sequentially into phrases and sentences, rules governing normal intonation, rules for transforming some types of sentences into other types (p. 34).

Language is not, however, the only means by which individuals communicate. Messages can be transmitted through physical symbols as well as by the gestures that individuals display to one another, including especially the formal symbols contained in "sign language." Language, on the other hand, has the distinctive advantage of portability. Not only can we communicate across time and space through the written words of a language, but we can also think thoughts and anticipate future events as a basis for action.

The social psychologist is concerned with the study of language and its acquisition especially because it has *functional* features which affect the individual's perceptions and motivations in the psychological field and it has *directive* features which influence social responses in a stimulus sense. In other terms, we may say that language is a tool for the individual's thoughts and also a technique of social influence. Both of these features are emphasized in this chapter. We begin, however, with some consideration of the nature of language.

The nature and basis of language

By its very nature, language is social. Carroll (1953) defines language as consisting of learned responses determined by social interaction.

Sapir (1921) considers that "Language is a purely human and non-instinctive method of communicating ideas, emotions, and desires by means of a system of voluntarily produced symbols" (p. 8). Hayakawa (1964) views language as a system of agreements among human beings which allow various noises produced to systematically stand for specified happenings in their nervous system. In this sense, it "mediates" between experience and action.

Two points in particular stand out in these definitions. One of these is the consideration that language is acquired from contact with other human beings. The other is the fact that language consists of symbolized meanings which are sources of stimulation and mediators of response. Moreover, these meanings can exist in thought as well as in spoken and in written form (cf. Osgood, 1952).

From a psychological standpoint, language is at first a set of vocalized stimuli which we encounter from infancy. People peer at us and utter sounds which subsequently become associated with the quality of that experience, whether pleasant or unpleasant. Soon, we learn to relate certain sounds with the people about us and the kind of experiences they provide, such as feeding us. This process of learning occurs within a "verbal community" (Skinner, 1957). With time, it evokes responses to these stimuli which are likely to produce desired effects. Sounds then stand for categories of experience.

For the individual, language soon becomes a way of defining experience, with significant consequences to perception. Words stand for things and we find it hard to conceive that it should be otherwise. If something is "cold," it has the attribute of coldness which is not similarly conveyed by any other word. When a child discovers that in French "cold" is "froid," this seems quite strange and even silly. The adult who is trying to make sense in his language to a foreigner unfamiliar with it will often repetitively pronounce his words more slowly and more loudly in the vain expectation that the foreigner should then understand and act. Imagine someone shouting at you what sounds phonetically like "sue yoke"—Turkish for "water's all gone"—and consider your own perplexity.

THEORIES OF LANGUAGE ORIGINATION

How Man came to use language continues to be an issue that is largely unresolved. As Pei (1960) indicates, this is not because linguists have been without theories, but that they are still unproven and in some instances unprovable. He says, "If there is one thing in which all linguists are fully agreed, it is that the problem of the origin of human speech is still unsolved" (p. 18).

There are several theories concerning the origin of language. Among the more common of these is the onomatopoeic theory, sometimes referred to as the "bow-wow" theory. It holds that language arose as an imitation of natural sounds. Thus, when a dog barks he makes a sound which the human speaker imitates as "bow-wow." Similarly, other words imitate sounds as in "hum," "gong," "bang," "slop," and "giggle." The difficulties with this theory are that only a small number of words within any language have this kind of onomatopoeic quality, the same supposedly natural noise is referred to differently in different languages, and such words have little to do with the abstract quality of language.

A second common theory holds that language arose from interjections, such as "oh" or "ah," that people made as a response to surprise, fear, pleasure, or pain. It is difficult, however, to see how human language could have been built up to such a variegated degree on the basis of a very few sounds of this kind, though it has been observed that animals appear to use such sounds as a simple form of communication.

A third theory suggests that there was some relationship between mouth movements and hand gestures. It has been suggested that the first regularized languages were based on a kind of sign language. At some stage, this theory contends, Man discovered that though his hands were not free, he might still communicate certain signs by means of vocalization. Eventually, the advantages of speech became apparent over gestures.

While each of these theories has some plausibility, they are all merely descriptive of an aspect of language. They do not help to understand how it might be that certain sounds came to represent persons, things, events, or concepts. Furthermore, the dispersion of different languages raises still other questions regarding the seemingly infinite variability of language.

THE EVOLUTION OF LANGUAGE

Languages persist and have the kind of continuity associated with culture, but they also may be altered through the processes of change in terms of cultural innovation. Pei (1960) gives an example of how linguistic change affects reality in the fact that the ancient Greek comic poets used the Greek letters BEH to signify a sheep's cry. While the sheep has not changed its cry, these letters have since been altered in their value so that in modern Greek they are actually pronounced as "vee" (p. 16). He says further:

> . . . all languages change in due course of time. A modern English speaker encounters some difficulty with the English of Shakespeare, far more with the English of Chaucer, and has to handle the English of King Alfred as a foreign tongue. A French speaker finds the 14th century language of François Villon a little difficult, has considerable trouble with the 12th century *Chanson de Roland*, barely recognizes the tongue of the 9th century oaths of Strasbourg, and if he goes further back has to handle the documents he finds from the Latin rather than from the French standpoint . . .(p. 21).

When language changes this is usually found to be related to cultural contact as well as to the modeling influence of an innovator—such as a king in his court—who is imitated by his courtiers. Shakespeare influenced English by many of his coinages, some of which are thoroughly commonplace today. Among them are these:

> "Strange bedfellows" (*The Tempest*)
> "Cold comfort" (*King John*)
> "Poor but honest" (*All's Well That Ends Well*)
> "The milk of human kindness" (*Macbeth*)
> "Not slept one wink" (*Cymbeline*)
> "In my mind's eye" (*Hamlet*)
> "Men of few words" (*Henry V*)
> "As good luck would have it" (*Merry Wives of Windsor*).

The degree to which once novel usages pass into language as trite phrases is brought home by a lady's comment that she liked Shakespeare because of all the "clichés" he used.

The structure and form of language

The "word" is the most elemental unit of language which communicates meaning. We have all been taught that it can be a "noun," a "verb," a "pronoun," or any number of other syntactic parts of speech. Yet, we need not know what words are to speak a language; and, indeed, what we do learn about words in our language may not conform to the rules in other languages. A great number of languages, for example, do without articles entirely, including Slavic tongues. In many languages no sharp distinction is made between nouns and verbs. They may be part of the same word, as in Japanese. Turkish is an agglutinative language in which word endings are added such that a long word by our standards may be a whole sentence. Thus, a single word is used in Turkish to ask, "Are you going?"

Many of the American Indian languages combine the noun and verb so that the phrase "the light flashes" might be rendered with more economy as "flashing." The use of prepositions, which we have in abundance in our language, is very often handled by endings or "post-positions" in other languages. An example of our own prepositional maze is humorously conveyed by the story of the precocious child whose mother had promised to read him a book at bedtime. When she arrived in his room with the wrong one, he said, "Mama, what did you bring that book that I didn't want to be read out of up for?"

Though awkward, we have no trouble discerning the meaning of this sentence. And this of course is the essence of language—that it convey meaning. *Semantics* is the study of meaning. It encompasses both written and spoken language, though these have quite different characteristics as we shall see.

Words are the major semantic units of language. In our language they are written by letters from an alphabet. Since language is essentially an arbitrary means of symbolizing thoughts and communication, there are many alphabets, in the sense of different ways of representing things and actions. The earliest form of language, which still prevails in Chinese and Japanese, relies on pictorial-like symbols. Hieroglyphs in ancient Egypt were used in this way.

Though we generally think of spoken language as a predecessor to written language, Brown (1958) says that it is by no means certain that speech is a more ancient form of language because the first true languages may have been these representational systems using pictures to convey commonly accepted meanings. Side by side with these, however, there may have been spoken languages where common sounds also held such meanings. Thus, the word for the actual "sun" would be uttered when speaking the picture "sun" aloud.

The alphabet which grew out of these representational systems constituted a considerable advance over them. The origins of the word "alphabet" come from the early Semitic alphabet used by the Hebrews and Phoenicians. "Aleph" originally meant ox and our modern letter *A* at one time was a drawing of the head of an ox. "Beth" meant house and the original picture for *B* represented a house. It still does; if you pass a Jewish Temple named "Beth Israel" its name means "House of Israel."

The Greeks adapted this Semitic alphabet and, in what was a comparatively short span of time as history goes, it was absorbed into what we know today as the Roman alphabet. A version of this Greek adaptation, the Cyrillic alphabet, is employed today in Bulgaria and Russia, where it was introduced with Eastern Orthodox Christianity in the ninth century. It was modified somewhat from the Greek alphabet, with some extra letters from Hebrew, to handle Slavic sounds. These alterations lead us to find, for example, that the Greek letter rho, which looks like our capital P, has an /R/ sound, and that the modern Russian letter which looks like H is actually pronounced with our /N/ sound.

As long as there is an agreed-upon pronunciation, or phonetic, for letters or combinations of letters, they represent a method for vocalizing words and broader statements. This makes it possible to go from written to spoken language and back again. Therefore, writing involves symbols put together to form another symbol.

The written and spoken forms of language are by no means perfectly congruent, however. The smallest discernible units of speech are called *phonemes.* Thus, various combinations of letters can yield a given phoneme, just as a group of phonemes may be necessary to sound a letter. In English, for example, we employ the two letters *t* and *h* to yield the single phoneme /th/. On the other hand, the letter *x* is made up of three phonemes, as follows: /eh/-/k/-/s/.

A major trouble in learning language is the fact that letters and phonemes do not conform on a regular basis. English is full of unsounded letters as in the *k* and *gh* appearing in the word "knight." In its original Anglo-Saxon form it is believed the word was fully pronounced including the sounds /k/ and a gutteral /gh/, which has since passed out of English, but is like the modern German *Knecht.* Furthermore, the sounding of letter combinations is irregular as is seen in the three words *though, through,* and *rough,* each of which ends with a distinctive phonemic sound. Also, there is confusion because a given letter, say a vowel, may be sounded differently. Consider, for example, the pronunciation of the letter *a* in the words *father, woman,* and *nature.*

When we sometimes ask why Johnnie can't read, we might well bear in mind Brown's (1958) incisive comment that:

> There are great psychological economies in a phonetic writing such as our alphabet, economies that have caused phonetic writing to prevail over the older representational writings. However, the alphabet used for writing English has come to be a very irregular phonetic system. Some say that its irregularities are so exasperating that children ought to be taught to read English without any direct tuition in the sound values of the alphabet. Others say that this is tantamount to returning us to a hieroglyphic writing since it deprives children of the advantages that inhere in a phonetic writing (p. 17).

In an attempt to deal with the complexities of English, a teaching device called the "Initial Teaching Alphabet" was developed some years ago by Pitman. Essentially, its 44 letters duplicate the actual phonemes in English. These are shown in Figure 9.1. Now being used in many school systems, this alphabet is said to be far easier for children to use in learning to read. Furthermore, the transition to the normal letters of the alphabet is supposedly quite smooth. Generally speaking, the acquisition of written language is among the most difficult tasks posed for the child.

Acquisition of language

The best estimates indicate that the English language contains anywhere from 50,000 to 100,000 words. Depending upon the criteria employed, it has been variously estimated that by the time he is four, an average child knows as many as 5000 words, in the specific sense of recognizing and acting on them, whether or not he can employ them himself. Though some authorities indicate that this is too high an estimate, it is nonetheless indicative of the massive learning process which occurs in early life. Again in terms of recognition, the average adult is said to know 35,000 words. It should be emphasized, however, that for every ten words that he can recognize, only one may be part of the functional vocabulary of the individual.

That all normal infants manage this tremendous task of acquiring

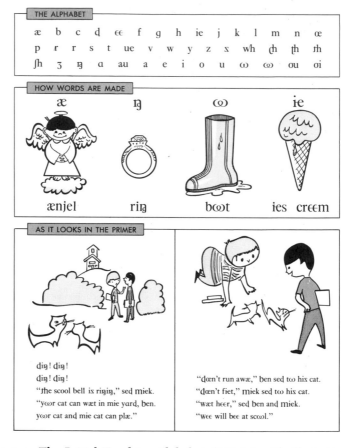

Figure 9.1: The Initial Teaching Alphabet (I.T.A.) with illustrations of its use in a children's primer. (From the *New York Times,* July 19, 1964.)

language is truly phenomenal. Commenting on this process, Miller (1964) says:

> Human language must be such that a child can acquire it. He acquires it, moreover, from parents who have no idea how to explain it to him. No careful schedule of rewards for correct or punishments for incorrect utterances is necessary. It is sufficient that the child be allowed to grow up naturally in an environment where language is used. The child's achievement seems all the more remarkable when we recall the speed with which he accomplishes it and the limitations of his intelligence in other respects. It is difficult to avoid an

impression that infants are little machines specially designed by nature to perform this particular learning task (p. 35).

By contrast, no matter how much animals are encouraged, they
manage only a few primitive "words." The Kelloggs (1933) raised a
female chimpanzee, Gua, with their own son, Donald. She arrived at
their home at the age of seven and one-half months and was treated
just as was Donald, then two months older. There was no special effort
made to teach Gua to talk, but she was exposed to the same environment of human speech as was Donald. Gua at first comprehended more
directions than did Donald, but at nine months lagged behind him.
Furthermore, she never employed more than two utterances that could
be considered to have a semantic quality, and even these were actually
cries characteristic of chimpanzees. One was a kind of "food bark" that
meant "yes," and the other was an "oo-oo" cry that meant "no." Cathy
Hayes and her husband raised a female chimpanzee, Viki, from the age
of six weeks. In contrast to the Kelloggs, they made a deliberate effort to
teach her to talk. In her report (1951) after three years, she indicates
that Viki had learned to say "papa," "mama," and "cup," but only with
imperfect articulation at best.

STAGES IN LANGUAGE LEARNING

There are several stages usually seen in the child's language development. The first stage involves random vocalization with a good deal of
cooing, squealing, crying, and gurgling. Several months after birth, a
stage of babbling starts which is characterized by the infant's repetition
of sounds in a self-stimulating way, i.e. saying the sound and then hearing it stimulates its vocalization again. The next stage, which occurs as
the infant nears age one, is one of imitation of the phonetic range the
child hears from others about him. The stage of true speech, seen
mainly after the first birthday, involves the relatively consistent use of
a given sound to mean particular things, as in "mama" and "dada."

Usually this last stage begins with terms that are used very generally
first and then proceed to be particularized. For example, the child may
use "dada" at first to mean a man and not just the father. As Brown
(1958) indicates, the child often uses concrete terms to stand for a
general category. This is not for a lack of abstracting ability but the

unawareness of an abstract term such as "quadruped" for a four-legged animal, rather than the terms "dog" or "horse."

In terms of this sequence of development, Piaget (1926) offered a distinction between a child's *ego-centric* vs. *social* speech. The former is largely a function of the child's pleasure in expressing himself. Piaget contends that this is characteristic of children through the ages of six or seven. Social speech addresses others in an attempt to influence them.

It is by no means clear that this Piaget distinction is so sharp as was once thought. McCarthy (1929), for example, found that the child's ego-centric speech varied considerably across situations such that it was higher when children were playing with one another than when they were in the company of adults. Vigotsky (1939) found with infants that their so-called "ego-centric" speech was also affected by whether there were others present. He contends that even early babbling speech *is* directed toward social ends insofar as the child believes others show signs of interest and understanding. In the absence of such conditions, he reports a sharp drop-off in these infant monologues. This and other evidence appears to indicate that a very large proportion of a child's speech actually is *social* in its intent (Miller, 1951).

Sometime during the second year of life, the child arrives at the "naming stage" where he asks many questions regarding the words which distinguish objects and things in his environment. Up to this time the practice has usually been to depend upon pointing and special words for his satisfaction, as in "moo-moo" for milk. This illustrates the early tendency for the infant to classify objects and to use the terms needed to secure them through directive language. This process of communication can proceed, as it does between parents and their infants, by special languages which are privately understood and serve as adequately meaningful communication.

The early vocalizations of the child have been found to cover a wide range which reproduce phonemes that occur in diverse languages. Bean (1932) says, "One cannot fail to hear all the vowels and consonants, diphthongs, aspirates, sub-vocals, nasals, German umlauts and tongue trills, French throat trills and grunts, and even the Welsh 'l' " (p. 198).

During the babbling phase, the child repeats vowels and then consonants, and then combinations of these, over and over. These sounds become associated with significant happenings for the child, such as obtaining his food, having his parents play with him, being cuddled, and so forth. When the child first utters some "word" by random babbling, the favorable response of a parent who happens to be present then leads to the increased probability of that response recurring. This general phenomenon was dubbed by Thorndike (1943) the "Babble-Luck Theory" of language acquisition.

It is important to understand, however, that there are two kinds of processes at work: one is the actual use of a term and the other is its recognition. When a child responds verbally to his own needs—for example, for milk—and then uses this to stimulate others to provide him with what he requires, he directs the actions of others. On the other hand, he learns to recognize and then respond to the kind of utterances made by those around him, within a verbal community; in that case, he is obliged to act appropriately to a directive statement such as "play quietly."

As we have indicated earlier, the building of a set of semantic categories with implications for action depends upon the reinforcement properties of the verbal community (cf. Skinner, 1957). Essentially, the child utters some sounds and finds that they elicit positive responses from others, while other sounds are not similarly reinforced. In Mowrer's (1958) conception of learning, this pattern depends upon feelings. He says:

> Words are reproduced if and only if they are first made to *sound good* in the context of affectionate care and attention. Once words, as heard, take on positive emotional connotations, the stage is set for their reproduction, on a purely *autistic*, self-rewarding, noncommunicative basis. Then, once imitated, once reproduced, words can thereafter function in the interpersonal, social modes that we call language (p. 151).

For spoken language, the child takes on formal rules in a quite literal way. Berko (1958) has studied this process by the interesting device of giving children pictures with nonsense words and having them indicate responses revealing their knowledge of plurals, past tense, and so on. One of these is shown in Figure 9.2. The text is always read to the child.

She found that 75 per cent of pre-school children, ages four and five, could give the correct ending for the plural form in the example shown in Figure 9.2. For first-graders, age six, 99 per cent could give the correct form. For past tense, she showed a picture of a man exercising. Then the text read: "This is a man who knows how to gling. He is glinging. He did the same thing yesterday. What did he do yesterday? Yesterday he _____." She found that 63 per cent of the pre-school children and 80 per cent of the first-graders could give the correct form, "glinged."

Figure 9.2: The first of the pictures used in a study of children's knowledge of language forms, in this case the plural ending. (From Berko, 1958.)

English, however, is highly irregular in its endings. This accounts for the fact that the child may use a form such as "haved" or "had-ed" when using "have" in the past tense. The author's son at age four, having heard of "golfing," said one day—with admirable consistency —that "Daddy is tennising." English, as well as other languages, confounds the child's systematic learning.

THE CONFUSION OF WRITTEN AND SPOKEN FORMS

The complexity of language acquisition is also revealed in the problems of written language. The controversies concerning the alphabet, to which we have already referred, actually devolve about whether the letters of the alphabet have sufficient consistency of phonemic value for them to make their sound quality significant. It is not only, however, the problem of going from spoken to written language, or back, that proves vexacious. Another perceptual problem involved in language is revealed by the different forms that many letters of the alphabet take, whether they are in the upper case or lower case printed versions, or in their written versions. This is revealed in Figure 9.3. The

Figure 9.3: Three letters of the alphabet shown in each of three forms. While the forms are perceived to be alike in sharing a common stimulus property, they are actually quite different; this is seen better when they are shown as mirror images upside down, as at the right.

letter *a* is by no means the same in the three forms shown, just as is the case with *b* and *r* among other letters in the alphabet. The child, however, must learn to associate a common quality of "being an *a*" despite the differences in the perceptual configuration that is presented. Incidentally, the typical adult reaction to this example is to say that they do look alike, at least at first. The degree to which we have learned to see them as alike makes it very difficult *not* to see them in this fashion.

The written and spoken systems of language exist side by side, but as we have said, they differ in several important ways. In the first place, spoken language is not taught in the same explicit sense as is written language. We tend to reproduce involuntarily those sounds which are like the ones being made by the people around us. Furthermore, in the early learning of our first language, we do not understand enough actually to be tutored in its intricacies.

While written language is built upon letters and words, the spoken language is built on phonemes, morphemes, and the broader statements of a sentence. By the time we become adept in a spoken language, we no longer speak in terms of words as such, but through these broader statements. Not only does written language not follow spoken language, but we listen for particular things and fail to attend to others in talking with one another. Here is a bit of conversation reproduced in semi-phonetic fashion to illustrate the point:

> First person: "J'eet?"
> Second person: "No."
> First person: "S'koweet."

If we were to reproduce them in their written form, these sentences would be fuller and just as intelligible to the person knowing English. Consider, however, the problem of first learning to set down these sounds in written form, given the fact that the two systems in English, the writing system and talking system, are so different. This can be seen if we think of learning to write French. When we hear the French statement "c'est," for example, we are inclined to write it as it sounds in terms of our English word "say." Within English itself there are many common incongruities of spelling and sound. Some of these are shown in Table 9.1.

Table 9.1: Examples of inconsistencies between written and spoken language

so = go = tow = dough	cow = how *not* mow
to = do = goo = through	fowl = howl *not* bowl
toes = goes *not* does	mow = sew = though = toe
does = fuzz	though = grow *not* tough
	tough = muff

laughter = after
slaughter = water
later = waiter *not* water

As will be seen there, "so" equals "go" in pronunciation, but these do not equal "to" or "do." To get the "go" sound from "do" requires the addition of "ugh." One would think, therefore, that because of the equality of "to" and "do" that the same pronunciation would occur by adding "ugh" to "to." But, of course, that does not follow either.

The 26 letters of written English approximate only a little more than half of the sounds, or phonemes, which are required in the spoken language. Moreover, many sounds which we take for granted as being constant are not. Look at /th/, which is perhaps one of the most difficult pronunciations in English for the foreign learner. To begin with, it is not simply the addition of the *t* sound plus the *h* sound, but a unique combination which is associated with the Greek "theta." In spoken language, the /th/ yields at least two discernible sound patterns: as in "thin," with a good deal of aspiration, and "then," with little aspiration.

We are a long way, therefore, from the ideal of a high correspondence between the written and spoken forms of our language. Other languages than English have the difficulties we have noted, but they appear to be particularly acute in English.

PROBLEMS OF IDIOMATIC USAGE

Even having overcome the difficulties of acquiring a spoken language, there are also idiomatic phrases which present problems to the new learner. Languages are full of expressions which are not supposed to be taken literally and are thoroughly inconsistent—thus "slow up" and "slow down" are identical in meaning. This quality of language is perplexing, especially to the child unequipped by past experience to understand certain associations. Consider the youngster listening to his mother talking to a friend about last evening, and a father's late arrival: "Bill got *hung up* on that case and was *all in* when he got home. He's been *burning the midnight oil* for weeks on it and I think he should *have it out* with Fred instead of being *tied up in knots* all the time."

More than the literal language, then, there are also idiomatic expressions, colloquialisms, and special figures of speech which become incorporated into written and spoken language. These often function without awareness but with considerable effect upon our thoughts. It is to this feature of language that we will now move.

Functional features of language

An essential characteristic of any language is that its words stand for categories. Since perception is fundamentally a process of categorizing experience, it is not hard to see that language should play a significant role as a source of influence on the individual's psychological field. As Strauss (1953) notes, "The social import of language development in the child is not that he learns words but that he learns group classifications for countless objects and events. . . . Implicit in the name given to the object, if it is properly learned, are directives for actions toward that object, both covert as well as overt" (p. 106).

LINGUISTIC RELATIVITY

The effect of language on thought is at the heart of the viewpoint expressed by the anthropologist Sapir (1912, 1921). It was further developed by Whorf (1956) and has since come to be called the Whorf-Sapir concept of *linguistic relativity*. This concept asserts that cultural influences affect psychological processes through language. Thus, once learned, language provides grooves for thought.

Sapir contended that since different languages employed different systems of categorization, and had different syntax, the worlds in which individuals from different societies live are distinct worlds, and not the identical world with different labels. In one of his early writings on this point (1912), he used this illustration:

> . . . a certain type of animal in the physical environment of a people does not suffice to give rise to a linguistic symbol referring to it. It is necessary that the animal be known by the members of the group in common and that they have some interest, however slight, in it before the language of the community is called upon to make reference to this particular element of the physical environment (p. 228). . . . The case may be summarized . . . by saying that to the layman every animal form that is neither human being, quadruped, fish, nor bird, is a bug or worm (p. 230).

Thus, the nature and characteristics of the physical environment are interpreted through the categories established in language. As Whorf

(1956) has noted, the Eskimos have three words for snow because that distinction is important to them in coping with the physical environment. Similarly, in our society labeling by color names—such words as "mauve," "fawn," and "chartreuse"—is generally more finely made by women than by men. Lindesmith and Strauss (1956) have explained this simply by saying that the American woman is more motivated to distinguish between color words because of her interest in clothes and home decorations as important features of her environment (p. 51).

Whorf (1956) considered that these discriminations are a vital consequence of growing up within a given culture. As the sounds of a language are learned and their meanings associated, he says that the child is inclined to perceive some things and not others within the non-linguistic world about him. In the absence of such learned discriminations, it would be difficult for a person to be aware of differences. Thus, he comments:

> . . . if a race of people had the physiological defect of being able to see only the color blue, they would hardly be able to formulate the rule that they saw only blue. The term blue would convey no meaning to them, their language would lack color terms, and their words denoting their various sensations of blue would answer to, and translate, our words "light, dark, white, black," and so on, not our word "blue" (p. 209).

Whorf also made a major point of the structure of language as a determinant of thought. His research on American Indian languages led him to conclude, for example, that the noun-verb linkage was important in viewing and interpreting events.

A good deal of research has been conducted which touches on aspects of the linguistic relativity concept. Brown and Lenneberg in summarizing their studies (1958) indicate essential support for the concept. In one of these, they found that colors were more easily differentiated from memory if a color *name* could be "coded" and stored. Other pertinent research in this vein is exemplified in studies by Brown (1957), Carroll and Casagrande (1958), Doob (1960), Flavell (1958), Johnson (1962), Lenneberg and Roberts (1956), and Maclay (1956). Viewed overall, this research work indicates that linguistic variables have an active role in such psychological processes as color discrimination and concept formation.

SELF-DIRECTION AND PROBLEM-SOLVING

There is also evidence to suggest that language serves the important function of *self-direction*, long since pointed out by Lorimer (1929). Our personal thoughts about what we are to do are frequently taken over from the instructions learned from others. This is seen when the child says to himself, "No. No," in response to his own actions that he has been taught are wrong, or "First this part, then the other," when building. Because a key function of thought is problem-solving, what the individual concludes also depends upon the kinds of concepts available for self-direction.

The availability of alternatives in problem-solving is conditioned by concepts which are linguistically based. While there is still some disagreement as to whether words are essential to problem-solving and self-directed action, there is no question but that they do enter into these processes. Imagine, for example, what you would most like to do on your next vacation and note how many words pop into consciousness as you "see" some panorama of activity before you.

SEMANTIC CONFUSION

One difficulty that language poses is the confusion of words with things. Though the first is merely symbolic of the latter, people act very much as if they were inseparable. This is especially true in childhood. But adults are also vulnerable to this pitfall, which can be particularly troublesome in interpersonal and inter-group relationships.

While words stand for things, they are not the things themselves. The word "table" does not resemble a table, nor does it necessarily mean a given table, unless a definite article is used. Rather, it represents a category of things that have some common set of attributes. Categories, however, tend to obliterate important variations among the units within them.

Regarding ideas about race, for example, the word "Negro" can refer to anything from a person who is black to white in appearance, who may be a physician or laborer, who may speak any language from Oxfordian English to Zulu, who could be a follower of any number of religious practices, and so forth. Yet, as Hayakawa (1963) pointedly notes, the word "Negro" itself has considerable reality for many white people. It produces many semantic disturbances that are illogical. "It is useless to point out," he says, "that, if we in America regard as Negroes all who are part Negro, it would be just as logical to regard as white all who are part white. Many people will simply stare at you angrily and say, 'We don't *regard* part Negroes as Negroes. They *are* Negroes!' For many people, the word 'Negro' is indeed a 'thing'" (p. 19).

DENOTATION AND CONNOTATION

What a word signifies is usually referred to as its *denotative* meaning. The special and less direct sense which it conveys is referred to as its *connotative* meaning. Broadly, denotative meaning is confined to the function of verbally pointing at a thing or characteristic, while the connotative meaning has to do with the subtleties of evaluation about the thing referred to—or *referent*—including plus or minus valence. Thus, while the denotation of a referent may be the same, the connotation can be different. This is revealed in such word pairs as "tramp" and "vagabond," or "cheap" and "inexpensive," or "flashy" and "vivacious." The coloration of words represented in connotation is what makes languages interesting. It accounts for the assertion we sometimes hear that it is impossible to directly translate the "full meaning" of a term from another language.

Even the same word may have different connotations in different circumstances for different people. Consider a word like "buddy." It conveys different qualities of meaning when used by one soldier to refer to another, when used by a father as a term of affection for his son, or when used by a beggar on the street to ask for a dime to buy a cup of coffee. Sometimes we are brought up sharply by the special connotation conveyed by a familiar term. The writer recalls an occasion in an English restaurant when the waitress said of the manager, who was then evidently upbraiding some members of his staff, "He's a bit of a lad." A new connotation for the word "lad" suddenly became apparent.

THE SEMANTIC DIFFERENTIAL

A technique for the refined measurement of semantic connotations has been developed by Osgood, Suci, and Tannenbaum (1957). It is called the *semantic differential,* and its specific purpose is to get at the meaning of a given term—e.g. "mother," "country," "politics"—by ratings of the term or concept along several scales formed by bi-polar adjectives. These usually cover three factors called the *evaluative, potency,* and *activity* dimensions. For any adjective pair a rater makes just one rating of the concept.

In Figure 9.4 an illustrative semantic differential profile is shown for

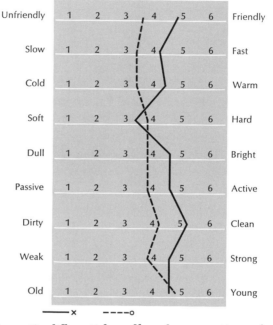

Figure 9.4: Semantic differential profiles of mean ratings of self (x) and leader (o) on nine scales for twenty subjects. (Based on data from Hollander, Julian, and Perry, 1966.)

the rating of "self" and the "group's leader." The first rating was obtained before a laboratory experiment, and the second after experience with an appointed group leader who, these subjects were led to believe, wanted the majority share of the group's profits. The evaluative factor is represented in the figure by the scales "friendly-unfriendly," "cold-warm," "bright-dull," and "clean-dirty." The potency factor there is covered by "hard-soft," "strong-weak," and "old-young." The two activity scales are "fast-slow" and "passive-active." In this case, the evaluative factor gave an overall difference between the self and leader ratings that was statistically significant. The other two factors showed scale differences, but these were not as marked as those for the total evaluative factor.

Research on the semantic differential by Osgood and his associates indicates that it has high reliability (cf. Osgood, 1960), particularly with respect to the evaluative factor, which essentially measures valence, i.e. like-dislike. Nunnally (1959) used the semantic differential in a field survey of attitudes toward the mentally ill and found that the "neurotic man" was viewed as relatively foolish and unpredictable compared to "self." Ratings of "psychotic man" were still more sharply different.

LINGUISTIC CODING AND SOCIAL INTERACTION

Language involves encoding a message which can readily be decoded by another individual. In social interaction there is a certain economy in using terms which convey information with brevity. When a word comes into increasing usage, it may be abbreviated or replaced by a shorter word. This phenomenon, known as Zipf's Law, was pointed out by Zipf (1935) who demonstrated its effect in several languages, including English and Chinese. In twentieth-century English, we see it in the following illustrative sequences:

    automobile—car
    television—TV
    motion picture—movie
    omnibus—bus.

Linguistic coding in general tends to facilitate thought and memory, as we noted in connection with the Brown and Lenneberg study of color names (1954). Where individuals interact frequently with one another, they share mutual benefits from such coding. This can be seen especially in occupations which require repetitive reference to objects or concepts which are vital to the ongoing effort. In an electrical supply store, there are many brief terms utilized to differentiate the thousands of pieces of equipment. The same thing is true of any "lingo" that develops as part of common activity, whether in medicine, art, or traffic engineering.

Linguistic coding is also a device for gaining social acceptance.

Fischer (1958) conducted interviews with children and found that the choice of "free variants" of a linguistic form, in this case the verbalized endings "ing" and "in'," was related to the child's sex, class, personality, and formality of the conversation. These variants, which have the same denotative meaning, have symbolic value because they signify to others the relative status of the speaker. In short, they can influence the recipient's perception of the child as "one of us."

Rosenthal (1957) found that the language used by young children was also a significant determinant of sociometric position in a group. The more "popular" children were found to use language which was more active than those children who were low on popularity. In terms of influence effects, the form of language itself conveyed a code about the child's relative standing in the group.

THE ABSTRACTION LADDER

Words in any language may also vary in terms of their abstractness. The quality of being "abstract" arises essentially from a word's removal from a concrete referent. A world such as "table" is low in abstractness, whereas words like "freedom" or "virtue" are very high, and more difficult to define. Thus, the word "democracy" has divergent meanings in the Communist and non-Communist countries of the world.

A word which is less readily tied to concrete referents is high on the abstraction ladder while one that is low can be made concrete more readily. However, the fact that a word is low on the abstraction ladder does not mean that it is necessarily limited in connotations. The word "money," for instance, is quite concrete but may conjure up all sorts of connotations. Other examples are "fireplace," "museum," and "mink coat."

One variety of semantic confusion is often created by using words which are highly abstract without supplying relevant referents to convey intended meaning. In fact, this kind of confusion is one of the propagandist's techniques for creating impressions by labeling. In this respect, Hayakawa (1963) says that educational practices tend to foster global abstractions that need to be understood more in terms of the concrete instance or referent. He says:

> Children are taught to read and write, and the more "fluently" they talk or write, the higher the grades they get. They are trained to

respond in specific ways to certain signals: "Christianity" ("a fine thing"), "the Constitution" ("a fine thing"), "Shakespeare" ("a great poet"), "Benedict Arnold" ("a traitor"), and so on. But, especially in the elementary and secondary schools, they are taught very little about how not to respond. Because Christianity, for example, is highly thought of, an organization practicing the opposite of Christian principles is likely to call itself a "Christian front"; because the Constitution is a "fine thing," it will occur to an anti-Democratic pressure group to call itself a "Committee to Uphold the Constitution" . . . (p. 24).

Language is also a potent device, then, for shaping the attitudes that people hold regarding aspects of their environment. In this respect, as well as in eliciting action, it holds significant directive features.

Directive features of language

The power of words to move people, to give impetus to their actions, is a vital feature of language. Carroll (1953) says, "it is overwhelmingly significant that every facet of a language system contributes to the way in which a community uses language in social control. Not only everyday conversation and address but also all the varieties of mass communication, such as propaganda and advertising, depend upon the precarious standards of a common language system" (pp. 112-113).

When language is used to influence others, it is said to be directive. The intent is to exercise a degree of control over their behavior. The mother says to the child, "Eat your lunch," in the hope of directing a behavioral sequence. An adjunct to such attempts is the potential in language for conveying a sense of future orientation. Thus, the mother may add the comment to the child, "And then you can have some candy." This provides the anticipation of a future reward which is far more difficult to establish without language.

THE "PROMISE" IN ADVERTISING

Hayakawa (1964) contends that virtually all directive statements have an implicit future-oriented element. By this means we transmit a sense of expectation, hope or fear, regarding consequences of presently urged action. The advertiser, wishing to influence customers, makes extensive use of such directive language. David Ogilvy, in his book

Confessions of an Advertising Man (1963), says that the "promise" contained in an advertisement is vital. Speaking to advertisers, he says: "Your most important job is to decide what you are going to say about your product, what benefit you are going to promise. Two hundred years ago Dr. Johnson said, 'Promise, large promise is the soul of an advertisement'" (p. 116).

Evidently, Dr. Johnson followed his own advice for, in auctioning off the contents of the Anchor Brewery, Ogilvy quotes him as having said: "We are not here to sell boilers and vats, but the potentiality of growing rich beyond the dreams of avarice." Ogilvy himself recounts various examples, among them one of his own advertisements for Helena Rubenstein's hormone cream headed "How women over 35 can look younger." Note the implicit promise and the use of a directive form in the words "how" and "can." He says: "The two most powerful words you can use in a headline are FREE and NEW. . . . Other words and phrases which work wonders are HOW TO, SUDDENLY, NOW, ANNOUNCING, INTRODUCING, IT'S HERE, JUST ARRIVED, IMPORTANT DEVELOPMENT, IMPROVEMENT, AMAZING, SENSATIONAL . . ." (pp. 131-2). And he then catalogues many others.

Advertisers spend literally billions of dollars each year to influence the attitudes of people toward their products. The American cigarette industry, for instance, has estimated yearly sales of about six billion dollars ($6,000,000,000), a substantial proportion of which goes into advertising. Just moving but 1 per cent of all sales to a given brand would mean a gain of $60,000,000 in additional annual revenues (Bauer, 1964, p. 322). Language is big business.

Even on a more modest scale, merely giving something a name with pleasant connotations may achieve a remarkable effect. Osgood (1960) refers to the fact that ". . . the cramped, standardized, insignificant little house with its postage stamp yard in 'Briarwood Valley,' in 'Larchmont Hills,' or in 'Sunnyvale Downs' somehow assumes a splendor and grace it could never have in 'Southside Brighton Avenue, Subdivision No. 7'" (p. 343).

THE USE OF SEMANTIC CONFUSION

This process of cognitive biasing is quite usual as a device communicators use to influence others. As observed in Chapter Six (p. 156), attitudes are prodded by attaching a positive symbol to something you are to approve, and a negative symbol to something you are to disapprove. In general, the intent of such labeling is deliberately to generate semantic confusion. It is often seen in two forms. One of these is the *degradation of language,* by abusing the meaning of a word or phrase. Recently a compact car was advertised as a "Big little beauty"; a further example is the use of a compound form such as "genuine imitation leather."

The other rather typical device is to make an assertion which, on examination, is *semantically empty.* Typically this will take the form of claims that a product is "the biggest selling of its kind" or "23% more effective by actual clinical tests." The specific referent and the bases for comparison are usually very ambiguous or entirely absent in these cases.

A way in which language can be degraded is set forth by George Orwell (1949) in his novel, *1984,* about a totalitarian state of the future. In the appendix to that work, he provides the basic ideas concerning "Newspeak," the language of thought control introduced by the ruling party of this society. Among the society's guiding slogans are: WAR IS PEACE, FREEDOM IS SLAVERY, IGNORANCE IS STRENGTH. By juxtaposing and equalizing opposites in this fashion, and limiting the availability of alternative words, an extreme form of language degradation occurs which Orwell calls "doublethink."

PROPAGANDA

All of these directive features of language are tools used by propagandists, whether they are advertisers, political figures, or industrial and labor spokesmen. The term "propaganda" has come into disrepute though its original meaning conveyed the essential idea of the dissemination of information. As used today, it most often refers to the presentation of selected information to influence others for the direct benefit of the propagandist or a cause which he serves. Thus, in wartime opposing governments routinely employ propaganda to influence not only the population in enemy lands but in their own country as well.

The techniques of propaganda have been described in various ways, but mainly they involve a highly contrived manipulation of symbols, through language, to create desired impressions. For example, in the propagandist's *message*, "facts" may be presented which are in themselves correct, but so sifted and slanted as to provide only one side of the case. This covers such techniques as the "focused truth" and "card-stacking," in which facts are selected and/or managed to yield a picture which is largely erroneous.

Deliberate cognitive biasing, discussed above, is frequently used by the propagandist in the techniques of "glittering generalities" or "transfer and testimony." In the first instance, a false conclusion may be foisted on the audience as a palatable and overly simple generalization to explain complex social phenomena, such as: "The Republican Party is the party of depression," and its counterpart, "The Democratic Party is the party of war." In transfer and testimony, the propagandist enlists a positive symbol, such as a baseball star, to endorse his breakfast cereal, thus hoping to raise the positive valence of his product and increase sales. The foundation for these attempts in "psycho-logic" is apparent (see Chapter Six, p. 156).

Finally, the propagandist can also present *himself* in ways designed to maximize positive group identity. By the "bandwagon" technique, he emphasizes that many others just like the members of the audience are with him on the "winning side," or in "buying the most popular car in America." By the technique known as "plain folks," the politician in particular may appeal to his audience as "one of the people," whether they are farmers—in which case he plays up his "roots on the farm"—or businessmen—in which case he points out that he "knows what it is to meet a payroll."

On a broader level, propaganda is necessarily practiced artfully by political leaders. In a democracy, political speeches are often informative and ennobling. At their best they can challenge people to great enterprises, as the speeches of a Roosevelt or a Churchill did. However, political communication does include the invocation of symbols highly charged with propagandistic intent. At the extreme, the demagogic orator does not persuade so much as he inflames. What he says may make little sense actually, but he sways his audience by the incessant use of loaded symbols. Hitler, for example, repeatedly used terms such as "Manifest Destiny," "Master Race," and "Aryan Blood" in his speeches.

In general, political terminology indulges in semantic confusion, much of it quite contrived. In this regard, the political writer C. L. Sulzberger (1960) observes:

France's Radical-Socialist party is neither Radical nor Socialist. Khrushchev, Tito, Nehru, and Hugh Gaitskell all employ the word "socialism" to convey contradictory ideas. And what about democracy, that precious Athenian term? It no longer has the least semantic significance. Pakistan's "controlled democracy" looks like benevolent despotism and Indonesia's "guided democracy" resembles chaos. The "popular democracies" of Eastern Europe are both unpopular and undemocratic. Each power coalition proclaims, while arming to the teeth, profound interest in peace. However, as Clausewitz remarked: "A conqueror is always a lover of peace" (p. 5).

Susceptibility to the effects of propaganda is not, however, inevitable or fixed. For one thing, as we noted more extensively in Chapter Six, a transactional view of communication considers various lines of resistance to such influence attempts. We are not therefore merely the passive receivers of propagandistic appeals, though they can do incalculable harm, especially with the highly credulous—the young, the under-educated, the inexperienced, as well as fanatics. Furthermore, as Kottman (1964) has found, the more adept individuals are in using language, the less likely they are to be influenced or misled by others' statements. With a more facile command of language, the individual evidently has a stronger attachment to the meaning of a verbal symbol and is less vulnerable to having it altered. This could be good or bad in its consequences. In either case, it encourages more precision in language usage and a greater respect for its enormous power.

As is apparent, the issues we have been considering about directive language mesh with many areas of interest in social psychology. These would include the phenomena of social interaction, leadership, conformity and attitude change, among others. Indeed, it is hard to conceive of social influence without some intervention by language.

SUMMARY

A significant defining characteristic of Man is his use of language. More than a means for transmitting information, language is an important part of culture which directly affects the individual psychologically. Its content can shape the perception and, in general, the thought and action of individuals. Language may be studied in terms of its *structure and form,* its *acquisition,* and its *functional* features including its *directive* use as an influence device.

There are several major theories about the origin of language. None of these, however, satisfactorily accounts for the abstract quality of language since they usually treat language in limited terms. Changes in language appear to follow the pattern of cultural innovation more generally.

Words are structural units of language that convey symbolic representations. They "stand for" but are *not the same as* their "referents," e.g. objects, things, events, actions. The words of a language may be spoken or written. The distinction between these two *forms* of language is very important, though confusion about their relationship persists. Our alphabet, for example, is merely a set of standard symbols which can be combined together to form other symbols, i.e. written words. They also can be pronounced in various combinations, in terms of sound patterns, as a word. These basic sound patterns, the smallest units of spoken language, are called *phonemes.* They are not identical to letters. Thus, a given letter of the alphabet may be pronounced with more than a single phoneme while more than one letter may be necessary to yield a single phoneme.

The learning of language is one of the most complex tasks confronting the young child in a society. Basically, it necessitates learning complex associations between sounds and the objects which they denote. Later as these sounds, or phonemes, are put together in various combinations, they come to stand for words as well as "broader statements." A sentence constitutes such a statement made up of a number of words which are constructed from phonemes. Even more complex than learning words and their associations orally is the acquisition of written language. Here the child is obliged to go from a spoken form to a system of writing which is frequently not consistent. The linguistic conventions of English are irregular and difficult to learn.

The acquisition of language can be viewed as involving the reinforcement contingencies existing in what Skinner calls a "verbal community." This process is instigated by the child's early "babbling" which comes to be reinforced in terms of sounding words and relating them to objects and experiences. Words may be recognized and acted on without being part of the individual's usable vocabulary.

The most significant *psychological function* of language lies in its effect on the individual's psychological field. These functional features of language have been identified with the writings of Sapir and Whorf. Their viewpoint has been referred to as the Whorf-Sapir concept of *linguistic relativity*. In general, this position considers language as a cultural influence upon psychological processes of perception and thought. This influence comes about through the categorization of experience in terms of the culturally defined emphases embodied in language.

Another functional feature of language has to do with the distinction between the specific *referent* that is *denoted* by a word and the meaning that may also be *connoted* by it. Denotative meaning is usually considered to be confined to verbally pointing at a thing, while connotative meaning has to do with subtleties of meaning. The study of meaning is called *semantics*. Various techniques have been devised for measuring the connotative meaning of words. A prominent procedure in current use is the *semantic differential* developed by Osgood and his colleagues.

Words also represent "codes" for conveying meaning briefly. Such *linguistic codes* affect thought and problem-solving and also have a facilitating effect upon social interaction. Words may vary, too, in terms of their abstractness. The *abstraction ladder* refers to how removed a word may be from a concrete referent. The word "table" is low in abstraction; the words "freedom" or "virtue" are very high in abstraction. *Semantic confusion* is often created by using words high on the abstraction ladder without supplying concrete referents.

Language is employed in a *directive* way when the intent is to influence the attitudes and behavior of individuals. Children use it in this fashion to make their desires known to parents, and parents in turn to affect the child's actions. A widespread use of directive language is seen in advertising and political activities. This mode of social communication capitalizes on the power of language to influence others, often through semantic confusion and cognitive biasing. *Propaganda* is the name usually applied to the presentation of information for the benefit of the propagandist or his cause. It involves the manipulation of symbols regarding both the "facts" in his *message* as well as in the way he presents *himself* to the audience in terms of group identity. Resistance to propaganda depends in part on an attachment to the meaning of words.

SUGGESTED READINGS

From E. P. Hollander and R. G. Hunt. (Eds.) *Current perspectives in social psychology.* (2nd Edition.) New York: Oxford University Press, 1967:

Introduction to Section IV—*Language and communication*
21. Charles E. Osgood and Thomas A. Sebeok: *Communication and psycholinguistics*
22. Norman N. Markel: *The basic principles of descriptive linguistic qnalysis*
23. S. I. Hayakawa: *The language of social control*
24. Charles E. Osgood: *On the nature of meaning*
25. Roger Brown: *How shall a thing be called?*
26. B. F. Skinner: *The verbal community*
27. George A. Miller: *The psycholinguists: on the new scientists of language*

SELECTED REFERENCES

Brown, R. W. *Words and things.* Glencoe, Ill.: The Free Press, 1958.
Carroll, J. B. *The study of language.* Cambridge, Mass.: Harvard Univer. Press, 1953.
*Hayakawa, S. I. *Language in thought and action.* (Second edition.) New York: Harcourt Brace, 1964.
*Miller, G. A. *Language and communication.* New York: McGraw-Hill, 1951.
Osgood, C. E., Suci, G. J., & Tannenbaum, P. H. *The measurement of meaning.* Urbana: Univer. of Illinois Press, 1957.
*Pei, M. *The story of language.* New York: New American Library, Mentor Books, 1960.
*Sapir, E. *Language: An introduction to the study of speech.* New York: Harvest, 1949.
*Whorf, B. L. *Language, thought, and reality.* Edited and with an introduction by J. B. Carroll. Cambridge: MIT Press Paperback Edition, 1964.

10

Personality functioning in society and culture

Personality is a way of referring to each individual's uniqueness. Just how much the culture of a society molds individual personality no one can say. However, there is widespread agreement that a person's distinguishing characteristics are inextricably bound up with the society in which he lives. This relationship is a direct outgrowth of the fact that an individual's personality develops as a function of social adjustment. The life-long necessity to balance individual needs and social requirements is vital in this process.

Regarding the interdependence of the individual and society, Kluckhohn and Murray (1948) say:

> . . . as social animals, men must adjust to a condition of interdependence with other members of their society and of groups within it, and, as cultural animals they must adjust to traditionally defined expectations. All men are born helpless into an inanimate and impersonal world which presents countless threats to survival; the human species would die out if social life were abandoned. Human adaptation to the external environment depends upon that mutual support which is social life . . . (p. 36).

In this chapter our major focus will be upon the way the individual personality is both influenced by and influences social processes. Because personality consists of manifest behaviors as well as underlying psychological states, our interest will be directed not only to the typical modes of response that an individual displays to others but also to the attitudes and values which are part of his psychological field.

Some definitions of personality

The concept of personality is so broad that it is very difficult to define precisely. Indeed, there are a great many definitions of personality which have been offered, from its early origins in the Greek word *persona* or mask (cf. G. W. Allport, 1937). One central problem concerns the development of personality and the extent to which the social environment conditions its qualities apart from organismic tendencies. Murphy (1947), for example, considers that the structure of personality arises from a complex "bio-social" process. It is not a simple matter therefore to say where these individual biological and physiological tendencies leave off and social influences begin since they are not observed in total isolation. Summing up this point, Linton (1945) asserts that "the main problem involved in the definition of personality is one of delimitation. The individual and his environment constitute a dynamic configuration all of whose parts are so closely interrelated and in such constant interaction that it is very hard to tell where to draw lines of demarcation" (p. 84).

Kluckhohn and his colleagues indicate that in some ways human beings are like all others; in some ways like some others; and in certain respects like no others (1953, p. 53). In the first category we might place certain of the basic survival needs of Man. In the second, we could point to the broad cultural similarities of people who, for example, speak the same language. In the third category, we deal with those *finely defined* differences that make for individuality. This latter element is distinctively a matter of personality which, for purposes of definition, we can consider to be the *sum total of an individual's characteristics which make him unique.*

However personality is defined, as a concept it depends upon a strong tendency to view individuals as the major locus of their own behavior. This is the essence of perceived "individuality." Krasner and Ullmann (1965) have expressed this tendency as follows: "It seems that if an observer does not know the antecedents, the behavior is attributed to the person, while if he has knowledge or control, he is inclined to consider the behavior to be superficial. We are . . . ingrained with the concept that people should be responsible for the production of their own behavior . . ." (p. 270).

Levels and aspects of personality

Any definition of personality refers to an individual's distinctive characteristics, whether behavioral or in the form of psychological states. People attach significance to these individual differences, and the individual himself usually has a sense of his own identity in terms of his self-concept. Another kind of distinction, then, concerns the external manifestations of qualities of personality and their inner workings. These can be characterized respectively as the *external* level and the *internal* level of personality. Furthermore, personality has varying aspects of permanence. It has a *dynamic* aspect, in the sense of allowing for change, as well as a *consistent* aspect, which provides continuity over time.

The external level of personality is represented by the typical behaviors of an individual and the way he affects other people in terms of what is called his "social stimulus value." Such behaviors can be "expressive" of feelings or be more in the nature of qualities of "performance." Apart from the acknowledged merit of their compositions, it is interesting, for example, to see the distinctive expressive characteristics of the musical notation used by three great composers, as shown in Figure 10.1. While expressive behavior of this kind can be revealing of some qualities of personality, it cannot convey the full richness of psychological states which lie beneath nor reveal a great deal about performance abilities. Using the boldly expressive notation of a Beethoven, in short, does not make a composer his peer.

The intra-psychic features of the individual—including his attitudes and values, his interests and acquired motives in the psychological field —represent a set of interrelationships on the internal level. In general, it is supposed that these two levels should be in harmony with one another so that the individual behaves with an adequate "integration" between them. Thus, people who seem to behave in one way but are perceived to be motivated in another are sometimes considered to be devious.

I

II

III

Figure 10.1: Musical notations from the works of three composers: I. Mozart; II. Bach; and III. Beethoven. (From Wolff, 1943.)

Personality functioning can be approached on either or both of these levels. In the first instance, observation of behavior is the primary technique employed. In the second, attitude scales or projective tests can be used to get at underlying dispositions. However, what is obtained from one line of study is by no means congruent with what is obtained from the other. For example, if a person behaves in a "dominant" fashion this may or may not accurately reveal the less apparent qualities of the person. An inference could be incorrectly drawn that he has a superior view of himself when, in fact, it could be the reverse; he might feel inferior to others and be compensating accordingly. Furthermore, two individuals may be similarly motivated or hold similar attitudes but behave quite differently, as we noted in Chapter Five. How we act is very much determined by social interaction and the situation in which it occurs.

Personality has a dynamic aspect because humans carry the effects of learning. While social psychology recognizes that there are stable features of personality across situations, changes can and do occur as a result of new experience. When an individual encounters a dramatically new situation or identity, through marriage, advanced education, extensive travel, adversity, or other profound experience, his outlook and response tendencies may be altered. Even going from one social situation to another, as we noted in connection with the concept of role, his behavior will be altered, if only in a transitory way.

But, at the same time, personality is consistent. The individual is usually found to have a characteristic mode of approaching the world, dealing with frustration, and seeking certain long-range goals in the form of values. These are probably best considered as elements of the individual's psychological field which are less susceptible to change. In this respect, George Kelly (1963) views personality as a way of construing the world, including the perception of self in relationship to it. Put in other terms, we may say that personality involves stable cognitive processes that generate a characteristic "style." It is in this sense that, even after a lapse of time and new experience, a person is still recognized by others as "the same old Jack."

A schematic representation of personality

As we have seen, personality is composed of external behaviors affecting others as well as internal features relating to the individual's disposition toward the world. In this section we will be making a further distinction about external behaviors, specifically in terms of those which are *typical responses* and those which are *role-related*. The internal, less visible quality of personality, we can think of as a *psychological core*.

In Figure 10.2 we have schematically represented these as concentric

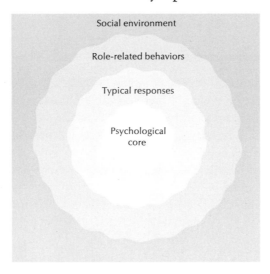

Figure 10.2: Schematic representation of personality within social environment.

rings. This diagram is useful in understanding the structure of personality, and the relationship between its components, though it is not to be taken as a literal "picture" of personality. As will be seen in the diagram, the core is the central feature of personality. It embodies the individual's psychological states, capacities, residues of past experience, and in short the things we associate both with the psychological field as well as unconscious elements. Moving outward toward increased contact with the social environment, the typical responses of the individual refer to such things as his characteristic activity level, sense of humor, and ways of responding to frustration, all of which are associated with his learned modes of adjustment. Role-related behavior is that behavior most subject to the particular social context in which the individual finds himself, and it is therefore more susceptible to social demands made there. The wavy lines between these components are intended to suggest permeability. There is a flow of experiences through these boundaries. Thus, the core of personality may lead to certain typical responses, but these responses may in turn affect the psychological field.

By way of further distinguishing these components, we can now delve into them somewhat more to discern their special quality, beginning with the core.

THE PSYCHOLOGICAL CORE

The psychological core of an individual's personality contains his psychological field, and also less conscious effects of past experience. Most significantly, it holds the individual's *self-concept*—his image of what he is like. This is the centerpiece of personality functioning because, as Murphy (1947) notes, "The individual perceives himself as figure in the figure-ground pattern that is each social group" (p. 766). How the person values himself, in regard to self-esteem, has been found to be an especially significant factor in receptivity to social influence, as we shall see.

As the individual interacts with the social environment from earliest childhood, he develops a picture of what the world is like and a set of perceptions of himself. Furthermore, as we said in connection with the discussion of attitudes and values in Chapter Five, these perceptions guide behavior by providing a relatively coherent and stable approach to the environment.

A way of describing personality, then, is in terms of the individual's perceptions of self and others. This is one of the major lines of study in contemporary social psychology. Its rationale can be simply stated as follows: to the extent that we know how the individual perceives and attaches meaning to the situation in which he finds himself, successful predictions can be made about his behavior.

This approach can be characterized as *dispositional* insofar as it stresses qualities of the individual that are brought into the context of social interaction. Projective testing, for example, relies upon this characterization of personality. It is, moreover, an essential feature of psychotherapy. In that process an extended contact occurs between a therapist and a client during which the client relates experiences in terms of *his* perception of them.

Whether consciously or unconsciously, it is widely conceded that people behave as they see and are motivated toward things. In one formulation of this, the psychoanalyst Karen Horney (1945) contends that there are three dominant ways of approaching the environment. Some individuals, she says, tend to move *toward* other people, some move *away* from other people, and some move *against* other people. This pattern of movement can be viewed as embodying typical responses which grow out of the dispositions in the psychological core.

TYPICAL RESPONSES

All of us have observed that some people we know seem good-natured, others intelligent, others aggressive or quick to emotional reactions, others jolly, and so on. We take this consistency largely for granted, even though it may be somewhat variable as a result of social circumstances. Sometimes we encounter a person only in a given situation, fulfilling a given role, and generalize excessively about the person's typical personality from just that limited basis. We say a teacher is "serious" or a comedian "jolly" little knowing whether this is generally the case or only a sign of the behavior produced by a social role.

When we first come to know someone, there is a tendency to describe his behavior and then to see it in terms of an underlying force that dictates certain patterns. The older concept of "trait" is precisely of this order. In discussing that concept, G. W. Allport (1966) has said: "Our initial observation of behavior is only in terms of adverbs of action: John behaves aggressively. Then an adjective creeps in: John has an aggressive disposition. Soon a heavy substantive arrives, like William James' cow on the doormat: John has a trait of aggression. The result is the fallacy of misplaced concreteness" (p. 1). Allport then considers the other extreme and points out that if we only describe the behavior of an individual, we may wind up with an empty organism without expectancies, attitudes, motives, capacities, and so on. We need to know more, therefore, about these less apparent qualities of the individual that may dispose him to characteristic behavior.

The alternative to traits is to recognize that individuals may have dispositions toward certain behaviors but that these dispositions are actuated as a result of the individual's perception of the situation. Viewed as an adjustive process, then, we can more readily see that the way an individual typically behaves depends upon his perception of present circumstances based upon his past learning. If we choose to use the word "trait" we should understand that it refers to recognizable typical responses rather than some underlying force which dictates such responses. In short, traits are behaviors. From these we infer certain things about the personality core.

ROLE-RELATED BEHAVIORS

In Chapters Seven and Eight we considered roles to be behaviors which are appropriate to the expectations of others in a given situation. Figure 10.2 indicates this feature of personality by showing role-related behavior to have the closest proximity to the social environment. In this respect, behavioral changes from one situation to another exemplify the dynamic aspect of personality.

Roles also have an interrelationship with an individual's typical behaviors and his construction of the situation in terms of his psychological core. Some roles are more lasting and more congenial to the individual's self-concept than are others. Thus, a role may be highly peripheral and short-lived, or it may be a major feature of his personal identity. Consider, for example, the person called to jury duty for the first time. The role of juror is new to him though he has some inkling about its requirements in advance. It is not, however, a dominant or persisting feature of his life. On the other hand, being a corporation executive, or a physician, or a military figure has a more pervasive effect upon the whole personality of the individual because of the totality and persistence of the role itself. It will affect many of his relationships. The man who has reached the rank of general in the armed forces is continually reminded of his prestigious position by other individual's actions toward him which in turn affect the core of his personality, most notably his self-esteem, but also his attitudes and values. Here we have one instance of the way in which a role carries a special impact as a significant feature of the psychological field.

Some roles, then, are far more central to an individual's own identity and view of himself than others. Furthermore, a particular role into which an individual is cast may "fit" the other components of his personality, or it may not. For example, an executive may very much enjoy his high prestige and power, but perhaps dislike some other demands made upon him, such as the pressure for decisions. This problem is especially inherent in roles which can involve conflicting values. A professor, for instance, may like the intellectual give-and-take of the classroom while disliking the task of evaluating and grading students which is another feature of his role.

While it is possible to talk about individual personality as if it were self-contained, the socially demanded relations between individuals have distinct effects on its functioning. The very conception of who we are and what we are depends upon social interaction within the framework of roles. This is seen with particular sharpness in connection with the influence of age-sex roles on behavior. One example of this influence comes from the work of Mirra Komarovsky (1946). She found that many students in an eastern women's college reported an inconsistency between their own intellectual interests and achievements and the "feminine" role. Because a major interpersonal task of that role is to find a suitable mate, Komarovsky indicates that her women students had to indulge in concealment tactics to conform to the expectations of their dates. Two typical comments were these:

> My mother thinks that it is very nice to be smart in college but only if it doesn't take too much effort. She always tells me not to be too intellectual on dates, to be clever in a light sort of way (p. 185).
> On dates I always go through the "I-don't-care-anything-you-want-to-do" routine. It gets monotonous but boys fear girls who make decisions. They think such girls would make nagging wives (p. 188).

Evidently, the conflict produced by a sex role is most sharply felt by women who have the interest and capacity to go on to professional careers. A study by Wallin (1950) in a coed university setting found that the vast preponderance of women students were oriented toward marriage rather than a career. Accordingly, very few of them reported any necessity to play down their intellectual interests and competence possibly because these were considerably more limited.

Such examples merely serve to point up the importance to personality functioning of the social expectancies associated with roles. However, they also suggest the broader process of adjustment that an individual undergoes in fulfilling his potentialities within the framework of organized society.

Some issues in characterizing personality

An item in *The New Yorker's* "Talk of the Town" (March 12, 1966, p. 45) neatly captures a major issue in characterizing personality. One young working girl is reported saying to another, "You should speak up to your boss more and assert yourself." The other replies, "I'm just not programmed that way."

Though its overtones are distinctly humorous, as befits the source, this item poses the question of what the "programming" of personality might mean. McDougall (1908) is remembered for putting forth a view which might have considered the young lady to have been programmed by response tendencies that were instinctive. Yet, McDougall actually recognized that there also must be a latitude for learning to respond. It was precisely in this connection that he introduced the concept of *sentiment*, which we take today to be "attitude." The most important of these sentiments, he said, was "self-regard," and added: "Insofar as they [sentiments] are associated with a strong master sentiment of self-regard . . . we are self-determined rather than impelled by our instincts" (1936, p. 140). Thus, even McDougall, who was so identified with an instinctual viewpoint, underscored the importance of processes of adjustment which gave rise to learning. He also was acknowledging the significant effect of the individual's perception of self, which we have stressed here as the self-concept (see Boden, 1965).

Returning to our young lady, the question of programming can now be viewed in terms of the influences of her past experiences on her response tendencies. Thus, though she might hesitate to speak back to her boss, as a result of past interactions with him or others in a similar role relationship, she might quite readily speak back to a brother or sister or parent or friend. There would be situational variations in her reactions which would suggest that this programming, if it can be called that at all, is still subject to the social context of interaction.

In the instance just given, we have been focusing on a relationship with an authority figure. This kind of relationship is a fundamental source of interaction tendencies, stemming from early childhood. Thus, Shaw and Ort (1953) cite an example reported by Fisher and Hanna of a barber who had been intimidated in childhood by his father and an older brother. When anyone with an authoritative manner requested his services, he became so agitated that he was unable to wield his clippers (p. 6). Here again we are dealing *not* with an instinct but a learned response that is strongly inculcated through early experience.

It is clear that personality depends on a multiplicity of social contacts and influences beginning in early life. A number of these have been treated in Chapter Five and will be further considered in the next chapter dealing with subcultures. It will be useful here, nonetheless, to make a point again concerning early experience in personality development, and to examine it more closely.

Previously we noted that the socialization of the child has redounding consequences in later life. It is widely agreed among authorities in the area that the child's family determines in considerable degree the social influences to which he is subjected as well as the responses that are socially defined as desirable. There is also agreement that certain patterns of early experience can produce personality characteristics which persist into later life, though this effect is not considered to be the result of one crucial event.

An emphasis on early experience is founded not only on the influential views of Freud, but also on accumulated knowledge about human socialization and animal behavior. One kind of demonstration of this effect comes from experimentation on the hoarding behavior of rats deprived of food in early life (Hunt, 1941). These rats showed a significantly higher rate of food hoarding than their litter mates who were not thus deprived. Other work on puppies has indicated that marked differences in development occurred among those who had been deprived of normal stimulation in their environment during the early weeks of their lives (Thompson and Melzack, 1956). Harlow in his research with infant monkeys has found profound effects on the later adult behavior of monkeys who were deprived of affection from a mother monkey (1962).

Given the weight of evidence, therefore, it is not surprising that humans should also be seen to react in distinctive ways to early deprivation. A variety of data have been accumulated to bolster this point. Thus, a contention in the field of child psychology (e.g. Ribble, 1944, and Spitz, 1945) runs to the effect that a lack of "mothering'" of the young infant may result in marked psychological damage, including depression and retardation of development. However, these effects may be readily overstated. As Orlansky (1949) observed from his review of such studies,

> In the normal range of infant experience . . . we believe that events subsequent to the first year or two of life have the power to "confirm or deny" the personality of the growing infant, to perpetuate or remake it, depending upon whether the situation of later childhood perpetuates or alters the situation in which the infant was reared (p. 35).

The subsequent development of personality, under normal circumstances, thus becomes involved in more complex relationships. Because of the range of variables, including physiological functioning, which enter into the process, a number of issues persist regarding the characterization of personality. Among these is the idea of traits as deep-seated forces, somewhat analogous to instincts. While this is not a popular position in social psychology, it is useful to consider this issue a bit further.

TRAIT AND DISPOSITIONAL CONCEPTS OF PERSONALITY FUNCTIONING

Historically, the most common way of approaching personality has been in terms of traits. *Traits* have traditionally referred to the individual's typical behaviors which are sometimes assumed to be based in innate factors, such as instincts. As McClelland (1951) notes, "Trait psychology represents one of the earliest attempts to introduce some kind of order into the multiplicity of human responses. Its approach is simple. It consists of looking for consistencies in behavior" (p. 117).

One of the most common of the trait typologies is extroversion and introversion. Though this concept has a long history, it was popularized

and is most identified with the writings of the psychoanalyst Carl Jung
(see 1959). As an illustration of how these terms are used to type people consider these characterizations from Eysenck (1965):

> The typical extrovert is sociable, likes parties, has many friends,
> needs to have people to talk to, and does not enjoy reading or study-
> ing by himself. He craves excitement, takes chances, often sticks his
> neck out, acts on the spur of the moment, and is generally an im-
> pulsive individual. . . . The typical introvert, on the other hand, is
> a quiet, retiring sort of person, introspective, fond of books rather
> than people; he is reserved and distant except with intimate friends.
> He tends to plan ahead, "looks before he leaps," and distrusts the
> impulse of the moment . . . (p. 59).

One major difficulty with such characterizations of a "pure type" is
that they omit a great deal of individual variation around the major
types, as well as mixtures that can occur. It is possible, of course, as Eysenck has done, to develop a psychological test of extroversion-introversion and consider people to be extroverts or introverts who score high
at either extreme. But this is not the same as saying that the population
distributes itself naturally into these two distinct behavioral groupings,
nor that people are necessarily consistent across different circumstances.
The danger, of course, is that labels of this kind can be misleading, especially since they tend to disregard situational variations. Thus, in
looking at the characterizations quoted above, many readers will doubt-
less feel with the writer that there are some things in both descriptions
which seem true of oneself.

Moving to another realm, even such a characteristic as "punctuality"
has been found by Dudycha (1936) to have low stability in four different
situations. He checked records for students and obtained measures on
their punctuality in returning library books, turning in their class assignments, returning course change cards to the registrar, and meeting
appointments. He found very low intercorrelations between these independent measures, the average being .19.

Similarly, Hartshorne and May (1928) report considerable variability in the "honesty" of children studied under varying situational circumstances. By ingenious methods they studied a large number of
children in a variety of conditions in which honesty or dishonesty could
be observed. For example, in one condition they returned their test
papers so the children themselves could each grade his or her own.

Their actual responses were known and this permitted the researchers to determine any changes made as the teacher read the correct answers aloud. While a few children were found who were consistently honest, and a few who were consistently dishonest, most varied considerably depending upon the circumstances. The results clearly established that honesty was not a stable trait but varied as a reaction to a given situation.

There are some central features of personality that do, however, appear to have stability over time. Thus, Stott (1957) studied children during a period of twelve years. Beginning in nursery school they were observed and rated on "ascendance" in spontaneous interaction. He found that this characteristic had a marked degree of stability, with only a few temporary changes from a consistent pattern. It should be borne in mind, though, that an interpersonal characteristic such as ascendance is likely to be heavily determined by the reinforcement provided in past interaction and therefore is not a trait in the classic sense of the term so much as it is a learned mode of adjustment which holds across many situations.

The most serious deficiency of trait typologies in understanding personality functioning is that they largely ignore the relationship between a person and his environment. They focus exclusively on responses and are excessively broad. Therefore, their application for prediction is limited, except in extreme instances. Lazarus (1963) says that the trait approach

> is most useful when the person's behavior patterns are absolutely consistent—that is, characteristic of a person regardless of circumstances. What limits the usefulness of any trait or type system is the problem of degree of trait generality. The statement that a person has the trait of submissiveness is useful for prediction only insofar as he is submissive in all or most situations. If he is submissive only in certain circumstances, then we can predict his behavior accurately only if we know what those circumstances are (p. 57).

A more inclusive view of personality attends to the *dispositions* which lead to certain typical responses rather than just to the responses themselves. The concept of a disposition acknowledges the intervening influence of the individual's psychological field on his reactions to social stimuli. It is, therefore, much more given to the "cognitive style" notion in terms of the individual's perception of the world and his interaction with it. In this vein, G. W. Allport (1955) observes,

> . . . the most comprehensive units in personality are broad inten-tional dispositions, future-pointed. These characteristics are unique for each person, and tend to attract, guide, inhibit the more ele-mentary units to accord with the major intentions themselves. This proposition is valid in spite of the large amount of unordered, im-pulsive, and conflictful behavior in every life (p. 92).

Among the dispositions which have been studied as features of per-sonality are authoritarianism, dogmatism, achievement motivation, risk-taking, internal or external control, category width, social desirability, manifest anxiety, and persuasibility. These represent various measures of personality that we will be considering later in this chapter. Each is employed in research on personality which aims at determining the processes by which individuals react differently to essentially similar stimuli. Each measure also embodies a conception of personality which contains cognitive as well as behavioral elements. Thus, while the tra-ditional trait approach attempts to measure consistent responses, such as extroversion or introversion, dominance or submission, the disposi-tional approach seeks to get at the psychological components of the individual's responses to the social environment.

TRANSACTIONAL CONCEPTIONS OF PERSONALITY

The dynamic aspect of personality has been treated here largely as a process of adjustment to the social environment. But this leaves out an important process, that is, the individual's action on the social environ-ment. The individual copes with his environment, within the range of responses available to him, in order to exert his influence or control over it. This idea is emphasized in G. W. Allport's concept of *pro-action* (1960b). In his earlier book, *Becoming* (1955), he says, "Personality is less a finished product than a transitive process. While it has some stable features, it is at the same time continually undergoing change" (p. 19).

In these terms, Allport characterizes personality as an "open system" involving a mutual interaction or *transaction* between the person and his environment (1960a). He presents several criteria of open systems which can be paraphrased as follows: they involve an intake and output of energy or action in terms of a continuing commerce; they achieve and attempt to maintain equilibrium or balance, in the sense of homeostasis; they tend to increase in their order or structure as they become more complex in time.

Applying this scheme more concretely, we can anticipate that some individual behaviors will be internally motivated as actions on the environment rather than reactions to it. This is a phenomenon which can be ascribed to the "effectance motivation"—the motivation to be competent in dealing with the environment—on which White (1959) places great stress (see Chapter Four). Furthermore, such striving will be bound up with the individual's desire to retain a coherent and stable self-concept. Maintenance of its integrity is especially crucial to the equilibrium of personality, with particular regard to central attitudes. Thus, as Levine (1963) aptly notes, challenging a man's honesty creates a disruption of equilibrium which is far stronger than if it were his choice in neckties that was at stake (p. 45). Finally, the addition of new experiences, new motivations and social demands, requires an increasingly more elaborate organization of personality to accommodate the increased diversity of elements.

Most importantly, the transactional conception makes the individual the focus of social influence processes. For example, it recognizes that the need for identity leads to a reaching out to take hold of a group, or a cause, or a responsibility. The person is not merely a receptacle into which these social entities are poured but an active agent transacting with them (see Chapter Four).

All in all, the nub of the matter resides in McDougall's (1936) sentiment of "self-regard," or what has more recently been dubbed *self-esteem*. This disposition, as part of the self-concept, has the greatest ramifications for social interaction and its influence effects. Though inclined to stability, the self-concept is still affected by the atmospherics of social situations and the other people there. We have all had the experience of becoming vaguely aware that we are not quite the person we believed we were, thus perceiving our "self" in a new light. By his notion of the "looking-glass self," Cooley (1922) accounts for the dynamics of this effect on the self-concept:

> As we see our face, figure, and dress in the glass, and are interested in them because they are ours, and pleased or otherwise with them according as they do or do not answer to what we would like them to be; so in imagination we perceive in another's mind some thought

of our appearance, manners, aims, deeds, character, friends, and so
on, and are variously affected by it. A self-idea of this sort seems to
have three principal elements: the imagination of our appearance to
the other person; the imagination of his judgment of that appearance, and some sort of self-feeling, such as pride or mortification.
. . . The thing that moves us to pride or shame is not the mere
mechanical reflection of ourselves, but an imputed sentiment, the
imagined effect of this reflection upon another's mind. . . . We
are ashamed to seem evasive in the presence of a straightforward
man, cowardly in the presence of a brave one, gross in the eyes of
a refined one, and so on. We always imagine, and in imagining
share, the judgments of the other mind (p. 184).

In this same regard, it also tends to be true that we prefer social interactions with people who sustain our self-concept, especially in positive terms. Research studies by Harvey, Kelley, and Shapiro (1957),
Howard and Berkowitz (1958), and S. Jones (1966) are among those
revealing a positive linkage between perceiving a person as liking one's
self and liking that person. This relationship is predictable in line with
the concept of cognitive balance discussed in Chapters Six and Seven
and fits a simple reinforcement scheme as well. However, where the
individual has a negative self-concept, in the sense of low self-esteem,
it is not necessarily the case that he likes those who reinforce that image, even though this would in theory be a balanced state (cf. S. Jones,
1966).

Social psychologists increasingly are concerned with the meanings
and evaluations individuals attach to their own actions and reactions,
as well as those of others. In operational terms, then, personality is
more than a set of behaviors or dispositions; it may better be seen as
the locus for a process of striving which is shaped by self-awareness
through a network of social relationships.

Approaches to the study of personality

In studying personality it is only possible to measure a few of its features at a time. It is not surprising, then, to find that the results of such
measurement provide a segmented view of the total personality.
Clearly, some things about a person are more relevant than others in
understanding his behavior. The first approaches took account of what

was manifestly there, in terms of ratings of the individual's apparently typical behavior. Either by the ratings of others, or by self-ratings, measures were made of the person's response patterns which seemed to have consistency. As we have already pointed out, this response-oriented approach has limited utility, mainly because of its failure to take account of situational variations. Nevertheless, it continues to be used, often in conjunction with the measurement of dispositions.

The trend in the contemporary study of the behavioral features of personality is exemplified by the recent research of Lorr and McNair (1965) on "interpersonal response categories." They examined various characterizations of personality and developed many categories in which observers could rate the typical behaviors of other people whom they knew well. Through the use of factor analysis, which permits the refinement of these categories, they found seven bi-polar factors which are shown (in Figure 10.3) as fourteen behaviors around a circle. Each

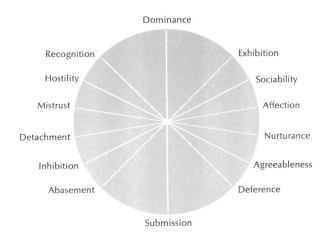

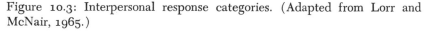

Figure 10.3: Interpersonal response categories. (Adapted from Lorr and McNair, 1965.)

behavior is connected by a line with its opposite number across from it in the circle. Behaviors which are close to one another around the circle are rated similarly. Those which are opposite are seen to differentiate people sharply.

Another technique for measuring overt characteristics of personality is the traditional personality inventory, such as the Bernreuter, MMPI, or Edwards scales, which provide a profile of the individual's characteristics. This method relies on self-ratings and, as we shall be noting, these have been found to be affected by a social desirability factor—that is, an individual's tendency to present himself in a favorable light —which has to be taken into account (Edwards, 1957a).

To a significant degree, the emphasis in the social psychological study of personality has moved more and more to the measurement of dispositions. This so-called "cognitive" approach emphasizes the stable components of the individual's psychological field which intervene between experience and action. The techniques employed in this approach have mainly been attitude scales and projective devices. We will now consider some of these measures of dispositions, beginning with authoritarianism.

AUTHORITARIANISM

More than any other single development in recent years, the research on authoritarianism has opened the way for a study of personality in terms of dispositions that are attitudinal in nature. As we noted in Chapter Three, the California F Scale, developed more than 20 years ago, has yielded a wide array of research on the "authoritarian personality." Scores from this scale have been used in studies of prejudice, leadership, rigidity, adjustment, group behavior, conformity, and many other phenomena (see Titus and Hollander, 1957; Christie and Cook, 1958).

Among the most systematic findings have been those which demonstrate that the scale is related to an individual's perceptions of others. In one study of this, Scodel and Mussen (1953) tested the hypothesis that ". . . authoritarians, because of their lack of insight into others and their need to consider themselves members of the ingroup, would perceive nonauthoritarian peers to have attitudes and personality characteristics similar to their own" (p. 184). In their experiment, 27 pairs of subjects, each pair consisting of a high scorer and a low scorer on the authoritarianism scale, were told to discuss such neutral topics as radio, television, and the movies. At the conclusion of these sessions, the subjects were given a second administration of the F Scale with instructions to respond as they believed their discussion partners would.

As predicted by the hypothesis, the high scorers perceived their partners as having F Scale scores similar to their own, while those with low scores estimated their partners' scores to be significantly higher than their own, though still lower than they actually were. This study establishes a dispositional tendency for authoritarians to have the characteristic of imperceptiveness, which is supported by the studies of Crockett and Meidinger (1956) and Rabinowitz (1956), among others.

Using a "prisoner's dilemma" situation, discussed in Chapter Seven, Deutsch (1960) found significant differences between high and low scorers on the F Scale regarding their trustworthiness. In general, trusting partners and being regarded as trustworthy are highly related, as are their opposites. Figure 10.4 shows the variations Deutsch found

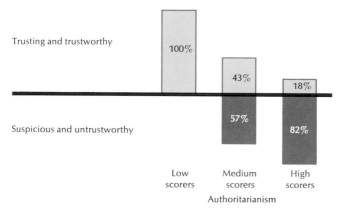

Figure 10.4: Percentages of subjects with high, medium, and low authoritarianism scores who were trusting and trustworthy or suspicious and untrustworthy with their partners. (Based on data from Deutsch, 1960).

in these pairs of responses for subjects at varying levels of authoritarianism. Clearly, a marked inclination exists for the high authoritarian subjects to be significantly more disposed to suspiciousness and untrustworthiness than the low and medium authoritarians.

In the non-social area, too, research has indicated that the authoritarian is likely to be more rigid in his perceptions. M. B. Jones (1955), for example, found with a flickering phenomenon produced by the "Necker Cube," that high scorers on the F Scale were significantly more intolerant of the fluctuation than were the low scorers who more readily acknowledged perceiving it. From this and several related findings, Jones contends that there is a basic perceptual process which underlies authoritarianism.

Some basis exists, therefore, for considering authoritarianism to be essentially perceptual, as Maslow (1943) pointed out when he characterized it as a *Weltanschauung*, or "world view." However, there is still little evidence of any direct experimental verification of a relationship between authoritarian attitudes and social behavior. It would seem that authoritarianism is therefore not a trait, in the same way as "ascendance," but is more a disposition toward the world. And this, of course, is the point of greatest interest here, namely that personality may be described as the individual's construction of the world which may vary as a result of different situational circumstances. This accounts for the fact that, in Fromm's (1941) original conception of authoritarianism, he described the authoritarian person as being both dominant and submissive—dominant to those whom he perceives as weaker, and submissive to those whom he perceives to be more powerful than himself. Thus, the influence of the situation, as the individual construes it, remains an important determiner of interaction patterns.

DOGMATISM

Rokeach (1954, 1960) has extended the concept of an authoritarian disposition in his work on dogmatism. Essentially, he defines dogmatism as *closed-mindedness*. The highly dogmatic individual has a set of tightly organized beliefs, usually derived from authority. A feature of dogmatism is rigidity in the psychological field, which takes the form of resistance to the acceptance of information which is contradictory to the individual's system of beliefs. An undogmatic individual would be more accepting of new experiences and information which might challenge his system.

Rokeach points out that a narrow, unsophisticated perspective leads an individual to experience threat to his closed belief system when he encounters those who are outsiders. Accordingly, he is less willing to tolerate close relationships with those who are different from himself, especially in terms of dissimilar beliefs.

The important feature distinguishing authoritarianism from dogmatism is that the dogmatic individual may be dogmatic irrespective of a particular ideology. He can be dogmatic about many things. The authoritarian, on the other hand, is usually found to be prejudiced and inclined to the political "right." In political terms, the dogmatic individual could tend either toward a "leftist" or a "rightist" viewpoint in an extreme way.

To measure dogmatism, Rokeach developed a 40-item attitude scale which was found to have a significant positive relationship with the F Scale and other measures of a similar kind (Rokeach, 1960). This scale is related to both ethnic as well as dogmatic intolerance, though it is not composed of items which refer directly to such issues.

The reliance of the dogmatic individual on authority has been experimentally verified by Vidulich and Kaiman (1961) who selected subjects on the basis of their scores at either extreme of Rokeach's Dogmatism Scale. They were then placed in an autokinetic situation where each subject privately judged the directional movement of the light for 30 trials alone and then for an additional 30 trials after a report of how another subject judged the same stimulus. Half of the subjects in each group were led to believe that this other person was a college professor and the other half that he was a high school student. They found that the individuals who were highly dogmatic agreed significantly more with the person of "high status" than with the one of "low status." Those who were low on dogmatism tended to agree more with the low rather than with the high status source. These results underscore the importance of the relationship between an individual's personality dispositions and his willingness to accept influence within a given social situation. This lends further emphasis to the necessity for jointly considering both the person's characteristics and his immediate situation in understanding influence processes.

ACHIEVEMENT MOTIVATION

One defining characteristic of personality lies in motivational dispositions. As we have previously indicated, achievement motivation constitutes a widely studied exemplification of these. Its measurement has mainly been approached by presenting a subject with pictures from the Thematic Apperception Test and having him tell a story answering such questions as: What is happening? Who are the people? What has led up to this situation? What is being sought? What is wanted? What will happen? What will be done? Then, the degree of achievement imagery is assessed by content analysis.

In developing this technique of projective study, McClelland and his coworkers (1953) aroused achievement motivation experimentally in a group of subjects to determine its effect on their stories. They found that where subjects were told that their abilities or leadership were being evaluated, they wrote stories that showed far higher achievement than did subjects studied under a normal control condition. The extent of achievement imagery was a direct function of this instructional set.

A considerable amount of research evidence suggests that achievement motivation is learned early and becomes a relatively stable characteristic of individuals, given the *appropriate situational circumstances*. Thus, in a study by Atkinson and Reitman (1956) subjects with a high need for achievement only performed better on tasks involving individual initiative, not on routine group tasks. Another thing which has been found regarding achievement motivation is that it is not highly correlated with risk-taking. The high achiever takes moderate risks but avoids excessive risks. Apparently, risk-taking as a disposition is a distinctive personality characteristic.

RISK-TAKING

Personality may be looked upon in terms of expressive characteristics and also as a complex of abilities, including intellectual performance. Decision-making has been found to be one of the key features involved in higher level intellectual functioning. Wallach and Kogan (1961) have found from experimentation that there is a decision-making style which characterizes people across situations. For example, their results indicated that the person who was more cautious in one kind of choice situation tended to feel a greater subjective probability of his own failure in a variety of tasks. On further study it developed that the disposition to take risks was associated with "test anxiety," which is a motive to avoid failure, and defensiveness. From a further series of experiments in which a subject was allowed to accumulate a monetary prize and then had options for betting it on subsequent trials, they found that both of these factors were features of risk-taking. However, the operation of these variables appears to depend upon other personality factors. Kogan and Wallach (1964) indicate that

> a particular personality dimension may have quite different meaning for individuals varying in other psychological characteristics. Impul-

siveness in males, for example, has distinctly different consequences for risk-taking when test anxiety and defensiveness are present and when they are absent. . . . Other traits, as we have seen, seem to require various types of motivational arousal if they are to have any influence on risk-taking (p. 202).

At best, then, risk-taking is a highly complex characteristic of personality. It involves at least two underlying dispositions which are also affected by the situation in which the individual finds himself. This is a truism regarding many of the cognitive approaches to personality functioning. The way an individual behaves is related to a set of underlying factors which are variously "triggered" as a result of situational factors.

INTERNAL-EXTERNAL CONTROL

One of the underlying determinants of an individual's action is the degree to which he perceives that a reward follows from his own behavior or is controlled by forces outside of himself. This conception can be seen to be related to the *re*action versus *pro*action ideas of G. W. Allport, discussed above. The major impetus for conceiving and studying the generalized expectancies for internal as against external control has come from the efforts of Julian Rotter who has recently provided a broad summary of this work (1966). His social learning theory (1954) emphasizes the persistence of certain "expectancies" that an individual holds. Guiding this work is the view that, depending upon their history of reinforcement, individuals will differ in the degree to which they attribute reinforcements to their own actions.

The measurement of dispositional differences among individuals in the expectancy of internal or external control began with the study by Phares (1957), a student of Rotter's who constructed a 26-item attitude scale composed of 13 items each of an external or internal kind. Subsequent refinements of the scale led to a 23-item forced-choice scale with internal and external choices involved for each. Two such illustrative items, where the subject must select either the *a* or *b* alternative, are these:

a. Many of the unhappy things in people's lives are partly due to bad luck.

b. People's misfortunes result from the mistakes they make.

    a. In the long run people get the respect they deserve in this world.

    b. Unfortunately, an individual's worth often passes unrecognized no matter how hard he tries.

Items of this kind, from the new scale and its predecessors, have been administered to a variety of different populations for research purposes. Quite consistent differences are found, usually in the predicted direction. Thus, among the other findings, Rotter (1966) reports that individuals with high achievement motivation are found to be more internal in their dispositions, and that where sex differences are found, males routinely are more internal than females. He also notes that a recent study of Peace Corpsmen indicates that they are significantly more internal than the general college population from which the bulk of his data are obtained.

Experimental evidence has also been accumulated which indicates differential behavior by internals versus externals. Thus, internals have been found to be more independent and resistant to influence attempts (Crowne and Liverant, 1963). Recently, Rotter and Mulry (1965) investigated the hypothesis that internals and externals would differ in the value placed on the same reward depending upon whether it was perceived as a matter of chance or their own skill. In this experiment, they found that individuals, who scored as internals on the I-E scale, take longer to make a decision in a matching task when that task is defined as demanding skill, than when it is defined as a matter of chance. As predicted, the opposite tendency was found with subjects who are characterized as externals; they were inclined to take more time to decide on a correct match when the task was defined as involving chance.

An important implication that flows from this work concerns cognitive functioning. What Rotter and Mulry have demonstrated is that a relationship exists between expectancies concerning source of reinforcement, and an individual's response time in different kinds of tasks. Thus, one kind of intellectual performance can be tied to a personality disposition.

CATEGORY WIDTH

Personality dispositions can also be viewed as constancies in perception. This is demonstrated in a study by Bruner and Rodrigues (1956) who showed that individuals varied consistently in the range or width of their categories for perceiving. Using color wheels, audio oscillators, and other psycho-physical measures, these investigators asked subjects to select the extremes, that is, the darkest and lightest, or highest and lowest, of a wide range of categories. They also obtained information on such things as their perceptions of the brightness of an overcast sky and the pitch of a female singing voice. Irrespective of the kind of perception, they found that, relatively speaking, subjects tended to be consistently broad, medium, or narrow in the widths of their categories.

This initial observation led to the conjecture that individuals carry a disposition to classify objects within certain equivalence ranges. As Pettigrew (1958) points out, this dimension seems to be compatible with the concept of "risk-taking." He says: "Broad categorizers seem to have a tolerance for type I errors: They risk negative instances in an effort to include a maximum of positive instances. By contrast, narrow categorizers are willing to make type II errors. They exclude many positive instances by restricting their category ranges in order to minimize the number of negative instances" (p. 532).

Building on this work, Pettigrew developed a Category Width Scale initially based on 14 items which supplied each category's average and required subjects to give their own estimates of each category's extremes. In one item, for instance, the subject was told that an average of 58 ships entered New York Harbor daily and was asked to guess what were the largest number and the smallest number of ships to enter New York Harbor in a single day. Employing data from a sample of 750 college students, a new scale was developed made up of 20 items with six alternatives. With this measure, Pettigrew (1958) found that males generally score higher than females, in the sense of having wider categories. Furthermore, he reports a positive correlation between the number of adjectives an individual checks as self-descriptive, in the sense of the span of his self-concept, and his category width score. Individuals who are broader categorizers tend to use significantly more adjectives to describe themselves. This measure, therefore, reveals something about the individual's characteristic perception of the world that can be related to various aspects of his receptivity to social influence and to his social behavior.

MANIFEST ANXIETY

Another kind of concern in the measurement of dispositions is the degree to which the individual inclines toward emotionality in coping with the environment. This is exemplified in the concept of manifest anxiety, identified with the work of Janet Taylor (1953, 1956). Her initial interest was in the selection of groups that would differ in "drive level" in experimental situations. She selected subjects on the basis of a self-rating personality scale using items from the MMPI (Taylor, 1953). This new scale, called the Manifest Anxiety Scale (MAS), has been validated in many studies, all of which reveal a tendency for observer ratings of anxiety to be significantly correlated with the subjects' scores on the MAS.

The importance of this work in social psychology stems mainly from the consideration that social stimuli, such as hostile interactions, can elicit varying responses from individuals as a function of their anxiety proneness (Bovard, 1959). This disposition appears to be measured by the MAS. Thus, it has been found that physiological measures, such as the Palmar-Sweat Index (PSI), are directly associated with MAS scores.

A study illustrating this line of work was conducted by Haywood and Spielberger (1966). Their aim was to investigate individual differences in physiological arousal produced by the anticipation of, and then participation in, a laboratory experiment. These investigators selected subjects who were high or low scorers on the MAS and then took a PSI measure, through a simple fingerprint applied to film, to determine the individual's basal level of arousal in the laboratory just before the experiment. Then subjects were involved in a procedure requiring the construction of sentences as part of a verbal conditioning task. After that, a second PSI print was taken. The results are shown in Figure 10.5.

As expected, the high and low groups on the MAS differed significantly in their respective PSI means. Furthermore, though both groups decreased in their physiological arousal from the first to the second measurement of the PSI, the high MAS group continued to be significantly more aroused than those who were low on the MAS.

This experiment again points up the situation as a factor which interacts with a personality disposition in eliciting behavior. In this experiment, the anticipation of what *was to come* aroused anxiety in both groups of subjects, and this diminished once they had been in the situation for a time. Nonetheless, those entering with a disposition toward greater anxiety continued to show anxiety at a significantly higher level than those who were lower on the anxiety scale.

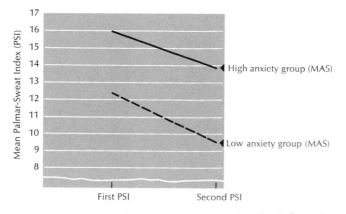

Figure 10.5: Mean levels of arousal, measured by the Palmar-Sweat Index (PSI), taken before and during an experiment, for subjects scoring high or low on the Taylor Manifest Anxiety Scale (MAS). (Based on data from Haywood and Spielberger, 1966.)

SOCIAL DESIRABILITY

A persisting problem in personality assessment has to do with the individual's attempt to present himself in a favorable light. This tendency has been called "social desirability" and appears to be an important feature of social relationships going beyond the personality testing situation. Edwards (1957a) developed a social desirability scale (SD) by making use of a sample of 150 items from various scales of the MMPI which were then submitted to ten judges, asked to rate them on what would be a socially desirable response for each. There was unanimous agreement on 79 items by the judges. Finally, a revised version incorporating 39 items which best discriminated between the high and low total scores on this scale became the major instrument for measuring social desirability.

It was found that this SD scale related to a number of other psychological measures. Among the major findings from one study of this measure, Allison and Hunt (1959) report that individuals scoring high on the SD scale were more likely to be affected by situational cues as to the appropriate response. Thus, aggression as a reaction to frustration varied considerably among these subjects depending upon the degree to which a norm for such expression was evident.

Crowne and Marlowe have extended the work of Edwards and developed a new scale which they consider to be a measure of the need for social approval. Half of its items are culturally acceptable, but probably untrue statements, and half are true but probably undesirable statements. Using subjects selected on the basis of their scores on this scale, they have conducted a number of experiments reported in their recent book, *The Approval Motive* (1964). They find consistent differences in social responses by individuals who are high or low on their scale. For example, those who score high are significantly more likely to conform to the judgments of others than those who score low. It seems apparent that, given a group of attractive others whose approval is desired, individuals will attempt in varying degrees to secure their approval—or social support—as a function of personality needs. This condition is, however, founded on the interaction of the individual and particular others.

PERSUASIBILITY

The personality disposition which seems most directly implicated in the acceptance of social influence is *persuasibility*. Janis and Hovland (1959) define this factor as "any variable attribute within a population that is correlated with *consistent individual differences* in responsiveness to one or more classes of influential communications" (p. 1). The essential characteristic of a persuasible individual would be his willingness to be influenced by others across many situations.

To get at the factor of persuasibility, Janis and Field (1959) have developed a test of persuasibility in which subjects are asked to express their opinions on various issues before any communication is presented, then again after reading a set of communications, and finally after reading an opposing set of communications (pp. 31-32). Scores on this test are obtained by summing the number of items on which the subject changed from his own initial position in the direction advocated by either the pro or con communication.

Among the pertinent findings from some administrations of this test is the significant difference obtained between male subjects and female subjects in overall persuasibility. On the average, females are found to be more persuasible. Accordingly, Janis and Field (1959) suggest that there are at least two broad classes of dispositional factors affecting an individual's persuasibility. They say, "One class involves personality factors, while the other concerns cultural sex-typing influences which may produce more or less stereotyped differences between male and female role behavior in our society" (p. 67).

Using a similar attitude-change test with college students, Linton and Graham (1959) have reported that those who were easily persuaded tended to have a weak self-concept. Taken together with other studies, this led these investigators to the conclusion that susceptibility to influence "is related to two main areas of personality functioning: the underlying attitude toward the self and the quality of a person's reactions to the environment—his ability to cope with it and his responsiveness to its emotional and personal aspects" (p. 99).

Thus, the individual's evaluation of himself, what we have called his "self-esteem," may affect his vulnerability to influence, within the framework of the resources he has available to cope with the environment. Further evidence for this comes from additional research by Janis and Field (1959) with a self-rating personality inventory that measured feelings of inadequacy and social inhibitions. Both of these were significantly correlated with high persuasibility for male high school students, though not for females.

While there is a basis for contending that self-esteem is a persisting personality characteristic related to persuasibility, it also appears that self-esteem can be determined by the situation. It is evidently subject to experimental manipulations which induce a greater or lesser degree of persuasibility in combination with other factors. This is illustrated by the experimental work of Gollob and Dittes (1965). Their subjects were 165 Yale freshmen who were first given an ambiguous test on which half were led to believe they had performed well ("success condition") and the other half that they had performed poorly ("failure condition"). They were asked to give their opinion on three questions, read a communication, and then again indicate their attitudes to the same questions based on what they had just read.

The communication had to do with cancer research and different segments of it were constructed to test the effects of different conditions.

The first condition tested the simple hypothesis of the usual inverse relationship between persuasibility and the manipulated self-esteem, by providing a clearly stated message that was not threatening. The "fear" condition was designed to create a threat by indicating that the problem of escaping cancer seems increasingly hopeless. The "complexity" condition involved an argument that was not as clearly stated. In all cases, attitudes were measured before and after on a six-point scale. It was predicted that the experimentally induced self-esteem would lead to resistance to the communication under the first condition but not for the latter two conditions. Separate questions were asked to measure their effects.

As will be seen in Figure 10.6, the results were consistent with these

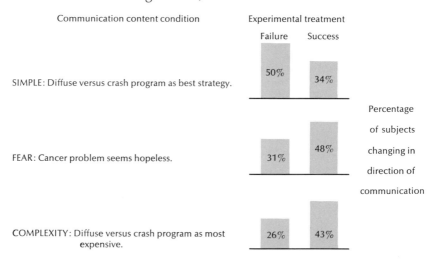

Figure 10.6: Percentage of subjects, among those given an initial set of failure or success, who changed attitudes in direction advocated by communication. (Based on data from Gollob and Dittes, 1965.)

hypotheses. An inverse relationship between manipulated self-esteem and persuasibility was found for the simple condition. For both fear and complexity conditions the relationship was reversed. Furthermore, neither the self-rating of low self-esteem which Janis and Field (1959) found to be positively related to persuasibility in male high school students, nor a test of self-esteem developed by Dittes (1959, 1961), was significantly related to any attitude change. Gollob and Dittes conclude that a persisting disposition of self-esteem was not as important here as its experimental manipulation.

This experiment, taken together with other recent work, leads to the conclusion that persuasibility is a complex outgrowth of the interaction of individual characteristics and situational requirements such as the characteristics of the communication, the characteristics of the communicator, and the person's sense of self-esteem in the particular circumstances.

Some features of personality and social interaction

What primarily concerns people about the personality of others is the way it affects them in social interaction. Most of the time, when we refer to an individual's "pleasant personality" we mean to say something about the ease or congeniality of a relationship with that person. In this sense, the external personality of the individual provides social stimuli which other individuals evaluate positively or negatively, as we indicated in connection with social interaction in Chapter Seven.

Two kinds of interpersonal relationships which are affected by personality are intragroup and inter-group relationships. The first category encompasses the effect of personality on group activity, while the second emphasizes the quality of interpersonal relationships which are shaped by group distinctions, as in prejudice. In this section we will consider both of these briefly as illustrations of personality's ramifications to ongoing social interaction.

GROUP PERFORMANCE

Many studies of group processes take account of the personality characteristics of the participants in the group. Indeed, one kind of research design involves the assignment of individuals with previously assessed personality characteristics to work with others who have the same or different characteristics. We saw this in connection with the experiment by Scodel and Mussen (1953) who paired individuals on the basis of their authoritarianism scores. Another illustration from research where subjects are experimentally paired is the work of Smelser (1961). His procedure was first to administer a personality inventory to a large group of male undergraduates to identify those scoring very high or very low on a dominance scale. They were then assigned to participate in a co-operative problem-solving situation. In all pairs, one partner was assigned a dominant role and the other a subordinate role.

Smelser found that the most productive situation was the one in which the subject with the dominant personality had been assigned the dominant role and the one with the submissive personality was assigned to the subordinate role. As expected, the least productive situation was the one where an incongruity was established between the individual's personality score and the role requirements, that is, a reversal of the congruous pattern. In general, dominant subjects paired together performed better than did submissive subjects. Thus, the congruence of personality with the role demands within a given situation bears directly on the effective performance of individuals who depend upon one another in close interaction.

There are, nonetheless, some circumstances where diversity or heterogeneity of personality is more efficient for the group's operation than a high degree of homogeneity. In the last study noted, only two individuals are involved in a narrowly defined task with a high degree of specificity regarding role relationships. But what of the situation where a large group is involved in a creative, less structured task? There has been a good deal of controversy about this. Some have argued that homogeneity contributes more effectively to group performance than does heterogeneity (Hemphill, 1950a). However, it seems apparent that the particular task posed for the group, as well as the variables of personality which are salient, act together to determine outcomes. Shaw (1960) has found from his studies (1959a, 1959b) that "there seems to be no systematic relation between homogeneity and group efficiency and satisfaction. Degree and direction of correlations vary with the group structure and the particular characteristic under consideration" (p. 450).

A major contribution to this line of work has come from research by Hoffman (1959). He found that groups made up of individuals with dissimilar personalities tended to produce higher quality solutions, of a creative kind, than did those made up of individuals who were most similar in personality. In a broadening of this work he and Maier (1961) conducted an experiment with four-person groups comprised of individuals who were homogeneous or heterogeneous in personality. To accomplish this they administered a standard personality inventory, the Guilford-Zimmerman Temperament Survey, and matched group members by the degree of correspondence of their profiles. Thus, homogeneous groups were made up of individuals who had very high positive profile correlations and heterogeneous groups were made up of people with negative or zero correlations between their profiles. Hoffman and Maier constructed 16 homogeneous and 25 heterogeneous groups on this basis, and all met weekly for case discussions, problem-solving, and role-playing.

Using a variety of different problems, and measures of the subjects' satisfaction with the solution and their influence over it, they found once again that in general heterogeneous groups produced a higher proportion of high quality solutions than did homogeneous groups. They also found that the satisfaction of individuals with solutions reached was highly correlated with the degree to which the individual reported having had influence in determining the group solution. These authors interpret their findings to suggest that "solutions with high quality and high acceptance can be obtained from groups in which the members have substantially different perspectives on the problem, and in which these differences are expressed and used by the group in arriving at the final decision" (p. 407).

On balance, it is not possible to say that either homogeneity or heterogeneity of personality will lead to better productivity or higher satisfaction in groups. More must be known about the task and role requirements to make this kind of prediction successful. However, a clear case can be made for the influence of the personality characteristics of group members on interactions within groups.

PREJUDICE IN PERSONALITY

Prejudice is a widespread social phenomenon which has long occupied a place in social psychological study. In recent years, increasing emphasis has been directed toward the features of personality which bolster prejudice. A good part of this has stemmed from the work on authoritarianism as a personality disposition. Typically, persons who are authoritarian are prejudiced in the sense of being negatively oriented toward groups other than their own. There are also other "functional" features of prejudice which have been revealed by research.

Because of this emphasis on the psychodynamics of prejudice, there is danger in thinking that only authoritarians or "disturbed" people are prejudiced. However, as G. W. Allport (1958) observes, many attitudes of prejudice are sustained among normal people as conformity in polite social chatter. He says:

> In the course of an evening's conversation in a gentile group it is not uncommon to hear the Jews blamed once or twice for some current evil. Everyone nods a head and goes on to the next subject. A group of Republicans might find the same conversational cement in abusing the Democratic administration, or vice versa. And a dig at Irish politicians is in many cities a safe adhesive to apply to a faltering conversation (p. 273).

Basically, then, prejudice begins as an inter-group phenomenon. It has to do with favorable as well as unfavorable attitudes which are related to group distinctions. The terms "ingroup" and "outgroup" are routinely used to signify those groups to which we are positively attached and those that we view from outside. Therefore, though we do not usually think of it in this way, all of us are assigned by others to many outgroups. While we perceive a range of individual differences within our own ingroups, outsiders are likely to have a blanket perception, or "stereotype," of these characteristics. Thus, although we freely talk about a "typical Frenchman," as Americans we may be jarred by the foreigner's stereotype of the "typical American."

For the highly prejudiced individual, this distinction takes on special importance because of an intense motive for *social acceptance*. One characteristic of the highly prejudiced person is the need for security or a sense of superiority that comes from belonging to a favored ingroup and attacking members of an outgroup. This phenomenon is especially seen in majority-minority group relations where, for example, any white, no matter how inferior his status, can feel superior to any Negro, no matter how well educated or economically well off.

In a related vein, the highly prejudiced individual is generally given to mental *rigidity* and categorical thinking. Distinctions between "we" and "they" are sharply made. Outgroup members are perceived to be different and to hold different attitudes. This has been experimentally verified in a study by Muraskin and Iverson (1958) who found that the more "social distance" college students set between themselves and other groups, the less they saw these group members as having attitudes similar to their own. Recently, Byrne and Wong (1962) found that prejudiced white subjects assumed that a Negro would have different beliefs than their own.

Psychodynamically, prejudice appears to function in unconscious, non-rational, and impulsive ways. Therefore, it is possible for intensely prejudiced people to maintain the appearance of composure but to operate with a great deal of *repression*. As G. W. Allport (1958) points out:

> . . . an outstanding result of studies of bigoted personalities seems to be the discovery of a sharp cleavage between conscious and unconscious layers. In a study of anti-Semitic college girls they appeared on the surface to be charming, happy, well-adjusted, and entirely normal girls . . . but probing deeper (with the aid of projective tests, interviews, case histories), these girls were found to be very different. Underneath the conventional exterior there lurked intense anxiety, much buried hatred toward parents, destructive and cruel impulses. For tolerant college students, however, the same cleavage did not exist (p. 373).

Two important unconscious elements in prejudice appear to be the mechanisms of *projection* and *rationalization*. If a person has impulses or desires that are socially disapproved, they can be projected onto disliked groups. Thus, sexual repression may readily lead to the labeling of other groups as sexy; one's own grasping tendencies may be made into others' mercenary traits; aggressive tendencies can be seen in others as warlike intentions, and so on. By this process the prejudiced individual rationalizes his prejudice by blaming it on the outgroups. Thus, some people justify prejudice and discrimination against Negroes by saying that they are unintelligent and "really prefer" menial work. Others excuse anti-Semitic real estate and social club restrictions by saying that Jews are clannish and "like to stay by themselves." By such rationalizations, the *effects of prejudice are made to seem its causes*.

Since individuals vary in the degree to which they are prejudiced, a reasonable question concerns the why of these individual differences. A reasonable answer is to consider prejudice as functionally important in *bolstering the self-concept* where the individual has feelings of personal inadequacy; we observed this in connection with Katz's functional viewpoint (1960) in Chapter Five. In this sense, it is an adjustive response for the individual, but one with potentially dangerous social implications.

Some have said that prejudice is merely a response to frustration. But all adjustment, in some degree, is responsive to frustration. How the individual copes with frustration is also a matter of great relevance to society. The problem with prejudice, simply stated, is that it can become such a pervasive feature of the individual's adjustment that it generates several more problems. First, a person who is highly prejudiced becomes inordinately dependent upon it for support; second, such categorical group distinctions considerably impede the effectiveness of his social relationships; third, rampant prejudice holds disabling social consequences not only to the target groups, but also in terms of the limitations it imposes on the productive energies and co-operative endeavors that any society requires to function smoothly.

By this brief discussion, we have by no means exhausted the topic of prejudice. In the next chapter more will be said about prejudice as one of the features of society associated with ethnic and sub-cultural variations. We will also be considering some of its aspects in greater detail in Chapters Twelve and Thirteen in dealing with group processes.

In the next chapter we will continue the discussion of personality in its development within various subcultures. This is appropriate to an understanding of the way that the individual's social identifications, beginning in childhood, shape his dispositions and responses.

SUMMARY

Personality refers to an individual's unique characteristics. These exist on an *external* and an *internal* level. The first level consists of typical modes of response that grow out of adjustment and role-related behaviors. The second level represents the individual's underlying characteristics which comprise the psychological core. Personality can also be seen to have a *dynamic* aspect which permits change through learning, and a *consistent* aspect which provides stability.

The study of personality proceeds on both levels. Usually, it is expected that these will be consistent with one another, though this may not be the case. Two individuals who behave in a similar way may be motivated quite differently, just as dissimilar behavior may arise from a common motive. Its dynamic aspect produces changes in personality, especially through profound life experiences and also from the immediate role demands of a social situation.

Qualities of personality arise from the complex relationship between biological tendencies and social influences beginning in early life. Various kinds of evidence from animal and human research indicate that early experience has a discernible effect on personality. Thus, exposure to deprivation during the formative years has been found to be associated with subsequent behaviors and attitudes, including the individual's self-concept.

The traditional approach to personality has been oriented toward *traits*, that is, the individual's typical behaviors which are sometimes imputed to innate factors such as instincts. One example of a trait typology is extroversion-introversion. Because "pure type" traits leave out individual variations across situations, the trait approach does not have much support today. A more contemporary view of personality is concerned with the *dispositions* which lead individuals to typical responses rather than focusing on the responses alone. Dispositions are considered to function within the individual's psychological field and to intervene between experiences and responses to social stimuli.

Another approach to personality emphasizes the individual's efforts to cope with his environment. This *transactional* approach makes the individual the primary focus for understanding social influence processes in a two-directional way. In this sense, the individual not only *re*-acts to the environment but also *pro*acts on it as well. At the heart of the transactional approach is a process of striving which is intimately associated with the individual's self-concept, with particular reference to self-esteem.

There are various techniques for studying personality. The initial, and still widely employed technique, was concerned with measuring typical behavior, either by the ratings of others or by self-ratings. The modern trend in social psychology is inclined toward a study of personality in terms of dispositions. This is sometimes referred to as the *cognitive approach*. Among the dispositions which have been measured as features of personality are authoritarianism, dogmatism, achievement motivation, risk-taking, internal and external control, category width, social desirability, manifest anxiety, and persuasibility.

A wide range of findings has been obtained which indicates a relationship between these measures and the individual's style of responding in social situations. The major thrust of this work has been to demonstrate that both the individual's dispositions and the immediate social situation in which he finds himself must be jointly considered in understanding social influence process. Experimentation employing subjects who vary on these dispositions routinely finds this interacting relationship with the situation.

In studying group processes, one kind of research design involves individuals placed in interaction with others who have been found to have the same or different characteristics of personality. A typical finding is that interaction proceeds better where there is a *high congruence* of personality characteristics with role demands, such as those for dominance and submissiveness. A good deal of research has also been done on the relationship of homogeneity or heterogeneity of group members' personalities in the efficient operation of a group. However, neither is necessarily more effective, in the sense of group productivity or satisfaction. Their effects appear to be intimately related to the kind of task and role requirements set in the situation.

Attitudes of prejudice have also been studied as a component of personality. The highly prejudiced person has been found to think in terms of *stereotypes* which oversimplify the qualities of those in his "outgroups." These attitudes persist despite the actual diversity in any human group, and the inconsistent nature of the attitudes themselves. The highly prejudiced person has been found to have an intense motive for *social acceptance* and to have several psychodynamic characteristics as well. These include *rigidity of thought, repression, projection,* and *rationalization.* Typically, those who are highly prejudiced give rationalizations which actually make the *effects* of prejudice seem the justifiable *causes* for prejudice. A major personality factor in prejudice appears to be the function it fulfills in *bolstering the self-concept* where the individual feels personally inadequate. While this may be a useful adjustive response for the individual, it has destructive implications for society at large.

SUGGESTED READINGS

From E. P. Hollander and R. G. Hunt. (Eds.) *Current perspectives in social psychology.* (2nd Edition.) New York: Oxford University Press, 1967: Introduction to Section III—*Personality and society*

15. J. McVicker Hunt: *Traditional personality theory in the light of recent evidence*
18. Milton Rokeach: *The nature and meaning of dogmatism*
19. Robert R. Sears: *A theoretical framework for personality and social behavior*
20. Paul F. Secord and Carl W. Backman: *Personality theory and the problem of stability and change in individual behavior: an interpersonal approach*
61. Gordon W. Allport: *On reducing prejudice*

SELECTED REFERENCES

*Allport, G. W. *Becoming.* New Haven: Yale Univer. Press, 1955.
*Allport, G. W. *The nature of prejudice.* Garden City, N. Y.: Doubleday-Anchor, 1958.
Barnouw, V. *Culture and personality.* Homewood, Ill.: Dorsey Press, 1963.
*Fromm, E. *Escape from freedom.* New York: Rinehart, 1941.
Kaplan, B. (Ed.) *Studying personality cross-culturally.* New York: Harper & Row, 1961.
*Kelly, G. *A theory of personality: the psychology of personal constructs.* (Norton Library Edition) New York: W. W. Norton, 1963.
Kluckhohn, C., Murray, H. A., & Schneider, D. *Personality in nature, society, and culture.* (2nd ed.) New York: Knopf, 1953.
*Linton, R. *The cultural background of personality.* New York: Appleton-Century, 1945.

11

Sub-cultural influences, personality, and individual differences

Any human society shapes the experiences of its members in a selective way. This process must necessarily affect the development of personality. As Parsons (1951) puts it, "behavior and personality are functions of the system of social relationships in which they are formed . . ." (p. 64).

While widespread social practices, especially in child-rearing, have an impact on individual personality, the idea of a society as a homogeneous unit is of course oversimplified. Any society is comprised of various social environments. Though there are dominant trends which characterize the culture of a society, sufficient diversity nonetheless exists to produce distinctive social influences. Indeed, a characteristic feature of life in modern society is the simultaneous participation of individuals in a plurality of social environments. Each of these environments or subcultures carries its own values and a view of the world.

Social psychology is concerned with the distinctive effects of various elements of a society and its culture. In this chapter we shall consider these on a general level and then move on to sub-cultural variations which have consequences in personality development.

314

Modal culture and modal personality

As we have indicated, socialization has a prominant role in the development of personality. It is clear also that the prevailing values and practices of a society are significant determiners of early experience. These values and practices, including the organization of the society, constitute the *modal culture*. In American society, for example, cleanliness is a major value within the modal culture. As Williams (1951) has indicated:

> A great deal of time and effort is lavished on washing hands, taking baths, preparing clean clothes, scrubbing and sweeping, collecting and disposing of trash. . . . Children are approved and otherwise rewarded for cleanly behavior, but meet frowns, censorious speech, minor deprivations, and physical chastisement for certain violations of this pattern. Although the rewards and penalties may be less obvious in later life, adults, too, face sanctions for conduct disregarding this value (p. 381).

Every society embodies major values which have wide acceptability in the practices of its members. Thus, Florence Kluckhohn (1953) has said that the American modal culture is characterized by such values as the emphases on individualistic achievement, future-oriented activity, and exertion of mastery over nature. Yet the concept of modal culture is essentially a statistical one. It is based on the observation that some practices and orientations are more characteristic of a people than are others. There remains a range of variation in the degree to which these practices have influence over people across the many reaches of a society.

In a highly traditional society, the possibilities for unique contacts and the accessibility of stimulation toward various modes of behavior and outlook are severely limited. Thus, the subculture of a non-urban area is likely to have a greater degree of homogeneity than that of an urban area. Commenting on this, Gardner (1963) says that the city affords wider prospects for individual choice, in these terms:

> The man who moves from a small town to a large city experiences unaccustomed freedom. He not only escapes the stultifying web of attitudes, expectations, and censorship that characterize the small

town, he finds in the city more choices in every dimension—kinds of dwelling, consumer goods, entertainment, social comparisons, culture and work (p. 61).

One implication of this range of choice is the differentiation of individual characteristics that it permits. If we contend that society affects personality then, at least in some way, the richness of a society's diversity should be reflected in the variations in its members' personality. Alternatively, very simple societies, such as some primitive tribes studied by anthropologists, should have a more distinctive modal personality.

SOCIETY AND BASIC PERSONALITY TYPES

Perhaps the best known formulation of society's influence on personality is represented in the work of the psychoanalyst Abram Kardiner (1939, 1945). One of his main contentions is that every society has a typical set of child-rearing practices which express the modal culture. As a result of these practices, a particular personality structure is formed and people in the society thus become oriented in the ways dictated by the culture. He defines this "basic personality structure" as "the effective adaptive tools of the individual which are common to every individual in the society" (p. 237).

It is important to understand, as Linton (1951) who worked with Kardiner has noted, that "the concept of basic personality . . . does not correspond to the total personality of the individual . . . it represents a common denominator, a series of fundamental characteristics upon which other and more variable elements of personality content are superimposed in the case of both individuals and groups" (p. 139).

There have been several lines of criticism of this heavily deterministic viewpoint. One consideration already noted is that any society has diverse elements which constitute its subcultures. Furthermore, the concept of basic personality tends to underemphasize individual differences and to overemphasize a presumed commonality of experience. Cora DuBois (1944) has introduced the alternative term *modal personality* to indicate better the wide range of variation within any society. She says that there may be central tendencies in the development of personality characteristics, but there are considerable variations, too, which are seen among adults in any society.

Parsons (1951) has taken issue with the schemes emphasizing personality types in a society on two grounds. First because cultures are not fully integrated in a homogeneous way; and, second, because personality represents an individual system of relationships which is not the same as those stable *inter*-individual relationships which characterize a social system (p. 69). A personality, in short, has an integrity which is not identical to a society's organization.

Thus, part of the difficulty lies in confusion regarding the very definition of personality. If typical behaviors are the focus of attention, people in a society tend to evidence many similar behaviors which are culturally defined. But these do not necessarily reflect more deep-seated commonalities in the psychological core of personality. Most observers, however, grant that there are certain mutually held attitudes and values which members of a society share to some extent. Though these need not lead to the same behaviors, they do define what is "right" and "proper," as we have previously indicated.

NATIONAL CHARACTER AND NATIONAL CHARACTERISTICS

Related to the idea of a society's modal personality is the concept of national character. As Linton (1951) says:

> The crux of the problem of national character lies in the degree to which modern civilized nations have distinctive national cultures and to what extent the culture elements shared by the various social units which compose such a nation reflect a common denominator of the personalities of the nation's members (p. 134).

Apart from everyday "stereotypes" about nations, anthropologists in particular have tried to delineate various "national characters," making use of techniques applied to the observation of primitive societies. Much of this work involves a melding of anthropological observation with Freudian interpretation. Thus, Gorer develops a major conception about American society around the theme of England as the "rejected father." Americans tend to reject authority, says Gorer (1964), because:

> In some significant ways the birth of the American republic can be compared with the mythological scene which Freud imagined for the origin of civilization. . . . The downtrodden sons combined together to kill the tyrannical father; then, overwhelmed by their crime . . . they make a compact which establishes the legal equal-

ity of the brothers, based on the common renunciation of the father's
authority and privileges (p. 29).

Gorer, as well as Margaret Mead, Ruth Benedict, and Gregory Bate-
son, are among those who have written largely impressionistic accounts
of the characteristics of people within a nation. Much of this has the
air of authenticity, though it rests largely on unsubstantiated impressions. Benedict in *The Chrysanthemum and the Sword* (1946) made
much of the Japanese devotion to ceremony, ritual, and position with
an emphasis on the rigidity of early toilet training as a sign of a "rigid"
society. But Stoetzel (1955) has raised questions concerning the accuracy of this contention. He has emphasized, too, the evident shifts
in cultural values which have occurred in Japan since World War II.
Apart from doubts about the validity of broad assertions concerning
a nation, then, the general point is that they may be too fixed and fail
to account for change.

Another point is that a factor which appears to be an explanation for
one nation's conduct may be evident in other nations without the same
consequences. Thus, Schaffner (1948) explained the character structure
of the Germans on the basis of respect and obedience for a dominant
father. But other nations also reveal such cultural patterns. Indeed, many
things which are said to typify one nation are often typical of other nations or segments of them. Moreover, a single characteristic pattern can
never adequately sum up the complexity of a modern nation. As Farber
(1950) aptly notes, the problem in discussing national character is that
the concept of a nation is essentially political-geographical. Thus, cultural patterns may vary from place to place and change from time to
time. They could not, therefore, yield a singular character structure.
He says:

> Not only do national and cultural boundaries often fail to corre-
> spond, but we are confronted with the further difficulty of nations
> containing several cultures. Is it possible, for example, to make a
> general statement about the character structure of the people of the
> Soviet Union? Such a statement would have to include reference to
> Ukrainians, Letts, Armenians, Mongols, and a large number of other
> culturally diverse groups. A Canadian national character would need
> to include French and British Canadians, as well as, to an extent,
> Indians and Eskimos. . . . It becomes clear that we can not speak of
> a national character in multi-cultural nations, or to state it positively,
> that the concept offers promise only in uni-cultural ones (p. 308).

Klineberg (1964) has also pointed to methodological problems and argued persuasively that we would do better to substitute the concept of *national characteristics* for national character. His major contention is that we can only deal in modal trends which are found across many reaches of a nation, through various research techniques, and not with some presumed similarity that everyone in the nation must share with everyone else. In this respect, he says, for example, that the city dwellers of Paris and New York have more in common with one another, in terms of their pattern of life, than they would have with the farmers or fishermen of their respective nations (p. 133). This consideration brings us face to face again with the vital matter of diversity within a culture.

The concept of subculture

For the most part, subcultures have to do with variations in the dominant pattern of life within a society. Some of the more significant subcultures are social class, community, and ethnic identifications including race and religion. One way to look at a subculture is as a "reference group" affiliation which provides an individual with distinctive perspectives in terms of values regarding what is right, proper, decent, or possible. These may also have other ramifications in later political affiliations as well as in important life choices such as occupation.

Of obvious importance in considering sub-cultural variations is the effect they have upon early socialization. The kinds of social interaction they engender carry considerable long-range potency in terms of the individual's values and mode of behaving represented in personality. Achievement motivation, for instance, is widely associated with the particular value-orientation emphasized by a given subculture. Some of the things about an individual, therefore, are quite intimately tied to the nature of these affiliations, even granting the possible shifts which can occur as a result of later social influences.

Previously we said that deprivation in early life was one example of an experience with long-range effects on personality. There is evidence from such studies as those of Berelson and his coworkers (1954), that growing up during the depression had a persistent subsequent effect upon political attitudes and voting behavior, especially for those of lower and middle class status. A poignant illustration of one kind of sub-cultural effect is conveyed by the observations of the anthropologist Oscar Lewis who has written on the "culture of poverty" as follows:

> The people in the culture of poverty have a strong feeling of marginality, of helplessness, of dependency, of not belonging. They are like aliens in their own country, convinced that the existing institutions do not serve their interests and needs. Along with this feeling of powerlessness is the widespread feeling of inferiority, of personal unworthiness (1963, p. 17).

Lewis points out too that not all people who are poor must necessarily live in or develop a culture of poverty. He says, for example, that middle class people who have become temporarily impoverished do not automatically become members of the culture of poverty even though they may have to live in the slums for a while. The implication of this is that the shared outlooks of a subculture may not be taken on by those who have already experienced a different way of life and are still attached to it psychologically.

Just as with the culture more broadly, the quality of a subculture is transmitted through the family as a primary agent of socialization. But the family represents a focus for several different kinds of affiliations which may shape its way of life, including its upbringing practices, in a distinctive fashion. These in turn can produce effects on the psychological development of the individual in terms of personality. We will now consider a number of sub-cultural distinctions, beginning with social class.

Social class

In a broad way, we can think of social class as a grouping of individuals with a set of privileges, responsibilities, and powers acquired through possession of a common degree of qualities valued in a particular culture (Gittler, 1952, p. 148). In terms of our society's culture, birth or family status constitute a major determinant of class, along with such factors as education and income. Thus, social class is a way of ranking persons in the larger community across many groups. Furthermore, people are born into a class as a result of parenthood, though there are opportunities for movement from one class to another. Considerable psychological effects flow from class identifications. As Shils points out, "Sentiments concerning class status and the individual's identification of himself in terms of a particular class status do . . . play a very permeative role in social life" (1960, p. 768).

A study by Davis, Gardner, and Gardner (1941) in a Southern town illustrates the perspectives that class identification lends to the perception of other classes. They find a differential basis for perceiving class membership such that *upper class* individuals "think of class divisions largely in terms of time—one has a particular social position because his family has 'always had' that position. Members of the middle class interpret their position in terms of wealth and time and tend to make moral evaluations of what 'should be' . . . middle-class groups accept the time element as an important factor in the superordinate position of the 'old aristocracy'. . . . Lower-class people, on the other hand, view the whole stratification of the society as a hierarchy of wealth" (p. 72).

MEASURES OF SOCIAL CLASS

Essentially, there are two major procedures for assessing class standing. One, the *objective* method, uses indexes of income, level of education, and occupation, usually in combination. It may also involve ratings from members of a community about each other's class position. The second is the *subjective* method which defines social class by asking people where they place themselves. A problem posed in using the subjective method lies in determining what categories should be employed. If, for example, only "upper," "middle," and "lower" class alternatives are used, then the overwhelming majority of people place themselves in the middle class. However, if the added alternative of "working" class is offered, about three-fifths of the respondents place themselves there (Converse, 1958).

Despite the widespread effect of class, people like to look on American society as essentially classless. The objective evidence on this point, however, is very much to the contrary. Substantial differences in income, occupation, and education prevail and determine class positions in most areas of our society. Government figures reveal sharp extremities in terms of average income and its distribution, as will be seen in Figure 11.1. The figures there for 1962 show that those in the highest

Income Ranks 1962	Average income 1962	Per cent share of all income 1962	1950
Highest fifth	$16,505 ▶	45.5	46.1
Second fifth	$8,241 ▶	22.7	22.1
Middle fifth	$5,938 ▶	16.3	16.1
Fourth fifth	$3,966 ▶	10.9	10.9
Lowest fifth	$1,662 ▶	4.6	4.8

Figure 11.1: Average 1962 personal income received by each fifth of the distribution of families and unattached individuals. Graph shows percentage share of all income received by each fifth in 1962, and for the fifths of the distribution in 1950 as a comparison. (Based on data from U. S. Bureau of the Census, *Statistical Abstract of the United States: 1964*. Washington, D. C., 1964, p. 339.)

fifth of income in 1962 received over 45 per cent of all income. Furthermore, the same government data show that those in the top 5 per cent on the income ladder received about 20 per cent of the income that year. Figure 11.1 also indicates that the relative shares of income for each fifth of the income distribution have remained essentially unaltered from 1950, though the average income has of course increased since that time.

SOCIAL MOBILITY

A striking feature of American society, nonetheless, is the accessibility of movement from one class to another. This is commonly referred to as "social mobility," and it has a high degree of influence in altering patterns of life and outlooks of those who experience it. As Lipset and Bendix (1959) note, "A person who moves up in the social hierarchy will tend to change his friends, join new organizations, move to a new neighborhood; perhaps he will even change his religious affiliation [and] alter his political attitudes" (p. 18).

From a psychological standpoint, it is important to recognize, however, that the prospect of social mobility cuts two ways. Its presumed availability does not insure necessarily that the members of the society will be satisfied. Expectations and hopes will be tested against reality. There is considerable evidence in the sociological literature to suggest that the rather widespread expectations for social mobility in American society can induce a sense of frustration when these are not met (e.g. see Bredemeier and Toby, 1960). This is accounted for in terms of the explanatory concept of *relative deprivation,* which refers to the discrepancy between what an individual actually achieves and what he aspires to achieve (see Chapter Seven, p. 201). In concrete terms, this means that a direct comparison between the material wealth of our society with another society is inappropriate to an understanding of how those in the "relatively deprived" sector of our economy may feel. To tell them that they are still better off than the majority of people on earth is essentially meaningless in terms of the standard that they see held out before them.

There is also a prevailing belief that the poor are free of tensions because of their lower status and lower mobility. It is the wealthier who are supposed to be subject to "executive stress" and the strains of "keeping up with the Joneses." Higher social class is in fact associated with a higher prevalence of *reported* neurosis. Yet, data on *severe* mental disorder indicate a reverse trend, especially among older persons. Hollingshead and Redlich (1958), for example, report data from a survey in New Haven of prevalence of psychotic disorders after age 55, by rate per 100,000, as follows:

Social Class	Rate
I-II (highest)	434
III	638
IV	1353
V	3161

Sharp and significant class differences in psychosis are found by these investigators beginning with ages 25-34, as will be seen in Figure 11.2. They also report that 91 per cent of the schizophrenic patients studied were in the same class as their parents (1954). Evidently, then, class

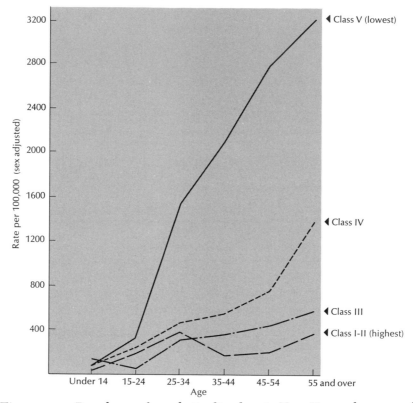

Figure 11.2: Prevalence of psychotic disorders in New Haven, by age and class. (From Hollingshead, 1958, p. 431.)

standing is psychologically relevant to the adequacy of the adjustment achieved by individuals. Hunt (1959), however, has cautioned that social class standing also may enter into a diagnostic label, such as "schizophrenia," which is attached to a patient by the physician, thus magnifying evident class differences in prevalence.

EFFECTS OF SOCIAL CLASS

Several kinds of observable social relationships flow from class distinctions. Persons of similar economic or educational circumstances, for example, tend to associate together and more often than not to marry one another. Friends and playmates tend to be drawn from the same class. The occupational aspirations of young people follow class lines and, indeed, about 60 per cent of American males have been found to be in occupations about the same or no better than that of their fathers (Centers, 1949), though Lipset and Bendix (1959) see this decreasing.

The experiences of a child also vary within the class structure. Among other findings in this regard, Gross has pointed out that "academic achievement, level of aspiration, participation in extra-curricular activities, and the drop-out rate all tend to be positively related to social class placement of the child" (1959, p. 144). In his work on social class in America, Kahl (1953) has shown that, with IQ levels constant, at every level high school boys whose fathers are in major white-collar positions have a far higher expectation of going on to college than do those boys whose fathers fall in lower occupational categories (see Figure 11.3). This is not only a matter of economics. It also indicates

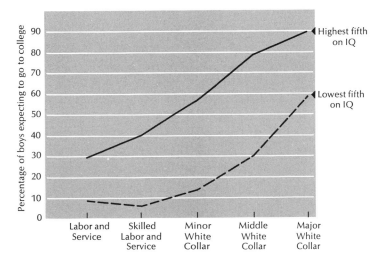

Figure 11.3: Percentage of boys who expected to go to college, among those in the highest fifth and lowest fifth on IQ, plotted by father's occupation. Total data based on 3348 second- and third-year public high school students in Boston. (Based on data from Kahl, 1953, p. 188.)

the accessibility of opportunities and how these are perceived as a function of the psychological identification with class, quite apart from intellectual capacity.

Hollingshead (1949) conducted a study of the friendship pattern of high school boys and girls in terms of their social class position. After categorizing these students into five social classes, he found that 63 per cent of all friendship ties were between members of the same social class and that another 33 per cent could be accounted for between members of two neighboring classes. Hence, boys and girls from distant classes in the social structure had very little informal relations with one another.

Perhaps the most widely studied social class phenomenon has to do with upbringing. In two papers appearing in 1948, Davis and Havighurst, and Martha Ericson, reported research results indicating that the child-rearing practices of middle class parents were significantly different from those of lower class parents. The most important finding of this study centered about the restrictiveness of middle class mothers in the early training of the child. They were reported to be less likely to breast feed, more likely to follow a strict nursing schedule, to wean earlier and more sharply, and to begin bowel and bladder training earlier than were lower class mothers. Middle class mothers were also found to expect their children to take responsibility for themselves earlier. These results led to the inference that middle class children encountered more frustration of their impulses and that this was likely to have serious consequences in the development of their personalities. In particular, some writers voiced the view that the training of middle class children was likely to produce an orderly, conscientious, responsible, tame, but frustrated child. More recent evidence from the work of Sears, Maccoby, and Levin (1957) indicated no significant differences in infant-feeding practices between the two social classes, though they did report two major differences in the behavior of *lower class* parents: *more* severity in toilet training; and *more* restriction of aggression toward parents and peers, coupled with *more* physical punishment and deprivation of privileges. In a number of significant respects, these results were in direct contradiction to the findings of the earlier work which portrayed the middle class mother as excessively rigid, restrictive, demanding, and punitive.

In summarizing the data on class factors in socialization over 25 years, Bronfenbrenner (1958) has lent an historical perspective to these findings, particularly in infant-feeding and toilet training. He says that up to World War II there was a greater degree of permissiveness on the part of lower class mothers, but that this has since been reversed. Subsequently, middle class mothers became more permissive as a result of the widespread availability of many recommendations about child-rearing, including those embodied in Spock's influential book, *Baby and Child Care,* originally published in 1946. Bronfenbrenner concludes that there is accordingly a considerable trend toward more homogeneous child-rearing in American society, with middle class mothers becoming consistently more permissive toward the child's expressed needs and wishes and less likely to use physical punishment.

One kind of finding, however, which continues to hold important relevance to social psychology, is the high premium placed on achievement by the parents of middle class children. This kind of striving for social mobility appears to cut across other distinctions in accounting for significant values transmitted to the child in early life by the parents. Moreover, it appears to be a broadening trend which may take in more than the middle class. In England, for example, Hilde Himmelweit (1955) has found in general that middle class children tend to be more concerned about how well they do in school and to have higher educational and vocational aspirations than do working class children. However, children described as from the "working class," but who were upwardly mobile in their school and vocational aspirations, were found to have parents who adhered to middle class values more strongly than did the middle class parents in Himmelweit's study.

In another investigation with American families, Miller and Swanson (1958) have also found differences within social class. They distinguish between families that are "entrepreneurial" or "bureaucratic," based upon the father's occupational setting, and characterize the family's child-rearing practices as emphasizing respectively self-control and individual initiative *or* adjustment and getting along well. While these patterns existed within both middle and lower class families, differences between the classes were still quite evident. More importantly, it may be that both patterns represent the fundamental value of "getting ahead," though construed differently by the family in terms of its social reality. Thus, the implicit goal sought may be the same though the explicit emphases of upbringing differ.

Clearly, then, families may differ in the degree to which they are bound into the values and practices of a social class. Therefore, social class has to be understood as a broad category of social identity within which other sub-cultural influences on the family may act in affecting the child's personality. Among these is ethnic affiliation.

Ethnic affiliations

An "ethnic group" is comprised of people who share a subculture based on racial, religious, or national origin similarities. These may overlap and provide varying perspectives. They are most often considered separately from class, though a unique feature of ethnic relations in America concerns the racial distinction between white and Negro which is related to class insofar as the lower segments of the class structure are populated disproportionately by Negroes. However, this distinction also has features of what is referred to as *caste*. In a caste system a barrier exists which sharply inhibits social mobility. Thus, while movement from one class to another may be possible, this is not so with regard to caste. The most pressing example of this in our society today is the caste discrimination directed against Negroes, which can override social class and make it count for very little. The Negro professional or businessman, with income, education, and position justifying a higher class status, may still be looked upon and treated by elements in the community as inferior to any white, however low his class position. The stressful quality of such relationships and the ensuing frustration are easy to understand.

Clark and Clark (1958) have studied the racial identifications of Negro children. In their experiment they used white and colored dolls as objects the children were to select in answer to questions. They found that "at each age from three through seven years the majority of these children prefer the white doll and reject the brown doll" (p. 608). Fifty-nine per cent of the children selected the white doll as the "nice doll," and the same percentage of the children indicated that the brown doll "looks bad," as shown in Figure 11.4. The Clarks conclude that even at four and five these children appear to have taken on the negative attitudes toward themselves of the larger community.

There are still other discriminatory policies which exist in American society as well. These are by no means unique to us, but we still entertain a number of significant beliefs to the contrary. The notion of the "melting pot," for example, is a widespread equalitarian value to which

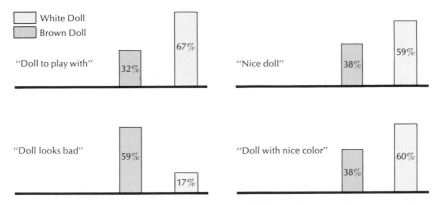

Figure 11.4: Percentages of 253 Negro children choosing brown or white doll in response to questions indicated. (Based on data from Clark and Clark, 1958.)

we pay homage. Ours is supposedly a nation in which a mixture of different ethnic strains is greatly to be desired. Here again, the actual social pattern does not confirm the value. Thus, Gordon (1964) writes:

> Both structurally and culturally, then, the "single melting pot" vision of America has been something of an illusion—a generous and idealistic one, in one sense, since it held out the promise of a kind of psychological equality under the banner of an impartial symbol of America larger than the symbols of any of the constituent groups— but one which exhibited a considerable degree of sociological naivete. Given the prior arrival time of the English colonists, and the cultural dominance of Anglo-Saxon institutions, the invitation extended to non-English immigrants to "melt" could only result, if thoroughly accepted, in the latter's loss of group identity, the transformation of their cultural survival into Anglo-Saxon patterns, and the development of their descendents in the image of the Anglo-Saxon American (p. 129).

Distinctive sub-cultural patterns continue to be found in various ethnic groupings, for example in terms of achievement motivation. Strodtbeck (1958) reports evidence indicating a higher value for achievement among children from Jewish and Greek homes, with a lower relative value among those from Italian or Negro homes. Results for Catholics compared with Protestants were dependent upon other ethnic ties and were not consistent.

Religious identifications can serve a reference group function however. Charters and Newcomb (1958) conducted an experiment with Catholic, Protestant, and Jewish undergraduates. A questionnaire on religious beliefs was administered to all of them, but only after they had been divided so that about one-third in each religious category was assigned to either one of two control conditions or to the experimental group. Those in the latter group were told that the test would include items relevant to *their* particular faith; on the other hand, the control groups were *not* made aware of their common religious identity. The results indicated a significant response difference for the Catholic experimental group compared to the Catholic controls, in terms of more responses in line with orthodox beliefs. No significant differences were found when these subjects were compared in items irrelevant to the Catholic religion. Comparable results were not found for the Protestant and Jewish students in this experiment. The authors conclude that "the data from the Catholic groups strongly suggest that an individual's expression of attitudes is a function of the relative momentary potency of his relevant group memberships" (p. 281).

Plainly, though, individuals are not one-dimensional in reacting to the world since they have varying sub-cultural identities. And there are conditions of "cultural conflict" where two such identities clash. This is likely to be seen when parents are new migrants to a society and have not absorbed its culture. Their children may then learn one thing from the school and playmates and another thing at home. This effect is enhanced if the parents are from an ethnic group which is disdained by the broader community. Thus, children are caught between a desire to assimilate to the broader culture by conformity to its patterns while still being identified with their parental subculture. This mode of "minority group" treatment is quite prevalent and leads to a widening gulf between the generations. It also produces frustration because of the paradox that assimilative acts of conformity by minority group members are not necessarily rewarded by social acceptance, as Georgene Seward (1956) found in her study of culture conflict.

Nonetheless, powerful tendencies toward assimilation persist, and the acquisition of new cultural forms from the school and playmates leads the child to a weakened attachment or even open hostility to the other culture that the parents represent (e.g. Eisenstadt, 1956). This is not only a problem of minority group members. A mobile, fast-changing society has been found to create a strain on the adolescent's relationship to his parents, and this is associated with greater identification with peers (cf. Coleman, 1961; Riley, *et al.*, 1961). In the next section we will consider peers as one of a number of sub-cultural influences.

The peer subculture

If the family may be said to be a fundamental institution in shaping socialization, another one of considerable significance is the so-called "peer group." A great deal of attention has been directed to the peer group's influence on the child. Exemplifying this trend, Riesman, *et al.* (1950) have made a particular point of the increasing influence of the peer group, and its consequences regarding the child's "other-directedness" as against his "inner-directedness."

There is evidence, however, that the peer group is not a unitary source of influence but rather one which varies in terms of age-level and the nature of the particular group of peers involved, as well as the context and nature of their activity. Thus, there are at least three age-level distinctions that should be made in this respect.

In the first place, pre-school children appear not to be overly influenced directly by the typical attitudes or behavior of age mates (e.g. Gellert, 1961), if we mean by "influence" the alteration of behavior in the face of more than one perceived behavioral alternative. Berenda (1950) found that children of ages seven through nine were more responsive to social pressures from age mates than those from ten through thirteen. However, Hunt and Synnerdahl (1959) obtained results indicating that children of five and six are little influenced by peers in an Asch conformity situation where they are the true subjects (see Chapter Three, p. 73).

In the school years, before adolescence, the child's peer group seems to serve as a supplemental agent of socialization to the family by providing especially for play activity. In this stage children usually gravitate toward peers of the same sex. Dependence upon the parents is normally still quite high.

The adolescent peer group marks a difference in both its quality and its functions. It tends to incorporate sub-cultural influences at variance with the adult culture. This is often accounted for by citing the ambiguity of adolescent status in our society. Plant, for example, points to the vulnerability of adolescents to social pressures, because they have no distinctive place in society but are "in between" (1950, p. 54). This does not mean, however, that adolescents generally accept peer standards uncritically. Brittain (1963), as one example, has found that peers are more influential for some things but not for others. What appears to matter is the importance at a given time of the affiliative needs mentioned before of social identity, social reality, and social support.

Some influences may appear to be more effective on the child than others, but this is determined by the situation. Thus, in a condition of confusion those persons providing a satisfactory "social reality" may be reacted to favorably, and in circumstances of status ambiguity "social identity" may be important, as is frequently observed with adolescents.

The long-run effects of influence therefore depend upon the initial conditions under which it occurred. The fact that the family provides social support where it is much sought, as in early childhood, carries a persisting impact. The peers then follow as a source of influence based on these affiliative needs.

THE NATURE OF THE PEER GROUP

The peer group has been studied in many different ways with varying definitions. It has been approached first as a grouping of age mates, with no necessary considerations as to their interrelations; second, as a grouping of individuals who are familiar to each other but who do not necessarily form a natural group involving choices of other individuals, such as a classroom; third, as small natural groups in face-to-face interaction, such as a play group. These may and indeed do overlap.

Because the definitions used involve different social relationships, apparently contradictory results are sometimes found concerning peer influence. From a socio-psychological standpoint, a peer group is best seen as a reference group of other youngsters with whom the child identifies and who have effects upon him in terms of his psychological field. While Kagan and Moss (1961) point out that "there are substantial methodological difficulties in demonstrating a cause-effect relationship between peer attitudes and changes in a child's behavior . . ." (p. 469), they nonetheless suggest that "the investigations of peer group influences . . . point to the potentially important role of social power or popularity in the course of a child's development of an autonomous or a passive disposition with others" (p. 471).

THE PEER GROUP AND THE FAMILY

Numerous studies have concerned themselves with the relative weight children attach to their family as against, for example, play groups, where alternative responses are involved. Thus, Rose (1956) studying 582 high school students of both sexes found that the family was the most influential group affiliation and that this was correlated especially with fondness for parents. This seems in contrast with the finding reported by Rosen (1955), with a sample of Jewish adolescents in a small upper New York State city, who found that the peer group exerted considerable influence in whether youngsters followed forms of religious observance.

Several other findings bolster the view that experience in the family is relevant to status among peers. In this respect, Marshall (1961) has found, in a study of pre-school children, that the child's linguistic development is associated with better social acceptance by playmates. Moreover, siblings have been found to affect a child's preferences in playmates (Koch, 1957). Thus, with a single sibling of the same sex, the child shows an even stronger inclination than usual to choose playmates of the same sex.

In line with our earlier discussion of identification with parents as part of moral development (Chapter Five, p. 135), Eleanor Maccoby (1961) has studied the child's reciprocity of behavior in enforcing rules with peers. Within her study sample of sixth graders, she found this kind of interaction to be related both to the sex of the child and dependence upon the parent. In general, boys showed more inclination than girls at this age to accept rule enforcement from peers of the same sex. This was particularly so if the parents had been relatively nonpermissive about the child's earlier impulsive behavior but also warm toward the child. Therefore, says Maccoby, the child's interaction with peers is conditioned by parental relationships in that:

> . . . the child acquires a set of adult-like behavior tendencies during early childhood . . . and these tendencies find their way into overt expression during interaction with peers at a later time when peers provide the necessary stimulating conditions (p. 503).

In a broader framework, the social class position of the family may affect the child's play pattern and relationship to the peer group. In this regard, Tuma and Livson (1960) have reported that how much the adolescent accepts the rules of a group in a given situation relates to the socio-economic status of the family. Moreover, Lesser (1959) is among those finding a relationship between aggressive behavior, popularity, and the class level of the family. In particular, he has been able to demonstrate that different manifestations of aggression meet with different degrees of approval and disapproval by lower-class peers, with provoked physical aggression being relatively approved and unprovoked and indirect aggression being progressively more disapproved. It would appear, then, that modes of reacting within the peer group are interpreted in part within the context of the family's socio-economic status and its environment.

PEERS AND EXTERNAL ASPECTS OF PERSONALITY

Perhaps most relevant to a socio-psychological view of the process of interaction between the individual and the peer group is the shaping effect that the peer group may have on individual behavior. As we noted earlier, Campbell and Yarrow (1961) found, in a summer camp session with pre-adolescents, that initial evaluations by peers are very likely to shape a child's subsequent actions. Furthermore, Dornbusch, et al. (1965) have found that children tend to perceive the behaviors of other children in line with their own behavioral tendencies.

Though early peer associations are governed by parents, this is variable. Thus, Marshall and McCandless (1957) find that pre-school children who are dependent on adults tend to have lower peer status. Girls also tend to be more emotionally dependent than boys. Subsequent work by McCandless, Bilous, and Bennett (1961) corroborates this finding with the conclusion that while it may be moderately acceptable for girls to show emotional dependency upon an adult in the pre-school situation, it is relatively unacceptable for boys. The fact that sex-typing occurs at this stage is another matter of interest. This has been further studied by Cox (1962) who observed aggressive and dependent behavior of children in a playground situation. He found that a positive attitude toward the father was associated with the establishment of competent group relationships. Boys who were reputed to be aggressive toward peers were found to reject one or both parents. Dependence was high in boys attached to their mothers.

A point of further interest is the child's acceptance by his peers. The underlying question here refers to the process by which status is achieved, in terms of the values implicit in the group's assessment. In summarizing some of the work on social acceptance, DiVesta (1961) reports that many studies indicated "a significant positive relationship between social acceptance and achievement, whether the study was conducted with grade school, secondary school, or college populations" (p. 517). This finding accords with the work of Marshall (1958) whose results show that level of performance in 4-H clubs by boys and girls was positively correlated to their standing on a sociometric measure. Also, Mouton, Bell, and Blake (1956) have reported that children having high status among their peers have greater self-confidence and appear to strive actively for recognition.

PEERS AND SELF-PERCEPTIONS

Of considerable psychological importance is the contribution made to a child's self-perception, his self-concept, by interactions with other children. The central conception of attitudes as well-springs for behavior is nowhere more important than in the core attitudes an individual acquires about himself from a significant reference group. Moreover, such acceptance by peers has been found to be associated with more positive self-oriented attitudes (Reese, 1961).

A counterpart of this is seen in the typical finding that children who are least popular among peers appear to be inaccurate in appraising their actual standing in the group. From this it is sometimes too readily inferred that they are less popular *because* they are less perceptive. Goslin (1962), for example, studied nineteen classes of seventh and eighth graders. Using a modified "social distance" scale, he identified the five most accepted and five least accepted children in each group and studied their relative accuracy in making several kinds of ratings. One of these was an estimate of how they were rated by classmates. As anticipated, those most accepted were significantly better in making accurate estimates than those who were least accepted (cf. Greer, *et al.*, 1954; Gallo & McClintock, 1962). This relationship is shown in Table 11.1.

This table makes clear what the direction of the relationship is—i.e. most accepted most accurate, and least accepted least accurate. What is not so readily apparent, however, is the inevitable bias introduced by the consideration that children—no less than adults—prefer to perceive themselves as higher in standing among their peers than they actually are, presumably to protect the self-concept. The least accepted children are accordingly most likely to seem inaccurate, on that basis, and the most accepted to appear quite accurate. Thus, a simple response bias can account for this kind of finding. What is more, a child at the low acceptance end could be quite accurate in knowing where he stands but nonetheless give a "socially desirable" response, namely that he is higher than that private estimate. It may be also that the child rejects what he considers the unfair judgment of his peers. Finally, another point in these data is that the levels of accuracy are based just upon those two categories of subjects who were high or low in acceptance, thus giving a sharper contrast by comparison of extreme groups.

Table 11.1: Distribution of accuracy scores in estimating ratings from classmates, by percentage, for most and least accepted children, with 93 in each category. (Based on data from Goslin, 1962.)

LEVELS OF ACCURACY BY FIFTH OF THE DISTRIBUTION	LEAST ACCEPTED CHILDREN	MOST ACCEPTED CHILDREN
1 Highest	14%	27%
2	15%	26%
3	18%	22%
4	25%	16%
5 Lowest	28%	9%
	100%	100%

The point, then, is that there is a great deal of subtlety in how acceptance from peers affects self-perceptions. Particularly where parents encourage a greater orientation toward peer influences, selfhood becomes more closely identified with social identity as defined by peers. Alternatively, where a child acquires an orientation of resistance to such influence, his independence from them may be better maintained.

PEERS AND THE SCHOOL

The school quite obviously provides a place for many peer contacts. As a context for interaction it also has a determining influence on peer relationships, since the social structure of the classroom is often determined by scholastic performance rewarded by the teacher. Moreover, that structure embodies a good deal of competitiveness and even implied threat of exposure for deficiency, as Henry (1963, Ch. 8) has observed. It is to be expected therefore that many studies find a positive relationship between high standing in class performance and peer acceptance in school.

Williams (1958), for example, reports that more than four out of five children found to be high in total acceptance were achieving at or beyond expectancy, whereas more than three out of five children who were low in acceptance were achieving below expectancy. Also, she reports that total performance in school correlates significantly with social acceptance at a level of .43. On the other hand, with high school seniors, Ryan and Davie (1958) report that verbal aptitude grades do not correlate significantly with acceptance by peers. Popularity was measured by having each student rate the others in the senior class and this measure was found to be correlated in the high .80's with a measure of social contact with classmates. In comparing these two studies it is noteworthy that there were differences and that in one case social acceptance was measured by classroom, and in another by an entire senior class.

There is no doubt that the school encourages values associated both with school performance and family aspirations, but how this school influence is felt by the youngster clearly depends on a variety of factors. As Elkin (1960) puts it:

> Compared to the family, the rewards of the school situation—grades, promotions, permission to participate in certain activities, compliments, and leadership positions—are quite formalized. There are particular age-grade expectations with specific tasks and standards, and the child is judged by the degree to which he measures up to these expectations. Almost inevitably there are rankings and comparisons with other students . . . in disciplining and teaching the child, the school authorities may use the child's dependence on his family and peer group . . . such techniques of course are effective only if the family and peer group in some ways support the school (p. 62).

Related to this concern with the child's peer group in its relationship to the school setting is the work of Rhine (1960), who studied the effect of peer-group responses upon the attitudes of college undergraduates. Of particular importance was his finding of a characteristic dependence of these students upon the others for a kind of "social reality," much in line with the findings of researchers such as Asch (1951). This definition of the world appears to be an important function provided by groups in general, and particularly by the adolescent groups operating outside the classroom.

On the psychological side, then, the child acquires a far broader spectrum of encounters in school than the subject matter of the classes. Experiences in the classroom, playground, gymnasium, and auditorium leave their stamp upon the youngster. Moreover, even in terms of routine subject matter, the school provides the child with a "social reality" within which to view the broader world. For example, the child's conception of his nation in the scheme of human events is affected by the kind of historical and political materials he is taught. This interpretation of the world is further reinforced by the already established attitudes of parents, and by peers who are being taught similar things.

In performing its function for society, then, the school affects the child's psychological field in combination with parents and peers. While much of this may occur unintentionally, it nonetheless has significant ramifications. It is also worth noting again that the school often extends the influence of peers, particularly in establishing dimensions for social acceptance.

Society and personality: a final word

The main recurring point here is the consideration that individuals are affected by those with whom they have the closest contact. Beginning with the family, and extending outward to other subcultures, the child has distinctive social experiences. It is hard, therefore, to reconcile this range of relationships with the idea of society as a single pervasive force which stamps each of its members in the same way.

Nonetheless, there continues to be a sense in which people feel that they "know" what Frenchmen or Chinese or Scandinavians are like. If these people are Americans they may be less sure of what an "American" is like. Studies by Perlmutter (1957) and by Bruner and Perlmutter (1957) clearly demonstrate this phenomenon. American subjects in these experiments were asked to predict the characteristics of stimulus persons described by various categorical terms. Thus, a given person might be described by occupation (a businessman), by personal characteristics (intelligent), and by nationality (an Englishman). If the

person was foreign, the most dominant factor in determining the subjects' predictions about him was found to be nationality. On the other
hand, if the subjects were told that the person was American, this was
of no relevance in their predictions; they were far more inclined to be
swayed by the information regarding occupation and intelligence in
making their judgments.

In explaining these findings, Pool (1965) says that typically we code
the behavior of foreigners by nationality rather than by sex, age group,
social class, or occupation, because we usually have less prior information on these categories. It is far easier to develop stereotypes of a people from brief encounters than from a rich stock of experience with
their individual and sub-cultural differences. Selective exposure also
has pronounced effects. As Linton (1951) says:

> . . . the picture of French personality obtained by an American
> who spent a year as an art student in Paris would be quite different
> from that of an agricultural expert who had spent a year studying
> French vegetable growing (p. 142).

In extending his consideration to Great Britain, Linton points to the
considerable cultural variations in England, Scotland, Wales, and
Northern Ireland, and adds:

> It may be urged that the cultural-social composition of Great Britain
> is unusually diverse, but there is little evidence for this. Other Euro-
> pean or Oriental nations may appear more homogeneous to an
> American, but this is mainly due to ignorance of local conditions.
> Even small enclaves such as the various Scandinavian nations are
> keenly conscious of cultural differences within their territories . . .
> even China, in spite of its common written language and nation-
> wide recruitment of the official class, presents many regional differ-
> ences (p. 143).

Quite commonly, people also think in terms of a given occupational
status as having a distinctive personality type. By now it should be clear
that this is essentially a manifestation of role, and it is all too easy to
confuse role behavior in an appropriate setting with more persisting
attributes of personality. Parsons (1951) has treated this misconception
in observing that:

> It is possible to categorize social groups according to status, into
> what as nearly as possible in social science terms it makes sense to
> call uniform status—let's say urban middle-class housewives or mem-

bers of the medical profession in middle-sized cities. . . . But I think no matter how fine you break down the differentiations of social status, if you are still left with a status category in which considerable numbers of people fit, you will find that those people, far from presenting a single, clear-cut pattern of personality type, will cover a widely dispersed range of different types . . . (p. 66).

The major implication of Parsons's point is that even in highly delimited groupings of people, individual differences persist. Think of the variations in personality among your classmates, for instance, and match those against the idea of the "typical college student." The core of the problem of such generalities is the use of *descriptive labels*— Frenchman, professor, housewife, college student—as if they encompassed significant elements of the person's personality. We are all subject to this tendency, however, since labeling is so much a part of language and communication. In one study, for example, it was found that college students responded to the question "Who are you?" by giving their nationality, religion, and status as students.

These "descriptive categories" convey the fabric of society, but they do not usually reveal a great deal about individual differences within a category. Nevertheless, as we have said previously, social identifications are important bases for an individual's orientations and actions. A sense of social identity can be a significant part of what we think of as individuality. We shall consider this matter further in connection with group processes in the next two chapters.

SUMMARY

Any society produces effects upon its individual members, particularly in the early socialization practices it employs. These practices, and the values underlying them, are part of the *modal culture*. The concepts of "basic personality" and "modal personality" are both directed at the characteristics that people in a society may share in common. Modern societies, however, provide a diversity of experience within their modal cultures.

Attempts to extend the idea of common personality characteristics to a whole nation, in terms of a "national character," have proven to be faulty on several grounds. Nations are politico-geographical units having complexity that arises from sub-cultural distinctions. With time and culture contacts, nations may change. Furthermore, the methodology used to study the characteristics of the people of a nation is often highly limited and impressionistic. In a modal sense, however, there may be identifiable *national characteristics* that have reference to typical attitudes and values, and culturally determined behaviors.

Subcultures are divisions of society represented in social class, community, and ethnic differences. They are important in social psychology because of their influence on the values and behaviors of individuals who are identified with them in a reference group sense.

Social class is a major sub-cultural variation based on the qualities valued in a society, such as family standing, income, and education. Measures of social class may use *objective* indexes of these factors or *subjective* reports by individuals of the class in which they place themselves. Objective census measures reveal substantial class differences, regarding income, for example, though some people prefer to view American society as classless.

Social mobility from one class to the next higher is often sought, though its effects are not entirely favorable. In terms of *relative deprivation,* the inability to be successfully mobile in attaining a higher level may lead to a sense of frustration. Studies of severe mental disorder indicate that psychosis is considerably more prevalent among the lowest classes, beginning with early adulthood.

Differentiation of experience by social class affects educational opportunities, occupational aspirations, and social contacts. It also has been found to be a factor in child-rearing practices, though there appears to be a growing similarity in such patterns across classes. There is still some stability in the finding that the middle class encourages in youngsters a greater value on achievement.

Ethnic distinctions based on racial, religious, and national origins also have persistent subcultural influences. The Negro subculture tends to represent a fusion of a *caste* distinction—which allows little prospect of "crossing" a barrier—with a mainly lower class status. Exclusionist policies also exist with regard to religious and national origin affiliations, revealing the inaccuracy of the "melting pot" concept of American society. The actual tendency lies more in the direction of encouraging assimilation toward an Anglo-Saxon mode, without necessarily guaranteeing social acceptance. Especially with parents who are recent migrants, this has the effect of causing children to break away from the family's older culture in favor of conformity to the new culture, thus widening the gulf between generations. A mobile, changing society in any case creates a strain for the adolescent in his parent vs. peer relationships.

A child's "peer group" represents a subculture which varies with age-level and activity. Very young children are not so markedly influenced by other children. By adolescence, though, peers are often a significant source of social identity, social reality, and social support, particularly because of the adolescent's ambiguous status in adult society. The family has an effect upon the peer's influences depending upon the kind of relationships involved and the attitude of the parents toward peer activities.

Social interaction with peers has a number of significant consequences in terms of the development of a child's external and internal aspects of personality, including the "self-concept." Acceptance by peers is associated with a number of performance characteristics such as high activity and school grades. The school setting thus encourages some features of peer evaluation. As an agent of society, the school also provides a locus for many values which are reinforced by the parents and by peers.

Individuals are therefore affected by a variety of subcultures. This makes the concept of a uniform influence of society upon the individual highly questionable. Though we may react to others in terms of labels arising from national, sub-cultural, or status differences, these categories are merely descriptive and not indicative of the range of individual differences within any one of them. It is still true, however, that social identities are important to understanding individual outlooks and actions.

SUGGESTED READINGS

From E. P. Hollander and R. G. Hunt. (Eds.) *Current perspectives in social psychology.* (2nd Edition.) New York: Oxford University Press, 1967:

13. Hilde T. Himmelweit: *Socio-economic background and personality*
14. Urie Bronfenbrenner: *The changing American child*
17. Thomas Pettigrew: *Negro American personality: the role and its burdens*
62. Oscar Lewis: *The culture of poverty*

SELECTED REFERENCES

Coleman, J. S. *The adolescent society: the social life of the teenager and its impact on education.* Glencoe, Ill.: Free Press, 1961.

*Elkin, F. *The child and society: The process of socialization.* New York: Random House, 1960.

*Gordon, M. M. *Assimilation in American life.* New York: Oxford Univer. Press, 1964.

*Gorer, G. *The American people: a study in national character.* New York: Norton Library Edition, 1964.

*Hollingshead, A. B. *Elmtown's youth.* New York: Wiley, 1949.

Kahl, J. A. *The American class structure.* New York: Holt, Rinehart & Winston, 1957.

*Lipset, S. M., & Bendix, R. *Social mobility in industrial society.* Berkeley: Univer. of California Press, 1959.

*Pettigrew, T. *A profile of the Negro American.* Princeton: Van Nostrand, 1964.

Sherif, M. & Sherif, Carolyn W. (Eds.) *Problems of youth: Transition to adulthood in a changing world.* Chicago: Aldine, 1965.

12

Group characteristics and functions

Groups are the most universal units of any social system. They exist primarily to carry on the necessary and significant functions in a society. In the course of our lives, all of us take part in many groups. The influence they exert on our individual actions and psychological states gives them a place of unparalleled importance in social psychology. Sherif and Cantril (1947) have highlighted this point in saying: "Once an individual identifies himself with a group and its collective actions, his behavior is, in a major way, determined by the direction of the group's action . . ." (p. 290).

The way groups influence an individual is related to the question of how they function. In this chapter we will attend to the characteristics of groups which have consequences for their functioning, and in the next chapter consider further the influence effects of groups in terms of group dynamics.

Some definitions of groups

Historical controversy concerning the definition of groups goes back to the time of the "group mind" tradition at the end of the last century, and even before that (see Chapter Two). Groups may vary in size from two persons to a large political party or major organization. They

344

may be essentially subcultures, or categories, which describe members of a society, or they may involve close face-to-face interaction directed at common goals such as one finds in the family, among playmates, or in a committee. However we define the boundaries of groups, they have the potential for an impact on their members through shared psychological states. As Newcomb (1951) puts it:

> For social psychological purposes, at least, the distinctive thing about a group is that its members share norms about something. . . . Thus an American family is composed of members who share norms concerning their everyday living arrangements, and also concerning the manner in which they behave toward one another. These distinctive features of a group—shared norms and interlocking roles—presuppose a more than transitory relationship of interaction and communication (p. 38).

Newcomb mainly refers to what we will call *functional* groups. We may define these as having members who are mutually involved in ongoing social interaction aimed at achieving a common goal. This is accomplished through their interdependent action within an organized pattern of roles and norms called group *structure*.

Two other kinds of groups, which are better called *groupings,* are *categories* and *aggregates*. As we have previously indicated, a category is made up of people who possess a common characteristic which can be used to *describe* them. An aggregate is a special category composed of individuals who share a time-space relationship, but who do not have a common goal, unless circumstances should create one. People waiting at a corner for a bus or riding in an elevator together constitute aggregates. Should an emergency arise, however, they might organize to take collective action and thus become a short-term functional group.

The term "group" will be used here almost entirely to refer to groups that are of the functional kind. It should be emphasized, however, that the groupings to which we have just referred may also have influence effects comparable in some ways to those produced by functional groups. What appears to matter especially is the degree to which the individual is motivated to be identified with a group, even if he is not strictly speaking a member. But membership is the first approximation to knowing whether a group constitutes a set of "relevant others" for an individual, and we shall consider its features now.

Kinds of group membership

Basically, there are two major ways that individuals become members of a group. The first of these is called *ascription*, the second *acquisition*. They are distinguished from one another by the quality of choice. Insofar as we are born into a family it becomes an *ascribed* group membership. Alternatively, when we join a club, it becomes a group membership we acquire. In social psychological terms, the initial motivations for membership are sharply different. In the first case we have a low degree of choice, while in the second it is high. Furthermore, it is possible for motivations to shift. For example, soldiers are usually assigned to their unit, but this does not limit strong attachments and even a sense that it is "the best outfit in the Army." And the reasons we join a group may not be the ones that eventually sustain our membership.

A TAXONOMY OF GROUP IDENTITIES

Both functional groups and descriptive categories may be entered through acquired or ascribed membership. Examples of these relationships are given in Table 12.1. In the upper right quadrant, the family

Table 12.1: Schematic representation of four kinds of social identifications growing out of two sources of membership in two social entities, functional groups and descriptive categories.

Source of membership	Greater functionality ⟶	
	Descriptive Categories	Functional Groups
Ascribed (assigned: low choice)	Sex Age-level	Family Work group
Acquired (joined: high choice)	Profession Magazine subscriber	Social club Civic association

⟵ Greater volition

and a work group illustrate functional groups that are ascribed in the sense of low choice. It is a commonplace that we cannot choose our family, and usually it is equally true that we cannot choose our coworkers, at least not within most complex organizations. On the other hand, as shown in the lower right quadrant, we may join such functional groups as a social club—where we choose our friends—or a civic association, presumably because of some commitment to its goals.

Descriptive categories are not functional groups, though they may imply functional group membership. Here, too, there is the prospect of low or high choice in terms of the individual's initiative or volition in membership. Our sex and age are dictated by forces over which we have no control. Thus, we belong to some categories, shown in the upper left quadrant, which may have a considerable effect upon us but are not of our own choosing. However, there are other categories that may describe us, which we have a greater degree of choice in determining. Typically, a profession involves a great deal of psychological investment and, on a less serious level, our decision to subscribe to a magazine represents a voluntary choice as well.

There are exceptions, of course, to this last assertion. For example, some people do not choose a profession but have it thrust upon them by circumstance. This is true of other identities as well. Religion and political party illustrate two descriptive categories which are most often acquired as a kind of social inheritance through the family, though they may be altered in time. Furthermore, identities such as these, including professional affiliation, may involve us in functional groups. The attorney belongs to a professional category but also is probably involved in a law firm, which is a functional group.

Because of their immediate, face-to-face quality, functional groups are typically seen to be more potent in their effects than categories, but they need not be so. For instance, a broad professional identification may influence an individual considerably more than his social club, or even his family, in some critical sectors of life activity. Underlying any delineation of an individual's identifications, then, is the basic question of his motivation. This may be variously related to past experience and the nature of his present relationship with groups.

Very early it was clear that some groups involve special relationships which are not characteristic of others. The family, for example, is the first point of contact the child has with society. It is a group which has highly institutionalized functions involving procreation and child-rearing. There are, therefore, a great many pervasive psychological effects which it induces in the actions, reactions, and outlooks of its members.

Cooley (1909) considered that groups such as the family were *primary* groups. In the primary group, members have close personal ties with one another with an emphasis on face-to-face interaction and spontaneous interpersonal behavior.

To Cooley's view, primary groups were primary in the sense that they gave the individual his earliest and most complete experience of social identity. Since this kind of attachment could develop from other associations quite beyond the family, the qualities of primary groups have largely been absorbed within the concept of functional groups. We observe this, for instance, in connection with the child and his peers, especially in the teen years, as we have noted before. *Secondary* groups are by contrast more impersonal, and are characterized by contractual relations among their members. Being identified with such groups is not an end in itself but rather a means by which other ends may be achieved, such as working to earn a livelihood.

A somewhat similar distinction was made by an early sociologist, Tönnies (1887), in terms of *Gemeinschaft* and *Gesellschaft*, usually translated respectively as "community" and "society." The communal relations between people are more in keeping with the sense of social identity that goes with primary group affiliation, while relationships based upon more formal and contractual foundations tend toward the impersonality of secondary group affiliations. As society has moved from a rural to an urban mode of life, shifts may be seen from the former to the latter pattern. A bureaucracy also exemplifies secondary relationships far more than primary ones.

In a sense, any functional group can be considered to be a primary group if it is a source of mutual attractions. Katz and Lazarsfeld (1955) provide a summary of findings, in addition to their own research, which sustains the hypothesis that "such groups actively influence and support most of an individual's opinions, attitudes, and actions" (p. 48). According to these authors, the importance of primary group ties was rediscovered after long neglect. On the significance of this, Verba (1961) says:

> The "rediscovery" of the primary group refers to the realization by
> researchers that systems previously thought of as purely impersonal

and formal are greatly influenced by networks of informal personal relations. . . . In the first place, the researchers had not expected to find that primary relationships were important. . . . Secondly, these primary relationships were discovered in what might be called the heart of the modern industrial society . . . (p. 18).

By way of example, Verba points out that the major appeal of intense political participation may be a response to the weakened primary group attachments in the family. Thus, affiliative needs which are otherwise unsatisfied by the kind of secondary relationships existing in an industrial society may encourage ties to political groups, such as a political party, as an alternative. The motivations involved would accordingly be less political than psychological (p. 58).

The nature of groups

Groups exist fundamentally to help individuals attain goals that would be unattainable otherwise. They represent an organization of effort beyond a mere aggregation of disparate individuals. As Blumer (1948) says:

A human society is composed of diverse kinds of functional groups. To a major extent our total collective life is made up of the actions and acts of such groups. These groups are oriented in different directions because of special interests (p. 544).

It should be clear, however, that the avowed functions of a group, in terms of the interests supposedly served, may not be the same as the real functions for the members. The exclusive ladies' club which holds a charity ball seeks a goal that openly goes beyond milk for the underprivileged. The prestige value of some groups, the fun their members get out of it, may be more real functions than those given public prominence. Moreover, it is clear that multiple motivations may be simultaneously served by group activity. In the next chapter, we shall explore these psychological relationships further, after delving a bit more into the structure and interaction within functional groups.

GROUP STRUCTURE

Whatever motivates people to come together to achieve avowed ends in common, they take on organizational properties which create certain relationships among them. We call this *group structure,* and this affects *group interaction.* As we pointed out in Chapter Seven, structure refers to the pattern of social relationships within a given situation. In concrete terms, we mean by a group's structure that the people involved divide certain functions, establish communication links, become more sensitive to the expectancies of each other regarding normative actions, and take on a sense of group identity. Thus, group members have psychological relevance to one another, which influences the interactions that occur between them.

There are a number of types of structure, as well as different elements which comprise it. One element is the *rank* or hierarchical *position* which people occupy within a group. Cartwright and Zander (1960) make this point about its relevance:

> It appears to be almost impossible to describe what happens in groups without using terms which indicate the "place" of members with respect to one another. Various words have been employed, but the most common are: position, status, rank, office, role, part, clique, and subgroup. Although these do not all convey intuitively quite the same meaning, all do refer to the fact that individual members of a group can be located in relation to other members according to some criterion of placement. The prevalence of such terms in the literature on groups, moreover, suggests that such placement of individuals is important for understanding what happens in and to groups (p. 642).

Whenever several individuals come together or are brought together in a group to achieve certain ends, a structure invariably is generated. A differentiation of function occurs, and rules are laid down which become part of the normative pattern of the group. Furthermore, there is usually an associated network of communication which arises in order to have the group further its function.

Therefore, two other key elements which go to make up structure are the *norms* of the group and its *communication pattern.* More usually, a norm can be considered to be an expectancy regarding the appropriate behavior of group members within a given facet of group activity. As we have indicated before, a role can be thought of as a highly specialized norm applicable to a person occupying a given status, in the sense of position. In effect, groups are role systems. When we observe a committee in action, some of its members are more vocal than others.

What they say is heeded and often reacted to positively. Others are more passive. These observed differences may be a result of higher status, dictating a more active role, as well as of personality characteristics.

Communication patterns involve the question of who communicates with whom, particularly in formal organizations where such patterns are determined in large part by authority from above. In military organizations, for example, it is necessary to "go through channels" in order to gain a hearing. This, of course, is true of most institutionalized hierarchies. Even where groups set their own communication patterns, it is still true that some people may occupy a more central place in the group's communication network than will others.

Just as with interaction in general, influence processes including the exertion of power are activated within a group's structure. Thus, power becomes a significant determinant of the relationships among members of a group. Hurwitz, Zander, and Hymovitch (1953) found that people low in power within the group structure engaged in more ego-defensive reactions. They also tended to overrate how much their superiors liked them. In a related vein, Kelley (1951) found that subjects who held insecure positions in the group structure by being low and unable to rise or high with a potential for falling, engaged in more irrelevant communication within the group, in terms of the task. Moreover, they were less satisfied with the group.

As a general rule, low status members of a group tend to better themselves with those who hold greater power in the hierarchy, as E. E. Jones (1964) has noted in his work on "ingratiation." This phenomenon has also been observed with children. Lippitt, Polansky, and Rosen (1952), for example, found that children of low power are typically inclined to engage in deferential and ingratiating behavior toward children of higher power.

INTERACTION WITHIN GROUPS

Simmel (see 1950) was an early sociologist concerned with the face-to-face group as a microcosm of interaction which could be studied to derive general propositions about social behavior. In his view, these "small groups" provide a prototype of society. The most noteworthy exponent of this viewpoint today is George Homans. In two books, *The Human*

Group (1950) and *Social Behavior: Its Elementary Forms* (1961), he sets forth a number of factors which account for group processes. He says that we study these processes to learn something about "elementary social behavior," which occurs all about us. In a recent exposition (1963) of his views he contends:

> Small groups are not *what* we study but *where* we often study it. . . . If you will look at the behavior that students of small groups actually investigate, you will find that it has the following characteristics. First, at least two men are in face-to-face contact, each behaving toward the other in ways that reward or punish him and therefore influence his behavior. Second, the rewards or punishments that each gets from the behavior of the other are direct and immediate rather than indirect and deferred. And third, the behavior of the two men is determined in part by something besides their conformity to institutional rules or roles (p. 165).

An individual's behavior in a functional group, therefore, is reinforced by such face-to-face interaction. But note that this reinforcement is reciprocal, and furthermore that it comes to be normative in the sense of commonly held expectancies. Whether these are fulfilled is a major source of satisfaction in groups. The interaction of members can be studied in terms of the Bales categories discussed in Chapter Three (see p. 66). Figure 12.1 shows the differences in the categories of interaction for a five-person group that was satisfied with their interaction and a group that was dissatisfied. Note especially the major disparities between the groups in the categories of "agrees" and "disagrees."

The process of interaction occurs within the framework of the group's structure. Moreover, the structure itself undergoes change as a consequence of the events represented in interaction. The factor of historicity, which we dealt with earlier, insures that past interactions will have an effect upon the content of future interactions. This process may produce a change in structure. There are, of course, differences in the degree to which such alterations of structure are possible. For example, leadership, which is a structural element associated with a role of high status and influence, may be changed more readily in some situations than in others. The source of the leader's authority is of central significance in determining this outcome, and this depends upon the source of structure. We turn now to the implications of this in terms of formal and informal groups.

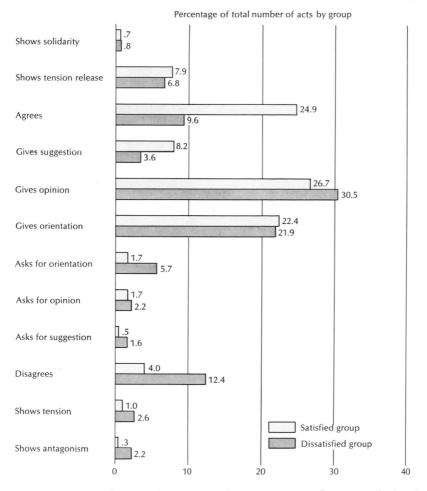

Figure 12.1: Distribution of interaction by categories within a satisfied and a dissatisfied group. (Based on data from Bales, 1952.)

FORMAL AND INFORMAL GROUPS

In functional groups, the goal of the group—essentially, its function— sets its structure, and this structure plays a significant part in interaction. Thus, structure and interaction are tied together so that changes in one may affect the other.

The source of a group's structure may lie within the group itself or in the external system in which it is imbedded. In organizations, typically, the goals and procedures of a group are governed by factors outside of the group's direct control. A work group, for example, has functional features of a *formal* kind which are specified by regulations. There are other kinds of functional groups whose organization is determined by the members themselves in an *informal* fashion. However, as we shall be noting further, the distinction between formal and informal structure is probably less important than the identification individuals have with the group.

Friendship groups are informal. They arise spontaneously out of common interests and certain shared goals, and they are sustained by interpersonal attraction. Research by Festinger, Schachter, and Back (1950) and by Newcomb (1961), for example, indicates that attraction within such groups is heavily dependent upon closeness of contact and is then enhanced by mutual interests. Thus, the teenager will select his friends among those who live nearby and who enjoy the same kind of records, play activities, and probably share similar problems. The major point about such groups is that they are autonomous in the sense of determining their own activities and being relatively free of organizational constraints.

On the other hand, most of the tasks of society are fulfilled by groups which are considerably more organized in the sense of a work orientation. Groups in organizations operate with a heavy infusion of structure from above. They are not autonomous so much as being components within a broader enterprise. Moreover, membership is determined for the most part by non-voluntary factors.

Homans (1961) considers that any group constitutes a social system that has both internal and external features. The elements in the internal system of a group are *activities, interactions,* and *sentiments.* Activities refer to movements that people do to or with non-human objects, such as typing, writing, building, driving, and so forth. By contrast, interaction refers to things people do together, such as eating, working co-operatively and playing games. Sentiments essentially refer to feelings and attitudes about things or events whether human or non-human. Homans sees these as being interrelated in such a way that if either sentiments or activities are changed, the tone of interaction will also change. Furthermore, this is a two-way relationship. Interaction and positive sentiments are directly related so that, other things equal, we tend to like those with whom we interact. These relationships, within the internal system of a group, are intimately tied to the external system.

Homans's essential principle of group functioning is that when several individuals form a functional group, or are formed into such a group, an internal system of social processes comes into play. This system, including member interaction, is affected by the group's own structure which derives in part from the normative expectations in the external environment.

An example of the influence of the external system on the internal system of a group comes from research on juries by Strodtbeck, James, and Hawkins (1958). Their major interest was in the interaction process which occurred in 49 jury deliberations, with real jurors listening to a recorded trial and then discussing it. They found that, beginning with the selection of a foreman, socio-economic differentials were important determiners of internal processes. Though the jurors were meeting as equals, their status in the broader society had considerable effect. Thus, in the jurors' selection of their foreman,

> There was no instance in which mention of any socioeconomic criteria was made, but this is not to say that socioeconomic criteria were not involved . . . some foremen were selected from all strata, but the incidence was three and a half times as great among proprietors as among laborers. In addition . . . only one fifth as many women were chosen as foremen as would be expected by chance (p. 382).

A related conclusion from this study was that socio-economic status affected the rate of juror participation sharply and that, as would be expected, those who participated more were more influential in the deliberations. Furthermore, these variables were interrelated such that the first person to speak had a higher probability of being selected as a foreman, and initial speakers tended to be from higher occupational strata.

In the last analysis, the distinction between formal and informal groups therefore becomes a matter of differentiating group activities and the kind of structures within which groups carry on their functions. To do this requires further attention to the properties of a group.

Group properties

In studying and differentiating groups, two levels are involved—the *group* level and the *individual* level. These terms are used to emphasize the source of primary data regarding a phenomenon. If we say that a group is productive, and we measure this by the output per unit time for the group, than we are dealing with the group level of analysis. Alternatively, if we ask the members of the group how successfully the group performed, then these responses are at the individual level. Such responses may then be summed together to provide a score or index of the group's success, as its members see it, but this is not the same as using a criterion on the group level.

Attempts to study groups in terms of their own properties, rather than as an aggregation of individual attributes, have focused on several kinds of variables. Proceeding from the broadest and most obvious group properties to the more specific and less obvious, several approaches have been followed. The first of these is the study of dimensions of groups, mainly through the *technique of factor analysis.* The other approaches in the study of groups emphasize *group size, group cohesiveness* and *group communication.*

THE FACTOR ANALYTIC APPROACH TO GROUP DIMENSIONS

A major exponent of the study of group dimensions through factor analysis is Raymond Cattell (1948, 1951). His essential contention is that a group may be described in a general way, much as one might describe an individual's personality. To achieve this Cattell proposes three sets of variables or concepts at a group level, which he calls "panels." These are *population, structure,* and *syntality.* In Cattell's system, population encompasses the psychological characteristics of group members in regard to personality and attitude-interest measures. This focus leads to a description of the attributes of individuals within the group that may bear on group productivity, some of which we considered in Chapter Ten. Structure, in Cattell's terms, embodies the pattern of interaction within the group. This covers especially the kinds of relationships that exist between the individual group members as a group property.

Perhaps most important in Cattell's system is the concept of group syntality. It refers, in broadest terms, to the performance of the group as a whole (see Cattell, 1948). This focus on syntality underscores Cattell's position that groups have qualities apart from those of their individual members and it has merit as one approach to understanding the broader character of groups.

When measured empirically, however, group syntality does not provide information about individual reactions, in terms of the processes occurring in a group. Thus, some things that are said to be part of syntality are an average of individual members' evaluations, and these may vary considerably. For example, two groups might have a common level of syntality, but be quite different in their internal processes of interaction, including member motivations and activities.

A wider approach to studying the dimensions of groups has been presented by Hemphill (1950a) who has set forth fifteen dimensions which can be used in distinguishing their characteristics. These dimensions represent those kinds of things at both the group and individual levels that might affect group performance. They are:

1. *Size* of the group
2. *Viscidity* or the degree to which the group functions as a unit
3. *Homogeneity* of group members with respect to socially relevant characteristics such as age, sex, and background
4. *Flexibility* of a group's activities in terms of informal procedures rather than adherence to established procedures
5. *Stability* of a group with respect to frequency of major changes over a period of time
6. *Permeability* of a group regarding ready access to membership
7. *Polarization* of a group in terms of its orientation and functioning toward a single goal
8. *Autonomy* of a group with respect to its functioning independently of other groups
9. *Intimacy* of group members in regard to mutual acquaintance and familiarity with details of one another's lives

10. *Control* or the degree to which a group regulates the behavior of individuals, while they are functioning as group members
11. *Participation* of group members in applying time and effort to the group's activities
12. *Potency* or importance of the group for its members
13. *Hedonic tone* in terms of the degree to which group membership is accompanied by a general feeling of pleasantness or unpleasantness
14. *Position* of group members with respect to an ordering of status in a hierarchy
15. *Dependence* of group members upon the group.

Hemphill and Westie (1950) have detailed the basis for measuring these dimensions. They found that individuals describing the same group, ranging from a small committee to a large university, tended to give similar ratings on the dimensions. However, Hemphill (1956) reports that depending upon the way in which a "group" is defined—in terms of descriptive categories and aggregates versus face-to-face functional groups—distinct differences in the homogeneity of ratings are found. Borgatta, Cottrell, and Meyer (1956) have surveyed this work on group dimensions, especially those studies using factor analysis, and conclude that a major need is for a more consistent use of factor names. In any event, there does seem to be a valid basis for describing group characteristics along several dimensions, and among these group size appears to be of great importance.

GROUP SIZE

As a group increases in size, certain changes occur in the relationship among members. For example, Hemphill (1950b) has studied the frequency with which "superior" leaders of larger groups (31 or more) are reported to engage in specified kinds of behavior in contrast with the "superior" leaders of smaller groups (30 or less). He reports that, in general, as the group becomes larger, demands upon the leader become greater and more numerous, and acceptance of the leader's influence becomes greater. Thus, the structure of interaction is affected by group size. This result is shown in Figure 12.2 which presents a com-

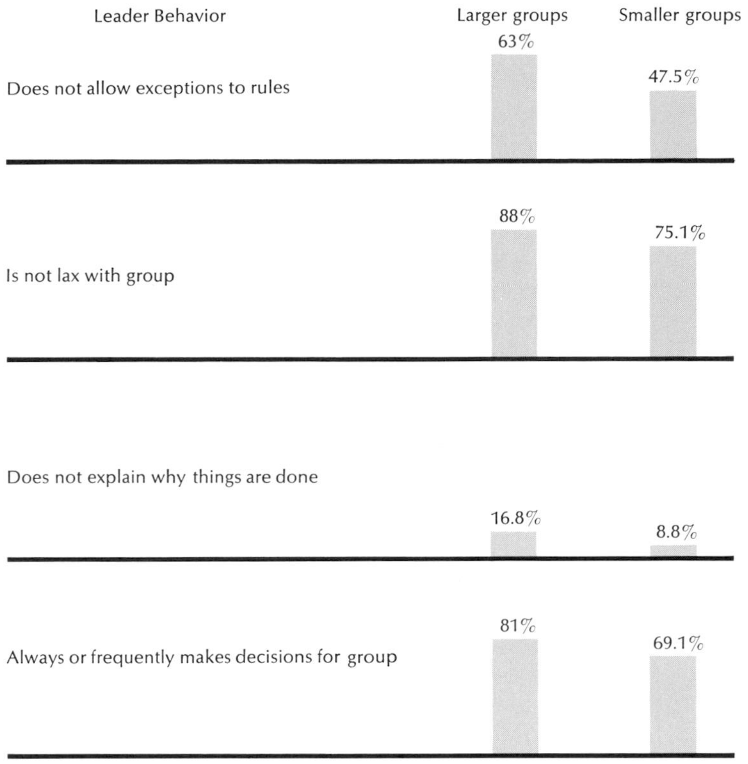

Figure 12.2: Differences in rating of four behaviors of "superior" leaders obtained from members of larger and smaller groups. (Based on data from Hemphill, 1950.)

parison of the percentage of members in larger groups and smaller groups reporting a given leader behavior. The four behaviors shown are those that revealed the most significant differences in Hemphill's study. It should be added that "smallness" as defined in this study is quite a bit larger than the five-person group typically studied in the laboratory experiment. Had something like this criterion of small size been applied, the differences obtained might have been sharper still.

In another vein, Bales and Borgatta (1955) have found that groups made up of an even number of members display interaction patterns on discussion tasks different from groups with an odd number of members. Most marked are the differences between groups made up of two people, *diads,* and those of two and any odd number, with two-person groups showing higher ratings on disagreement and antagonism. They explain this because two-person groups can only achieve a majority in one way, by both parties agreeing.

However, three-person groups, or *triads*, present problems too. Experimental work by Mills (1953) found that in triads a distinct tendency occurs for two members to pair against the other member. In general, the triad is considered to be unstable because of the tendency toward coalition-formation (Caplow, 1956; Vinacke & Arkoff, 1957). This varies though depending upon the members' relationship with one another. For example, research by Strodtbeck (1954) with three-person families only partially confirms Mills's findings. This may be explained as a feature of the family which requires more accommodation to maintain the integrity of the group. Strong social pressures therefore operate to reduce in family triads the split which is observed in more loosely associated groups of three in experimental situations.

Vinacke (1959) has studied triads composed of males or females involved in a bargaining game where there was one "powerful" member. As in Caplow's (1956) work, he found that the two members of "weaker power" tended to ally against the stronger, irrespective of the sex of group members. However, women were far more inclined to seek accommodation with less coalition-formation than were the men. Bond and Vinacke (1961) found that mixing sexes with a majority of men or of women essentially yielded a parallel to the all male or all female patterns already noted. The results of a further study by Uesugi and Vinacke (1963) showed that changing the content of the game to give it greater feminine interest only served to increase accommodation rather than competition among females. Thus, they contend that accommodation in triads is partly a function of culturally induced personality characteristics which appear to be more pronounced among females (p. 80).

Other studies of group size have emphasized performance and interaction processes occurring in groups of varying sizes. Some of these relationships are readily predictable on an arithmetic basis. Bossard (1945), for example, has provided a formula for the possible relations between members of groups as the number in the group grows. A curve indicating the sharp rise in this number of possible relations is shown in Figure 12.3. This has a bearing on member participation and satisfaction. Accordingly, different qualities may characterize internal group relationships as a function of group size. Carter, Haythorn, Meirowitz, and Lanzetta (1951) found differences in rates of participation within groups varying from four to eight members in size.

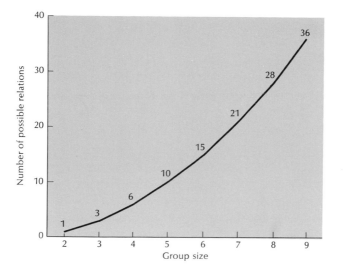

Figure 12.3: Increasing number of two-person relations illustrated for groups from two to nine in size. (Based upon data from Bossard, 1945.)

Slater (1958) conducted an experiment with discussion groups each of which met four times. They ranged in size from two to seven members. He found that groups made up of five members expressed greatest satisfaction on their subsequent ratings of the group experience. When groups exceeded five members, higher rates of competitive and impulsive behavior were reported. Therefore, not only does the prospect for participation change as a consequence of group size, there also may be a corresponding change in the feeling generated by that participation. Bales, Strodtbeck, Mills, and Roseborough (1951), relatedly, have found that the larger the group the greater the disparity between the most frequent contributors to group discussion and the other members in the amount of prominence. There is a tendency toward a disproportionate share of time being taken up by a few prominent members, and this is directly associated with member dissatisfaction.

The results of research on group size clearly point to the frustrations associated with largeness, especially where the groups convene in face-to-face interaction. However, this need not color relationships adversely in large organizations, if members are organized into smaller work groups which provide for participation and mutual attraction. It is this latter property of cohesiveness to which we now turn.

GROUP COHESIVENESS

Cohesiveness is a term which is used to describe a group property in the nature of solidarity or unity. Generally speaking, cohesive groups are supposed to be better co-ordinated than non-cohesive groups and have a greater sense of "we" feeling. As the term itself suggests, the members of cohesive groups are more likely to stick together, to co-operate, and participate in their common enterprises more fully.

While everyday observations confirm differences in the extent to which groups evidence this property, its measurement presents problems. These have been handled in various ways, involving one or both levels of analysis represented by the individuals comprising a group, or the group itself. On the individual level, cohesiveness is often measured by having members indicate their group's attractiveness to them. On the group level, the group's performance is usually taken as measure of cohesiveness because, practically speaking, performance is a readily observed outgrowth of activity. Yet, the performance of a group need not imply that it should necessarily be highly cohesive, though it often does (see Libo, 1953). Schachter, Ellertson, McBride and Gregory (1951) are among those who have pointed out that the productivity of a group is not necessarily a direct function of the average of members' attraction to it. They indicate, for example, that a highly cohesive group could have norms encouraging low rather than high rates of productivity. This might occur in a work setting where the workers resist the standards set by management.

The research literature on cohesiveness is quite extensive and, for the most part, tends to accept a definition of cohesiveness along the lines suggested by Festinger, Schachter, and Back (1950, p. 164) as the "total field of forces which act on members to remain in the group." But as Israel (1956) notes, this definition is difficult to apply in research since it usually comes down to group attraction. An alternative definition might be the degree to which group members conform to group norms (Landecker, 1955). As Hagstrom and Selvin (1965) observe, however, this definition creates a problem of circularity because, where hypotheses about the relationship of cohesiveness and conformity are being tested, both variables would be commonly measured.

"Attraction" measures of cohesiveness remain the most typical though they can hide individual variations within the group when they are used as a simple average. This might lead to the conclusion that a group is cohesive when in fact several members inflate the average by their high ratings. Even granting this deficiency, it is acknowledged that being attracted to a group remains the most distinctive *social psychological* avenue to understanding its effects on individuals. Whether this attraction is a *unitary* variable or a combination of several factors is another matter.

Gross and Martin (1952) report that three indexes of attraction within residence groups of college women did not have uniformly high positive correlations with one another. In another study with the same kind of subjects, Hagstrom and Selvin (1965) have recently found that two factors emerge from ratings of a group's attraction. One they label "sociometric cohesion," which reflects the intrinsic attraction of the group to its members, and the other "social satisfaction" which takes in the instrumental attraction of the group in terms of the activities it provides. In short, a group may be evaluated positively for the people who are its members and the values they represent, as well as for the kinds of tasks in which they engage co-operatively. Both of these effects have been verified in research. In one such study by Hollander (1964, Ch. 7), a high positive correlation was found between the perception of group members' values being similar to one's own and attraction to the group.

The broader question of how a group becomes attractive has been dealt with by Cartwright and Zander (1960). They stress that attraction arises primarily from the satisfactions a group provides through the achievement of what it is in the member's interest to have it achieve. Individual motivations are therefore of substantial importance in the emergence of a sense of group cohesiveness, as we have previously noted. The consequences of cohesiveness to group processes will be considered further in connection with group dynamics. For the moment we will look at the related phenomenon of intra-group communication.

INTRA-GROUP COMMUNICATION

An important structural property of groups is their network of communication. In the Leavitt study (1951), reported in Chapter Three, the positioning of people with regard to who could communicate to whom was found to be important to group efficiency and member satisfaction. Thus, the "wheel" was fastest, but the "circle" most satisfying (see p. 73). Leavitt interpreted his findings in line with centrality and peripherality in the group's communication network. Individuals who are more "central" are positioned to receive and send more communications and tend to be more satisfied than those who are by contrast "peripheral."

Shaw (1954) has reasoned that another factor of significance in communication networks is availability of information. In his experiment, a peripheral subject in each of the networks was given five units of information while the others were given one unit each. This considerably altered the previous results obtained by Leavitt. Shaw found that under these conditions the circle was fastest as well as the most satisfying. Furthermore, those with more information were as satisfied as those who were central. The importance of these findings is twofold. First, it indicates that it is more information, rather than merely centrality, which creates satisfaction. Second, it highlights the place of information as a group "resource" whose possession is important to the group as well as gratifying to those who can dispense it. Since a group functions in part by the flow of information, through communication, access to it increases the group's prospects for achievement. Those who provide such access are accordingly rewarded.

Being central in a communication structure is one characteristic of leadership. Typically, the leader is a group member who receives and sends more communications than others, and who thereby exerts influence on the group's activity. A person in a leadership position is, moreover, likely to have greater control over group resources, which includes information as well as his own competence in matters affecting the achievement of the group goal.

The close association between communication and leadership, as an influence process, will be considered further in Chapter Thirteen. It is worth noting here that several experiments (e.g. Berkowitz, 1956; Medow and Zander, 1965) indicate that a person placed in a central position in a communication network evidences more assertive leader-type behavior. Furthermore, that person reports more involvement in the group's activity, and is perceived by other members to be more motivated and more responsible for the group's outcomes. Therefore, the network of intra-group communication is a property of the group's structure which has a high degree of significance to group functioning.

Communication within groups is not solely taken up with the group's task, even though laboratory experiments emphasize this feature of group functioning. In the ongoing interaction between members of a continuing group, patterns of communication may reflect normative practices about who speaks first and to whom. Seniority and tradition itself may determine such patterns, independently of any immediate task, as Parsons, Bales, and Shils (1953) observe. These are instigated through a sequence of interaction which provides reinforcement for the utterances of some members more than others, thus creating roles. As these authors put it:

> Insofar as a given person "gets on the right track" and receives positive reaction from other members, he will be reinforced in his direction of movement, and will tend to keep on talking. He will "generalize" from the premises, logical and emotional, which underlay his original successful attempt . . . and reciprocally, the other members will "generalize" from his earlier attempts, gratifying in some sense to them, to an expectation of further effective behavior on his part. The member begins to build a "specialized role" (p. 133).

Communication processes in a group therefore serve to create as well as to maintain differences in role behavior. These differences are associated with hierarchical status in the group. Such a hierarchy is shown in Figure 12.4. It is drawn from the field work of W. F. Whyte (1943) with a neighborhood gang in Boston. Doc was the leader of this group and his immediate "lieutenants" were Mike and Danny. Each member of the group had his own position in the hierarchy indicated by the relative rank of the circles in Figure 12.4. Though their positions might remain consistent over some time, the hierarchy was not a static one. When the relationship between members changed, their positions changed.

A primary activity of this street-corner group was bowling. Doc had

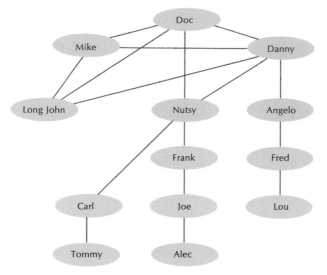

Figure 12.4: Relative positions in social organization of the Norton Street Gang. (From *Street Corner Society* by William F. Whyte by permission of The University of Chicago Press. Copyright 1943.)

achieved his position of leadership partly because of his bowling skill. But the hierarchy was not built on this ability alone. Therefore it was possible for a low status member, Alec, to be a better bowler than some of those of higher status. When this happened in the presence of other group members, Alec was consistently heckled and jeered by them. Thus, communications were brought to bear to maintain the status hierarchy. Whyte reports:

> One evening I heard Alec boasting to Long John that the way he was bowling he could take on every man on the first team and lick them all. Long John dismissed the challenge with these words: "You think you could beat us, but, under pressure, you die!" [In] . . . a match held toward the end of April . . . Alec was leading by several pins . . . but then he began to miss, and, as mistake followed mistake, he stopped trying . . . [Later] as Doc told me: "Alec isn't so aggressive these days. I steamed up at the way he was going after Long John, and I blasted him. . . . Then I talked to Long John. . . . I made him see that he should bowl better than Alec. I persuaded him that he was really the better bowler." The records of the season . . . show a very close correspondence between social position and bowl-

ing performance. . . . Bowling scores did not fall automatically into this pattern. There were certain customary ways of behaving which exerted pressure upon the individuals. Chief among these were the manner of choosing sides and the verbal attacks the members directed against one another. . . . When a follower threatened to better his position . . . the boys shouted at him that he was lucky, that he was "bowling over his head." . . . This type of verbal attack was very important in keeping the members "in their places" (pp. 19-24).

In general, then, intra-group communications follow the pattern of status in the group and thereby serve to maintain it (see Klein, 1956, p. 33). But the net effect of communication is not in a static direction. Indeed, communication considerably facilitates various processes of group dynamics which we will consider in the next chapter.

SUMMARY

All human societies are organized into collective entities called groups that carry on the necessary and significant functions of the society. Individuals have affiliations with many groups, each of which has the potential for affecting the individual's actions and psychological states.

Usually, in speaking of groups, we refer to *functional groups* made up of members who have regularized social interaction aimed at the achievement of a *common goal.* Such groups require interdependent action within a pattern of organization of relationships called *structure.* Two other ways of grouping people are by *descriptive categories,* made up of people who share a common characteristic such as age level, and by *aggregates,* composed of individuals who share a time-space relationship.

People become members of functional groups and categories in two major ways—by *ascription* and by *acquisition.* An ascribed group membership refers to less voluntary or non-voluntary circumstances, such as being born into a family. An *acquired* group membership involves a greater range of choice, in the sense of joining a group. Thus, the initial motivations for membership are different, though they may change later. Both functional groups and descriptive categories may be entered through acquired or ascribed membership.

The initial psychological impact on individuals is considered to be greatest from those functional groups, including the family, called *primary groups.* Such groups provide close relationships and mutual attraction. Recent work has re-emphasized the importance of such close ties, apart from the task of groups, within work settings.

Groups carry on their operations within a *structure.* Three features of structure are the *status differentiation* within the group, its *norms,* and its *communication pattern.* Norms and status are interrelated insofar as specialized roles are created for a person occupying a given status. In this sense, a role can be thought of as a highly specialized norm within the role system which characterizes any group.

The nature of structure affects *interaction* within groups. In functional groups, the process of interaction is determined in part by the source of structure, whether imposed or determined by the group itself. The distinction between *formal* and *informal* groups depends upon this source of structure. Organizations typically set the goals and procedures of a group which make it formal. By contrast, friendship groups are informal with a more spontaneous structure growing out of common interests and interpersonal attraction. The distinction between formal and informal groups is not always sharp since the *internal system* of any group may be affected in various ways by its *external system.*

The study of groups may be approached on two levels, the *group* level and the *individual* level; this depends on the primary data of interest in studying social phenomena. The productivity of a group exemplifies the group level of analysis, while the satisfaction of members of the group exemplifies the individual level.

Among the techniques applied to studying groups in terms of their own properties, *factor analysis* has been quite prominent. It yields several group dimensions, such as its overall performance, in terms of *syntality,* its stability, its autonomy, and its homogeneity of membership.

Group *size* is one of the more important factors in determining the functioning and psychological effects of groups. Studies of the interaction processes occurring in groups of various sizes have indicated differences between *diads,* two-person groups, and *triads,* three-person groups. Furthermore, as groups increase in size, the number of possible relationships among members accelerates sharply. The prospect for participation in groups of larger size decreases and a greater disparity is found between the frequent contributors to group discussion and the others. There are also differences in leadership within groups of larger size, and increased frustrations associated with largeness.

The *cohesiveness* of a group, in terms of its solidarity or unity, is a factor which produces and reflects the interactions within a group. The measurement of cohesiveness has largely been approached in terms of the attraction of the group to its members. On the group level, there are other measures including performance and conformity, which have been taken as signs of cohesiveness. In terms of its effect upon its members, attraction continues to be a major avenue for understanding the social psychology of group processes.

Related to cohesiveness is the *communication network* within a group. Experimental findings indicate that persons who are more central in this network tend to be more satisfied. Centrality, however, appears to be associated with an individual's accessibility to and control over the flow of information within the group. Those who are more central, and thereby control more of the group's communication resources, are found to evidence more assertive leader-type behavior. Communication also functions within a group to stabilize the status hierarchy, including the differentiation of roles.

SUGGESTED READINGS

From E. P. Hollander and R. G. Hunt. (Eds.) *Current perspectives in social psychology.* (2nd Edition.) New York: Oxford University Press, 1967:

Introduction to Section VII: *Normative behavior, conformity, and intra-group processes*
43. James G. March: *Group norms and the active minority*

SELECTED REFERENCES

Golembiewski, R. T. *The small group.* Chicago: Univer. of Chicago Press, 1962.
Hare, A. P. *Handbook of small group research.* New York: Free Press, 1961.
Hare, A. P., Borgatta, E. F., & Bales, R. F. (Eds.) *Small groups.* New York: Knopf, 1955. (2nd edition, 1965.)
Homans, G. C. *The human group.* New York: Harcourt, Brace, 1950.
*Katz, E., & Lazarsfeld, P. F. *Personal influence.* Glencoe, Ill.: Free Press, 1955.

Klein, Josephine. *The study of groups.* London: Routledge & Kegan Paul, 1956.

McGrath, J. E., & Altman, I. *Small group research: A synthesis and critique of the field.* New York: Holt, Rinehart & Winston, 1966.

*Olmsted, M. S. *The small group.* New York: Random House, 1959.

*Stogdill, R. M. *Individual behavior and group achievement.* New York: Oxford Univ. Press, 1959.

13

Group dynamics and inter-group relations

Group dynamics is often used as a general label for the processes and their consequences occurring within groups. In its special usage, the term refers to the tradition of experimentation on groups established by Kurt Lewin. From that impetus, group dynamics continues to emphasize the influence on individuals of processes occurring in small face-to-face groups (see Cartwright and Zander, 1960).

In this chapter we will examine the wider scope of group dynamics with regard to social change, group effectiveness, and intergroup relations, as well as other psychological aspects of groups. As an initial point of reference, we turn to the basic processes that determine what happens in groups.

Basic processes

Lewin considered two variables to be particularly important for the understanding of the dynamics of a group—*group cohesiveness* and *group locomotion*. Each of these implies a process. We have already stressed the degree to which cohesiveness, seen as the sum of forces which bind an individual to a group, plays a vital role in determining the group's influence on its members. Shortly we will elaborate several points concerning its relationship to communication and conformity.

371

The concept of group locomotion is essentially one of movement toward a desired goal. A group is conceived to be operating in a field of forces in one region to attain a goal in another region. It is generally assumed that this locomotion is directed at the "goal region." In a political campaign, for example, the supporters of a candidate will be working toward his election and their goal is clear.

Generally speaking, the clarity of a group goal has an important enhancement effect in furthering group locomotion. In an experiment by Raven and Rietsema (1957), the group's performance was considerably facilitated by members' awareness of what goal was being sought and how it was to be achieved. Furthermore, various studies have pointed to the importance of the interdependence of group members, and their co-operation, as factors which improve locomotion (e.g. Deutsch, 1949b; Thomas, 1957). In his theory of social communication, Festinger (1950) employs locomotion as a major variable determining pressures toward conformity in a group. He postulates that such pressures will be greater to the extent that group members perceive that group movement would be facilitated by conformity, and this has been experimentally verified in the research of Schachter (see Chapter Three, pp. 74-76).

THE INTERDEPENDENCE OF COHESIVENESS,
COMMUNICATION, AND CONFORMITY

Conformity, which will be treated more fully in the next chapter, can be thought of as an individual's adherence to group expectancies. Berkowitz (1954), among others, has found conformity to be greater where a group is more cohesive. Furthermore, its probability is increased by communications from other group members directed at bringing the individual "into line." There are also reciprocal relations between these variables, as is shown in Figure 13.1. Each has an effect upon the others, and none can be considered solely an independent or a dependent variable.

Any proposition which states a functional relationship between a pair of these variables has some demonstrable validity. Greater conformity not only is positively affected by greater cohesiveness, it also tends to increase cohesiveness. When members of a group share similar attitudes and abide by normative behaviors, their cohesiveness rises (Newcomb, 1956, 1961). This is understandable with reference to the comfort and smoothness of more predictable interaction associated with greater uniformity. In the realm of ability also, Zander and Havelin (1960) have found that greater similarity strengthens group bonds. Similarly, communication is higher among members of more cohesive groups (Bales, 1950b).

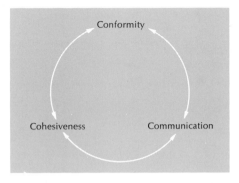

Figure 13.1: Diagrammatic representation of the reciprocal relations among cohesiveness, communication, and conformity.

Thus, when we tap into any of these three variables, we are likely to find associations with the others. An illustration of this is in the study in Westgate West by Festinger, Schachter, and Back (1950). They observed the development of group norms in this new apartment project for married veterans attending MIT. The project consisted of a number of residential courts with several buildings, each building having a number of apartments. Before coming to the project, the residents did not know each other, and they were assigned to apartments largely at random. The research found that friendship ties developed among members of this community as a result of propinquity. In Chapter Seven on social interaction, we covered a number of the obvious features of propinquity, in terms of physical contact, as a basic condition for the development of interpersonal attraction. Without contact and communication, it is of course far less likely that people can have the opportunity to develop such ties and similarity of attitude. Illustrating this, people living near the apartment mail boxes were found to know more people and have more contact with them.

Friendship choices were also found to be based on the arrangement

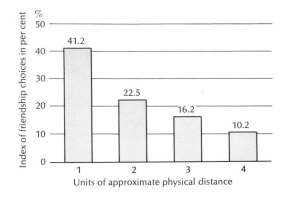

Figure 13.2: Relationship of friendship choices to physical distance on a floor of Westgate West. (Based on data from Festinger, Schachter, and Back, 1950.)

of apartments. On the average, the respondents gave 41 per cent of the possible number of friendship choices to people who lived very close by on their floor. As is shown in Figure 13.2, this percentage systematically dropped off as the units of distance from other residents there increased. Regarding conformity, it was found that certain prevailing norms existed with respect to the attitudes that members of a given residential court held. They had been asked how they felt about a new "tenant's counsel," and highly similar attitudes were found among the respondents living in the same court. Furthermore, the more the members of the court were attracted to one another, in a cohesiveness sense, the greater was the uniformity of attitude in that court on this issue and the more they communicated with one another through social interaction.

The matter of cohesiveness has vital practical implications in functional groups. During World War II, large-scale research was done on factors involved in troop morale, a major report of which is *The American Soldier* (see Stouffer, *et al.*, 1949). In one of a series of studies, an essential finding was that combat motivation was most related to close, primary group affiliations. One of the major reasons soldiers gave for willingness to enter battle was protection of buddies, or a desire to do what their buddies expected of them. In general, motives like this were found to be more salient to the combat soldier than were more abstract things like hatred of the enemy, political ideology, or the formal orders and disciplinary demands from above. Thus, cohesiveness implies a concern for others and a readiness to do what is expected by them.

Research with industrial work groups also indicates that cohesiveness plays a significant part in their activity. For example, Kerr and his colleagues (1951) conducted a field study in a large factory. They were investigating factors affecting absenteeism, turnover, and morale, in relationship to job efficiency and satisfaction. While it is often assumed that conversation impedes productivity, these investigators found that those groups characterized by a high degree of conversation were not lower producers. Furthermore, they had relatively low turnover, low absenteeism, and high work satisfaction. Thus, intra-group communication among employees increased the cohesiveness of their work group and actually resulted in benefits to the company, rather than the kind of loss which is often imputed to conversation on the job. This effect would of course depend upon the nature of the job to be performed, since not all tasks lend themselves to conversation. The key point, however, is that work-group cohesiveness can have a beneficial effect on the relationship of the worker to his organization. Here again, the significant determiner of this effect appears to be the cohesiveness of the group, which is nourished by communication.

SOCIAL CHANGE

The word "dynamic" usually conveys the idea of forces affecting change. Therefore, group dynamics should appropriately concern itself with the processes over time by which changes occur in groups. An important contribution of Lewin's to understanding social change begins with his assertion that it has two aspects. To render change requires not only the introduction of innovation but also the overcoming of resistance represented in attachments to prevailing practices. In Lewin's terms, these practices are in a state of "quasi-stationary equilibrium" and need to be "unfrozen" before new practices at another level of equilibrium can be established. Thus, Lewin (1947) says:

> . . . it is of great practical importance that levels of quasi-stationary equilibria can be changed in either of two ways: by adding forces in the desired direction, or by diminishing opposing forces. . . . In both cases the equilibrium might change to the same new level. The

> secondary effect should, however, be quite different. In the first case, the process on the new level would be accompanied by a state of relatively high tension; in the second case, by a state of relatively low tension (p. 342).

Lewin is therefore quite emphatic in pointing up the importance of the *process* by which change is brought about. In overcoming resistance to the opposing forces, Lewin considers the group as a major vehicle for bringing individuals to a more ready acceptance of new conditions and requirements. His own research on group decision-making, and the related work of Coch and French (1948), both discussed in Chapter Three (see pp. 70 and 71), illustrates how group support can be instrumental in influencing individuals to perceive new alternatives more favorably.

An extension of Lewin's ideas about the effect of groups upon individuals in rendering change is found in Cartwright's principles drawn from group dynamics (1951). On a practical level they sum up a number of coherent points growing out of the group dynamics framework. Several of his principles are these:

> The more attractive the group is to its members, the greater is the influence that the group can exert on its members.
>
> In attempts to change attitudes, values, or behavior, the more relevant they are to the basis of attraction to the group, the greater will be the influence that the group can exert upon them.
>
> Efforts to change individuals or some parts of the group which, if successful, would have the result of making them deviate from the norms of the group will encounter strong resistance.

The stress which Cartwright brings to bear here reveals a number of forces. Prominent among these is the identity of the individual with the group as a factor which can either increase or inhibit the prospects for change. Unless individuals share the "we" feeling associated with such identification, the functioning of the group in the face of demands for change will be impaired. In this respect, Atthowe (1961) conducted an experiment with pairs of people working together on a common task and found that the early use of the pronoun "we" was associated with more efficiency in decision-making. In those pairs where the pronoun "I" was used more frequently, especially in the earlier phases of interaction, their efficiency in adapting to the demands of the task was considerably lower. Relatedly, Fouriezos, Hutt, and Guetzkow (1950) studied the content of interaction in group meetings in terms of self-oriented versus group-oriented activity. They found that those meetings showing a high frequency of self-oriented activity were much less satisfying to group members and much less likely to produce cohesiveness.

It is reasonable to suppose from this and other research that a group composed of members with a weak sense of identity is more vulnerable to external influences. As Verba (1961) notes, soldiers are more likely to be affected by enemy propaganda when they no longer feel strong group identity. In short, they are more inclined to be swayed and change their attitudes when social ties with their unit are broken. Alternatively, as Cartwright's principles above suggest, a person's attitudes will not readily change if they are anchored in a group membership of importance to the individual. Illustrating this, Kelley and Volkart (1952) conducted a field experiment with troops of boy scouts. By using a questionnaire, they were able to identify the scouts in advance who were or were not highly identified with their troop. They also obtained data on their attitudes toward scouting. Then the entire troop was presented with a speech by a guest speaker who disputed the merits of two key features of scouting—woodcraft and camping. Afterward another questionnaire was administered to determine any change in attitude on these points from those attitudes obtained originally with the earlier questionnaire. The findings were quite clearcut. Scouts *without* a high identification with their troop showed a significantly greater shift in attitude toward agreement with the speaker than did the others.

We have been treating identification here as a factor growing out of *individual* motivations. It is not the same as cohesiveness, though it relates to it on the group level since members of a highly cohesive group are presumed to share such positive identifications. The significant point, all in all, is that change is effected through groups, but individual motivations and perceptions are necessarily implicated in the process. In the sections which follow, we will give further consideration to group effectiveness and other psychological aspects of group dynamics.

Group effectiveness

Given the great diversity of groups, and the variable nature of their membership, the idea of effectiveness as a group characteristic can be misleading. What may be effective in one group, by some criterion, may not be effective in another. Every group faces a challenge from the environment in terms of a set of goals which are to be achieved as part of the group's task. As McGrath (1964, p. 70) points out, since tasks vary in their properties, they also impose different requirements upon the group. Thus, effectiveness must always be gauged with regard to the particular group and the challenge it faces. However, there is a certain validity in considering factors yielding effectiveness, once the need for this specification of circumstances is recognized.

In formal terms, Barnard (1938) has defined effectiveness as "the accomplishment of the recognized objectives of cooperative action" (p. 55). These objectives may lie in several directions, however. Essentially, there are two ways that groups may be viewed as effective in handling their tasks. One is aimed at the success with which the group achieves its goals in terms of *performance*. Another concern relates to the *satisfaction* of the group members in the process of attaining their goals. The latter criterion has much more to do with the interactions along the way. Still another point of reference relates to the *resources* available to the group in achieving its goals. There are, then, several features to be considered in dealing with the broad issue of group effectiveness.

PERFORMANCE AND SATISFACTION

Performance is largely a matter for consideration at the group level of analysis. It is most often measured in terms of an output which may be represented, for example, in production per unit time or a team score. Alternatively, satisfaction is usually approached on the individual level. It contributes to the group phenomenon of *morale*, as a general index of the satisfaction that prevails in the group, but it stems from individual attitudes. While performance and morale may contribute to one another in a reciprocal fashion, they need not be positively related, as research often reveals (see Brayfield and Crockett, 1955).

In highly competitive situations, group members will often sacrifice their own satisfactions in order for the group to win. In the case of professional baseball, we readily see by the league standings that some teams are winning many games while others are winning relatively fewer. By the simple criterion of performance, therefore, the top team in the league appears to be more effective than the bottom team. But by the criterion of member satisfaction, which is not directly revealed by the league standings, it may not necessarily be highest. Winning itself may contribute to member satisfaction, but it need not in any complete sense. Even the big league team that has just won a key game may contain players who are personally displeased with their own performance, or lack of opportunity to play, or who feel inadequately recognized for their contribution. Because of the two levels involved, it is essential to understand that peak performance by itself does not directly betray member satisfaction, nor does it reveal future outcomes in this vein.

As we observed in connection with the laboratory research on communication networks, groups may be effective in performance, though members who are peripheral, or lack information, are dissatisfied with the structure and the related processes within the group. There are implications in this in terms of the subsequent cohesiveness and stability of these groups, if they were perpetuated in time.

Attempts to discern the source of member satisfaction have usually found several variables at work. In their recent survey of the research literature in this line, Heslin and Dunphy (1964) encountered three such factors which recur in findings on member satisfaction. The first of these is *status consensus*, indicating the degree of consensus concerning group structure, particularly with regard to leadership. The second relates to the members' perception of progress toward group goals, in terms of what we referred to earlier as *group locomotion*. The third refers to the perceived freedom of *participation* within the group. All of these elements relate in an interacting way to the sense the individual has of a stable environment within which he can make contributions that are rewarded. The importance of these factors will be considered further below, in connection with psychological effects.

GROUP RESOURCES: INPUTS AND OUTPUTS

Another way of viewing group effectiveness is in terms of what the group is able to achieve with its available resources. As a group goes about fulfilling its task, it has the capabilities of persons as well as features of the physical environment with which to work. Its resources are the *inputs* to its activity in dealing with the task at hand. What it does with these can be considered as its *outputs.* In some sense, a group's effectiveness is determined by how successfully it is able to muster its resources in order to secure beneficial outputs, regarding both the criteria of performance and satisfaction.

By way of illustration, consider our big league ball team again. It is low in the league standings, but it has a relatively inexperienced team without major stars. Given the resources at its disposal, it is doing rather well in terms of the output-to-input ratio represented by winning games. Looking just at the criterion of performance, while the top team in the league appears to be more effective, its ratio may not be nearly so favorable since it starts with far greater inputs, in terms of experienced players who are highly proficient. Moreover, the team low in standing, because it is playing so well with the little it has, may have comparatively high morale.

Stogdill (1959) has proposed that many otherwise contradictory findings regarding group performance and morale can be reconciled by viewing performance and member satisfaction as group outputs from the use to which group resources are put. The concept of resources helps to get away from the simple notion that good performance necessarily means great effectiveness. It also looks upon a group with reference to the characteristics of its members, their competence, and their motivation.

One of the longstanding controversies in social psychology, dating back to the work of Marjorie Shaw (1932) and earlier, has had to do with the question of whether groups are more effective in problem-solving than are individuals. A recent study on this issue by Tuckman and Lorge (1962) has special relevance to the matter of resources. They had individuals solve problems initially on a separate basis, then constituted them into groups to re-solve the same problems. A set of groups was established as a control without the prior tradition of individual experience. They found that both kinds of groups in general were superior to individuals in average "quality points" for solutions. However, their data also indicated that this resulted not from the greater effectiveness of groups in solving problems so much as the greater probability of getting a good solution from a group of five rather than from any single individual. Thus, where an individual member had given a highly superior solution before, his group did better. The significant correlation for the quality point scores of the re-solving groups and their best individuals is plotted in Figure 13.3.

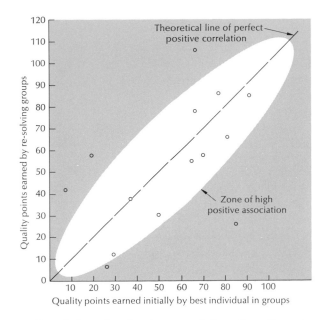

Figure 13.3: Correlation plot showing association of quality points earned by fourteen groups re-solving problems and those points earned before by the best individual performer assigned to the group when he had worked alone. The coefficient of correlation is .54, significant at the .05 level. (Based on data from Tuckman and Lorge, 1962.)

As Steiner and Rajaratnam (1961) point out, the requirements of the task make a considerable difference in determining the superiority of the group as against an individual in problem-solving. For a simple task, individuals may do very adequately, but for a complex task the resources afforded by several people working together are likely to be more suitable. Therefore, the performance of a group depends upon the inter-relationship of its task and the people who compose it, with particular regard to their individual qualities including competence and commitment to the group's endeavor.

Psychological effects of groups

In various ways, we have seen that groups exert influence over the psychological processes and behavior of individuals. A primary source of this influence, as we noted earlier, rests in the identification of an individual with a group. This dependency relationship is basic to an understanding of social psychology. Thus, the very quality of "groupness" has important psychological consequences. A long time ago, Cooley (1909) observed:

> The result of intimate association, psychologically, is a certain fusion of individualities in a common whole. . . . Perhaps the simplest way of describing this wholeness is to say that it is a "we"; it involves the sort of sympathy and mutual identification for which "we" is the natural expression (p. 23).

Because an individual may be identified with many groups, it is necessary to seek an explanation for why some of them exert influence and others do not. In psychological terms, this is a motivational question, as we pointed out in Chapter Four. For several reasons, some groups hold more motivational valence and thereby are greater sources of identification and influence. Furthermore, the attitudes of an individual may be affected by groups to which he does not literally "belong," as in the case of "reference groups."

One way of distinguishing membership from identification has been proposed by Lambert and Lambert (1964) in terms of "membership groups" and "psychological groups." One may be a member of a group but be relatively unaffected by it, just as one may be influenced by a group and not be one of its members. These kinds of attachment may coincide, but they need not. In what follows we will be considering groups that have a psychological impact on the individual because of their value to him, in this reference group sense. The source of this value rests in several motivational bases.

MOTIVATIONAL BASES OF GROUP INFLUENCE IN GENERAL

The motivation to take part in groups is made up of two distinguishable clusters of motives. As we observed in connection with the findings of Hagstrom and Selvin (1965) regarding cohesiveness, individuals may be primarily oriented toward the *task* of the group or toward the *affiliations* the group provides. These clusters may be interrelated and bolster one another. In the case of task motivation, the individual is interested in joining others for the sake of the mutual goal to be achieved. They depend upon one another in seeking its attainment. Whether the individual feels attachment to these others and develops attraction toward them, is of secondary importance, at least at the outset. If, for example, a person wishes to take part in dramatics, it is essential that he find others to support his interest in putting on a play. This is equally true with regard to many other activities, including sports.

Affiliation motives operate most clearly where the individual is attracted to others as a source of social contact and approval. As we noted in Chapter Four, there are three such motives which are operative, in varying combinations, where the individual is psychologically identified with a group. These are the motivations to gain or sustain *social identity, social reality,* and *social support.*

In line with Cartwright's principles discussed earlier, an individual is more susceptible to being influenced by a group where his identification with it is high. Social identity, in the sense of a psychological identification, appears to be the foremost motivational basis for such influence.

AWARENESS OF GROUP IDENTITY

A major psychological feature of groups is their function in providing individuals with social identity. By this we mean that group members become involved with one another and aware of each other as members of the same social entity. Groups, of course, may vary considerably in the degree to which they are open in their membership and therefore exclusivity very often becomes a determiner of the prestige-value of a group. We must also bear in mind that individuals have overlapping group memberships, and some of these are more important than others.

Once given that importance, groups have a quality which Goldschmidt (1959) compares to "a kind of psychological membrane which marks those within from those outside" (p. 67). This parallels the in-group and out-group distinction mentioned in Chapter Ten.

Especially in groups permitting face-to-face contact, shared identities become vital aspects of an individual's approach to the world. As Durkheim puts it:

> . . . it is impossible for men to live together, associating in industry, without acquiring a sentiment of the whole formed by their union, without attaching themselves to that whole, preoccupying themselves with its interests, and taking account of it in their conduct. This attachment has in it something surpassing the individual (1947, p. 14).

One criticism of laboratory experimentation is that groups are often formed on an arbitrary basis without having the "real life" quality of established groups, such as a tradition (see Lorge, Fox, Davitz, & Bremer, 1958). Accordingly, individuals in these groups may not be motivated to seek an identification with an assemblage of this kind. Despite this criticism, it is evident from other research findings that motivations are at work which contribute to an individual's acceptance of influence by such *ad hoc* laboratory groups. We shall consider this point further in connection with social reality.

In broader terms, identity is highly susceptible to the effects of environmental forces. Thus, a threat to a group has been found to increase its members' identification with it (e.g. Pepitone and Kleiner, 1957). In time of external strife, the people of a nation manifest a heightened sense of identity with their country and its cause. In this respect, Karl Deutsch (1954) has pointed to the overriding quality of social identity that is bound up with nationalism, because of the sense of a "common fate" which members of a nation share. Belonging, and having a place, are therefore profound sources of the psychological attachment between individuals and the social entities in their environment.

SOCIAL REALITY AND SHARED ATTITUDES

One of the demonstrably pervasive effects of groups is their effect on attitudes. An enormous amount of research has indicated that even with limited interaction, and a marginal sense of group identity at best, individuals are affected by the perceptions of others, particularly under conditions of ambiguity. For example, there is the impressive fact that in the classic laboratory experiments by Sherif (1935) and Asch (1951), referred to earlier, individuals with only limited contact were receptive to the judgments of others.

Festinger (1950) places a considerable amount of weight on "social reality" as a motivational force directing an individual toward affiliation with others and influence by them. What is perhaps less apparent is the degree to which groups as *role systems* create expectancies for individuals to hold and manifest attitudes which are in keeping with their roles. The work of Katz and Lazarsfeld (1955) on "opinion leadership" suggests, for example, a more ready acceptance of novel attitudes from those who have the status of "opinion leaders" as against those who do not.

Uppermost in any consideration of the need for social reality are the rational elements in Man's attempt to understand and cope with his environment. However, the idea of rationality should not be mistaken for logical thinking so much as an attempt to develop a coherent view of reality. Deutsch and Gerard (1955) found in their laboratory research that there are two distinguishable aspects to this process. Individuals react to *normative* as well as *informational* sources of reality. The normative source refers to what "others" do and expect. The informational source refers more to the acceptance of information from "others" as a source of knowledge. In their experiment, they found that subjects who gave only anonymous judgments were less influenced by others than those who gave judgments with which they could be identified. This private versus public dimension exemplifies the differential effect of normative influence which characterizes a good deal of the research findings on conformity. We will treat these further in the next chapter. What needs particular stress here is that identification with others leads to a greater reliance on them for "social reality," especially in terms of normative standards.

GROUP SUPPORT

While social identity provides the individual with a psychological attachment, social support sustains his activity. Groups provide all of us with the basis for carrying on activities, in terms of group tasks, but also with regard to our sense that others approve of these activities. Whether it is writing poetry, wiring a circuit, or speaking out at a political meeting, the approval of others provides a significant reinforcement function in lending support to our actions. Such support can play a vital preservative role, as we noted with regard to Durkheim's research on suicide in Chapter Two (see p. 38).

Group support is closely tied to the motivation to take part in functional group tasks. Whenever individuals come together to achieve some function, they rely on one another for adequate performance. To the extent that individuals find the achievement of the group's goal rewarding, they will act in consonance with its achievement and be supported by the positive response of others. Uppermost in this process, from a psychological standpoint, is the individual's own investment in what the group seeks to attain. With this in mind, it is clear that a reciprocal sequence is involved; in joining groups, individuals often are attracted by the group's activity, then play a role in it which rewards them by others' approval. It is in this sense that task and affiliation motives are intertwined over time (see Wyer, 1966).

A further point of interest lies in the conditions for withdrawal of group support. In an illuminating pair of experiments on this issue, Jones and deCharms (1957) found that the task-related behavior of a group member who is performing poorly is evaluated most negatively if he is perceived to be low in motivation. By contrast, if there is only a doubt raised about his basic ability to perform the task, he is not evaluated nearly so negatively by the others. Thus, disapproval from the group is conditional upon a member's perceived ability to be responsible for behavior which causes the group to fail. In the case of low motivation, the simple judgment is made that the person has not "tried enough" and therefore has "let us down." In Heider's terms (see p. 197), the person who is competent but does not try enough is perceived more as the "locus of causality" for the group's failure than the one who is incompetent but tries hard.

Group support often acts as a gauge for the individual to know how he is doing. The reactions of others thus become a source of informational influence. This process is spelled out in the discussion in Chapter Four of the influence effects of reinforcement. In social settings, evidences of approval from others is routinely found to increase the probability of the approved response. Thus, a recent series of experiments by Bavelas,

Hastorf, Gross, and Kite (1965) has demonstrated that signs of evident approval of comments made by a previously quiet member of a discussion group increased his frequency of commenting and improved the ratings by others of his "leadership characteristics." To a significant degree, his participation in group discussion had been raised. This effect is revealed in Figure 13.4. Subjects who were "target persons" were

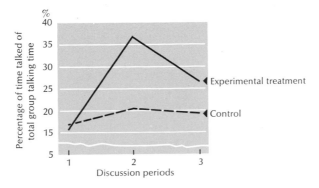

Figure 13.4: Time talked by target persons reinforced in nine experimental groups and non-reinforced in nine control groups. (Based on data from Bavelas, Hastorf, Gross, and Kite, 1965.)

selected from those showing a very low level of participation in the first discussion period. Then, in the experimental treatment, they were reinforced by green lights on a panel before them whenever they spoke out. The controls were matched for low initial participation and received no reinforcement. They maintained roughly the same low level while those receiving the experimental treatment spurted upward.

It would be a mistake, however, to conclude that any source of approval of any behavior will influence a person's subsequent action. The effects of group support require two conditions for their operation: first, that the individual himself be positively motivated regarding the activity; and second, that he be positively motivated toward identification with the group as a set of "relevant others," that is, people whose standards and support he desires. It is possible, of course, for a person to do something he finds personally distasteful because others whose approval he seeks are doing it. Where the choice exists, though, the typical inclination is to be associated with those who lend support to activities the individual finds satisfying. This interdependent relationship, between what the individual does and how relevant others value it, is an essential feature of the reference group concept.

Much that we have said here is applicable to features of the reference group. It should be emphasized that the affiliative motives of social identity, social reality, and social support form the psychological substructure for the reference group concept. Thus, as Kelley (1952) has observed, reference groups may be groups that can award or withhold recognition and approval to a person, as well as serve as a standard for him in making judgments.

On social psychological grounds, then, the idea of the reference group provides a useful meshing of the individual and group levels of analysis. Any group known to a person that he takes as a standard of comparison or judgment—whether it is a membership group for him or not—influences his psychological field (Shibutani, 1955). However, the fullest impact of the reference group is most likely to be felt where the individual is not only committed to its "perspectives," in Shibutani's terms, but also is in contact with members who may reward or punish his actions. In that case, the individual has a social identity, with considerable psychological investment, plus the effects of direct reactions from others to his behavior and expressions of attitudes. This feature of functional groups is especially relevant to the satisfactions they provide, as well as to their performance effectiveness, as we have seen. It also has a great bearing on intergroup relations.

Inter-group relations

The effects of group identity are quite readily observed in inter-group relations. These relations involve the operation of values and attitudes, co-operation and competition, leadership and communication, prejudice and discriminatory practices. Any circumstance which is likely to elicit a we-they distinction has elements which can drastically alter the outlook and actions of group members. From the results of his UNESCO studies in India, for example, Gardner Murphy (1953) concluded that to be accepted in one's own group as a "good Hindu" or a "good Moslem" required expressed hostility toward the other group, in the aftermath of partition there.

THE NATURE OF INTER-GROUP RELATIONS

In general terms, *inter-group relations* refer to the character of the relationship that exists between two or more groups and their members. There are additional refinements necessary, however, to make this definition more complete. The "groups" may be functional groups, social institutions, descriptive categories that represent a "slice" of society—such as socio-economic classes—or total societies such as nations. A "relationship" may be largely a matter of the continuity of history, or an attitude such as a stereotype. It can mean the active involvement of representatives of allies or of contending parties, personal relationships across groups, or institutionalized conflict in terms of outright warfare. Furthermore, as we have already observed, "membership" can mean commitment to a group, independently of formal affiliation. From a social psychological perspective, then, inter-group relations can be considered to encompass actual or implied interaction, whether collectively or individually, between persons who share distinct social identities which are particularly salient at the time.

Organized society would be unmanageable without co-operative group relationships. However, it is mainly conflict between groups which rivets our attention. Rather than being a deviate feature of life, many kinds of inter-group conflict are part of its give and take. A primary requisite in any human society is for mechanisms to regulate and manage conflict toward productive rather than destructive ends.

PROCESSES OF CONFLICT

Most popular views of conflict among humans begin with the idea of aggressiveness. As we indicated earlier, however, there is at best only a limited basis for viewing aggressiveness as innate in man. The fact that man has the *capacity* for being aggressive has sometimes led, too readily, to the view that its expression is a necessity of life. But what is more probably the case is that a good deal of aggressive behavior is *reactive* to threat, rather than a direct expression of some instinctive requirement.

Another relevant consideration in viewing aggression is that it may cover all sorts of behavior, ranging from coping with the environment in an assertive way on through hostile or destructive action. It is mainly the latter which has concerned observers of intergroup relations, particularly since it has the flavor of harming or destroying a perceived irritant or threat in the environment. Aggression of this kind, in its more violent manifestations, has been attributed to pent-up feelings of frustration among members of a group. Miller and Dollard (1941), for example, showed a relationship between the rise in the number of lynchings of Negroes in the South during the 1930's and the drop in the price of cotton. They suggest that when economic conditions are bad, this results in frustration and that, accordingly, there is a tendency to show displaced aggression toward any convenient scapegoat. A similar explanation has been offered by Schuman (1939) for the rise of Hitler in Germany and the willingness of its people to follow him into World War II. There are, nevertheless, some unanswered questions in this explanation. As Klineberg (1950) points out, aggression toward the Negro depends upon the time and place, including the influence of culture. He notes that white Brazilians are, on the whole, much more frustrated economically than are white Americans. Yet, he says, there is far less evident conflict there, and no lynchings of Brazilian Negroes (p. 198).

Regarding war, it is even more doubtful that it is built upon individual needs for aggression. In this vein, Klineberg (1964) observes that:

> . . . every modern nation in time of war has to resort to some form of draft or conscription to satisfy the manpower needs of its armed forces. If all of us were eagerly awaiting a chance to express a latent aggression stored up for years, would coercion be necessary to build up an army? Would we not all rush to enlist instead of, in most cases, awaiting the summons? . . . Is there any indication that people who start wars are more frustrated than those who do their best to stay out of them? Are pacifists less frustrated than those ready to' go to war? (pp. 14-15).

In general, the approach to conflict in social psychology places little value on the views that humans are either innately aggressive or else aggressive out of a sense of frustration. While conflict between groups is a widespread social phenomenon, it is not caused by a single factor. There are many different reasons for conflict which can be studied and understood. Among these are the undeniable disputes about how valued resources should be distributed, the varying definitions of a situation held in the perspectives of different groups, as well as contextual factors of an historical and institutional nature. Therefore, the study of conflict requires a delineation of regularities in the processes which occasion it and may reduce it.

THE IN-GROUP AND THE OUT-GROUP

The perception of differences between groups is an inescapable social phenomenon. By itself it need not lead to conflict, but indeed often leads to productive action and social progress. Yet, the usual way of seeing an "in-group"–"out-group" distinction is in terms of conflict. In such a case, as we observed in Murphy's (1953) report of India at the time of partition, conflict makes this distinction a dominant psychological force. Its destructive overtones are furthered by the imputation of a value judgment of "goodness" versus "badness."

It is understandable, of course, that groups which are salient reference groups for individuals are usually seen by them as having virtues which others may not see. In their UNESCO study in nine countries, as an example, Buchanan and Cantril (1953) found that respondents in all of these countries agreed uniformly on one point, namely that their own nation was the most "peace-loving" among the nations they rated. When situations of conflict arise, this tendency to judge one's own group favorably takes on added potency. Then all virtue is likely to be seen in the in-group, all evil in the out-group. Each side sees itself as the instrument of higher values, up to and including divine will, as in the case of nations at war. Group loyalties and the sense of determination to overcome the evil represented by the adversary are increased. As a consequence, the prospects for reducing conflict are diminished considerably.

Therefore, while a distinction between an in-group and an out-group is not destructive, it holds the potential for causing social unrest whenever it spills over into areas of perceived conflict of interest. Ardrey (1966), who has argued that territorial possession is a basis for conflict, says that patriotism dictates a hostile response whenever a nation's "territory" is intruded upon or threatened by an adversary. The concept of "territory," however, can be extended to include not only physical space, but a nation's or a group's symbols. Its flag, its honor, its dignity and history, all symbolize in-group characteristics which have psychological significance in terms of the social identity of individuals.

Associated with the process of intensified conflict is the simplistic quality of "psycho-logic," discussed in Chapter Six. Since the evaluative dimension takes on great strength in conflict, the perceived negative qualities of the out-group make it inconsistent to believe that they may be justified in their position. This is abetted by the incendiary use of language which may portray them as "devious," "treacherous," or "aggressive," while the in-group may be characterized as "noble" in pursuing a "just cause" for the sake of "honor."

It is unlikely that in-group versus out-group distinctions can be made to vanish. However, as Gordon Allport (1958) has persuasively indicated, there is no fundamental reason why loyalty to one group must preclude loyalty to another. Identifications may be concentric such that loyalty to one's family can be accommodated within loyalty to one's community, occupation, state and nation, each at successive levels. Thus, he contends that just as identification to one's state can be readily absorbed within identification to one's nation, identification with one's nation can be accommodated within identification with the United Nations and a commitment to world order. Indeed, Guetzkow's study (1955) of members of the United Nations Secretariat indicates that loyalty to one's nation is no barrier to being a competent international civil servant. The compatibility of national and world interests is readily seen, for example, in international trade and postal agreements, weather reporting, air traffic control and public health measures, among many other day-to-day practices. In the larger perspective, the maintenance of life on our planet urgently depends upon the extension of group loyalties beyond the tribe and the nation to the requirements of all mankind.

MANAGING INTER-GROUP CONFLICT

Given the reality of inter-group conflict, how is it to be managed? Practically speaking, it is managed by a variety of social mechanisms which exist to contain and direct it toward productive ends. Of these, negotiation continues to be the most widespread. It is seen routinely in labor-management relations. Even given periodic strikes, negotiation works remarkably well in contrast with the past, when unions were attempting to establish bargaining rights with a reluctant management. Before such rights became normative, there was a great amount of turbulence on the industrial scene. To those who despair that we can ever manage some conflicts in an organized way, Etzioni (1964) reminds us that until relatively recent times, in the United States,

> . . . labor organizations were viewed as conspiracies and fought with all the instruments management could marshall, including the local police, militia, armed strike-breakers, professional spies, and the like. The workers, in turn, did not refrain from resorting to dynamite and other means of sabotage nor from beating the strike-breakers (p. 244).

To be effective, negotiation requires co-operation within a set of rules. From a social psychological standpoint, these rules represent agreed-upon norms for making conflict productive rather than destructive. They set a structure for the conflict and thereby "encapsulate" it (Etzioni, 1964). However, negotiation which occurs within this structure can proceed in various ways. Oftentimes, the process of negotiation is perceived by the negotiators, the groups they represent, or by outsiders, as a zero-sum game in which there must be a "winner" and a "loser" (see Chapter Seven, p. 178). This construction of the situation is not likely to encourage co-operation since it implicitly emphasizes competition (Sherif, 1958). Unless both contending parties see the necessity for accommodation, then accusations and recriminations will be the order of the day and a retreat to entrenched positions will very probably occur. To paraphrase Milburn (1961), the belief that international relationships are competitive in the sense that only one side can win means that both sides may very well lose.

Deutsch (1962) reports an experiment using the prisoner's dilemma situation (see Chapter Seven, p. 179) in which each player had to decide whether to push a red button or a green button. If both players pressed red, they each lost one dollar; if both pressed green, they each won one dollar. Alternatively, if either player pressed green when the other pressed red, then the one who pressed green lost two dollars, and the one who pressed red won two dollars. As Deutsch indicates:

> A superficial rational calculation of self-interest would lead each player to press his red button since he either wins as much as he can or loses as little as he can this way. But if both players consider only their self-interest and press their red buttons, each of them will lose. Players oriented toward defeating the other player or to their self-interest only, when matched with similarly oriented players, do in fact choose the red button and do end up losing consistently. I be-

lieve our current international situation is in some respects similar to the game I have described . . . any attempt on the part of any individual or nation to increase its own welfare or security (without regard to the security or welfare of the others) is self-defeating. In such situations the only way an individual or nation can avoid being trapped in a mutually reinforcing, self-defeating cycle is to attempt to change the situation so that a basis of mutual trust can develop (p. 380).

In a study of inter-group competition, Blake and Mouton (1961b) found that a competitive, "You win, I lose" strategy caused group members to misunderstand the proposed solution of the other group. The findings are clear in indicating that inter-group problem-solving is made more difficult by the distortions created by a totally competitive strategy. They suggest that an understanding of the other party's position requires a mutual recognition of common goals to be achieved. Relatedly, Rapaport (1962) has urged that the spokesman for each side in a controversy should be required to state his adversary's position to the latter's satisfaction before responding with his own.

The importance of "superordinate goals" in managing inter-group conflict is underscored by the findings of elaborate field experimentation by Muzafer Sherif and his coworkers (Sherif and Sherif, 1953; Sherif, Harvey, White, Hood, and Sherif, 1961). In two experiments in boys' summer camps, they were able to study the development of inter-group conflict among these youngsters when, at each camp, they were divided into two groups. The groups were commonly drawn from an identical sample which was highly homogeneous in terms of such factors as age, race, religion, and socio-economic status. Conflict was induced largely through intensive competitive rivalry for rewards which were limited.

In the next phase of these experiments, after a high level of conflict had been attained, the effect of factors which could reduce the conflict was carefully studied. Thus, mere contact between the groups in enjoyable activities was found to serve as an occasion for further exchanges of hostile comments. It was only when a mutual crisis was introduced—for example, an apparent breakdown in transportation carrying food for the camp—that mutual co-operation developed. Furthermore, some necessity for continuing co-operation toward the achievement of common superordinate goals had to be sustained over *time* for their effect on the reduction of inter-group hostility to be achieved (Sherif, 1962, p. 11).

REDUCING INTER-GROUP TENSION

Underlying outbreaks of inter-group conflict is the less dramatic but persistent quality of inter-group *tension.* Such tension does not require a manifest issue of pronounced conflict, a *cause célèbre,* or a dramatic incident. Whenever individuals perceive a group of others with distrust and hostility, practice discrimination, or harbor residuals of hatred, inter-group tension exists.

As we noted in connection with prejudice in Chapter Ten, tension between groups usually takes the form of hostility toward others because of a perceived group affiliation independently of their individual characteristics. Any discriminatory practices which sharpen lines of demarcation between groups, for example on the basis of skin color or religion, serve as structural supports for prejudice. Furthermore, they prevent individuals from confronting one another on the basis of a wide range of other personal qualities they may possess, including their capacities and intelligence, mutual interests, and personality. Research on interpersonal contact as a basis for the reduction of prejudice encourages the view that once the environmental supports for prejudice are removed, tension between groups is considerably reduced. This is especially so in terms of "equal status" contacts.

During World War II, before the U.S. Armed Forces were integrated by Presidential Order, some units of the army in Europe were composed of Negro troops who had volunteered for combat. These troops were organized into platoons, under white officers, in companies that were otherwise made up of white troops. A survey conducted by the Army's Research Branch (Information and Education Division, 1945) revealed a very high degree of satisfaction among white officers and non-commissioned officers in these companies with the performance of the Negro soldiers. More to the point, however, the greater the degree of contact with these soldiers the greater the degree to which white soldiers favored the idea of having companies include Negro platoons.

Part of the results of this survey are shown in Figure 13.5. The two questions asked were:

> Some Army divisions have companies which include Negro and white platoons. How would you feel about it if your outfit was set up something like that?

In general, do you think it is a good idea or a poor idea to have the same company in a combat outfit include Negro platoons and white platoons?

Plainly, those who had directly experienced Negro troops in their companies were far more inclined to be in favor of this practice than those who did not. Those who had not had this encounter were overwhelmingly opposed to it. A reasonable presumption then is that a shift occurred as a result of equal status contacts, within the context of vital superordinate goals.

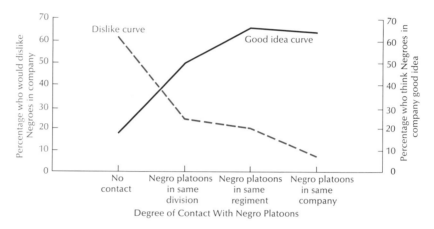

Figure 13.5: Responses of white soldiers to two questions concerning Negro platoons in white companies by degree of respondents' actual contact with Negro platoons in their own units. (Based upon data gathered in 1945 and reported in Stouffer, Suchman, DeVinney, Star and Williams, 1949.)

Comparable findings have been obtained in the realm of housing, without such evident goals but with person-to-person contact. Jahoda (1961) reports that while a majority of white Americans prefer residential segregation, that preference is reduced by *half* where white persons have had the experience of working with Negroes and having them as neighbors. Deutsch and Collins (1951) studied housing projects that were integrated throughout or segregated by buildings allocated exclusively for white or for Negro residents. Their results indicated a far greater degree of contact of whites with Negroes in the integrated housing with a corresponding decrease in prejudice among the white persons toward the Negroes. Here again, racial tension was highest where the two groups lived apart and where prejudice was thereby sustained through environmental support.

From this and other evidence, it is clear, therefore, that the reduction of inter-group tension can be accomplished through favorably sustained social contact, particularly where common goals are being co-operatively sought. It is equally clear that programs of information or exhortation will not in themselves effectively reduce intergroup tension without action, which also means involvement. Hyman and Sheatsley (1947) are among those finding that selective perception operates to block out information which is contrary to what a person already believes (see Chapter Six). Thus, those who are most likely to need the facts from an information campaign are often impervious to them.

A final point concerns the widespread belief that inter-group tension and associated conflict only affect members of so-called "minority groups" in a society. They are unquestionably victimized and may suffer profoundly, up through deprivation of liberties, incarceration, and death. It is, to say the very least, unpleasant to live in a hostile environment where one's children must learn that others hate them for nothing they have done. Yet, all parties to inter-group tension, including the broader society, are adversely affected by being cut off from the resources and initiatives of individuals.

In inter-group or international conflict, the fragile balance between individual freedom of action and of expression, on the one hand, and social demands, on the other, shifts. The group's insistence on the absolute rightness of its position forces greater signs of loyalty from its members. In that circumstance, as Blake and Mouton (1962) put it:

> Disagreement, the raw material of creative thinking which can lead to the re-examination and enrichment of the position of one's group, tends to be snuffed out. Failure to go along after a certain point can aroused insidious group pressures toward conformity and, in the extreme, may even lead to the expulsion of members who resist the tide (p. 99).

Thus, the freedom to be one's self is diminished by intense social forces in inter-group tension. Conformity for its own sake becomes the prevailing standard. As we shall see in the next chapter, this kind of pressure poses problems for the fulfillment of individual potentialities, as well as for the successful functioning of a group.

SUMMARY

Group dynamics refers generally to the processes occurring within groups, and in particular to the research tradition established by Kurt Lewin. It views groups in terms of *group locomotion,* that is, the movement of a group toward its goal. Associated with locomotion are the *interrelated variables of cohesiveness, communication, and conformity.* Each of these depends upon and affects the others.

Another approach to group dynamics concerns the forces affecting *social change.* Bringing about change requires an alteration in the *quasistationary equilibrium* of prevailing practices. This involves a *process* by which sources of individual resistance are overcome through group support. In general, cohesive groups appear to exert greater influence over their members either to enhance or to impede change. Members who have a weak sense of group identification have been found to be more likely to change their attitudes in directions opposite to those of the group.

The effectiveness of a group can be considered in terms of two criteria, its *performance* and its *members' satisfaction.* These depend upon the particulars of the situation and the task confronting the group, and the satisfaction of individual members of a group is often aggregated in terms of *morale.* Studies reveal that this index of satisfaction is not necessarily tied to group performance in a one-to-one fashion.

Another aspect of group effectiveness rests in the *resources* available to a group in carrying out its functions. The outcome of this process depends upon the ratio of *inputs* from the group and its environment and the *outputs* it produces in terms of performance and satisfaction along the way. The qualities of individuals comprising a group are therefore vital to its effectiveness.

The psychological effects of the group arise primarily from the *identifications* individuals have with it. The differential effects of various groups on individuals arise from several motivational bases. One of these is the motivation to take part in the *task,* the other is to gain from the *affiliations* that the group provides socially. The affiliation motives which appear to be most operative are those for *social identity, social reality,* and *social support.* These may be interrelated, as well as being associated with the individual's task motivation.

The identification of individuals with groups is a basic feature of life. Some of these identities are more important than others and this distinction grows out of the satisfaction of other affiliation motives. Thus, the need for social reality, in the sense of having an outlook which is corroborated by others, is one of these. The individual also requires support from others, in terms of approval of his activities. Group support provides a significant reinforcement function in shaping and giving continuity to individual actions.

The concept of *reference groups* sums up these psychological effects. Whether an individual belongs to them or not, such groups constitute "psychological groups" which provide *standards for making judgments,* in the sense of social reality, and *approval,* in the sense of group support. The reference group stands as a useful bridge between the individual and group levels of analysis. Its essential quality lies in the identification, or social identity, it provides for the individual.

Inter-group relations refer to the character of the relationship between groups and their members. It can encompass various kinds of actual or implied interaction where group identities are particularly salient. Though co-operative group relations are necessary to the maintenance of organized society, intergroup conflict is nevertheless a compelling quality of life.

The basis for *conflict* rests in the complex relationship of psychological as well as historical and institutional factors. Aggressivity in human affairs, including war, appears to be reactive rather than instinctive. It does not stem from a necessity for aggressiveness, nor solely from a response to frustration.

The distinction between an *in-group* and an *out-group* holds the potential for inter-group tension whenever a value judgment of "goodness" versus "badness" is involved. Especially where there are perceived conflicts of interest, this distinction takes on added potency. The in-group is seen as virtuous and the out-group as evil. Simplistic "psycho-logical" thinking then makes the reduction of conflict more difficult. There is no reason why group identifications must exist on an exclusive basis. They can be, and often are, accommodated within *concentric loyalties,* such as to one's family, community, state, and nation, as well as to the world.

The *management of inter-group conflict* is a vital social requirement. It is usually accomplished through *negotiation* within a set of rules, or norms, which are mutually accepted by the parties concerned. A pitfall in negotiation is that it may be perceived as a zero-sum game in which there must be a "winner" and a "loser." Given such a strategy, both parties may lose. A mutual recognition of the necessity for *co-operation* is essential for negotiation to direct conflict toward productive ends. Such recognition is facilitated by the presence of *superordinate goals* which are valued by both parties.

Inter-group tension usually takes the form of hostility and prejudice, even without a direct point of conflict. Such tension is sustained by environmental supports. When these are removed, tension is reduced by interpersonal contact on an equal status basis. But information programs designed to reduce inter-group tension are less effective than such action because they often fail to reach those for whom they are intended.

The existence of inter-group tension serves as a limitation on a society by cutting off the availability of individual resources. Individuals who are caught up in inter-group conflict are vulnerable to coercive pressure toward intense group conformity, and are therefore less free to exercise their independence and fulfill their potentialities.

SUGGESTED READINGS

From E. P. Hollander and R. G. Hunt. (Eds.) *Current perspectives in social psychology.* (2nd Edition.) New York: Oxford University Press, 1967:

55. Dorwin Cartwright: *Achieving change in people: some applications of group dynamics theory*
Introduction to Section X: *Intergroup relations*
63. Muzafer Sherif: *Superordinate goals in the reduction of intergroup conflict*
64. Urie Bronfenbrenner: *The mirror image in Soviet-American relations*
65. Morton Deutsch: *Some considerations relevant to national policy*

SELECTED REFERENCES

Bonner, H. *Group dynamics: Principles and applications.* New York: Ronald, 1959.
Cartwright, D. & Zander, A. (Eds.) *Group dynamics: Research and theory.* Evanston, Ill.: Row, Peterson, 1960. (2nd ed.)
*Gouldner, A. W. *Wildcat strike: A study in worker-management relationships.* New York: Harper Torchbooks, 1965.

Kelman, H. (Ed.) *International behavior: A socio-psychological analysis.* New York: Holt, Rinehart, & Winston, 1965.

*Klineberg, O. *The human dimension in international relations.* New York: Holt, Rinehart, & Winston, 1964.

Lippitt, R., Watson, Jeanne, & Westley, B. *The dynamics of planned change.* New York: Harcourt, Brace & World, 1958.

McNeil, E. (Ed.) *The nature of human conflict.* Englewood Cliffs, N.J.: Prentice-Hall, 1965.

Sherif, M. & Sherif, Carolyn W. *Groups in harmony and tension: An integration of studies on intergroup relations.* New York: Harper, 1953.

Sherif, M. & Wilson, M. O. (Eds.) *Group relations at the crossroads.* New York: Harper, 1953.

14

Conformity and nonconformity

Conformity is a widespread social phenomenon which has attracted attention from many quarters. For the most part, social psychology's interest in conformity lies in understanding the influence effects which produce it and flow from it. This necessitates the systematic study of factors in both conforming and nonconforming behavior. In pursuing this study, judgments are not made about the absolute goodness or badness of conformity since it clearly has complex sources and ramifications. Neither conformity nor diversity is valued for its own sake. Indeed, it is well recognized that individuality of expression fulfills a significant social function, as exemplified in the generation of new ideas and innovations. Gardner (1963) for one underscores the point that stifling this feature of individuality is likely to lead to social decay because "the capacity of society for continuous renewal depends ultimately upon the individual" (p. 54).

If we look upon conformity as adherence to social expectancies, it becomes clear that organized society would be unthinkable without it. Yet a common social criticism today is that we live in an age of conformity. When used in this fashion, "conformity" is seen as something which undercuts individuality. This represents a legitimate concern which we will consider further in a moment. It is futile, however, to condemn any action automatically because it evidences conformity, since the world in which we live would be chaotic if we did not have accepted rules of behavior. Nevertheless, there continues to be a sense of an incompatibility between conformity and individuality, and some reflection on this issue is worthwhile for clarification.

Individuality and conformity

Wilson (1964) observes that the clamor about conformity is actually the latest version of the ancient and largely fruitless discussion of the individual versus society. A long tradition of philosophical thought surrounds this point, which is sometimes stated as freedom versus determinism. For instance, a belief in "fate" implies a primary acceptance of external determination of the individual's actions. To speak of individual freedom, on the other hand, one must accept a view of Man as a self-determining agent of his actions. In either case, the very formulation of this issue prejudges the alternatives.

There is, for example, a large question concerning what is meant by individual freedom. In the view of many, conformity inhibits freedom. But Gardner (1963), who would encourage individual expression, goes on to contend that while "the man on the street thinks of freedom as the natural state, and lack of freedom as the unnatural, artificial, contrived state . . . freedom as we now know it has been exceedingly rare in the history of Mankind. It is a highly perishable product of civilization, *wholly dependent on certain habits of mind widely shared, on certain institutional arrangements widely agreed upon*" (p. 65) [italics supplied]. The question, then, is not an either-or matter since freedom in a practical sense relies upon social organization.

DETERMINISM

E. G. Boring (1957) considers this matter in connection with determinism and concludes that freedom is often employed as a negative concept insofar as it deals with "the absence of causes" of action or the "absence of constraints" on action. "This problem," says Boring, "is not made easier when we realize that Man's belief that he is free may itself be pre-determined. The belief in freedom could be Man's great delusion—nearly, if not quite, immutable" (p. 189). Yet, he emphasizes that the idea of freedom has justified itself and is one for which men fight and die. The essential point appears to be that neither freedom as a matter of positive license nor as the negation of all constraints portrays an accurate picture of individual action.

The ultimate perplexity that would be introduced if everyone were literally free to do as he chose is illustrated by the anecdote concerning the child in a progressive school who asked the teacher, "Do I *have* to do what I want to do today?"

Individuals have freedom of action, but within certain prescribed standards of society. These confine us but also provide us with distinct benefits which include: freedom from continuous doubt about the actions of others; emancipation from finding *ad hoc* solutions daily for the patterned activities in which we take part; and positive gains available from other people as sources of social rewards. Our motivation to affiliate and "go along" with others therefore provides us with the social identity, social reality, and social support to sustain our individuality. Rather than be antithetical to one another, it is more likely the case that conformity can serve individuality.

NONCONFORMITY AND CONFORMISM

While we may not have total internal control over all of our actions, in a complex society we very often are able to react to those external controls which are more favorable to us. This is another way of saying that we may "refer" ourselves to the kinds of groups, and the norms that they set, which we find more congenial to our individual tastes. This also illuminates another feature of conformity which is often overlooked. Within the tendency to label people as "nonconformists," it is easy to disregard what is in fact their *high* conformity to some particular group. We often observe this in connection with the discussion of the nonconformity represented among so-called "beatniks." Though it is true that they may represent a segment of society that does not conform to certain prevailing social expectancies, they nonetheless can be observed to conform tenaciously to expectancies of their own reference groups. Thus, nonconformity to one standard may simply imply conformity to another, as we shall have occasion to point out further. Many years ago this idea was illuminated by Thoreau's observation that the apparent nonconformer was merely hearing another drummer. Cooley put it in these terms:

> There is, therefore, no definite line between conformity and non-conformity; there is simply a more or less characteristic and unusual way of selecting and combining accessible influences . . . a just view of the matter should embrace the whole of it at once and see conformity and nonconformity as normal and complementary phases of human activity (1922, p. 302).

In the last analysis, what probably arouses concern is not conformity as such but over-conformity or "conformism." It is this *excessive* reliance on others as a standard for conduct and as a basis for judgments which is deplored by Riesman and his colleagues in *The Lonely Crowd* (1950) and by Whyte in *The Organization Man* (1956). The line is not sharply defined, but what they contend in part is that the individual may be so eager for the anticipated rewards associated with displays of conformism that he loses touch with his own critical faculties. And this is antithetical to the long-range interests of society itself.

The nature of conformity

Conformity obviously is not a single thing, but rather a social phenomenon which can be defined in many ways. In the main, though, it refers to a kind of uniformity of behavior which is conventionally expected in society (Beloff, 1958). This is what was referred to above in connection with expected standards of conduct in a society. We can call this kind of conformity *congruence conformity*. It represents a form of response to which an individual is likely to see no alternatives. As Asch (1959) has pointed out, we do not usually deviate from the language and food preferences that characterize other members of our own society. In fact, we tend to see them as right and proper and to find them suiting our individual taste.

A second kind of conformity has been the object of a considerable amount of scrutiny in laboratory experimentation. This can be called *movement conformity*, since it represents an alteration of behavior from what apparently represents an individual's preferred tendency to a socially prescribed standard. This kind of influence acceptance is seen in the work of Sherif (1935) discussed in Chapter Two (see p. 46). In that experiment individuals placed in a stimulus situation involving the autokinetic phenomenon tended to "converge" toward a group norm from their initially preferred responses. The work of Asch (1951), which was considered here in Chapter Three (see p. 73), is also noteworthy in this regard.

A number of studies have varied the Sherif procedure, employing a range of stimuli, to study the movement of individual responses toward a group standard. In one such variant, Mausner (1953, 1954a, 1954b), Kelman (1950), and Luchins and Luchins (1961) have reinforced the subject's own accuracy to determine its effects on the degree of movement. In general, it is found that reinforcing the subject for accuracy of his own response leads to a *decrease* in conformity in the direction of greater *independence* from the partner or group.

Both congruence conformity and movement conformity involve an acceptance of influence which reveals *dependence*. In the first instance, this dependence has origins in a *past* influence, such as a food preference, which encourages an individual to persist in certain modes of action; in the second, the individual responds to a *present* influence by altering his actions to fit new demands, such as a shift in fashion.

SOURCES OF MOVEMENT CONFORMITY

Conformity is usually considered in terms of a single dimension that places perfect conformity at one end and perfect nonconformity at the other. Sometimes, nonconformity is referred to as independence. In either case, conformity means matching a group-approved response along a unidimensional scale. The utility of studying movement conformity lies especially in the relative ease with which it permits investigation of complex relationships. Thus, experimentation on movement conformity reveals in the first place that the more ambiguous the stimulus presented to the subject, the greater the tendency to conform to social pressure. However, such behavior also appears to depend upon other properties of the situation which cause an individual to rely upon others. Among such properties found to increase the probability of movement conformity are the status, power, or competence of the others representing an influence source, and their apparent unanimity. This is not unique to the movement conformity situation alone, but has wider generalizability to the acceptance of influence.

In terms of characteristics of the individual, it is also the case that the attractiveness of the group, and the general utility of conformity to achieving an individual goal, tend to encourage higher conformity. Fear or anxiety, for example, have been found to be associated with greater conformity. Walters and Karal (1960) isolated subjects and found that those who experienced greater anxiety subsequently showed greater susceptibility to influence. Relatedly, subjects identified as high on anxiety were found to conform more to the experimenter's suggestions in the Sherif autokinetic situation (Walters, Marshall, Shooter, 1960). Such findings, in line with Schachter's work on first-born children (see Chapter Five, p. 132), are usually interpreted in terms of heightened affiliation needs. Recent confirmation of this has come from an experiment by Darley (1966). He found that female subjects who were made anxious in anticipation of an electric shock conformed more in an Asch situation than those who were not made anxious. Furthermore, conformity was highest if the fearful subjects believed that the others in the group were also vulnerable to the shock, thus presumably increasing the subjects' affiliation tendencies toward them. To paraphrase Schachter (1959)—misery loves company, especially equally "miserable" company.

Alternatively, there are several circumstances where individuals are less likely to be influenced to shift a response. Among these are when: they have a high degree of certainty of their own perception; they feel themselves more competent or powerful or of higher status than others; they have one or more others in the group agreeing with them against the majority judgment; they find the others an unattractive influence source, possibly unlike themselves; and, finally, they see little to be gained by conformity in terms of any important personal goals. In line with our previous consideration of persuasibility in Chapters Six (see p. 163) and Ten (p. 302) the acceptance of influence also depends in some degree upon self-esteem, which we will consider here shortly in connection with personality and conformity.

As we have seen, where subjects believe that they are more accurate, they are less likely to show movement conformity in terms of convergence. In an experiment by Mausner (1954a) he had subjects judge the length of lines alone and then in pairs. The pairs were so chosen that the judgments of the two subjects when alone were quite different. Half of the subjects were told that they were right in almost all of the trials when judging alone first, while the other half were told that they were wrong on the same number of trials when judging alone. Figure

14.1 illustrates the degree of convergence which Mausner found for three pairs of subjects. In the first pair, both were reinforced; in the second, one was reinforced and the other negatively reinforced; and in the third, both were negatively reinforced. He found a significantly higher tendency for subjects who had been negatively reinforced to be

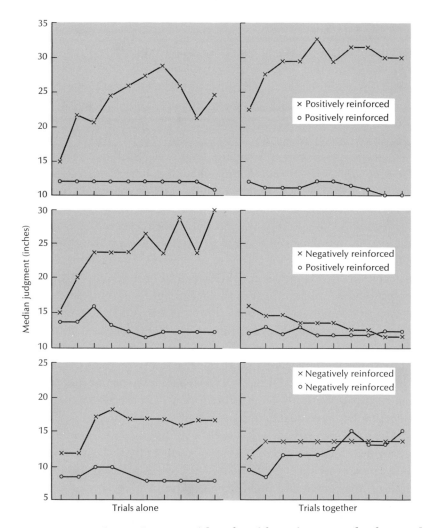

Figure 14.1: Median judgments of lengths of lines for ten trials alone and ten together for three pairs of subjects with various combinations of prior reinforcement for accuracy. (From Mausner, 1954a.)

influenced by their partners' judgments in the subsequent group situation.

Still other studies have looked at the degree of movement conformity created by the influence of status. For example, age differences in children (Berenda, 1950) operate so that younger children are more susceptible to the influence of older children than the reverse. In general, greater conformity influences are found when the other person in the situation holds a higher status on some relevant dimension than does the subject. Most importantly, participants in groups that are highly cohesive are usually found to be more susceptible to movement conformity than are those subjects in groups that are less cohesive. In other terms, the group's favorable characteristics create a situation where members may be more inclined to accept its influence. This is by way of emphasizing again that dependence upon a group tends to increase with its attractiveness, as we noted in the last chapter.

Back (1951) investigated this effect of cohesiveness on conformity in two-person groups where he manipulated cohesiveness in several ways. For example, some subjects were told that they were assigned to work with someone whom they would like very much because of their similarity to one another (High Cohesiveness), and others that they had a partner who did not fit their own description of someone with whom they would like to work (Low Cohesiveness). He asked these varying pairs to write a joint story about a picture which had been described to them differently. His results indicated that whatever the type of cohesiveness induced, high-cohesive groups had significantly more instances of influence attempts and resulting shifts in judgment than did low-cohesive groups.

The main thrust of this work is that there are conditions which do lead to predictably greater conformity in the sense of influence effects. As Berkowitz (1957) and Jakubczak and Walters (1959) observe, these effects appear to be explainable in terms of a heightening of dependence. Summing up this point, Blake and Mouton (1961a) say:

> . . . conformity behavior increases when it is necessary for an individual to rely more heavily on the responses of others in making his own adjustment. Attitudes are more easily shifted than are reactions to factual or logical items, probably because attitudes are more social in character. Increasing the degree of difficulty of items, reducing external cues which provide external information, and in-

creasing the strength of command in the direction of the compliant behavior all serve to increase the effectiveness of conformity pressures in shifting a person's response (p. 11).

PERSONALITY AND CONFORMITY

A related line of research on conformity has tended to look at stable characteristics of the individual which may affect his acceptance of influence. The many research efforts in this vein have only revealed partial confirmation for a set of personality attributes underlying conformity. Part of the difficulty resides in the variable way in which conformity is defined operationally.

The evidence reveals only a limited tendency for individuals to conform across different situations. Thus, in a study by Vaughan (1964), he found that only 20 per cent of his subjects conformed in four different conformity situations. Alternatively, the others were affected in varying degrees by the situation in terms of the amount of movement conformity they showed. Back and Davis (1965) studied conformity in three situations and found a small though consistent trend for subjects to behave with some uniformity across them. In two situations, Samelson (1958) found that conformity was not consistently related to either the need for affiliation or the need for achievement.

Walker and Heyns have argued with some reason that, because of the reinforcements provided in the convergence situation, "groups can be made to appear as 'individualists' or 'conformists' almost at will through subtle but nevertheless effective differential reward for the two forms of behavior" (1962, p. 75). For example, by creating a situation where an individual has to make a perceptual judgment, with high stimulus ambiguity, and allegedly low status or accuracy, he is quite likely to move toward the group judgment. This response is in line with the need for social reality, but it may also serve affiliation goals of social support and social identity as well. In effect, then, characteristics of personality may not carry as much weight as the situation because they are "washed out" by strong situational factors. The diversity of findings suggests the necessity to look further at the characteristics of the situation, especially as they are defined by the subjects, in studies of conformity. These issues are illustrated by the research of Crutchfield (1955).

In a group pressure situation similar to that employed by Asch, subjects in Crutchfield's experiment observed what appeared to be the responses of others on a signal light panel before each of them. Actually, these were completely controlled by the experimenter. The tasks consisted of line comparisons as well as attitude judgments. For a sample of adult executives, Crutchfield found that conformity was higher for the line comparisons than attitudes and that total conformity correlated inversely with ratings on intellectual effectiveness, leadership, ego strength, and maturity of social relations. On a questionnaire, he also found that high conformers gave answers with "neurotic tone." No significant correlations were found, however, for conformity and scales of the MMPI, a standard measure of personality. Barron (1953) reports a similar negative finding for this measure and conformity in the Asch situation.

Since Crutchfield's approach is a well-known example of the study of personality and conformity, it is pertinent to mention several problems which it poses. For one thing, even those who conformed to a high degree were aware of discrepancies between their own judgments and the group consensus. When interviewed later, some expressed doubts about their own perception, while others blamed the group's inaccuracy. Most conforming subjects, however, indicated a mixture of these reactions. Thus, conformity meant different things to them in this particular situation. Furthermore, their motivation may have been directed as much to the goal of avoiding prolongation of an unpleasant experience as to showing agreement with the group for its own sake.

A further probing in this vein is represented in the study of Moeller and Applezweig (1957). By use of a questionnaire, they selected college women with high motivation for either self-approval or social approval, or for both. Then their conformity was assessed in an Asch situation. They found that the subjects high on the need for social approval conformed significantly more to the majority than those who were high on both needs. Those who were high on self-approval conformed least and were least concerned about their nonconforming, while those high on both needs were most concerned. Thus, subjects can be aware of group pressures but not conform to them, given other goals.

Linton and Graham (1959) have reviewed a number of studies of conformity and personality, across various situations, and conclude that patterns of personality do make a person more or less susceptible to influence. In keeping with the Moeller and Applezweig study just noted, they especially emphasize the central role of the self-concept, in terms of self-esteem, as a general factor which is inversely related to conformity. As we noted in Chapter Ten (p. 302), this position is sustained for the most part by the work of Cohen (1959) and Janis and Field (1959) among others.

The broadest overview of the evidence obtained with regard to personality variables and conformity is presented by Mann (1959) who surveyed 27 studies involving relationships between measures of personality and conformity. His findings are summarized in Table 14.1. As

Table 14.1: Percentage of significant relationships reported in a positive or negative direction for 27 studies, representing 102 findings on the relationship of various personality characteristics and conformity. (After Mann, 1959.)

PERSONALITY FACTORS AND NUMBER OF STUDIES OF EACH	NO. OF FINDINGS	% YIELDING SIG. POSITIVE RELATIONSHIP	% YIELDING SIG. NEGATIVE RELATIONSHIP	% YIELDING NEITHER
Adjustment				
Self-ratings—2	(18)	73% (13)	5% (1)	22% (4)
Sociometric ratings and personality inventories—8	(30)	7% (2)	14% (4)	79% (24)
Extroversion				
Self-ratings—2	(16)	62% (10)	6% (1)	32% (5)
Projective techniques and personality inventories—5	(10)	0% (0)	10% (1)	90% (9)
Dominance—4	(8)	0% (0)	25% (2)	75% (6)
Conservatism—6	(20)	80% (16)	0% (0)	20% (4)

will be seen there, in some studies conformity was found to be a positive function of certain personality variables, while in others it was an uncorrelated or negative function of the same variables. For example, people who reported themselves as "better adjusted" showed a considerable tendency toward conformity. On the other hand, ratings of adjustment by *other* means, such as sociometric measures, revealed an overall result in the reverse direction; however, most studies of these relationships were ambiguous or untested statistically. Clearly, there is a dissimilarity in the operational definition of certain of these personality variables, just as there is in what is meant by conformity. As Mann notes, "Those who conform to the opinion of others describe themselves as kind, friendly, helpful, and optimistic. However, the results employing projective and personality inventory variables do not confirm this relationship" (p. 261).

A further feature of this relationship lies in the confounding of variables. Mann observes that "those individuals who conform more to group opinion also tend to conform to an acceptable personality characterization in their self-descriptions" (p. 261). This is seen, too, in the operation of a tendency toward "social desirability" (Crowne and Marlowe, 1964) which is found to be associated with conformity—a point we considered in Chapter Ten (see p. 301).

While Mann concludes that there is a basis for considering another variable—conservatism—as positively associated with conformity, he adds that "No single measure of the conservatism dimension emerges as an especially potent predictor of conformity in all conditions; in fact, there is a suggestion that it is important to control for a number of conditions if the relationship is to hold at all" (p. 261). In this respect, Weiner and McGinnies (1961) and Steiner and Johnson (1963) report that authoritarians conform more only under certain conditions. Indeed, in the latter study, high scorers on the F Scale were found to conform quite selectively in an Asch situation when the majority was not unanimous.

A significant consideration in this work, viewed broadly, is that the demonstration of a relationship between personality and conformity in one situation does not in itself establish a general pattern across different situations (see Goldberg and Rorer, 1966). The most reasonable position appears to be that presented by Hunt (1965) who says that personality factors are more likely to be important in their *interaction* with situational factors than in any sense of a total dominance over them.

Interpersonal effects of conformity

Studies of conformity and nonconformity have proceeded on two levels. The first treats the *sources* of conformity within the situation or the individual. The second concerns the *consequences* of such responses upon other persons in terms of interpersonal influence. The work on movement conformity with which we have been dealing, largely emphasizes the first approach. There is, however, a good deal of interest concerning conformity as it affects the interaction of individuals with one another.

To this point we have noted that research on movement conformity is defined essentially by establishing discrepancies between an individual's probable response tendencies and the behavior of other group members. When the individual alters his response to match those of the group, this is usually treated as evidence of conformity. And, as we have seen, there are a number of factors in the situation which appear to yield such behaviors. On the whole, where the individual, for one reason or another, is more dependent upon others, his conformity is likely to be greater.

A counterpart of this feature of conformity is how its public display *influences others*. Kelman (1958) has distinguished between several kinds of conformity, one of which—compliance—refers to the outward display of agreement while retaining inward disagreement (see Chapter Six, p. 150). Where an individual is forced to make a public commitment, he is usually found to be more likely to conform than would be the case otherwise. The consequences of nonconformity are amply

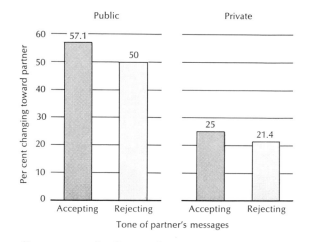

Figure 14.2: Percentage of subjects changing their opinion toward partner on final judgment under public and private conditions with differential tone in messages received from partner. (Based on data from Argyle, 1957.)

revealed in Schachter's experiment (1951), reported in Chapter Three (p. 74), in which the deviate was ultimately rejected as a group member by the others, especially under conditions of high cohesiveness.

Argyle (1957) led an experiment to study the effects on conformity behavior of requiring people to take a public stand. He set up 52 two-person groups, each containing one true subject and one mock subject as a partner. The true subject received standardized written messages from the partner in connection with the quality of a picture they were to judge. Half of the subjects had to make their final judgment publicly, the other half privately in an envelope. Messages from the partner were also contrived to be "accepting" in tone for some of these subjects and "rejecting" in tone for the others. Argyle found significantly more conformity to the partner's judgment occurring under public conditions, with acceptance yielding somewhat higher results than rejection for both the public and private conditions, as will be seen in Figure 14.2.

EXTERNAL AND INTERNAL ASPECTS OF CONFORMITY

An interest in external conformity has generally dominated the concern of social scientists. More recently, however, greater attention has been directed to its internal aspects. This emphasis represents a greater focus on the "functional" features of conformity for the individual (cf. Katz, Sarnoff, and McClintock, 1956). In this vein, Kelman (1958, 1961) has sought to separate three distinctive processes of conformity represented in the acceptance of external influence. He calls these compliance, identification, and internalization. We have already noted above that compliance involves overt conformity without internal agreement. Identification means showing conformity in a satisfying role relationship where it is expected if the relationship is to be maintained. Internalization leads to both external and internal conformity because the individual finds it harmonious with his own values.

The vital element in these functional approaches to individual conformity is their attention to motivation. Inevitably, the rewards associated with conformity must be specified. Furthermore, there is a widespread assumption that external conformity reflects a motivational intent, usually to gain social approval or acceptance. Such an assumption appears unfounded as a global generalization for several reasons: first, because an individual may choose to do as others do without necessarily being dependent upon their standard in any persisting way; second, because motivation to conform may result from a desire to participate in a group task, not from seeking approval from others; and third, because in the absence of accurate perception of social demands a person could behave in line with a social standard without being motivated to do so. The converse of this last point has implications as well, i.e. if an individual apparently nonconforms, this may *not* reflect a motivational intent, but rather indicate an error of perception even in the face of a desire to conform. Thus, a psychological definition of conforming behavior would consider whether the individual *intended* to fulfill normative group expectancies as he perceived them.

Some light is cast on the issue of underlying change by an experiment reported in Sherif (1961). Working with Hood, he was essentially interested in determining if public compliance in the autokinetic situation was aimed at avoiding disapproval from others in the group. Accordingly, in this experiment no indication was given that the aim was to study social influence. To do this no confrontation occurred with another subject at the time the subject made his judgment. This was accomplished by first having the subject simply overhear another person making 20 judgments while apparently waiting his turn to make his own estimates. Next, the subject made his own judgments alone. One experimental group overheard judgments ranging from 1 to 5 inches and another group overheard judgments from 6 to 10 inches. As will be seen in Figure 14.3, the judgments made by those subjects when alone were significantly related to what they had overheard the other subjects saying. Subjects were later asked what degree of movement they had actually seen. It was found that these reports did not differ significantly from what they had judged in the situation.

"We may conclude," says Sherif, "that in this situation individuals 'call them as they see them' and they see them as influenced by judgments previously overheard. There is no evidence of a discrepancy between judgment and verbal report" (p. 168). The generalizability of this finding is debatable, in part because of the use of an ambiguous stimulus. In the Crutchfield (1955) study, for example, noted above, he reported that, with essentially unambiguous stimuli, between 25 and 30 per cent of his subjects "freely admit on later questioning that they responded the way the group did even when they thought this not the proper answer" (p. 197). The entire issue of the accuracy of verbal reports of perception is one that has commanded a good deal of interest in psychology, and it is by no means resolved.

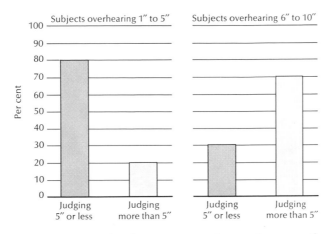

Figure 14.3: Proportions of judgments 5" or less and greater than 5" for subjects under two conditions of prior exposure to another's judgment. (From Sherif, 1961, after Hood and Sherif, 1957.)

CONFORMITY AND SOCIAL EXCHANGE

In the world of everyday affairs, the effects of conformity can be seen in several ways. One factor of importance is the reward conformity provides in smoothing the path of interaction between individuals. This is the essential touchstone to understanding conformity in terms of reciprocity and social exchange (cf. Homans, 1958, 1961; Thibaut and Kelley, 1959; Gouldner, 1960; Blau, 1964). These views construe conformity as a reward for others which yields positive effects from them. Jones (1964, 1965) has also called attention to the way in which conformity may be used as a technique of *ingratiation*, where a person of lower status wishes to obtain certain benefits from one of higher status in a relationship. In line with the kind of thinking represented in Goffman's work (1959), Jones sees conformity as a way of creating a favorable impression, or at least avoiding an unfavorable one. This leads, in turn, to certain desired outcomes from the interaction (see Chapter Seven, p. 185).

An illustration of this phenomenon appears in John F. Kennedy's introduction to his *Profiles in Courage* (1956) in which he writes of influence pressures toward conformity in the United States Senate. He says:

> Americans want to be liked—and Senators are no exception . . . We enjoy the comradeship and approval of our friends and colleagues. We prefer praise to abuse, popularity to contempt . . . We realize, moreover, that our influence in the club—and the extent to which we can accomplish our objectives and those of our constituents—are dependent in some measure on the esteem with which we are regarded by other Senators. "The way to get along," I was told when I entered Congress, "is to go along." (p. 3).

The important element that this account reveals is that conformity can be exchanged in order to gain acceptance from others, especially in their later support. Extending this process over time leads to the prospect that *early* conformity may permit later nonconformity to be better tolerated. This is the basis for the "idiosyncrasy credit" concept which we will now consider.

IDIOSYNCRASY CREDIT AND NONCONFORMITY

As we have seen, one feature of conformity is to reward others in social interaction (Homans, 1961). A consequence of this reward is to alter interpersonal perceptions which may affect later interactions.

Idiosyncrasy credit may be considered to be the positive impressions of a person held by others, whether defined in the narrower terms of a small face-to-face group or a larger social entity such as an organization or even a total society. These credits represent *status* and have the operational property of allowing deviation, innovation, and the assertion of influence. Basically, credits *accumulate* as a result of perceived conformity and competence, though other factors also enter in (Hollander, 1958).

Perceived conformity, in the first place, can be looked upon as one input to the accumulation of status in the form of credit in the eyes of others. This "credit balance" later permits greater latitude for nonconformity. This accounts for the fact that the neophyte in a group, with a minimum of credits, is more constrained to conform than an old-timer, other things being equal.

Associated with this concept is the view that conformity and nonconformity are not fixed to a single norm applicable to everyone, as in the traditional conception exemplified in the "J Curve." Rather, nonconforming behavior is seen to be variously defined by the group, depending on how the actor himself is perceived. Thus, conformity is considered to be evaluated in terms of the specific person and his credits. This fits the everyday observation that individuals of higher status have a wider latitude for nonconformity. It has also been demonstrated in recent experiments by Berkowitz and Macaulay (1961), Harvey and Consalvi (1960), Julian and Steiner (1961), Sabath (1964), and Wiggins, *et al.* (1965). The essential result in all of these studies is that higher status members could nonconform more freely.

This feature of idiosyncrasy credit was tested in an experiment conducted by Hollander (1961). Students were given a brief description of a person they were to imagine in any group to which they belonged. Eight descriptions were used. Half the subjects were told this stimulus person had "been in the group for some while," the other half that the person was "new to the group." Within each of these two categories the person was described as having one of four levels of competence. Subjects were then asked to signify on a 7-point scale how willing they would be to have this person in a position of authority. This was the measure of accorded status. The results are shown in Table 14.2. They indicate, for the first phase, that both competence and length of time in the group contributed systematically to increased accorded status.

Table 14.2: Means for accorded status by experimental treatments. (From Hollander, 1961.)

TREATMENT	IN GROUP FOR SOME WHILE	NEW TO GROUP
Extremely capable performer	6.25	5.84
Capable performer	6.11	5.50
Average performer	5.06	4.50
Poor performer	2.95	2.53

In the second phase of the experiment, these scores for accorded status were looked at in relationship to how much the subjects would disapprove various behaviors that the same stimulus person might show in the group. Figure 14.4 shows the disapproval curves for three behaviors which yielded significant correlations with accorded status. The two innovative behaviors were less disapproved the higher the status, but alternatively, the reverse was found for a behavior involving an interpersonal act, i.e. "interrupts others." This study, therefore, demonstrates the greater latitude that a person of higher status has in such realms as innovation, but not in others. The implications of this for leadership will be considered in the next chapter.

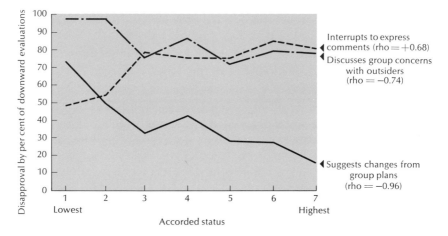

Figure 14.4: Percentage of respondents giving disapproving evaluation of stimulus person for displaying indicated behaviors, by status accorded the stimulus person. (From Hollander, 1961.)

The fact that when a person is perceived to have higher status his behavior is evaluated differently, provides a useful bridge for understanding the potential for innovation associated with leadership. Thus, leaders may be greater conformers to group norms in establishing their position initially, while also being initiators of change in seemingly nonconforming ways later on. In another experiment, with problem-solving groups, it was found that early nonconformity to agreed upon group procedures sharply reduced the influence of the group's most competent member (Hollander, 1960). Alternatively, early conformity to these procedures allowed that competent member to be more influential on the task and also to alter the normative procedures themselves.

Nonconformity can also be viewed with regard to the distinction between common expectancies of a group regarding its members, as well as those special expectancies associated with higher status. While there is, then, greater tolerance of nonconformity for the high status person in some ways, the results shown in Figure 14.4 reveal restrictions imposed in other ways. These particular expectancies can be thought of as role behaviors associated with a position of higher status. There are at least two reasons why these restrictions are imposed. First, because status is usually perceived to carry with it greater self-determination of behavior such that those in positions of higher status are assumed to be more responsible for their actions (Thibaut and Riecken, 1955). Second, status holds more potential for affecting important outcomes for the members of the group (Hollander, 1964, p. 227).

The visibility associated with higher status also means that the outcome of any given act of nonconformity will be judged in terms of the rewards it produces for the group. Given the development of the history of past deviations which have proven to be fruitful innovations, the high status group member's behavior is more likely to be perceived in the nature of providing good outcomes to the group rather than bad outcomes. In Pauline Pepinsky's term (1961), they will be seen to be in the nature of "productive nonconformity." The central point here is the consideration that acts of an evidently nonconforming variety will be variously interpreted as a function of others' *perception of the actor* based on their past experience with him and their *imputation of motivations* to him (cf. Heider, 1958). In sum, conformity and nonconformity are observed and evaluated with reference to past interactions, and this may influence others' subsequent behavior toward the actor.

Group support as a basis for nonconformity

The consideration that perception of higher status may alter expectancies accounts for one basis for nonconformity. This is in line with other results found in studies of movement conformity. However, such studies do not usually involve social interaction leading to effects from interpersonal perception. A major factor is the role of the experimenter as the one who constructs the situation and himself serves as an influence source. Orne (1962) has pointed to the way in which "demand characteristics" of the experiment may enhance the experimenter's influence.

In an experiment closer to the substance of a real-life problem, Milgram (1965) provides a test of experimenter influence which also illuminates a basis for evident nonconformity through group support. Briefly, as the experimenter, he instructed subjects to administer what they were previously led to believe would be a painful shock to another person. In one set of experimental conditions, two other mock subjects either agreed to administer the shock or refused to do so. He found significantly more subjects refusing to administer shock, if the other "subjects" would *not*, than actually did when instructed to do so with no others present. What is particularly striking is that he found no significant differences in willingness to give shock between subjects with two other agreeable subjects doing so or alone. These results are shown in Figure 14.5. The effect of the experimenter in influencing the behav-

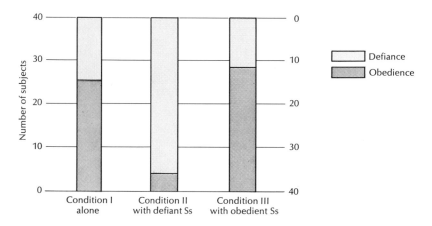

Figure 14.5: Proportion of subjects showing defiance and obedience to the experimenter's instructions under three conditions with 40 subjects in each. (Adapted from Milgram, 1965.)

ior of the subject toward an undesirable act was quite marked unless the subject had *support from others* in resisting that influence. Put in other terms, nonconformity to the experimenter was a function of conformity to others sharing an evidently common fate. Clearly, then, conformity to one standard led to nonconformity to another. The finding that others in the "group" could sustain such independence is especially significant.

An important question regarding nonconformity concerns the accessibility of alternatives to the individual for *resisting* influence. In this respect, Cartwright (1959) has discussed two features of power: power *over* others to influence them; and power to *resist* the imposition of influence *by* others. Both processes are implicated in conformity and nonconformity. The latter, however, has received little attention as compared with the former.

At bottom, one of the major problems in studying conformity is to view it as if the individual had only one alternative to conformity. This overlooks the variability of expectancies and the different kinds of non-conformity.

Conformity, anticonformity, and independence

As we have noted, there are inadequacies in the usual unidimensional approaches to conformity, with conforming behavior viewed at one end of a continuum and deviations at the other. An alternative model which departs from the unidimensional tradition, has recently been suggested by Willis (1963) and adapted in research by Willis and Hollander (1964a; 1964b) and Hollander and Willis (1964). A major feature of this model, shown in Figure 14.6, is the provision it makes for distinguishing between two kinds of nonconformity response, i.e. independence and anticonformity. Basically, it concerns aspects of movement conformity and not congruence.

In this model two dimensions are used for the construction of an adequate representation of conformity and nonconformity. The first of these dimensions is dependence-independence; the second is conformity-anticonformity. These are at right angles to one another. They produce an isosceles triangle with points labeled conformity and anticonformity, along the net conformity dimension, and independence, at right angles to it, as shown in Figure 14.6. These points describe the three basic modes of responding to social pressures:

> *Conformity* refers to consistent movement in the direction of a social expectancy.
>
> *Independence* refers to a lack of consistent movement toward or away from a social expectancy.
>
> *Anticonformity* refers to consistent movement away from a social expectancy.

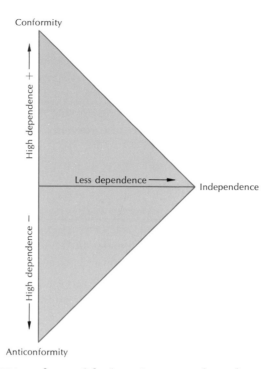

Figure 14.6: Triangular model of *conformity, independence,* and *anticonformity* responses. (From Willis, 1963.) This can be expanded to a diamond shape by extending the horizontal dimension to the left to generate *variability,* which is a mode of independence that reveals itself in a consistent change from one's own position (see Willis, 1965).

It is important to note that both *conformity and anticonformity reveal dependence* upon others. In the first instance this takes the form of a positive response to their expectancies and in the second a negative response to those expectancies. Notice, therefore, that a person who nonconforms by anticonforming is still tied to a group norm as a source of influence for his actions. On the other hand, the person who responds *independently* in a situation *may or may not* behave in terms of such demands.

Thus, the person perceives relevant social expectancies but is not dependent upon them as guides to behavior. A simple example of independence would be a situation where a girl wears her hair long and prefers it that way. Suppose that other girls, as a result of new fashion dictates, start wearing their hair long so that it becomes a behavioral norm. If the girl wants to "be different" she might then cut her hair. In so doing, she would be anticonforming since she is responding in a dependent way to what others are doing, and *not* to her own preference. Independent behavior in this situation would be presented by the girl continuing to wear her hair as before, if that is what she likes best. However, if she does keep her hair long, she might be regarded by others as a "conformist," though her intent is otherwise, i.e. to be independent.

A confusion between anticonformity and independence has been at the heart of many controversies about conformity and individuality. The anticonforming person in any circumstance can easily be taken for someone who is being "individualistic" when, in fact, he may actually be tied to doing the absolute reverse of what relevant social practices require. The difference between such negativism and independence quite obviously lies in the motivational intent, and that poses a complicated problem of interpretation. However, it is possible to create certain aspects of a situation experimentally, by giving different sets to subjects, in order to study anticonformity in contrast to independence.

As a demonstration of the variables *producing* conformity, and nonconformity of both the independence and anticonforming variety, Willis and Hollander (1964a) experimentally varied the subject's own perceived competence, the perceived competence of the coworker, the strength of the set to reaffirm inital judgments, and the reward structure. Movement in the direction predicted was found to confirm the two-dimensional triangular model as a better description of behavior than the more usual unidimensional conception.

Regarding the *effects* of these three behaviors, in another experiment these same investigators had subjects working together on a task with a coworker who behaved in a conforming, independent, or anticonforming way, and who also was said to be more competent or less competent than the subject himself. They found that subjects reported highest perceived influence by their coworker where he was competent in the task and behaving independently. Conformity by the coworker, even when he was competent, led to significantly lower perceived influence. These and other findings from that study corroborate the differential effects of conformity, independence, and anticonformity in combination with competence. Therefore, though independence and anticonformity both constituted nonconformity, each evoked a distinctive pattern of reaction from subjects (Hollander and Willis, 1964).

The multi-causal nature of conformity

Most characterizations of conformity and nonconformity continue to treat these phenomena as if they satisfied a single motive. But as we have observed, this is much too narrow a conception of the diverse pressures and anticipated goals that shape behavior. For one thing, the continuity of behavior is inextricably bound up with many associations of a dependence nature, in the past and present as well as in the future. Furthermore, diverse motives may be satisfied simultaneously.

The teenager, for example, who conforms to what his peers are doing may be establishing a social identity apart from the family at the same time that he gains social support from his peers and achieves a sense of what his world is about in terms of their social reality. These affiliative needs are among various factors which may be implicated in the kind of influence relationship which leads to conformity.

A major point to be stressed, then, is the need to understand conformity and nonconformity as modes of response aimed at securing certain desired consequences for the individual, often in terms of several goals. Conformity and nonconformity both result from situational factors and individual needs which together produce a response to influence. This means that a person's evident nonconformity may represent rewards to him associated with less apparent conformity to another standard. The relationship between conformity and nonconformity is therefore complicated and not a matter of simple opposites, as we are often led to believe.

SUMMARY

Conformity is studied in social psychology in terms of its sources and effects. While some social critics are concerned about excessive conformity, the study of conformity proceeds without judgments of goodness or badness. The most widespread concern about conformity lies in the belief that it is opposite to individuality. This overlooks, however, the individual benefits gained by conforming and by knowing that others will conform.

Conformity and nonconformity are not simple phenomena that can be treated in a categorical fashion. Sometimes they refer to the degree of uniformity of expected behavior which can be called *congruence conformity,* and sometimes to a shift toward a social standard called *movement conformity.*

The latter form has been the basis for a great deal of laboratory experimentation which reveals a number of factors in the situation which regularly relate to such conformity, e.g. the ambiguity of the stimuli presented; a lower perceived competence or status than other group members; the presence of a unanimous majority; and the attractiveness of the group. While situational factors such as these produce a higher probability of conformity, attributes of personality are not found to be consistently related to conformity across situations.

The effects of conformity can be looked at in terms of a "social exchange" producing benefits in interaction. Thus, where an individual must make a public commitment, the probability of a conforming response is heightened. Acceptance of nonconformity is related to status in the sense of how an individual is perceived by those with whom he has ongoing interaction. Such status can be thought of as an accumulation of "idiosyncrasy credits" which represent the positive perceptions held of a person. These arise from perceived conformity and competence, among other factors, and can be used for later nonconformity and innovation as represented in leadership.

The concept of a single norm, or expectancy, applicable to everyone in a group can be modified to recognize the effects of status in producing differential expectancies for various members. Furthermore, there also exists a differential power to resist influence represented in conformity pressures. Group support appears to be one important basis for not complying with an assertion of influence. This reveals an essential point whereby evident nonconformity to one social standard may reflect conformity to another less evident one.

Nonconformity can be of two distinct varieties: it may be *anticonformity,* which takes the form of high dependence upon a social expectancy as a negative basis for action, or *independence,* which represents an absence of concern for that expectancy. While anticonformity and independence may resemble one another superficially, the latter represents far greater individual initiative. *Both* conformity and anticonformity constitute responses of a heavily *dependent* nature since they are tied to a group expectancy. Several kinds of goals may be served simultaneously by these modes of nonconformity, as well as by conformity.

SUGGESTED READINGS

From E. P. Hollander and R. G. Hunt. (Eds.) *Current perspectives in social psychology.* (2nd Edition.) New York: Oxford University Press, 1967:

44. Richard H. Willis: *The basic response modes of conformity, independence, and anticonformity*
45. Herbert C. Kelman: *Three processes of social influence*
48. Edwin P. Hollander: *Conformity, status, and idiosyncrasy credit*
49. Edward E. Jones: *Conformity as a tactic of ingratiation*

SELECTED REFERENCES

Berg, I. A., & Bass, B. M. (Eds.) *Conformity and deviation.* New York: Harper, 1961.
*Gardner, J. W. *Self-renewal.* New York: Harper & Row, 1963.
*Riesman, D., Glazer, N., & Denny, R. *The lonely crowd: a study of the changing American character.* New Haven: Yale Univer. Press, 1950.
Sherif, M., & Sherif, Carolyn W. *Reference groups: exploration into the conformity and deviation of adolescents.* New York: Harper & Row, 1964.
*Walker, E. L., & Heyns, R. W. *An anatomy for conformity.* Englewood Cliffs, N. J.: Prentice-Hall, 1962.

15

Leadership, supervision, and negotiation

The idea that leaders are born is still a popular one. It has ancient origins, illustrated by Aristotle's sweeping observation that "From the hour of their birth some are marked out for subjugation, and others for command." Contemporary views of leaders and leadership depart considerably from this. The prevailing view in social psychology today stresses the leadership functions to be fulfilled in the situation rather than the characteristics of the leader alone.

Just as groups vary in their characteristics, so do leaders. Different circumstances may require different leader attributes for group functions to be performed. The nub of the matter is that leadership is a role which provides for vital group needs, and these may be performed by various persons. Any time two or more people function together to attain a mutual goal, a group structure develops. Leadership, in the sense of influence directed toward the attainment of group goals, is the most central part of that structure.

The process of leadership can therefore be considered as an influence relationship that occurs between mutually dependent group members. It can be understood with reference to the interrelation of three broad factors: the *leader* with his attributes including motivations, perceptions, and resources relevant to the attainment of the group's goal; the *followers*, with their attributes including motivations, perceptions, and relevant resources; and the *situation* within which they function. In

429

this chapter we will consider this interrelation and the implications it holds for group processes as well as for leader effectiveness.

The nature of leadership

The two terms "leadership" and "leader" are not the same and should be distinguished from one another at the outset. In the broadest sense, *leadership* implies the existence of a particular influence relationship between two or more persons, though it usually refers to groups of more than two. As Stogdill (1950) puts it, "Leadership [is] the process of influencing the activities of an organized group toward goal-setting and goal achievement" (p. 4).

A *leader* is a person with characteristics, including especially a given status, which allow him to exercise influence in line with the attainment of group goals. In doing so, he can be seen as someone whose role constitutes a major group resource, insofar as he exerts influence in the direction of helping to achieve common goals.

While we are treating the leader here mainly in his interaction in a functional group situation, the role of leader may also be fulfilled in symbolic terms, as exemplified by those noted for their great scientific or artistic achievements. Among scientists, for instance, a great figure such as an Einstein could exert considerable influence as a model or examplar of shared values. The influence may not be as direct, but the quality of being a cherished "resource" is there and that potential could be activated. In general, wide esteem creates a "high status" which provides the basis for influence. However, status depends upon interpersonal perception. A person does not "hold" status so much as he is "accorded" status, and this results from a process of evaluation through actual or implied interaction.

LEADERSHIP AS A TRANSACTION

The venerable view of the leader as the primary actor, the one who imposes his influence upon others, omits the essence of the transaction which occurs between a person in a leadership role and his followers. As Homans (1961) aptly notes, "Influence over others is purchased at the price of allowing one's self to be influenced by others" (p. 286). In this sense, the willingness of group members to accept the influence of a leader depends upon his characteristics perceived in the course of interaction.

In the transactional view, the leader can be considered to be an influence agent who directs communications to his followers, to which they may react in various ways. The leader attempts to take account of the perceptual-motivational states of his followers and they, in turn, evaluate his motivations and characteristics in terms of responses to their needs. Leadership therefore cannot be meaningfully considered independently of the followers within a particular group and of the nature of the transactions involved.

The potentialities for leadership exist in many reaches of life. It is not confined only to those holding exalted status, nor is it firmly fixed. In everyday life, persons function in numerous roles embodying leadership. Many leadership events occur between people involved in reciprocal role relationships such as parent-child, teacher-student, husband-wife. These are not static patterns, of course, but may vary over time.

Yet, there is a special quality associated with leadership in groups, as well as in large organizations and nations, and this inevitably has engendered a focus on "the leader" as the central figure in the leadership process. There is a long tradition associated with the idea that the source of this process lies within the leader and history itself is full of accounts of leaders and their acts. We will review some of this tradition now.

TRAIT VERSUS SITUATIONAL APPROACHES TO LEADERSHIP

Concern and controversy about leadership extend far back in philosophical thought. Typically, the leader was seen to be someone possessed of unique traits. Cowley (1928) captured this theme in his contention that "The approach to the study of leadership has usually been and must always be through the study of traits" (p. 144).

While there is a degree of validity in the notion of leaders as significant agents in human events, it produced an overemphasis on the traits of the leader at the expense of other factors in the situation, including followers and prevailing circumstances which shape the leader's actions. The trait approach was particularly favored as a strategy for investigating leadership among psychologically oriented investigators. Accordingly, research on the subject earlier in this century placed considerable stress on such factors as height, weight, appearance, intelligence, self-confidence, and any other variables which might be correlated positively with leadership. The broad aim was to determine once and for all what factor or factors *made* a person a leader. The results were summarized in an influential review by Stogdill (1948) and presented a very mixed picture, to say the least. The major finding was that, on the average, leaders tended to be slightly more intelligent than non-leaders. Even this finding was not, however, thoroughly stable.

More recently, Mann (1959) has reviewed 125 studies of leadership and personality characteristics representing over seven hundred findings. These are summarized in Table 15.1. Once again, intelligence

Table 15.1: Percentage of significant relationships reported in a positive or negative direction for 125 studies, representing 751 findings on the relationship of various personality characteristics and leadership. (After Mann, 1959.)

PERSONALITY FACTORS AND NUMBER OF STUDIES OF EACH	NUMBER OF FINDINGS	% YIELDING SIG. POSITIVE RELATIONSHIP	% YIELDING SIG. NEGATIVE RELATIONSHIP	% YIELDING NEITHER
Intelligence—28	(196)	46% (91)	1%* (1)	53% (104)
Adjustment—22	(164)	30% (50)	2%* (2)	68% (112)
Extroversion—22	(119)	31% (37)	5% (6)	64% (76)
Dominance—12	(39)	38% (15)	15% (6)	46% (18)
Masculinity—9	(70)	16% (11)	1%* (1)	83% (58)
Conservatism—17	(62)	5% (3)	27% (17)	68% (42)
Sensitivity—15	(101)	15% (15)	1% (1)	84% (85)
* Rounded upward				

stands forth as the factor with the highest percentage of positive relationships with leadership. Mann also identifies general adjustment, extroversion, and dominance as correlates of leadership. He points out, however, that most of these studies involved a group organized around an assigned discussion task. The "superiority" of the leader, therefore, has to be viewed in that context. Gibb (1954) has summed up the matter in observing that:

> Followers subordinate themselves, not to an individual whom they perceive as utterly different, but to a member of their group who has superiority at this time and whom they perceive to be funda-

mentally the same as they are, and who may, at other times, be prepared to follow (p. 915).

This point suggests the necessity to see leadership and followership as complementary roles which are not fixed but amenable to change.

The largest deficiency in the trait approach was its insistence upon looking for stable features of "leaders" across many situations. Again, this is not the same as studying "leadership" as a process. At any rate, the trait approach failed to recognize that leadership involves a network of relationships with other individuals who are engaged in a situation with a focal activity. As Gouldner (1950) says:

> There is a certain degree of persistence or patterning in the activities which a group undertakes be it bowling, playing bridge, engaging in warfare, or shoplifting. These persisting or habitual group activities, among other things, set limits on the kind of individuals who become group members and, no less so, upon the kind of individuals who come to lead the group (p. 76).

The biggest part of the situational view is the attention it pays to the varying demands upon leadership imposed by the situation. These demands may grow out of the group's task or function, its structure, and other contextual features, such as external threat. As the dominant theme of the last decade in research on leadership, the situational approach does *not* play down the characteristics of the leader so much as it recognizes their importance to a group in a given situation. Thus, for example, it is recognized that the leader should have some acceptable level of competence on a task of importance to the group's functioning. But, as Cartwright and Zander (1960) say, whether this competence displays itself in flying an airplane or in organizing an expedition for survival, depends very much upon these situational factors (p. 495).

The concept of the leader as a group resource is among the most recent extensions of the situational approach (cf. Hollander and Julian, in press). It has roots in two kinds of considerations. One is the evident need for a functional group to operate in an organized way to attain its objectives. The second consideration is that followers define situations in responding to leadership. They are not merely passive recipients of influence assertions from the leader but they react to these in evaluative terms. This conception has obvious parallels to the model of persuasive communication we considered in Chapter Six (see pp. 152-153).

The more contemporary, functional view looks upon leadership within a situation as a property of the group's structure, rather than as an individual attribute. As Cartwright and Zander (1960) indicate, two ideas are embedded in this view: first, that "any member of a group may be a leader in the sense that he may take actions which serve group functions," and, second, that "a given function may be served by many different behaviors . . . taken by a variety of people" (p. 494).

Therefore, leadership is a matter of degree and not an all-or-nothing affair. It requires the engagement of various group resources in co-ordinate activity, which means that the follower has a place as an active participant in the leadership process. As Fillmore Sanford (1950) observes:

> There is some justification for regarding the follower as the most crucial factor in any leadership event. . . . Not only is it the follower who accepts or rejects leadership, but it is the follower who *perceives* both the leader and the situation and who reacts in terms of what he perceives. And what he perceives may be, to an important degree, a function of his own motivations, frames of reference, and "readinesses" (p. 4).

In its most recent form, then, the situational approach is oriented to the demands made on leaders for leadership functions. It conceives of leadership more in terms of functions to be performed than persisting attributes of the leader himself. Furthermore, it grants the follower a more active role as the participant in a transaction who perceives and reacts to the leader as an influence source. Of obvious importance, too, is how the leader's position is attained and characterized.

Some characterizations of the leader

One major question in characterizing the leader rests in how he comes to be in the leadership role. Much depends on the way in which that role is construed, both by the leader and the followers. As we pointed out earlier, groups may have an informal or formal structure. In the first case, the leader derives his status from others in the group who may accord or withdraw it. This pattern, which depends upon group consent, can be called *emergent leadership*. By contrast, a formal structure produces *appointed leadership* imposed by external authority.

Mainly, this distinction is important for highlighting situational forces which reflect on the legitimacy of the leader's position, and not his style of interaction. For example, though the group is not directly involved in choosing an imposed leader, he may be perceived favorably for attributes which would make him acceptable to followers as an emergent leader as well.

THE APPOINTED LEADER

The first and most traditional way to determine who is a leader is to find out who has been designated for this function. If you go to an executive's office, or encounter a military officer, the assumption is that that person is a leader. This in fact was the basis for a program of research conducted by Shartle and Stogdill (1952) on naval leadership. They discovered that highly variable functions were involved as features of various leader roles. Command at sea holds requirements which vary considerably from those, let us say, at a recruiting center ashore.

Since appointed leaders are assigned to the group and given functions by higher authority, their activities are accordingly greatly determined by those considerations. Leadership thus becomes a means rather than an end in itself. Bavelas (1960) says the question "Who is the leader?" might better be put in other terms as "What functions are to be fulfilled?" He suggests that in the aggregate "organizational leaders" are those who perform certain kinds of tasks rather than having certain characteristic attributes of personality, in terms of social interaction. Indeed, leaders of this kind may or may not require effective interpersonal relations. This point will be elaborated later in connection with organizational leadership.

SOCIOMETRIC CHOICE AND POPULARITY

In the informal group, emergent leaders have frequently been identified by sociometric choice patterns. The techniques of sociometry, which we considered in Chapter Seven (p. 190), provide a basis for determining who the members of a group perceive to be their leader. In its earlier phases, popularity was given a great deal of weight in sociometric studies. Much of this work looked at choices among roommates or study companions. As a consequence, a general measure of liking was taken as a sign of leadership (e.g. Jennings, 1943).

More recently, it has been found that the relationship between such popularity and leadership depends upon the situation and therefore need not be high. Simply liking a person does not mean that he would be acceptable in fulfilling a leadership role within a group. In this respect, Jennings (1947) has distinguished between attraction based upon personal liking, which she calls *psyche-tele* attraction, and *socio-tele* attraction, based upon a group standard of judgment.

It may also be that acknowledging a leader does not signify a liking for him. Bales (1955) had students involved in a group discussion task answer four sociometric questions regarding: 1) contributing best ideas; 2) guiding the discussion; 3) liking; and 4) disliking. He found that those rated at the top for "best ideas" and "guiding discussion" were near the bottom for "liking." On the other hand, the second man on these leadership functions was routinely found to be highest on liking. Bales concluded that "there must be something about high participation and specialization in the technical and executive directions which tends to provoke hostility" (p. 453). In a related work, Bales with Slater (1955) has distinguished between the "task specialist" and "socio-emotional" leadership roles; they say that both of these exist in groups. It is doubtful, however, that there is a fundamental conflict between these roles and, indeed, they may be occupied by the same person depending upon the character of the task (Marcus, 1960; and Turk, 1961).

The import of Bales's work lies in the finding that participants in a group distinguish between those who contribute to a leadership function and those they like. In short, leaders are not necessarily the best liked individuals in a group, nor can they always be, though they may be admired and esteemed. Corroboration for this comes also from research by Hollander and Webb (1955). In that study, still another issue was introduced in terms of "followership." For a long time the traditional sociometric approach to leadership had been based on a pyramid model with a peak of leaders at the top and a residue of non-leaders below. Non-leaders were presumed to be followers, which is an assumption this research tested.

The procedure in the Hollander and Webb study was to have naval aviation cadets complete three sociometric forms upon graduation from a sixteen-week preflight course at Pensacola. The first two of these were on leadership and followership, the third on friendship. On both the leadership and followership form each cadet was asked to assume that he was assigned to "a special military unit with an undisclosed mission." Then, for leadership, he was directed to nominate in order three cadets from his section whom he considered best qualified to lead this special unit and three cadets from his section whom he considered least qualified. A similar set was presented for followership with the instruction that the cadet assume that *he himself had been assigned to the leadership* of this special unit; from among the members of his section, he was instructed to nominate three cadets whom he would want as part of his unit and three whom he would not want. The friendship nomination form simply asked for the names of three friends in the section.

Correlation analysis revealed leadership and followership nominations to be related to a high degree, r = .92. Friendship had a significantly higher relationship with followership, r = .55, than with leadership, r = .47. But apart from this, friendship nominations were not found to bear appreciably on the basic leadership-followership relationship. Of the three friendship nominees designated by each subject, an average of more than two were not mentioned at all in the leadership nominations made by these same subjects, as is shown with the other relationships in Figure 15.1.

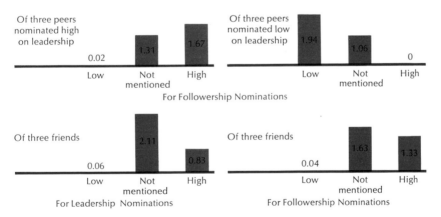

Figure 15.1: Pattern of relationship among peer nominations for leadership, followership, and friendship. (Based upon data from Hollander and Webb, 1955.)

The results clearly established that the more desired followers tended to be chosen from the upper extremes of the leadership distribution; indeed, the correspondence was marked. Furthermore, the influence of friendship, so often taken for leadership under the heading of "popularity," had little effect on this relationship. In a later study by Kubany (1957) quite comparable results were found with 87 medical school graduating seniors. A correlation of .85 obtained between peer-nomination scores for choices on "family physician" and "turn over practice to." Neither of these was as highly correlated with "friend and social associate."

INFLUENCE AND INNOVATION

Another way of identifying the leader is to consider the influence patterns of a group. One major exponent of this viewpoint, Homans (1961), considers leadership in direct influence terms:

> . . . the larger the number of other members a single member is regularly able to influence, the higher is his authority in the group. The man with highest authority we shall call the leader. By this definition authority is not just influence, for each member may have influenced every other at one time or another. Authority refers instead to differences between members in the amount of influence they exert (p. 286).

Direction of group activity is a central feature of the leadership role. Thus, leadership implies influence. As Gibb (1950) notes, group members are usually quite able to identify their peers who exert the greatest influence. Indeed, the idea of an influence hierarchy, whether explicit or implicit, is quite pervasive in human affairs (Seeman & Morris, 1950).

One pointed characterization of leadership in terms of influence is Hemphill's (1958, 1961) concept that the leader is the group member most responsible for *initiating structure*. In this view, leaders can be identified by the high degree to which they determine the group's pattern of interaction and locomotion toward its goal. The significant element here is that the leader is not simply part of the group's structure but rather is an active agent in shaping it. Hemphill also distinguishes between *attempted* leadership and *accepted* leadership. In the first instance, an individual initiates activity to influence others, and in the second, that assertion is responded to affirmatively. There is no flow of leadership, so to speak, unless both conditions are fulfilled. It is this sequence, says Hemphill, which is a basic requirement for effective leadership. As we shall be observing shortly, in connection with organizational leadership, a considerable range of research indicates initiation of structure to be a major factor in leadership across many situations.

Another way of considering the leader is to view him as the *completer* of essential group functions. This view is identified with the work of Schutz (1961) who places particular stress on the role of the leader as a resource person who insures that the group's critical functions are adequately fulfilled and maintained in harmony with one another. This idea meshes rather well with the concept of initiation of structure, especially in those circumstances where the group requires the leader's organizational efforts to move toward its goals. Accordingly, once a set of group functions can be specified, it is possible to consider that person as leader who can help to fulfill these functions by his initiative and influence.

The concept of *idiosyncrasy credit,* discussed in the last chapter, has special relevance to the leader's latitude for exerting influence, particularly in an innovative way. This concept looks upon the leader's status as an accumulation of positive impressions from past interactions with other group members. In operational terms, they provide the basis for the leader's taking actions which would be seen to be nonconforming for other members of the group. The important point, however, is that innovation in the face of situational demands is expected of the leader as a feature of his role. Inaction by the leader would therefore considerably reduce his status in the eyes of the other group members. Which person achieves and retains leadership will therefore depend upon the perceptions held by others, particularly in terms of an acceptable level of initial conformity to group expectancies and competence in providing for a function of significance in the attainment of the group's goal.

POWER AND LEGITIMACY OF AUTHORITY

As a general rule, power is seen to be part of the leader's role. Yet it may vary considerably with the nature of the group as well as with the source of the leader's authority. It is sometimes the case, for example, that an emergent leader, within an informal group, is as powerful in directing others as one who is appointed. In a study by Carter, Haythorn, Shriver, and Lanzetta (1951) they found such an inversion of their predicted results. They had some groups working under an appointed leader and others working under a leader freely elected by the group itself. It was assumed that the former situation would lead to a greater assertion of influence by the leader. This was not the case. In general, the appointed leaders saw their position as one of co-ordination —in the sense of a distribution of responsibilities—rather than as a powerful director of the group's activities. By contrast, the elected leaders were found to be more forceful in supporting their own proposals and urging action.

There may be a question about the generalizability of this finding, given the particular nature of the groups in this situation. However, this study points up an interesting feature of leadership in terms of its legitimacy. One explanation for the finding obtained is that the appointed leader has less need to assert his authority since it is imposed from above, while the emergent or elected leader finds it necessary to establish his position in a competitive situation with other would-be leaders. In either case, there is a necessity for the leader's position to be validated in some way (see Goldman & Fraas, 1965).

The importance of this factor in the leader's authority is illustrated in a study by Raven and French (1958). In one condition they had a confederate apparently usurp a leadership position when it was not legitimately granted to him. In another condition the confederate was supposedly elected by the group. Raven and French found that attempts to exert influence in the group were much more successful in the latter condition after the leader had been invested, as they put it, with the "legitimate power of that office."

These same investigators have also presented an analysis of the various bases for power (French and Raven, 1959). They distinguish between reward power, coercive power, referent power, expert power, and legitimate power. They see reward and coercive power as representing gains or losses for compliance or non-compliance to an authority. Referent power, in their scheme, represents an extension of reward power through a process of identification. Once such identification has been made with the agent of power, it is no longer necessary for that agent continually to monitor the behavior of the less powerful person. As the term suggests, expert power arises from conditions of specialized knowledge that has value. Finally, legitimate power is based upon the mutual acceptance of norms which require one person to do the bidding of another within the framework, for example, of an organization.

We have been speaking about power, influence, and innovation as if these were different processes. Clearly, however, they are intertwined and especially in terms of a transactional view of leadership. Whether an individual is appointed or elected, for example, it is necessary that his position be seen as legitimate by followers and, furthermore, not as exploitative. Thus, the unfettered use of power, by organizational leaders for example, can create numerous points of resistance in the relationship with followers.

Leader attributes and the situation

One of the major experimental approaches to leadership has been to study the consistency with which an individual has leadership status from one group to another. Exemplifying this approach, Bell and French (1950) had subjects participate in six discussion groups, each of which included four other men they had not met previously. Six different discussion problems were used, and at the end of each session the members of the group were asked to nominate a discussion leader for a hypothetical second meeting of the same group. They found that "varying group membership in this situation accounts for at most a relatively small portion of the variation in leadership status. Leadership status seems to be rather highly consistent despite the situational changes involved" (p. 767). However, as they point out, this result is limited since the task involved was of a particular variety, and certain characteristics of the group members were fairly homogeneous. Gibb (1950) also found comparable results but again with subjects involved in similar kinds of tasks. More recently, Cohen and Bennis (1961) found that, after systematically shifting persons in the communication networks of their groups, those identified as leaders remained fairly constant.

LEADER PERSONALITY

These findings tend to support the view that there are personality characteristics which are associated with leadership in groups of a comparable kind, in terms of the task to be performed. Whether this would be so across widely varying situations is considerably more problematic. In discussion groups, for example, the emphasis on verbal output clearly affects the pattern of leadership. Illustrative of this, Riecken (1958) among others has found that the most talkative members of a group are usually seen to be most influential in the group's solution of a problem.

In this vein, Bass (1959) has reported on a line of research with "leaderless group discussion" (LGD), in which subjects participated in the discussion of a problem without a designated leader. Leadership standing, determined by observer ratings, was found to be highly related to the category "time spent talking." Furthermore, this index was quite consistent for a person observed from one group to another.

In an early study on personality variables related to LGD behavior, Bass, McGehee, Hawkins, Young, and Gebel (1953) found a significant correlation between leadership status (a "high" LGD score) and an individual's self-ratings on ascendance and social boldness as measured by a standard personality inventory, the Guilford-Zimmerman Temperament Survey. They also found that authoritarian attitudes measured by the California F Scale correlated negatively with LGD scores. Here again, because of the standard quality of the task, situational differences were not great, though the composition of the group's membership could vary considerably.

Borgatta, Couch, and Bales (1954) also studied discussion groups across four sessions. They report that the eleven group participants who scored highest in terms of a composite of four criteria, i.e. intelligence, leadership ratings by other participants, total participation time in interaction, and popularity, were found to consistently lead groups that were more effective.

In a natural setting, Beer, Buckhout, Horowitz, and Levy (1959) used sociometric ratings to compare campus leaders with non-leaders on the three attributes of self-acceptance, need achievement, and interpersonal skill. They found that campus leaders were rated as more confident, more willing to take responsibility, more forceful, persuasive, and diplomatic.

Depending upon the structural properties of the situation, however, personality differences may become far less important. Berkowitz (1956) measured the ascendance of male students with the Guilford-Zimmerman Temperament Survey and then placed high or low scorers in a central or peripheral position within a variant of the "wheel" communication network (see Chapter Three, p. 74). For three problem-solving tasks he obtained data on communications from subjects that either relayed information or were more assertive in initiating communication. In Figure 15.2 the results are presented by the proportion of

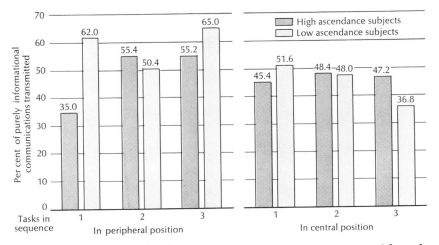

Figure 15.2: Per cent of informational communications transmitted by subjects of high and low "ascendance" assigned to peripheral and central positions in three group problem-solving tasks. (Based upon data from Berkowitz, 1956, p. 216.)

informational communications out of the total given by a subject; this is a measure which reflects *lower* initiative, in leadership terms.

As expected, Berkowitz found that low ascendance subjects were more likely to give informational communications when in a peripheral position, than were high ascendance subjects, since it is more consistent with their personality. However, low ascendance subjects reacted to the central position by dropping substantially in the number of such communications, in keeping with their position; moreover, by the third task, they had dropped considerably below the high dominance subjects in that position. Berkowitz interprets this effect as "position adaptation" and concludes that the operation of a particular personality factor in leadership depends significantly upon the structural properties of the group.

Group performance and satisfaction are also related to the personality of the person in a leadership position. Shaw (1959a) placed subjects who scored high or low on the California F Scale in central positions in communication networks. He found that high authoritarian leaders led groups which performed better, in terms of higher work output, under a centralized communication structure; but group members were significantly less satisfied working for the leader who was a high authoritarian. When the communication structure was decentralized, Shaw found that low authoritarian leaders led groups which performed better, as well as being better satisfied. Here again, the nature of the structure interrelates with leader personality.

RATE OF PARTICIPATION AND ACTIVITY

The participation of leaders is usually found to be at a higher rate than other group members. This is one of the major findings of the leaderless group discussion research already noted. Bolstering Riecken's (1958) findings, which showed that members who spoke most were perceived as contributing more and were more influential, Kirscht, Lodahl, and Haire (1959) found with three-person discussion groups, that those who emerged as leaders had a significantly higher rate of participation in the discussion. McGrath and Julian (1963) report similar differences in participation rate for appointed leaders in four-person negotiation groups.

Even varying the nature of the task somewhat, Carter, Haythorn, Shriver, and Lanzetta (1951) found that leaders tended to be those more likely to initiate action for solving a problem. They presented groups with four tasks in varying sequences—reasoning, mechanical, assembling, and discussion. In general, leaders were likely to participate more frequently and to stand out as more prominent in initiating action. This is in line with Hemphill's concept of initiation of structure considered above.

It should also be recalled that the activity level of an individual, in terms of leadership acts, may be varied as a result of the reinforcement provided by the other group members. This is the essential finding of the study by Pepinsky, Hemphill, and Shevitz (1958) discussed in Chapter Four (p. 105). In that experiment, under an acceptance condition, attempts to lead were rewarded by the other group members, and under conditions of rejection such attempts were disapproved by the others. Significant differences in leader behavior were found between these two conditions.

In general, the functioning of the leader depends upon the demands of the total situation, and the rewards it provides. To be rewarded, the leader's actions should be seen as a useful resource contributing to the group's success. Banta and Nelson (1964) conducted an experiment to see the effect of reward on the rate of participation of a group member who had a valued resource. They paired 96 female college students in a situation in which the pairs were to discuss a series of problems and express opinions to reach agreement. As the external authority, the experimenter arbitrarily rewarded the pair when opinions of one of the subjects was accepted and not the other's. These may be called the "favored" and "nonfavored" subjects, respectively. In Figure 15.3 the re-

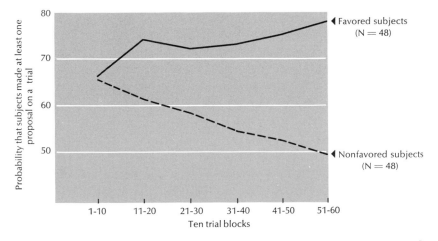

Figure 15.3: Changes in rate of participation in making opinion proposals under conditions of 100 per cent reinforcement of favored subjects' proposals and 0 per cent reinforcement of nonfavored subjects' proposals. (From Banta and Nelson, 1964, p. 496.)

sults are shown for the average effect upon 48 subjects in each of these positions. As will be seen there, the probability of a nonfavored subject expressing an opinion on a trial decreases steadily over time while the favored subjects increase beyond their initial rate of expressing an opinion. Note that these curves do not depend upon one another since it is possible for each subject to make proposals for every trial. Neverthe-

less, the nonfavored subject clearly gives way to the one whose resources appear to be more rewarding to the group. Banta and Nelson also
found that the girls who were the "favored subjects" expressed more
confidence later in their personal ability and the group's joint ability.

The importance of the leader as a resource is revealed in research on
leaders in various settings. Flanagan (1952), for example, conducted a
study of "critical incidents" in military leadership situations. One prominent factor he found to be represented by many incidents was "Accepting responsibility for contributing to achievement of group goals."
Among other factors were incidents represented by such reports as "Set
example for men by remaining calm and efficient under fire."

A laboratory experiment on crisis conditions affecting leadership was
conducted by Hamblin (1958). He studied 24 groups, twelve of whom
experienced a "crisis" that took the form of changing previous rules and
creating a condition of sharp ambiguity about correct procedures. The
effect of this crisis was to alter drastically the prospect of being successful on a task involving a modified shuffleboard game. Leadership in
both the crisis and control groups was measured by an "influence ratio"
for each individual which represents the number of suggestions made
by that member as against the average of other group members. A high
influence ratio is associated with leadership.

Hamblin found that the leader maintained a relatively consistent influence ratio in the crisis situation. This is revealed in Figure 15.4,
which shows the mean influence ratios for the leaders across the twelve
crisis and twelve control groups. In the condition of crisis, the leaders
were more likely to retain high influence across trials. This was less so
for the controls. However, under crisis some groups more readily replaced their leaders if they did not have an apparent solution to the
problem posed by the crisis.

LEADER PERCEPTIVENESS

The suggestion that the leader's perceptiveness has a bearing on his
functional effectiveness has come from several lines of research. Chowdhry and Newcomb (1952) found that leaders were significantly better
in judging the attitudes of group members than non-leaders, particularly on matters of relevance to the group. They interpreted these
results to indicate that an important factor in the achievement of lead-

ership status was the ability to assess others accurately. Earlier, Hites and Campbell (1950) had obtained equivocal findings with similar groups. In discussing this disparity, Campbell (1955) suggests that such "accuracy" may be more apparent than real. This would be so, he says, if an individual uses his own attitudes as an anchor for judging group attitudes, as is suggested by the work of Hovland and Sherif (1952). Where the leader has shaped group attitudes, his judgments of them would seem more accurate (see Talland, 1954). However, there remains a body of findings supporting the view that the emergent leader, in particular, is more likely to be attuned to the needs of the group.

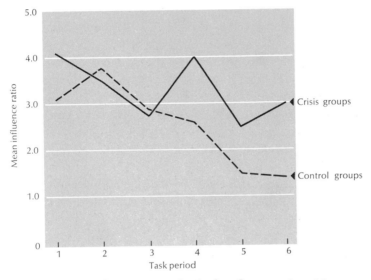

Figure 15.4: Mean influence ratios for high influencers in crisis groups and control groups by task periods. (From Hamblin, 1958, p. 330.)

Bell and Hall (1954), for example, found a significant correlation between leadership standing in a leaderless group discussion situation and scores obtained on tests of empathy. Showel (1960) found that rated leadership potential in military units correlated significantly with interpersonal knowledge, even after the effect of general intelligence had been taken into account. Research by Exline (1960) indicated that such accuracy of perception was significantly affected by group cohesiveness; in his study, only in cohesive groups was the leader a more accurate judge of opinion.

A major line of work by Fiedler (1961) is based in the view that perceptiveness is a characteristic which differentiates the effective from the ineffective leader. In his work, he made initial use of a measure called "assumed similarity between opposites" (ASo). The ASo score is obtained by asking subjects to describe their most preferred coworker by filling out a form which has approximately 20 semantic differential items, each of which consists of a personality adjective and its opposite, e.g. friendly–unfriendly, co-operative–unco-operative, etc. After he rates his most preferred coworker, the subject follows a similar procedure for his least preferred coworker. The score yielded by this procedure appears to measure a stable quality of interpersonal perception and has been found to be quite reliable (Fiedler, 1958). The ASo score may be interpreted to be a measure of the perceived similarity between coworkers in that a high score indicates that the subject sees these coworkers as essentially the same.

In his review of these studies, Fiedler (1958) reports a consistent relationship between this score and group productivity across a variety of task situations. Research on basketball teams, student surveying teams, and small military combat units have all shown, in general, that leaders of effective groups perceive little similarity between their most and least preferred coworkers. Fiedler does not consider these findings to be in conflict with current situational conceptions of leadership. He argues that leader effectiveness may depend upon a number of other factors such as the skill of the group members, the nature of the task, and the social context within which the group operates. Furthermore, these factors may influence to a considerable degree who is to become a leader and determine the course of his behavior once he has assumed that position.

More recently, Fiedler has modified his ASo measure in terms of a score based on the favorability of the leader's rating of his "least preferred coworker" (LPC). It is the major component of the earlier ASo measure. A person with a *high* LPC score describes his least preferred coworker in a relatively favorable manner. He tends to be permissive, human relations oriented, and considerate of the feelings of his men. A person with a *low* LPC score describes his least preferred coworker in an unfavorable manner. He tends to be managing, task-controlling, and less concerned with human relations aspects of the job.

Generally, Fiedler finds (1964, 1965) support for his "contingency model" which predicts differential levels of effectiveness for combinations of situational and leader characteristics. Thus, he reports consistent evidence for a positive relationship between leader LPC and group creativity under pleasant and relaxed group conditions and a negative relationship when the group operated under an unpleasant, stressful group climate. More particularly, he also obtains significant relationships between this LPC measure and three situational factors: the quality of leader-member relations, the degree of task structure, and the leader's power. Depending upon the combination of these elements with the leader's permissiveness measured by LPC, Fiedler finds pronounced variations in the productivity of groups. From this work we may now move to several issues regarding organizational leadership.

Organizational leadership

Organizational leadership starts with the formal structure imposed by authority. Except in extreme instances of power, however, such authority is not sufficient to insure loyalty and ready acceptance of influence. Work groups in all kinds of organizational settings are likely to generate informal structures which accord some authority to emergent leaders. This need not be a source of conflict with imposed authority, but smoothly functioning relationships require that this "structure" and its functions be recognized by the organizational leader for him to be fully effective.

Any organization operates in terms of two patterns of relationship. First, each person has his designated place and function within the organizational whole, represented by the imposed structure. There is also a highly important informal or emergent structure established within the groupings into which people are placed to carry out their function.

The work group, as we pointed out in Chapter Twelve, has a considerable effect on individual satisfactions. Likert (1956) reports that favorableness toward the work group is associated with lower absence rates, better interpersonal relationships, more favorable attitudes toward the job and company, and higher production goals. Thus, people at work find an opportunity to secure more than financial remuneration there. The work setting represents the potential for social rewards in terms of affiliations yielding recognition and participation.

SUPERVISORY STYLE

The organizational leader may be an executive decision-maker down through a first-line supervisor. Whatever his position, he affects the leadership climate. A significant aspect of that climate for workers is what we have called "structure," in such particulars as these: knowing what is expected and having some feedback on how one is doing; consistent treatment in supporting the right and correcting the wrong; and, indicating changes that may affect personal welfare.

One fact of life that Likert (1961) has pointed out is that supervisors tend to use the same kind of leadership style that they experience. It is often an organizational characteristic to be "employee-centered" or "job-centered" in supervision. These are not antithetical, but are more in the nature of emphases. However, this distinction is evidently meaningful in terms of morale. Thus, Likert reports that high morale groups more frequently describe their supervisor's activities by indicating his interest in the well-being of the employees by such acts as recommending promotions, transfers, pay increases, and informing men of what is happening in the company, keeping them posted on how well they are doing, and paying heed to complaints and grievances.

General supervision and close supervision have also been studied as another feature of supervisory style. Kahn and Katz (1960) report from a survey of many industrial studies that high producing units are more usually found to have general rather than close supervision. Results

Table 15.2: Relation of closeness of supervision to section productivity in insurance companies. Twelve sections each are represented in the high and low categories. (Based on Table 41.5, p. 559, from Kahn & Katz in *Group Dynamics*, by D. C. Cartwright and A. Zander. Harper & Row, 1960.)

	CLOSE SUPERVISION	GENERAL SUPERVISION	NOT ASCERTAINED	
High producing sections	50%	42%	8%	100%
Low producing sections	92%	8%	0%	100%

illustrating this finding are shown in Table 15.2 for sections of office workers in an insurance company. The data on supervision were obtained from the section heads themselves. As will be seen, close supervision is associated with low production. Kahn and Katz observe further that:

> Close supervision often is employed as an institutional device for insuring that workers follow their job assignments correctly and assiduously. But this very practice also has negative morale and motivation implications. . . . In [a] tractor company studied, workers who perceived their foremen as supervising them less closely were better satisfied with their jobs and with the company (p. 560).

A mistaken conception which could be drawn from findings such as these is that the supervisor's function in providing a structure should be downgraded. Apart from the absolute merits of any given structure, it seems clear that it is necessary to the fulfillment of stable relationships and a sense of continuity and wholeness. In short, some supervision is essential to secure stability of expectation for the people in an organization. However, there is a balance needed in the kinds of factors which comprise organizational leadership. We will now consider some of these in greater detail.

CONSIDERATION AND INITIATING STRUCTURE

In a large-scale study of organizational leadership, Halpin and Winer (1952) analyzed a large number of ratings of leader characteristics from which they extracted several factors. In order, the two major ones were:

1. *Consideration,* representing the degree to which the leader manifests warmth in personal relationships, trust, readiness to explain actions and listen to subordinates.
2. *Initiating structure,* comprising the extent to which the leader maintains standards of performance and follows routines, makes sure his position and functions are understood, and distributes tasks.

A number of studies (e.g. Fleishman, Harris and Burtt, 1955; Hemphill, 1955) reveal these as two dimensions of considerable weight in leader performance. Halpin (1955), for example, showed that supervisory leaders in two different roles, i.e. school administrators and command pilots on airplanes, differed on these dimensions. The administrators were more likely to show consideration than initiation of structure, and for the pilots it was the reverse.

As these results suggest, it is far too simple to say merely that these two factors are both related to leadership without specifying further some of the situational conditions which are present. Furthermore, it would be a mistake to see these factors as representing two "kinds" of leadership. As Fleishman and Peters (1961) point out, these factors may be combined in various ways together to yield various leadership practices.

An industrial study by Fleishman and Harris (1962) shows something of the complexity of the relationship between these factors in determining the rate of grievances. They separated sections into those of low, medium, or high consideration, and then further subdivided them by three levels of structure. Their results for these nine kinds of units are shown in Figure 15.5. In determining the dissatisfactions repre-

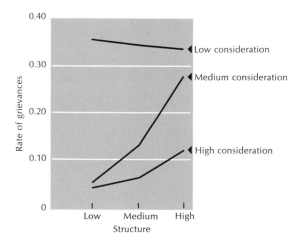

Figure 15.5: Relationship of consideration and group structure to rate of grievances. (From Fleishman and Harris, 1962.)

sented there, consideration appears to have a clear priority. If a foreman is low in consideration, his initiation of structure makes no discernible difference in the group's rate of grievances. On the other hand, a foreman who is characterized by high consideration can initiate high structure with only a small increase in employee dissatisfaction, though attention to productivity is needed to round out the picture. We now turn to a consideration of some features of effective leadership.

Some features of effective leadership

While there may not be universal traits possessed by all leaders, it is possible to speak of requirements for effective leadership. Within organizational settings, for example, various programs of selection and training are employed precisely toward that end. We intend here to present some generalizations in this vein.

In our view, effective leadership may best be considered as an influence process in which the leader is able to muster willing group support to achieve certain clearly specified goals with best advantage to the individuals comprising the group. This conception can be seen to have applicability independently of the source of the leader's authority. The operation of a group in terms of its movement toward a goal rests on characteristics which go beyond that distinction alone.

In our preceding discussion here, we have noted a number of factors which are associated with how the leader is reacted to by followers. Among these are his competence, his fulfillment of certain group expectancies for structure and action, his perceived motivation, and his adaptibility to changing requirements of the situation. It should be noted that these are not fixed attributes residing in the leader himself so much as they are relevant perceptions of the leadership role and its requirements. In this respect, the role of leadership places its occupant in a highly visible position. The leader, as a high status person, is assumed to be more responsible for the actions that he displays and these actions are more likely to affect important outcomes for the members of the group. Thus, Thibaut and Riecken (1955) have demonstrated that high status is perceived to carry a greater initiative for action, and this is especially consequential where that status is bound up with the high centrality of the leadership role.

Earlier, in connection with the discussion of idiosyncrasy credit, we observed that the leader's apparent nonconformity may be more readily tolerated by members of his group. We may now add that this probably occurs because the leader's actions are more likely to be interpreted in terms of positive outcomes. Here we observe a kind of cognitive balancing (see Chapter Six, p. 155) such that the actions of the highly regarded leader are more likely to be perceived in an equally positive way. Nonetheless, the performance of the leader is inevitably tested against a sequence of outcomes in terms of his perceived competence.

An important attribute of effective leadership, as we have stressed repeatedly, is the ability to provide a useful resource in the group's achievement of its goals. This process comes under the general heading of competence. The term does not necessarily mean some superior ability or skill on a task as such. In a highly sociable setting, for example, it may be that having a good sense of humor is what matters in terms of competence. In short, the leadership role demands functional value for the group, but this may encompass a wide variety of attributes required in the situation.

Furthermore, what may be a significant function for a group at one time may no longer be important at another. Indeed, the very act of attaining a major goal may reorient the group's activity. Accordingly, there may be redefinitions of what is required of leadership. Thus, former leadership may be deposed because of its inability to meet new demands, as Hamblin (1958) found in his study of crises, noted above. Therefore, factors which may have influenced an individual's attainment of leadership may no longer be adequate to his retention of the leadership role.

Another feature of effective leadership is to provide mechanisms for communication and participation within the group. Several ends of effective leadership are served by facilitating an exchange of information. Because groups may face new situations which require innovation, the generation of ideas or approaches is highly desirable. Furthermore, the involvement of group members in matters which affect them directly is essential if their commitment to the group's activities is to be maintained.

Effective leadership also necessarily depends upon the personality characteristics of the person in the leadership role, especially in terms of his adjustment. From his review of leadership studies, Mann (1959) concludes:

> While no single measure of adjustment can be expected to be an efficient predictor of leadership, there is strong evidence to indicate

a positive relationship between an individual's adjustment and the leadership status he is likely to attain (p. 249).

One example of the importance of adjustment lies in our earlier consideration of the necessity for restraint in the use of power. In effective leadership, this is evidenced by emotional balance and predictability rather than impulsivity in the leader's actions. In any social relationship, regularities of behavior are valued for the ease with which they may be anticipated. This is especially important, as one illustration, in terms of the distribution of rewards. Since the leader has a great deal of visibility, his actions toward others are interpreted as signifying the "goodness" or "badness" of the performance of others. Thus, by rewarding actions which are in the interest of the group and avoiding rewards for those which are not, the leader secures respect for his fairness. This is not so much a matter of gaining favor as it is a way of providing a better basis for effective leadership.

In sum, the main point of effective leadership as an influence process is that it evokes a positive response from followers, in line with the group's central activity. In the transactional view, leadership effectiveness depends upon a fair exchange with the leader securing status and exercising influence while helping the group to achieve desired outcomes. But goal attainment by itself is not a sufficient condition for effective leadership unless it is accompanied by social rewards to the individual, illustrated by recognition. A significant function of effective leadership, therefore, is to provide for meaningful social participation among the members of a group.

Finally, a pervasive quality which determines the effectiveness of leadership is its perceived identification with the group. Leaders are expected to display loyalty to the collective needs and aspirations of their group. One of the ways this shows itself, concretely, is in *advocacy*. By this we refer to the expectation that the leader will communicate his group's desires to other groups, and to higher authority, in order to facilitate goal attainment. In one study by Pelz (1952), for example, it was found with industrial workers that the ability to deal with upper echelons was rated even higher than human relations skills in evaluating their foremen. In many other settings as well, the effectiveness of leadership depends upon external dealings in the group's behalf. We will now consider this with particular reference to inter-group relations.

Advocacy and negotiation in inter-group relations

In Chapter Four we observed that the influence process involves a re-lationship between an agent of influence and a recipient of that influ-ence. In our discussion here, we have sought to draw out some of the implications of this for effective leadership. If we consider the leader as an influence agent, what he seems to be and how he stands on issues lends substance to the acceptance of his credibility as a source of in-fluence. Indeed, we can think of competent leadership as an analogue to credibility (see Chapter Six, p. 159).

The leader as an influence source communicates to followers not only verbally but by his actions. Thus, the leader increases his credibility by actions which make apparent his identification with things, including the group itself, valued by the followers. This is essential to the trans-actional quality of the leader-follower relationship.

As we noted earlier, inter-group relations are often shaped by the expectations which leaders establish (see Chapter Thirteen, p. 392). The utterances of leaders may have the effect of signifying their loyalty to group goals, but at the same time they may increase the level of conflict in inter-group relations. What is particularly important to recognize is the requirement for a balance between such manifestations of identifi-cation with one's group and the willingness to undertake co-operation with other groups when it is necessary. In such situations of inter-group negotiation, Sherif (1962) observes:

> Leaders, delegates, and representatives of the groups must remain part of the power structure of the group if their actions are to be ef-fective. The significance of the power structure for assessing the be-havior of individuals in such positions is immediately seen when their actions deviate widely from the expectations of the membership (p. 17).

The solution to this dilemma rests in the fact that leaders themselves help to establish these expectations, and are not merely their creatures. As influence agents, they are in a position to define the situation for the members of a group and to set realistic goals for potential achievement. Again, this occurs within a context of the positive perception of the leader as a trusted advocate holding high status. In the absence of such status, the leader is highly vulnerable to rejection by the group, if he appears to violate its interests. In any case, as Blake and Mouton (1961c) have found, a representative who is tied to entrenched group commitments is unable to undertake productive negotiation.

The advocacy function of leadership is therefore delicate and can produce effects in several directions. By his utterances, the leader may initially bolster his status in the group and increase a sense of morale, but also heighten the level of conflict and limit the alternatives available to him. While it is considered to be something of a canon of diplomacy that avenues be kept available to other courses of action, it is often the case that leaders do not heed the implications of this injunction in their statements.

Once the need for negotiation is granted, incendiary language damages its long-range as well as its short-range prospects. A union leader who goes into negotiations with management having told his members that "We can't accept any of their proposals," reduces the likelihood that his members will accept whatever he is able to secure from such negotiations. Furthermore, the expectations shaped by the leader's statements may have the quite unintended effect of reducing his range of influence at a later point. Much of this follows from the kind of psychological formulations which we previously noted. Thus, to publicly characterize proposals from another nation as "Just the same old devious devices," is to insure greater difficulty in the acceptance of any subsequent proposals, even when they are in fact in line with the desires and needs of the former nation.

Whenever groups or nations are in open conflict, the problem of limiting hostility becomes critical, as Richardson demonstrates in his *Statistics of Deadly Quarrels* (1960). The sad history of most international conflicts is that of unwanted results in war, and often in the peace which follows. The generation of an unalloyed hostility toward an adversary group may make it appear that any accommodation with it represents a "sell-out." The implications of this for productive negotiation must be carefully understood. As Sherif (1958) points out, it does little good to attempt discussions in an atmosphere of hostility and recrimination. It is essential to recognize that the atmosphere itself is created in great part by what leaders say and do. An example of public utterances likely to open the way for later acceptance of the outcome of negotiation, is this passage from an address by President Kennedy:

It is a test of our national maturity to accept the fact that negotiations are not a contest spelling victory or defeat. They may succeed, they may fail. But they are likely to be successful only if both sides reach an agreement which both regard as preferable to the *status quo,* an agreement in which each side can consider that its own situation has been improved (1961).

Illustrative of such agreement was the 1963 atomic test ban treaty which had the quality of representing the achievement for its signators of superordinate goals, not the least of which was tension-reduction. A proposal for furthering this process has come from Osgood (1962) in his strategy of "graduated reciprocation in international tension-reduction" (GRIT). Just as leaders can "escalate" conflicts by their statements and their actions, Osgood proposes that they can "de-escalate" them by announcing and carrying out small conciliatory acts on a unilateral basis. Rather than be seen as a sign of weakness, such acts are likely to signalize the power and high status of a nation because they are initiated voluntarily. Furthermore, Osgood points out that initiatives can be graduated in risk so that very little is lost if they are not reciprocated initially.

Apart from its effect in reducing a hostile climate of opinion within a nation, a GRIT strategy has major merits as a possible device for establishing a better atmosphere for mutual trust between nations. While its efficacy in international relations is yet to be established, in part because of the difficulty in having a nation take the first steps as a consistent policy, GRIT has been found to work in laboratory experimentation. In one such study, Scodel (1962) found, in an experiment with a prisoners' dilemma problem, that a player who adopted a conciliatory strategy after an initial period of employing an intensely competitive strategy received significantly higher co-operation from the other player than one who had co-operated from the very outset. If nothing else, it may be that the "contrast effect" of sudden conciliation induces in time a move favorable psychological reaction in the other person.

In another experiment directly involving GRIT, Crow (1963) used the procedure of Inter-Nation Simulation developed by Guetzkow and his colleagues (see 1963) to study international relations. In this procedure, each member of a group acts as a policy-maker for a fictitious nation. Each person is given basic data on the initial strength of its nation's position. Then, over periods of time each is allowed to make policies regarding the allocation of resources, for example, to the production of consumer goods or armaments, and to enter into trade or military alliances with the other nations represented. It is possible in this procedure for the nations to go to war when the tensions increase to an extreme.

In Crow's research, there were five nations, two of which were very powerful. Each was represented by a policy-maker. They interacted over thirteen periods of seventy minutes each. In every period, measures of the "tension level" were taken by the ratings of the participants. As his major experimental intervention, Crow had the policy-maker of one of the powerful nations adopt a GRIT strategy at the beginning of the seventh period. As is seen in Figure 15.6, the tension level had been

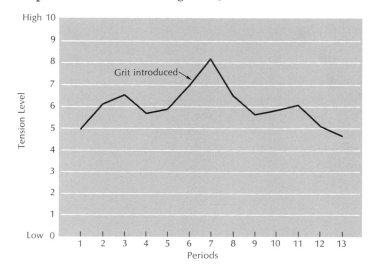

Figure 15.6: Tension level as rated by participants in Inter-Nation Simulation, run over thirteen periods, showing effect of introduction of GRIT strategy by one participant. (From Crow, 1963, p. 588.)

showing a not unusual rising tendency during the first six periods. Under such circumstances, warfare might very well be predicted. However, after a further slight rise during the seventh period when GRIT was initiated, the figure shows a marked drop-off in tension level to the lowest point in the last period.

This finding dramatizes one prospect for the creative use of techniques which may alleviate undue tensions in international relations. When we speak of leaders who have "vision" we mean in some great measure the ability to see how such present policies can yield beneficial effects in the future. Imaginative ideas are not the special province of leaders, but recognizing and using such ideas effectively is. Those who hold the reins of authority are necessarily agents of influence and of social change. Whether by accident or design what they say and do creates expectations through which the future is molded. It is not too much to hope that there will be a design, and that the vision will be one of promise.

SUMMARY

The modern view of leadership in social psychology emphasizes its variable nature. Depending upon the group, its activity and its situation, different leader attributes are called forth. Therefore, the role of leader can be filled by various group members who at the time can direct group resources toward the attainment of group goals.

The study of leadership requires attention to the *leader,* the *followers,* and the *situation* in which they interact. Their processes of interaction constitute *leadership* in the broad sense of an influence relationship in groups. A *leader* is someone whose role permits him to exercise leadership. His interaction can be seen as representing a *transaction* between himself and others in the group. By providing them with useful resources, the leader gets in return a greater degree of influence and esteem.

In the history of concern about leadership, the first and most dominant focus was upon the *traits* of the leader. Because of the irregular pattern of leader traits found across situations, this older view gave way to a focus on the demands of *situations* in which leadership occurred. This newer, situational approach stresses the various functions to be performed by those occupying a leadership role rather than stable characteristics of leaders. The situational approach also sees the follower as having an active role in leadership processes.

A major distinction in characterizing leadership is its source, specified by the terms *emergent* leadership and *appointed* leadership. The first is determined by some mode of group consent, the second by an external authority. The identification of emergent leaders is often accomplished by sociometric techniques. While the early use of this procedure left the impression that choices for leader and for friend were highly related, the stability of this relationship very much depends upon the situation. A differentiation is often found between liking certain group members and recognizing those who contribute in a leadership sense.

Leaders can also be identified as those who are highly influential in the group's operations. One way of conceiving this is with regard to *initiating structure*. In these terms, the leader is a member who contributes most to the pattern of interaction and locomotion within the group. Relatedly, the leader can be seen as the *completer* of essential group functions in that he helps the group to attain its goals by balancing off various factors in an harmonious fashion. Still another way to consider the leader's influence is to look at his potential for *innovation* through actions which would be viewed as nonconforming were others to take them. This is a function of the *idiosyncrasy credits* at his disposal, as a feature of his accorded status.

In some sense, the leadership role involves a power component which often relates to the *legitimacy* of the leader's position. Power can arise from various factors in the relationship between the leader as an agent of influence and the followers who are recipients of that influence. Thus, the basis for legitimate power in an organizational setting rests in the mutual acceptance of norms requiring one person to do the bidding of another. Power, influence, and innovation are not totally separate processes, but rather are interrelated facets of leadership.

A considerable volume of experimentation reveals that whoever emerges as a leader, from one situation to another, depends upon the nature and comparability of the tasks presented to the group. Personality attributes of the leader, such as ascendance, have been found to be consistently related to leadership emergence, especially where the tasks are largely uniform. However, the *structure of the situation* can considerably reduce the effect of personality differences. Furthermore, both the quality of group performance and member satisfactions are bound up with the relationship of the leader's personality to the requirements of the group's structure.

In many different group settings, leaders are found to have higher rates of participation and activity. This is particularly true in discussion groups where verbal output has been found to be highly related to leadership. The rate of participation has also been shown to be affected by the rewards made available by the other participants or by the group's successes. Therefore, the resources of the leader may be variably elicited depending upon the group's needs and the rewards it accordingly provides.

Several lines of study have pointed to *perceptiveness* as a factor in leadership. The leader's functioning is facilitated by his being attuned to the other group members and the situation confronting them. The importance of perceptiveness appears to be considerably altered, however, by other conditions such as the group's cohesiveness. In any case, the leader's perceptiveness does have relevance as a feature differentiating effective from ineffective leadership.

Organizational leadership is imposed by authority. It is part of the *formal structure* which requires certain functions to be fulfilled by the appointed leader. These functions may vary from those of the first-line supervisor in a direct interpersonal relationship with many subordinates to those of an executive planner involved mainly in decision-making without much contact of that kind. Supervision is most representative of the appointed mode of leadership. Its *style* can be characterized as mainly *employee-centered* or *job-centered*. Another component of supervisory style is *general* or *close* supervision. These emphases, in various combinations, may stamp the interactions within an organization in a distinctive way.

From analyses of ratings made on supervision in organizations, two factors which are revealed to have major importance are *consideration* and *initiating structure*. The first relates to warmth in interpersonal relationships, and the second to such task elements as setting standards of performance and distributing assignments. Both are evidently involved in the supervisor's role across most situations. Consideration is important as a basic condition which engenders a greater willingness to accept the supervisor's direction without various kinds of resistance. In the absence of consideration, such resistance may reveal itself in grievances and absenteeism, in addition to lowered performance.

Essentially *effective leadership* can be viewed as an influence process in which the leader achieves willing group support in the attainment of group goals. The general features of effective leadership are not attributes of the leader so much as they are expectancies held of the leadership role and its requirements. Among those features are evidences of: *competence*, in terms of providing a contribution to the group's goals; *identification* with the group and its aspirations; provision for *communication* and *participation* by group members as a routine of group functioning; *adjustment,* with regard to stability and an awareness of the needs of others, particularly in providing rewards. Therefore, effective leadership yields an equitable transaction, not just in terms of helping the group attain its goals, but also by providing social rewards along the way such as a sense of participation and recognition.

A potent feature of leadership is in the *advocacy function* as a representative of the group in external relations with other groups or with higher authority. Advocacy is particularly critical where open conflict exists in inter-group relations. The person in this leadership position is required to show loyalty to his group's interests while opening the prospects for favorable dealings with the adversary group. Where negotiation is necessary, his statements designed to manifest loyalty to the group's position may make it harder for the group to accept the outcome of negotiation later. Thus the leader's influence may be reduced by failure to maintain the balance which shapes the group's expectations toward a position favoring reduction of tension. In inter-group dealings, co-operative strategies tend to encourage the development of mutual trust and the achievement of goals that benefit both parties.

SUGGESTED READINGS

From E. P. Hollander and R. G. Hunt. (Eds.) *Current perspectives in social psychology.* (2nd Edition.) New York: Oxford University Press, 1967:

Introduction to Section VIII: *Leadership, power, and innovation*
50. Edwin P. Hollander: *Leadership, innovation, and influence: an overview*
51. Alex Bavelas: *Leadership: man and function*
52. Fred E. Fiedler: *Styles of leadership*
53. John R. P. French and Bertram Raven: *The bases of power*
Introduction to Section IX: *Organizational processes*
56. William G. Scott: *Organization theory: an overview and an appraisal*
57. Daniel Katz: *The motivational basis of organizational behavior*
60. Rensis Likert: *An overview of new patterns of management*

SELECTED REFERENCES

Browne, C. G., & Cohn, T. S. (Eds.) *The study of leadership.* Danville, Ill.: Interstate Printers & Publishers, 1958.
Gouldner, A. W. (Ed.) *Studies in leadership.* New York: Harper, 1950.

Guetzkow, H. (Ed.) *Groups, leadership, and men.* Pittsburgh: Carnegie Press, 1951.

Guetzkow, H. *et al. Simulation in international relations.* Englewood Cliffs, N. J.: Prentice-Hall, 1963.

Haiman, F. S. *Group leadership and democratic action.* Boston: Houghton Mifflin, 1951.

Hollander, E. P. *Leaders, groups, and influence.* New York: Oxford Univer. Press, 1964.

Petrullo, L. & Bass, B. M. (Eds.) *Leadership and interpersonal behavior.* New York: Holt, Rinehart & Winston, 1961.

Sherif, M. (Ed.) *Intergroup relations and leadership.* New York: Wiley, 1962.

Verba, S. *Small groups and political behavior: a study of leadership.* Princeton, N. J.: Princeton Univer. Press, 1961.

Bibliography

Abelson, R. P., & Rosenberg, M. J. Symbolic psycho-logic: A model of attitudinal cognition. *Behav. Sci.*, 1958, *3*, 1-13.

Adorno, T. W., Frenkel-Brunswik, Else, Levinson, D. J., & Sanford, R. N. *The authoritarian personality.* New York: Harper, 1950.

Allen, F. L. *Only yesterday.* New York: Harper & Bros., 1931. (Also published as a Bantam Book, New York, 1959.)

Allison, J., & Hunt, D. E. Social desirability and the expression of aggression under varying conditions of frustration. *J. consult. Psychol.*, 1959, *23*, 528-532.

Allport, F. H. *Social psychology.* Boston: Houghton Mifflin, 1924.

Allport, F. H. The J-curve hypothesis of conforming behavior. *J. soc. Psychol.*, 1934, *5*, 141-183.

Allport, F. H. *Theories of perception and the concept of structure.* New York: Wiley, 1955.

Allport, G. W. *Personality: A psychological interpretation.* New York: Holt, 1937.

Allport, G. W. *The nature of prejudice.* Reading, Mass.: Addison-Wesley, 1954. (Paperback edition by Doubleday Anchor, 1958.)

Allport, G. W. *Becoming.* New Haven: Yale Univer. Press, 1955.

Allport, G. W. The open system in personality theory. *J. abnorm. soc. Psychol.*, 1960a, *61*, 301-311.

Allport, G. W. *Personality and social encounter.* Boston: Beacon Press, 1960b.

Allport, G. W. Traits revisited. *Amer. Psychologist*, 1966, *21*, 1-10.

Allport, G. W., & Pettigrew, T. F. Cultural influence on the perception of movement: The trapezoidal illusion among Zulus. *J. abnorm. soc. Psychol.*, 1957, *55*, 104-113.

465

Allport, G. W., & Postman, L. J. *The psychology of rumor.* New York: Henry Holt, 1943.

Allport, G. W., Vernon, P. E., & Lindzey, G. *Study of values.* Boston: Houghton Mifflin, 1951.

Allyn, Jane, & Festinger, L. The effectiveness of unanticipated persuasive communication. *J. abnorm. soc. Psychol.,* 1961, *62,* 35-40.

Altrocchi, J. Dominance as a factor in interpersonal choice and perception. *J. abnorm. soc. Psychol.,* 1959, *59,* 303-307.

Ames, A., Jr. Visual perception and the rotating trapezoid window. *Psychol. Monogr.,* 1951, *65,* No. 7.

Ardrey, R. *The territorial imperative.* New York: Atheneum, 1966.

Argyle, M. Social pressure in public and private situations. *J. abnorm. soc. Psychol.,* 1957, *54,* 172-175.

Aronson, E., Turner, Judy, & Carlsmith, J. M. Communicator credibility and communication discrepancy. *J. abnorm. soc. Psychol.,* 1963, *67,* 31-36.

Asch, S. E. Effects of group pressure upon the modification and distortion of judgments. In H. Guetzkow (Ed.), *Groups, leadership and men.* Pittsburgh: Carnegie Press, 1951.

Asch, S. E. *Social psychology.* New York: Prentice-Hall, 1952.

Asch, S. E. A perspective on social psychology. In S. Koch (Ed.), *Psychology: A study of a science.* Vol. 3. New York: McGraw-Hill, 1959. Pp. 363-384.

Atkinson, J. W., & Reitman, W. R. Performance as a function of motive strength and expectancy of goal-attainment. *J. abnorm. soc. Psychol.,* 1956, *53,* 361-366.

Atthowe, J. M., Jr. Interpersonal decision-making: The resolution of a dyadic conflict. *J. abnorm. soc. Psychol.,* 1961, *62,* 114-119.

Azrin, N. H., & Lindsley, O. R. The reinforcement of cooperation between children. *J. abnorm. soc. Psychol.,* 1956, *52,* 100-102.

Bachrach, A. J., Candland, D. K., & Gibson, Janice T. Group reinforcement of individual response experiments in verbal behavior. In I. A. Berg & B. M. Bass (Eds.), *Conformity and deviation.* New York: Harper, 1961. Pp. 258-285.

Back, K. W. Influence through social communication. *J. abnorm. soc. Psychol.,* 1951, *46,* 9-23.

Back, K. W., & Davis, K. E. Some personal and situational factors relevant to the consistency and prediction of conforming behavior. *Sociometry,* 1965, *28,* 227-240.

Bales, R. F. A set of categories for the analysis of small group interaction. *Amer. sociol. Rev.,* 1950a, *15,* 257-263.

Bales, R. F. *Interaction process analysis: A method for the study of small groups.* Reading, Mass.: Addison-Wesley, 1950b.

Bales, R. F. Some uniformities of behavior in small social systems. In G. E. Swanson, T. M. Newcomb, & E. L. Hartley (Eds.), *Readings in social psychology.* (2nd ed.) New York: Holt, 1952. Pp. 146-159.

Bales, R. F. The equilibrium problem in small groups. In A. P. Hare, E. F. Borgatta, & R. F. Bales (Eds.), *Small groups: Studies in social interaction.* New York: Knopf, 1955. Pp. 424-463.

Bales, R. F., & Borgatta, E. F. Size of group as a factor in the interaction profile. In A. P. Hare, E. F. Borgatta, & R. F. Bales (Eds.), *Small groups: Studies in social interaction.* New York: Knopf, 1955. Pp. 396-413.

Bales, R. F., & Slater, P. E. Role differentiation in small decision-making groups. In T. Parsons, R. F. Bales, *et al.* (Eds.), *Family, socialization, and interaction process.* Glencoe, Ill.: Free Press, 1955.

Bales, R. F., Strodtbeck, F. L., Mills, T. M., & Roseborough, Mary E. Channels of communication in small groups. *Amer. sociol. Rev.,* 1951, *16,* 461-468.

Bandura, A., & Walters, R. H. *Social learning and personality development.* New York: Holt, Rinehart, & Winston, 1963.

Banta, T. J., & Nelson, C. Experimental analysis of resource location in problem-solving groups. *Sociometry,* 1964, *27,* 488-501.

Barker, R. G., & Wright, H. F. *Midwest and its children: The psychological ecology of an American town.* Evanston, Ill.: Row, Peterson, 1954.

Barnard, C. I. *The functions of the executive.* Cambridge: Harvard Univer. Press, 1938.

Barnouw, V. *Culture and personality.* Homewood, Ill.: Dorsey Press, 1963.

Barron, F. Some personality correlates of independence of judgment. *J. Pers.,* 1953, *21,* 287-297.

Bass, B. M. An approach to the objective assessment of successful leadership. In B. M. Bass & I. A. Berg (Eds.), *Objective approaches to personality assessment.* New York: Van Nostrand, 1959.

Bass, B. M., McGehee, C. R., Hawkins, W. C., Young, P. C., & Gebel, A. S. Personality variables related to leaderless group discussion behavior. *J. abnorm. soc. Psychol.,* 1953, *48,* 120-128.

Bauer, R. A. The obstinate audience: The influence process from the point of view of social communication. *Amer. Psychologist,* 1964, *19,* 319-328.

Bavelas, A. Leadership: Man and function. *Admin. Sci. Quart.,* 1960, *4,* 491-498.

Bavelas, A., Hastorf, A. H., Gross, A. E., & Kite, W. R. Experiments on the alteration of group structure. *J. exp. soc. Psychol.,* 1965, *1,* 55-70.

Bean, C. An unusual opportunity to investigate the psychology of language. *J. genet. Psychol.,* 1932, *40,* 181-202.

Beer, M., Buckhout, R., Horowitz, M. W., & Levy, S. Some perceived properties of the difference between leaders and non-leaders. *J. Psychol.,* 1959, *47,* 49-56.

Bell, G. B., & French, R. L. Consistency of individual leadership position in small groups of varying membership. *J. abnorm. soc. Psychol.,* 1950, *45,* 764-767.

468

BIBLIOGRAPHY

Bell, G. B., & Hall, H. E. The relationship between leadership and empathy. *J. abnorm. soc. Psychol.*, 1954, *49*, 156-157.

Beloff, Halla. Two forms of social conformity: Acquiescence and conventionality. *J. abnorm. soc. Psychol.*, 1958, *56*, 99-103.

Benedict, Ruth F. *Patterns of culture*. Boston: Houghton Mifflin, 1934. (Also published by Penguin Books, New York, 1946.)

Benedict, Ruth F. *The chrysanthemum and the sword: Patterns of Japanese culture*. Boston: Houghton Mifflin, 1946.

Berelson, B. R., & Steiner, G. *Human behavior: An inventory of scientific findings*. New York: Harcourt, Brace & World, 1964.

Berelson, B. R., Lazarsfeld, P. F., & McPhee, W. N. *Voting: A study of opinion formation in a presidential campaign*. Chicago: Univer. of Chicago Press, 1954.

Berenda, Ruth W. *The influence of the group on the judgments of children*. New York: Kings Crown Press, 1950.

Berg, I. A. & Bass, B. M., (Eds.) *Conformity and deviation*. New York: Harper, 1961.

Berko, Jean. The child's learning of English morphology. *Word*, 1958, *14*, 150-77.

Berkowitz, L. Group standards, cohesiveness, and productivity. *Hum. Relat.*, 1954, *7*, 509-519.

Berkowitz, L. Personality and group position. *Sociometry*, 1956, *19*, 210-222.

Berkowitz, L. Liking for the group and the perceived merit of the group's behavior. *J. abnorm. soc. Psychol.*, 1957, *54*, 353-357.

Berkowitz, L., & Cottingham, D. R. The interest value and relevance of fear-arousing communications. *J. abnorm. soc. Psychol.*, 1960, *60*, 37-43.

Berkowitz, L., & Macaulay, Jacqueline R. Some effects of differences in status level and status stability. *Hum. Relat.*, 1961, *14*, 135-148.

Berlyne, D. E. *Conflict, arousal, and curiosity*. New York: McGraw-Hill, 1960.

Berne, E. *Games people play*. New York: Grove Press, 1964.

Bierstedt, R. An analysis of social power. *Amer. sociol. Rev.*, 1950, *15*, 730-738.

Blake, R. R., & Mouton, Jane S. Conformity, resistance and conversion. In I. A. Berg & B. M. Bass (Eds.), *Conformity and deviation*. New York: Harper & Bros., 1961a. Pp. 1-37.

Blake, R. R., & Mouton, Jane S. Comprehension of positions under intergroup competition. *J. Conflict Resolution*, 1961b, *5*, 304-310.

Blake, R. R., & Mouton, Jane S. Loyalty of representatives to ingroup positions during intergroup competition. *Sociometry*, 1961c, *24*, 177-184.

Blake, R. R., & Mouton, Jane S. The intergroup dynamics of win-lose conflict and problem-solving collaboration in union-management relations. In M. Sherif (Ed.), *Intergroup relations and leadership*. New York: Wiley, 1962.

Blau, P. M. *Exchange and power in social life*. New York: Wiley, 1964.

Bleuler, M., & Bleuler, R. Rorschach Ink-blot Test and racial psychology; mental peculiarities of Morroccans. *Charact. & Pers.*, 1935, *4*, 97-114.

Blumer, H. Public opinion and public opinion polling. *Amer. soc. Rev.*, 1948, *13*, 542-554.

Boas, F. *Anthropology in modern life.* New York: W. W. Norton, 1928.

Boden, Margaret. McDougall revisited. *J. Pers.*, 1965, *33*, 1-19.

Bogardus, E. S. Measuring social distance. *J. appl. Sociol.*, 1925, *9*, 299-308.

Bohannan, P. The impact of money on an African subsistence economy. *J. econ. History*, 1959, *19*, 491-503.

Bond, J. R., & Vinacke, W. E. Coalitions in mixed-sex triads. *Sociometry*, 1961, *24*, 61-75.

Bonner, H. *Group dynamics.* New York: Ronald Press, 1959.

Borgatta, E. F., Cottrell, L. S., Jr., & Meyer, H. J. On the dimensions of group behavior. *Sociometry*, 1956, *19*, 223-240.

Borgatta, E. F., Couch, A. S., & Bales, R. F. Some findings relevant to the great man theory of leadership. *Amer. sociol. Rev.*, 1954, *19*, 755-759.

Boring, E. G. When is human behavior predetermined? *Scientific Monthly*, 1957, *84*, 189-196.

Bossard, J. H. S. The law of family interaction. *Amer. J. Sociol.*, 1945, *50*, 292-294.

Bovard, E. W. The effects of social stimuli on the response to stress. *Psychol. Rev.*, 1959, *66*, 267-277.

Bowerman, C., & Day, B. A test of the theory of complementary needs as applied to couples during courtship. *Amer. sociol. Rev.*, 1956, *21*, 602-605.

Brayfield, A. H., & Crockett, W. H. Employee attitudes and employee performance. *Psychol. Bull.*, 1955, *52*, 396-424.

Bredemeier, H. C., & Toby, J. *Social problems in America.* New York: Wiley, 1960.

Bredemeier, H. C., & Stephenson, R. M. *The analysis of social systems.* New York: Holt, Rinehart, & Winston, 1962.

Brehm, J. W., & Cohen, A. R. *Explorations in cognitive dissonance.* New York: Wiley, 1962.

Brittain, C. V. Adolescent choices and parent-peer cross pressures. *Amer. sociol. Rev.*, 1963, *28*, 385-391.

Bronfenbrenner, U. Socialization and social class through time and space. In Eleanor Maccoby, T. M. Newcomb, & E. L. Hartley (Eds.), *Readings in social psychology.* (3rd edition) New York: Holt, Rinehart, & Winston, 1958. Pp. 400-424.

Bronfenbrenner, U. Some familial antecedents of responsibility and leadership in adolescents. In L. Petrullo & B. M. Bass (Eds.), *Leadership and interpersonal behavior.* New York: Holt, Rinehart, & Winston, 1961.

Bronfenbrenner, U., Harding, J., & Gallwey, Mary. The measurement of skill in social perception. In D. McClelland, A. Baldwin, U. Bronfenbrenner, & F. Strodtbeck (Eds.), *Talent and society*. Princeton, N. J.: Van Nostrand, 1958. Pp. 29-111.

Brown, R. W. Linguistic determinism and the part of speech. *J. abnorm. soc. Psychol.*, 1957, 55, 1-5.

Brown, R. W. *Words and things*. Glencoe, Ill.: The Free Press, 1958.

Brown, R. W., & Lenneberg, E. H. A study in language and cognition. *J. abnorm. soc. Psychol.*, 1954, 49, 454-62.

Brown, R. W., & Lenneberg, E. H. Studies in linguistic relativity. In Eleanor E. Maccoby, T. M. Newcomb, & E. L. Hartley (Eds.), *Readings in social psychology*. New York: Holt, Rinehart, & Winston, 1958.

Browne, C. G., & Cohn, T. S. (Eds.) *The study of leadership*. Danville, Ill.: Interstate Printers & Publishers, 1958.

Bruner, J. S. On perceptual readiness. *Psychol. Rev.*, 1957, 64, 123-152.

Bruner, J. S., & Goodman, Cecile C. Value and need as organizing factors in perception. *J. abnorm. soc. Psychol.*, 1947, 42, 33-44.

Bruner, J. S., & Perlmutter, H. V. Compatriot and foreigner: A study of impression formation in three countries. *J. abnorm. soc. Psychol.*, 1957, 55, 253-260.

Bruner, J. S., & Rodrigues, J. Unpublished study cited in J. S. Bruner, Jacqueline J. Goodnow, & G. A. Austin. *A study of thinking*. New York: Wiley, 1956. P. 28.

Buchanan, W., & Cantril, H. *How nations see each other*. Urbana, Ill.: Univer. Ill. Press, 1953.

Byrne, D., & Wong, T. J. Racial prejudice, interpersonal attraction, and assumed dissimilarity of attitudes. *J. abnorm. soc. Psychol.*, 1962, 65, 246-253.

Calvin, A. D. Social reinforcement. *J. soc. Psychol.*, 1962, 56, 15-19.

Campbell, A., Converse, P. E., Miller, W. E., & Stokes, D. E. *The American voter*. New York: Wiley, 1960.

Campbell, A., Gurin, G., & Miller, W. E. *The voter decides*. New York: Harper & Row, 1954.

Campbell, D. T. An error in some demonstrations of the superior social perceptiveness of leaders. *J. abnorm. soc. Psychol.*, 1955, 51, 694-695.

Campbell, D. T. Social attitudes and other acquired behavioral dispositions. In S. Koch (Ed.), *Psychology: A study of a science*. Vol. 6. New York: McGraw-Hill, 1963. Pp. 94-172.

Campbell, D. T. Distinguishing differences of perception from failures of communication in cross-cultural studies. In F. C. S. Northrop & H. H. Livingston (Eds.), *Cross-cultural understanding: Epistemology in anthropology*. New York: Harper & Row, 1964. Pp. 308-336.

Campbell, J. D., & Yarrow, Marian R. Perceptual and behavioral correlates of social effectiveness. *Sociometry*, 1961, 24, 1-20.

Cannon, W. B. *The wisdom of the body*. New York: Norton, 1932.

Cantril, H. The intensity of an attitude. *J. abnorm. soc. Psychol.*, 1946, 41, 129-135.

Cantril, H. *The politics of despair*. New York: Basic Books, 1958.

Cantril, H. *The pattern of human concerns*. New Brunswick, N. J.: Rutgers Univer. Press, 1965.

Caplow, T. A theory of coalitions in the triad. *Amer. sociol. Rev.*, 1956, *21*, 489-493.

Carpenter, C. R. Societies of monkeys and apes. In C. H. Southwick (Ed.), *Primate social behavior*. Princeton, N. J.: D. Van Nostrand, 1963. Pp. 24-51.

Carroll, J. B. *The study of language*. Cambridge, Mass.: Harvard Univer. Press, 1953.

Carroll, J. B., & Casagrande, J. B. The functions of language classification and behavior. In Eleanor E. Maccoby, T. M. Newcomb, & E. L. Hartley (Eds.), *Readings in social psychology*. (3rd edition) New York: Holt, Rinehart, & Winston, 1958. Pp. 18-31.

Carter, L. F., & Schooler, K. Value, need, and other factors in perception. *Psychol. Rev.*, 1949, *56*, 200-207.

Carter, L. F., Haythorn, W., Meirowitz, Beatrice, & Lanzetta, J. The relation of categorizations and ratings in the observation of group behavior. *Hum. Relat.*, 1951, *4*, 239-254.

Carter, L. F., Haythorn, W., Shriver, E., & Lanzetta, J. The behavior of leaders and other group members. *J. abnorm. soc. Psychol.*, 1951, *46*, 589-595.

Cartwright, D. C. Achieving change in people: Some applications of group dynamics theory. *Hum. Relat.*, 1951, *4*, 381-393.

Cartwright, D. C. Introduction. In D. C. Cartwright, *et al.*, *Studies in social power*. Ann Arbor: Institute for Social Research, 1959.

Cartwright, D. C., & Zander, A. (Eds.) *Group dynamics: Research and theory*. (2nd ed.) Evanston, Ill.: Row, Peterson, 1960.

Cattell, R. B. Concepts and methods in the measurement of group syntality. *Psychol. Rev.*, 1948, *55*, 48-63.

Cattell, R. B. New concepts for measuring leadership in terms of group syntality. *Hum. Relat.*, 1951, *4*, 161-184.

Centers, R. *The psychology of social classes*. Princeton: Princeton Univer. Press, 1949.

Chapanis, Natalia P., & Chapanis, A. Cognitive dissonance: Five years later. *Psychol. Bull.*, 1964, *61*, 1-22.

Charters, W. W., Jr., & Newcomb, T. M. Some attitudinal effects of experimentally increased salience of a membership group. In Eleanor Maccoby, T. M. Newcomb, & E. L. Hartley (Eds.), *Readings in social psychology*. (3rd edition) New York: Holt, Rinehart, & Winston, 1958. Pp. 276-281.

Child, I. Socialization. In G. Lindzey (Ed.), *Handbook of social psychology*. Vol. 2. Reading, Mass.: Addison-Wesley, 1954. Pp. 655-692.

Childe, V. G. *What happened in history*. New York: Penguin Books, 1946.

Chowdhry, K., & Newcomb, T. M. The relative abilities of leaders and non-leaders to estimate opinions of their own groups. *J. abnorm. soc. Psychol.*, 1952, 47, 51-57.

Christie, R., & Cook, Peggy. A guide to published literature relating to the authoritarian personality through 1956. *J. Psychol.*, 1958, 45, 171-199.

Clark, J. V. A preliminary investigation on some unconscious assumptions affecting labor efficiencies in eight supermarkets. Unpublished doctoral dissertation, Graduate School of Business Admin., Harvard Univer., 1958.

Clark, K. B., & Clark, Mamie P. Racial identification and preference in Negro children. In Eleanor Maccoby, T. M. Newcomb, & E. L. Hartley (Eds.), *Readings in social psychology*. (3rd edition). New York: Holt, Rinehart, & Winston, 1958. Pp. 602-611.

Cline, V. B. Interpersonal perception. In B. A. Maher (Ed.), *Progress in experimental personality research*. Vol. 1. New York: Academic Press, 1964.

Coch, L., & French, J. R. P., Jr. Overcoming resistance to change. *Hum. Relat.*, 1948, 1, 512-532.

Cofer, C. N., & Appley, M. H. *Motivation: Theory and research*. New York: Wiley, 1964.

Cohen, A. M., & Bennis, W. G. Continuity of leadership in communication networks. *Hum. Relat.*, 1961, 14, 351-367.

Cohen, A. R. Need for cognition and order of communication as determinants of opinion change. In C. I. Hovland (Ed.), *The order of presentation in persuasion*. New Haven: Yale Univer. Press, 1957. Pp. 79-97.

Cohen, A. R. Some implications of self-esteem for social influence. In C. I. Hovland & I. L. Janis (Eds.), *Personality and persuasibility*. New Haven, Conn.: Yale Univer. Press, 1959. Pp. 102-120.

Cohen, A. R. *Attitude change and social influence*. New York: Basic Books, 1964.

Cohen, A. R., Stotland, E., & Wolfe, D. M. An experimental investigation of need for cognition. *J. abnorm. soc. Psychol.*, 1955, 51, 291-294.

Coleman, J. S. *The adolescent society: The social life of the teenager and its impact on education*. New York: Free Press, 1961.

Comte, A. *The positive philosophy of Auguste Comte*. (Translated and condensed by Harriet Martineau.) London: J. Chapman, 1853.

Converse, P. E. The shifting role of class in political attitudes and behavior. In Eleanor Maccoby, T. M. Newcomb, & E. L. Hartley (Eds.), *Readings in social psychology*. (3rd edition) New York: Holt, Rinehart, & Winston, 1958. Pp. 388-399.

Cook, P. H. The application of the Rorschach Test to a Samoan group. *Rorschach Research Exchange*, 1942, 6, 52-60.

Cooley, C. H. *Social organization*. New York: Scribners, 1909.

Cooley, C. H. *Human nature and the social order*. New York: Scribners, 1922.

Cottrell, L. S. Some neglected problems in social psychology. *Amer. sociol. Rev.*, 1950, 15, 705-712.

Cowley, W. H. Three distinctions in the study of leaders. *J. abnorm. soc. Psychol.*, 1928, 23, 144-157.

Cox, F. N. An assessment of children's attitudes towards parent figures. *Child Development*, 1962, 33, 821-830.

Crockett, W. H., & Meidinger, T. Authoritarianism and interpersonal perception. *J. abnorm. soc. Psychol.*, 1956, 53, 378-380.

Crow, W. J. A study of strategic doctrines using the Inter-Nation Simulation. *J. Confl. Resol.*, 1963, 7, 580-589.

Crowne, D. P., & Liverant, S. Conformity under varying conditions of personal commitment. *J. abnorm. soc. Psychol.*, 1963, 66, 547-555.

Crowne, D. P., & Marlowe, D. *The approval motive: Studies in evaluative dependence.* New York: Wiley, 1964.

Crutchfield, R. S. Conformity and character. *American Psychologist*, 1955, 10, 191-198.

Darley, J. M. Fear and social comparison as determinants of conformity behavior. *J. Pers. soc. Psychol.*, 1966, 4, 73-78.

Darwin, C. R. *Origin of species by means of natural selection; or, The preservation of favoured races in the struggle for life.* New York: D. Appleton & Co., 1860. (London, 1859; paperback by Doubleday, 1960.)

Darwin, C. R. *The descent of man and selection in relation to sex.* New York: D. Appleton & Co., 1871.

Davis, Allison, Gardner, B., & Gardner, Mary R. *Deep South: A social-anthropological study of caste and class.* Chicago: Univer. of Chicago Press, 1941.

Davis, Allison, & Havighurst, R. J. Social class and color differences in child-rearing. *Amer. sociol. Rev.*, 1948, 11, 698-710.

deCharms, R., & Moeller, G. H. Values expressed in American children's readers: 1800-1950. *J. abnorm. soc. Psychol.*, 1962, 64, 136-142.

deCharms, R., Carpenter, Virginia, & Cuperman, A. The "origin-pawn" variable in person perception. *Sociometry*, 1965, 28, 241-258.

DeFleur, M. L., & Westie, F. R. Verbal attitudes and overt acts: An experiment on the salience of attitudes. *Amer. sociol. Rev.*, 1958, 23, 667-673.

Dember, W. N. The new look in motivation. *Amer. Scientist*, 1965, 53, 409-427.

Deutsch, K. W. *The political community at the international level.* Garden City, N. Y.: Doubleday, 1954.

Deutsch, M. A theory of cooperation and competition. *Hum. Relat.*, 1949a, 2, 129-152.

Deutsch, M. An experimental study of the effects of cooperation and competition upon group process. *Hum. Relat.*, 1949b, 2, 199-231.

Deutsch, M. Trust, trustworthiness, and the F scale. *J. abnorm. soc. Psychol.*, 1960, 61, 138-140.

Deutsch, M. A psychological basis for peace. In Q. Wright, W. M. Evan, and M. Deutsch (Eds.), *Preventing World War III: Some proposals.* New York: Simon & Schuster, 1962. Pp. 369-392.

Deutsch, M. & Collins, Mary E. *Interracial housing: A psychological evaluation of a social experiment.* Minneapolis: Univer. Minnesota Press, 1951.

Deutsch, M., & Gerard, H. B. A study of normative and informational social influence upon individual judgment. *J. abnorm. soc. Psychol.,* 1955, *51,* 629-636.

Deutsch, M., & Solomon, L. Reactions to evaluations by others as influenced by self evaluations. *Sociometry,* 1959, *22,* 93-112.

Deutsch, M., & Krauss, R. M. *Theories in social psychology.* New York: Basic Books, 1965.

DeVos, G. Symbolic analysis in the cross-cultural study of personality. In B. Kaplan (Ed.), *Studying personality cross culturally.* Evanston, Ill.: Row, Peterson & Co., 1961. Pp. 599-634.

Dittes, J. E. Effect of changes in self-esteem upon impulsiveness and deliberation in making judgments. *J. abnorm. soc. Psychol.,* 1959, *58,* 348-356.

Dittes, J. E. Impulsive closure as a reaction to failure-induced threat. *J. abnorm. soc. Psychol.,* 1961, *63,* 562-569.

DiVesta, F. J. Meaningful learning: Motivational, personality, interpersonal, and social variables; peer relationships. *Rev. educat. Res.,* 1961, *31,* 511-521.

Doob, L. W. The effect of codability upon the afferent and efferent functioning of language. *J. soc. Psychol.,* 1960, *52,* 3-15.

Dornbusch, S. M., Hastorf, A. H., Richardson, S. A., Muzzy, R. E., & Vreeland, Rebecca S. The perceiver and the perceived: Their relative influence on the categories of interpersonal cognition. *J. Pers. soc. Psychol.,* 1965, *1,* 434-440.

DuBois, Cora. *The people of Alor. A social psychological study of an East Indian island.* Minneapolis: Univer. of Minnesota Press, 1944.

Dudycha, G. J. An objective study of punctuality in relation to personality and development. *Archives of Psychology,* 1936, No. 204.

Dunn, L. C., & Dobzhansky, T. *Heredity, race and society.* New York: New American Library, 1946. (Rev. ed., 1952.)

Durkheim, E. *De la division du travail social.* Paris: Alcan, 1893. (Trans. *The division of labor in society.* Glencoe, Ill.: Free Press, 1947.)

Durkheim, E. *Le suicide; étude de sociologie.* (Trans. *Suicide, a study in sociology*). Paris: Alcan, 1897.

Edwards, A. L. *The social desirability variable in personality assessment and research.* New York: Dryden, 1957a.

Edwards, A. L. *Techniques of attitude scale construction.* New York: Appleton-Century-Crofts, 1957b.

Eisenstadt, S. N. *From generation to generation.* Glencoe, Ill.: Free Press, 1956.

Elkin, F. *The child and society: The process of socialization.* New York: Random House, 1960.

Elms, A. C. Influence of fantasy ability on attitude change through role playing. *J. Pers. soc. Psychol.*, 1966, *4*, 36-43.

Ericson, Martha. Child rearing and social status. *Amer. J. Sociol.*, 1948, *52*, 190-192.

Etzioni, A. On self-encapsulating conflicts. *Conflict Resolution*, 1964, *8*, 242-255.

Exline, R. V. Interrelation among two dimensions of sociometric status, group congeniality, and accuracy of social perception. *Sociometry*, 1960, *23*, 85-101.

Eysenck, H. J. *Fact and fiction in psychology.* Baltimore, Md.: Penguin Books, 1965.

Farber, M. L. The problem of national character: A methodological analysis. *J. Psychol.*, 1950, *30*, 307-316.

Festinger, L. Informal social communication. *Psychol. Rev.*, 1950, *57*, 271-282.

Festinger, L. *A theory of cognitive dissonance.* Evanston, Ill.: Row, Peterson, 1957.

Festinger, L. The psychological effects of insufficient rewards. *Amer. Psychologist*, 1961, *16*, 1-11.

Festinger, L. Behavioral support for opinion change. *Publ. Opin. Quart.*, 1964a, *28*, 404-417.

Festinger, L., with the collaboration of Vernon Allen and others. *Conflict, decision, and dissonance.* Stanford: Stanford Univer. Press, 1964b.

Festinger, L., & Katz, D. (Eds.) *Research methods in the behavioral sciences.* New York: Dryden, 1953.

Festinger, L., & Carlsmith, J. Cognitive consequences of forced compliance. *J. abnorm. soc. Psychol.*, 1959, *58*, 203-210.

Festinger, L., & Maccoby, N. On resistance to persuasive communications. *J. abnorm. soc. Psychol.*, 1964, *68*, 359-366.

Festinger, L., Schachter, S., & Back, K. *Social pressures in informal groups: A study of a housing project.* New York: Harper, 1950.

Fiedler, F. E. *Leader attitudes and group effectiveness.* Urbana, Ill.: Univer. of Ill. Press, 1958.

Fiedler, F. E. Leadership and leadership effectiveness traits. In L. Petrullo & B. M. Bass (Eds.), *Leadership and interpersonal behavior.* New York: Holt, Rinehart, & Winston, 1961.

Fiedler, F. E. A contingency model of leadership effectiveness. In L. Berkowitz (Ed.), *Advances in experimental social psychology.* Vol. 1. New York: Academic Press, 1964.

Fiedler, F. E. The contingency model: A theory of leadership effectiveness. In H. Proshansky & B. Seidenberg (Eds.), *Basic studies in social psychology.* New York: Holt, Rinehart, & Winston, 1965.

Fischer, J. L. Social influences on the choice of a linguistic variant. *Word*, 1958, *14*, 47-56.

Flanagan, J. C. (Ed.) *Leaders reaction test.* Pittsburgh: Amer. Inst. for Research, 1952.

Flavell, J. H. A test of the Whorfian theory. *Psychol. Reps.*, 1958, *4*, 455-62.

Fleishman, E. A., & Harris, E. F. Patterns of leadership behavior related to employee grievances and turnover. *Personnel Psychol.*, 1962, *15*, 43-56.

Fleishman, E. A., & Peters, D. R. Interpersonal values, leadership attitudes, and managerial success. *Personnel Psychol.*, 1962, *15*, 127-143.

Fleishman, E. A., Harris, E. F., & Burtt, H. E. *Leadership and supervision in industry.* Columbus, Ohio: Bureau of Educat. Res., Ohio State Univer., 1955.

Fouriezos, N. T., Hutt, M. L., & Guetzkow, H. Measurement of self-oriented needs in discussion groups. *J. abnorm. soc. Psychol.*, 1950, *45*, 682-690.

Freedman, J. L. Involvement, discrepancy, and change. *J. abnorm. soc. Psychol.*, 1964, *69*, 290-295.

Freedman, J. L. Long-term behavioral effects of cognitive dissonance. *J. exp. soc. Psychol.*, 1965, *1*, 145-155.

Freedman, J. L., & Sears, D. O. Warning, distraction, and resistance to influence. *J. Pers. soc. Psychol.*, 1965, *1*, 262-266.

French, J. R. P., Jr., & Raven, B. H. The bases of social power. In D. Cartwright (Ed.), *Studies in social power.* Ann Arbor, Mich.: Univer. of Michigan Press, 1959. Pp. 118-149.

Fromm, E. *Escape from freedom.* New York: Rinehart, 1941.

Fromm, E. Psychoanalytic characterology and its application to the understanding of culture. In S. S. Sargent & M. W. Smith (Eds.), *Culture and personality.* New York: Viking Fund, 1949.

Gallo, P. S., & McClintock, C. G. Behavioral, attitudinal and perceptual differences between leaders and non-leaders in situations of group support and non-support. *J. soc. Psychol.*, 1962, *56*, 121-133.

Galton, F. *Hereditary genius: An inquiry into its laws and consequences.* London: Macmillan, 1869. (Also published in paperback by Meridian Books.)

Gardner, J. W. *Excellence.* New York: Harper & Row, 1961.

Gardner, J. W. *Self-renewal.* New York: Harper & Row, 1963.

Gellert, Elizabeth. Stability and fluctuation in the power relationships of young children. *J. abnorm. soc. Psychol.*, 1961, *62*, 8-15.

Gibb, C. A. The sociometry of leadership in temporary groups. *Sociometry*, 1950, *13*, 226-243.

Gibb, C. A. Leadership. In G. Lindzey (Ed.), *Handbook of social psychology.* Vol. II. Reading, Mass.: Addison-Wesley, 1954.

Gittler, J. B. *Social dynamics.* New York: McGraw-Hill, 1952.

Goffman, E. *The presentation of self in everyday life.* Garden City, N. Y.: Doubleday Anchor, 1959.

Goldberg, L. R., & Rorer, L. G. Use of two different response modes and repeated testings to predict social conformity. *J. abnorm. soc. Psychol.*, 1966, *3*, 28-37.

Goldman, M., & Fraas, L. A. The effects of leader selection on group performance. *Sociometry*, 1965, *28*, 82-88.

Goldschmidt, W. *Man's way*. Cleveland: World Publ. Co., 1959.

Golembiewski, R. T. *The small group*. Chicago: Univer. of Chicago Press, 1962.

Gollob, H. F., & Dittes, J. E. Effects of manipulated self-esteem on persuasibility depending on threat and complexity of communication. *J. Pers. soc. Psychol.*, 1965, *2*, 195-201.

Gordon, M. M. *Assimilation in American life*. New York: Oxford Univer. Press, 1964.

Gorer, G. *The American people: A study in national character*. New York: W. W. Norton, 1948 (revised edition in Norton Library Paperback, 1964).

Goslin, D. A. Accuracy of self perception and social acceptance. *Sociometry*, 1962, *25*, 283-296.

Gottheil, E. Changes in social perceptions contingent upon competing or cooperating. *Sociometry*, 1955, *18*, 132-137.

Gouldner, A. W. (Ed.) *Studies in leadership*. New York: Harper, 1950.

Gouldner, A. W. *Wildcat strike*. Yellow Springs, Ohio: Antioch Press, 1954. (Available as Harper Torch Book, New York, 1965.)

Gouldner, A. W. The norm of reciprocity: A preliminary statement. *Amer. sociol. Rev.*, 1960, *25*, 161-179.

Greer, F. L., Galanter, E. H., & Nordlie, P. G. Interpersonal knowledge and individual and group effectiveness. *J. abnorm. soc. Psychol.*, 1954, *49*, 411-414.

Gross, N. The sociology of education. In R. K. Merton, *et al*. (Eds.), *Sociology today: Problems and prospects*. New York: Basic Books, 1959. Pp. 128-52.

Gross, N., & Martin, W. E. On group cohesiveness. *Amer. J. Sociol.*, 1952, *57*, 546-554.

Grossack, M. M. Some effects of cooperation and competition upon small group behavior. *J. abnorm. soc. Psychol.*, 1954, *49*, 341-348.

Group for the Advancement of Psychiatry. *Psychiatric aspects of the prevention of nuclear war*. New York: Committee on Social Issues, 1964. Rep. #57.

Guetzkow, H. (Ed.) *Groups, leadership and men*. Pittsburgh: Carnegie Press, 1951.

Guetzkow, H. *Multiple loyalties*. Princeton: Princeton Univer. Press, 1955.

Guetzkow, H., Alger, C. F., Brody, R. A., Noel, R. C., & Snyder, R. C. *Simulation in international relations*. Englewood Cliffs, N. J.: Prentice-Hall, 1963.

Guttman, L. The basis for scalogram analysis. In S. A. Stouffer, L. Guttman, E. A. Suchman, P. F. Lazarsfeld, Shirley A. Star, & J. A. Gardner (Eds.), *Measurement and prediction*. Princeton, N. J.: Princeton Univer. Press, 1950. Pp. 60-90.

Hagstrom, W. O., & Selvin, H. C. Two dimensions of cohesiveness in small groups. *Sociometry*, 1965, *28*, 30-43.

Haiman, F. S. *Group leadership and democratic action.* Boston: Houghton Mifflin, 1951.

Hall, E. T. *The silent language.* Garden City, N. Y.: Doubleday, 1959.

Hallowell, A. I. Temporal orientation in Western civilization and in preliterate society. *Amer. Anthropologist,* 1937, *39,* 647-670.

Halpin, A. W. The leader behavior and leadership ideology of educational administrators and aircraft commanders. *Harvard educ. Rev.,* 1955, *25,* 18-32.

Halpin, A. W., & Winer, B. J. *The leadership behavior of the airplane commander.* Columbus: Ohio State Univer. Research Foundation, 1952.

Hamblin, R. L. Leadership and crises. *Sociometry,* 1958, *21,* 322-335.

Hammond, L. K., & Goldman, M. Competition and non-competition and its relationship to individual and group productivity. *Sociometry,* 1961, *24,* 46-60.

Hare, A. P. *Handbook of small group research.* New York: Free Press, 1961.

Hare, A. P., Borgatta, E. F., & Bales, R. F. (Eds.) *Small groups.* New York: Alfred A. Knopf, 1955. (Rev. ed., 1965.)

Harlow, H. F. The heterosexual affectional system in monkeys. *Amer. Psychologist,* 1962, *17,* 1-9.

Hartshorne, H., & May, M. A. *Studies in deceit.* New York: Macmillan, 1928.

Harvey, O. J., & Consalvi, C. Status and conformity to pressures in informal groups. *J. abnorm. soc. Psychol.,* 1960, *60,* 182-187.

Harvey, O. J., Kelley, H. H., & Shapiro, M. M. Reactions to unfavorable evaluations of the self made by other persons. *J. Pers.,* 1957, *25,* 398-411.

Hastorf, A. H., & Cantril, H. They saw a game. *J. abnorm. soc. Psychol.,* 1954, *49,* 129-134.

Hayakawa, S. I. *Symbol, status, and personality.* New York: Harcourt Brace & World, 1963.

Hayakawa, S. I. *Language in thought and action.* (2nd ed.) New York: Harcourt Brace & World, 1964.

Hayes, Cathy. *The ape in our house.* New York: Harper, 1951.

Haywood, H. C., & Spielberger, C. D. Palmar sweating as a function of individual differences in manifest anxiety. *J. Pers. soc. Psychol.,* 1966, *3,* 103-105.

Heider, F. Social perception and phenomenal causality. *Psychol. Rev.,* 1944, *51,* 358-374.

Heider, F. Attitudes and cognitive organization. *J. Psychol.,* 1946, *21,* 107-112.

Heider, F. *The psychology of interpersonal relations.* New York: Wiley, 1958.

Heilbroner, R. L. *The worldly philosophers.* (Revised ed.) New York: Simon & Schuster, 1961.

Helson, H. Adaptation-level as a basis for a quantitative theory of frames of reference. *Psychol. Rev.,* 1948, *55,* 297-313.

Helson, H. Adaptation level theory. In S. Koch (Ed.), *Psychology: A study of a science.* Vol. I. *Sensory, perceptual, and physiological formulations.* New York: McGraw-Hill, 1959. Pp. 565-621.

Hemphill, J. K. The measurement of group dimensions. *J. Psychol.*, 1950a, 29, 325-342.

Hemphill, J. K. Relations between the size of the group and the behavior of "superior" leaders. *J. soc. Psychol.*, 1950b, 32, 11-22.

Hemphill, J. K. Leadership behavior associated with the administrative reputation of college departments. *J. educ. Psychol.*, 1955, 46, 385-401.

Hemphill, J. K. *Group dimensions: A manual for their measurement.* Columbus: Ohio State Univer., Ohio Studies in Personnel, Monogr. #87, Bureau of Business Research, 1956.

Hemphill, J. K. Administration as problem-solving. In A. W. Halpin (Ed.), *Administrative theory in education.* Chicago: Midwest Administration Center, 1958.

Hemphill, J. K. Why people attempt to lead. In L. Petrullo & B. M. Bass (Eds.), *Leadership and interpersonal behavior.* New York: Holt, Rinehart, & Winston, 1961.

Hemphill, J. K., & Westie, C. M. The measurement of group dimensions. *J. Psychol.*, 1950, 29, 325-342.

Henry, J. *Culture against man.* New York: Random House, 1963.

Heslin, R., & Dunphy, D. Three dimensions of member satisfaction in small groups. *Hum. Relat.*, 1964, 17, 99-112.

Himmelweit, Hilde T. Socio-economic background and personality. *Int. soc. Sci. Bull.*, 1955, 7, 29-35.

Hites, R. W., & Campbell, D. T. A test of the ability of fraternity leaders to estimate group opinion. *J. soc. Psychol.*, 1950, 32, 95-100.

Hoffman, L. R. Homogeneity of member personality and its effect on group problem-solving. *J. abnorm. soc. Psychol.*, 1959, 58, 27-32.

Hoffman, L. R., & Maier, N. R. F. Quality and acceptance of problem solutions by members of homogeneous and heterogeneous groups. *J. abnorm. soc. Psychol.*, 1961, 62, 401-407.

Hollander, E. P. Conformity, status, and idiosyncrasy credit. *Psychol. Rev.*, 1958, 65, 117-127.

Hollander, E. P. Competence and conformity in the acceptance of influence. *J. abnorm. soc. Psychol.*, 1960, 61, 361-365.

Hollander, E. P. Some effects of perceived status on responses to innovative behavior. *J. abnorm. soc. Psychol.*, 1961, 63, 247-250.

Hollander, E. P. *Leaders, groups, and influence.* New York: Oxford Univer. Press, 1964.

Hollander, E. P., & Webb, W. B. Leadership, followership, and friendship: An analysis of peer nominations. *J. abnorm. soc. Psychol.*, 1955, 50, 163-167.

Hollander, E. P., & Willis, R. H. Conformity, independence and anticonformity as determiners of perceived influence and attraction. In E. P. Hollander, *Leaders, groups, and influence.* New York: Oxford Univer. Press, 1964. Ch. 19.

Hollander, E. P., & Julian, J. W. Leadership. In E. F. Borgatta & W. W. Lambert (Eds.), *Handbook of personality theory and research.* Chicago: Rand McNally, 1967.

Hollander, E. P., Julian, J. W., & Haaland, G. A. Conformity process and prior group support. *J. Pers. soc. Psychol.*, 1965, *2*, 852-858.

Hollander, E. P., Julian, J. W., & Perry, F. A. Leader style, competence, and source of authority as determinants of actual and perceived influence. *Technical Report 5, ONR Contract 4679.* Buffalo: State University of New York, Department of Psychology, September, 1966.

Hollingshead, A. B. *Elmtown's youth.* New York: Wiley, 1949.

Hollingshead, A. B. Factors associated with prevalence of mental illness. In Eleanor Maccoby, T. M. Newcomb, & E. L. Hartley (Eds.), *Readings in social psychology.* (3rd edition) New York: Holt, Rinehart, & Winston, 1958. Pp. 425-436.

Hollingshead, A. B., & Redlich, F. C. Schizophrenia and social structure. *Amer. J. Psychiat.*, 1954, *110*, 695-701.

Hollingshead, A. B., & Redlich, F. C. *Social class and mental illness.* New York: Wiley, 1958.

Homans, G. C. *The human group.* New York: Harcourt Brace, 1950.

Homans, G. C. The cash posters. *Amer. soc. Rev.*, 1954, *19*, 724-733.

Homans, G. C. Social behavior as exchange. *Amer. J. Sociol.*, 1958, *63*, 597-606.

Homans, G. C. *Social behavior: Its elementary forms.* New York: Harcourt Brace, 1961.

Homans, G. C. Small groups. In B. Berelson (Ed.), *The behavioral sciences today.* New York: Basic Books, 1963. Pp. 165-175.

Homans, G. C. Unpublished address given at the Upstate Sociological Association Convention, Cornell University, Ithaca, New York, May, 1965.

Hood, W. R., & Sherif, M. Verbal report and judgment of an unstructured stimulus situation. Reported in M. Sherif, Conformity-deviation, norms, and group relations. In I. A. Berg & B. M. Bass (Eds.), *Conformity and deviation.* New York: Harper & Row, 1961. P. 167.

Horney, Karen. *Our inner conflicts.* New York: Norton, 1945.

Hovland, C. I. (Ed.) *The order of presentation in persuasion.* New Haven: Yale Univer. Press, 1957.

Hovland, C. I. Reconciling conflicting results derived from experimental and survey studies of attitude change. *Amer. Psychologist*, 1959, *14*, 8-17.

Hovland, C. I., & Sherif, M. Judgmental phenomena and scales of attitude measurement: Item displacement in Thurstone scales. *J. abnorm. soc. Psychol.*, 1952, *47*, 822-832.

Hovland, C. I., & Weiss, W. The influence of source credibility on communication effectiveness. *Publ. Opin. Quart.*, 1951, *15*, 635-650.

Hovland, C. I., & Janis, I. L. (Eds.) *Personality and persuasibility.* New Haven: Yale Univer. Press, 1959.

Hovland, C. I., & Rosenberg, M. J. (Eds.) *Attitude organization and change.* New Haven: Yale Univer. Press, 1960.

Hovland, C. I., Lumsdaine, A. A., & Sheffield, F. D. *Experiments on mass communication.* New Jersey: Princeton Univer. Press, 1949.

Hovland, C. I., Janis, I. L., & Kelley, H. H. *Communication and persuasion.* New Haven: Yale Univer. Press, 1953.

Hovland, C. I., Campbell, Enid H., & Brock, T. The effects of "commitment" on opinion change following communication. In C. I. Hovland (Ed.), *The order of presentation in persuasion*. New Haven: Yale Univer. Press, 1957. Pp. 23-32.

Hovland, C. I., Harvey, O. J., & Sherif, M. Assimilation and contrast effects in reactions to communication and attitude change. *J. abnorm. soc. Psychol.*, 1957, 55, 244-252.

Howard, R. C., & Berkowitz, L. Reactions to the evaluations of one's performance. *J. Pers.*, 1958, 26, 494-507.

Hunt, J. McV. The effect of infant feeding frustration upon adult hoarding in the albino rat. *J. abnorm. soc. Psychol.*, 1941, 36, 338-360.

Hunt, J. McV. Traditional personality theory in the light of recent evidence. *Amer. Scientist*, 1965, 53, 80-96.

Hunt, R. G. Socio-cultural factors in mental disorder. *Behav. Sci.*, 1959, 4, 96-107.

Hunt, R. G., & Synnerdahl, Vonda. Social influences among kindergarten children: An experimental note. *Sociol. & soc. Res.*, 1959, 43, 171-174.

Hurwitz, J. I., Zander, A. F., & Hymovitch, B. Some effects of power on the relations among group members. In D. Cartwright & A. F. Zander (Eds.), *Group dynamics: Research and theory*. Evanston, Ill.: Row, Peterson, 1953. Pp. 488-492.

Hyman, H. H. *Survey design and analysis*. Glencoe, Ill.: Free Press, 1955.

Hyman, H. H. *Political socialization: A study in the psychology of political behavior*. Glencoe, Ill.: Free Press, 1959.

Hyman, H. H., & Sheatsley, P. B. Why information campaigns fail. *Public Opinion Quart.*, 1947, 11, 412-423.

Ichheiser, G. Misunderstandings in human relations: A study in false social perception. *Amer. J. Sociol.*, 1949, 55, 1-70.

Israel, J. *Self-evaluation and rejection in groups*. Stockholm: Almqvist & Wiksell, 1956.

Jacobs, R. C., & Campbell, D. T. The perpetuation of an arbitrary tradition through several generations of a laboratory microculture. *J. abnorm. soc. Psychol.*, 1961, 62, 649-58.

Jaeger, Gertrude, & Selznick, P. A normative theory of culture. *Amer. sociol. Rev.*, 1964, 29, 653-669.

Jahoda, Marie. Race relations and mental health. In UNESCO, *Race and Science*. New York: Columbia Univ. Press, 1961.

Jakubczak, L. F., & Walters, R. H. Suggestibility as dependency behavior. *J. abnorm. soc. Psychol.*, 1959, 59, 102-107.

Janis, I. L., & Feshbach, S. Effects of fear-arousing communications. *J. abnorm. soc. Psychol.*, 1953, 48, 78-92.

Janis, I. L., & Field, P. B. Sex differences and personality factors related to persuasibility. In C. I. Hovland & I. L. Janis (Eds.), *Personality and persuasibility*. New Haven: Yale Univer. Press, 1959. Pp. 55-68.

Janis, I. L., & Gilmore, J. B. The influence of incentive conditions on the success of role playing in modifying attitudes. *J. Pers. soc. Psychol.* 1965, *1*, 17-27.

Janis, I. L., & Hovland, C. I. An overview of persuasibility research. In C. I. Hovland & I. L. Janis (Eds.), *Personality and persuasibility.* New Haven: Yale Univer. Press, 1959. Pp. 1-26.

Janis, I. L., & Mann, L. Effectiveness of emotional role-playing in modifying smoking habits and attitudes. *J. exp. Res. in Pers.*, 1965, *1*, 84-90.

Janis, I. L., & Terwilliger, R. An experimental study of psychological resistance to fear-arousing communications. *J. abnorm. soc. Psychol.*, 1962, *65*, 403-410.

Jenkins, W. O., & Stanley, J. C. Partial reinforcement: A review and critique. *Psychol. Bulletin,* 1950, *47*, 193-234.

Jenness, A. The role of discussion in changing opinions regarding a matter of fact. *J. abnorm. soc. Psychol.*, 1932, *27*, 279-296.

Jennings, Helen H. *Leadership and isolation.* New York: Longmans Green, 1943. (2nd ed., 1950.)

Jennings, Helen H. Sociometry of leadership. *Sociometry Monogr.*, 1947, *14*, 12-24.

Johnson, R. C. Linguistic structure as related to concept formation and to concept content. *Psychol. Bull.*, 1962, *59*, 468-76.

Jones, E. E. *Ingratiation.* New York: Appleton-Century-Crofts, 1964.

Jones, E. E. Conformity as a tactic of ingratiation. *Science,* 1965, *149*, 144-150.

Jones, E. ·E., & Daugherty, B. N. Political orientation and the perceptual effects of an anticipated interaction. *J. abnorm. soc. Psychol.*, 1959, *59*, 340-349.

Jones, E. E., & deCharms, R. Changes in social perception as a function of the personal relevance of behavior. *Sociometry,* 1957, *20*, 75-85.

Jones, M. B. Authoritarianism and intolerance of fluctuation. *J. abnorm. soc. Psychol.*, 1955, *50*, 125-126.

Jones, S. C. Some determinants of interpersonal evaluating behavior. *J. Pers. soc. Psychol.*, 1966, *3*, 397-403.

Julian, J. W., & Perry, F. A. Cooperation contrasted with intra-group and inter-group competition. Paper presented at the Midwest. Psychol. Ass., Chicago, 1965.

Julian, J. W., & Steiner, I. D. Perceived acceptance as a determinant of conformity behavior. *J. soc. Psychol.*, 1961, *55*, 191-198.

Jung, C. G. *The basic writings of C. G. Jung.* V. de Laszlo (Ed.) New York: Random House, 1959.

Kagan, J. The concept of identification. *Psychol. Rev.*, 1958, *65*, 296-305.

Kagan, J. Body build and conceptual impulsivity in children. *J. Pers.*, 1966, *34*, 118-128.

Kagan, J., & Moss, H. A. Personality and social development: Family and peer influences. *Rev. of educat. Res.*, 1961, *31*, 463-474.

Kahl, J. A. Educational and occupational aspirations of "common man" boys. *Harvard Educat. Rev.*, 1953, *23*, 186-203.

Kahl, J. A. *The American class structure*. New York: Holt, Rinehart & Winston, 1957.

Kahn, R., & Katz, D. Leadership practices in relation to productivity and morale. In D. Cartwright & A. Zander (Eds.), *Group dynamics: Research and theory*. Evanston, Ill.: Row Peterson, 1960. Pp. 554-570.

Kaplan, B. (Ed.) *Studying personality cross-culturally*. New York: Harper & Row, 1961.

Kardiner, A. *The individual and his society*. New York: Columbia Univer. Press, 1939.

Kardiner, A., with the collaboration of R. Linton, Cora DuBois, & James West. *The psychological frontiers of society*. New York: Columbia Univer. Press, 1945.

Kardiner, A., & Preble, E. *They studied man*. New York: New American Library, Mentor Book, 1963.

Katona, G. *The powerful consumer*. New York: McGraw-Hill, 1960.

Katona, G. *Mass consumption society*. New York: McGraw-Hill, 1964.

Katz, D. The functional approach to the study of attitudes. *Publ. opin. Quart.*, 1960, *24*, 163-204.

Katz, D., & Stotland, E. A preliminary statement to a theory of attitude structure and change. In S. Koch (Ed.), *Psychology: A study of a science*. Vol. 3. New York: McGraw-Hill, 1959. Pp. 423-475.

Katz, D., Sarnoff, I., & McClintock, C. G. Ego-defense and attitude change. *Hum. Relat.*, 1956, *9*, 27-45.

Katz, E., & Lazarsfeld, P. F. *Personal influence*. Glencoe, Ill.: Free Press, 1955.

Kelley, H. H. The warm-cold variable in first impressions of persons. *J. Pers.*, 1950, *18*, 431-439.

Kelley, H. H. Communication in experimentally created hierarchies. *Hum. Relat.*, 1951, *4*, 39-56.

Kelley, H. H. Attitudes and judgments as influenced by reference groups: Two functions of reference groups. In G. Swanson, T. M. Newcomb, & E. L. Hartley (Eds.), *Readings in social psychology*. (2nd ed.) New York: Holt, 1952. Pp. 410-420.

Kelley, H. H. Salience of membership and resistance to change of group-anchored attitudes. *Hum. Relat.*, 1955, *8*, 275-290.

Kelley, H. H., & Volkart, E. H. The resistance to change of group-anchored attitudes. *Amer. sociol. Rev.*, 1952, *17*, 453-465.

Kellogg, W. N., & Kellogg, Louise A. *The ape and the child*. New York: McGraw-Hill, 1933.

Kelly, E. L. Consistency of the adult personality. *Amer. Psychologist*, 1955, *10*, 659-681.

Kelly, G. *A theory of personality: The psychology of personal constructs*. (Norton Library Edition) New York: W. W. Norton, 1963.

Kelman, H. C. Effects of success and failure on "suggestibility" in the autokinetic situation. *J. abnorm. soc. Psychol.*, 1950, *45*, 267-285.

Kelman, H. C. Compliance, identification, and internalization: Three processes of opinion change. *Journal of Conflict Resolution,* 1958, *2,* 51-60.

Kelman, H. C. Processes of opinion change. *Publ. Opin. Quart.,* 1961, *25,*
57-78.

Kelman, H. C. (Ed.) *International behavior: A socio-psychological analysis.*
New York: Holt, Rinehart & Winston, 1965.

Kennedy, J. F. *Profiles in courage.* New York: Harper, 1956.

Kennedy, J. F. Address at the University of Washington, November 16, 1961.

Kerr, W. A., Koppelmeier, G., & Sullivan, J. J. Absenteeism, turnover, and
morale in a metals fabrication factory. *Occup. Psychology,* 1951, *25,*
50-55.

Kinsey, A. C., Pomeroy, W. B., & Martin, C. E. *Sexual behavior in the
human male.* Philadelphia: W. B. Saunders & Co., 1948.

Kirscht, J. P., Lodahl, T. M., & Haire, M. Some factors in the selection of
leaders by members of small groups. *J. abnorm. soc. Psychol.,* 1959,
58, 406-408.

Klapper, J. T. *The effects of mass communication.* Glencoe, Ill.: Free Press,
1960.

Klein, Josephine. *The study of groups.* London: Routledge & Kegan Paul,
1956.

Klineberg, O. *Tensions affecting international understanding.* New York: Social Science Research Council, Bulletin 62, 1950.

Klineberg, O. *Social psychology.* (Rev. ed.) New York: Holt, 1954.

Klineberg, O. *The human dimension in international relations.* New York:
Holt, Rinehart, & Winston, 1964.

Kluckhohn, C. *Mirror for Man.* New York: McGraw-Hill, 1949a. (Also available in paperback from McGraw-Hill.)

Kluckhohn, C. The limitations of adaptation and adjustment as concepts for
understanding cultural behavior. In J. Romano (Ed.), *Adaptation.*
Ithaca: Cornell Univer. Press, 1949b. Pp. 99-113.

Kluckhohn, C., & Murray, H. A. (Eds.) *Personality in nature, society, and
culture.* New York: Knopf, 1948.

Kluckhohn, C., Murray, H. A., & Schneider, D. *Personality in nature, society,
and culture.* (2nd ed.) New York: Knopf, 1953.

Kluckhohn, Florence R. Dominant and variant value orientations. In C.
Kluckhohn, H. A. Murray, & D. M. Schneider (Eds.), *Personality in
nature, society, and culture.* New York: Knopf, 1953.

Koch, Helen L. The relation in young children between characteristics of
their playmates and certain attributes of their siblings. *Child Development,* 1957, *28,* 175-202.

Kogan, N., & Wallach, M. A. *Risk taking: A study in cognition and personality.* New York: Holt, Rinehart, & Winston, 1964.

Komarovsky, Mirra. Cultural contradictions and sex roles. *Amer. J. Sociol.,*
1946, *52,* 184-189.

Kottman, E. J. Language internalization and intentional orientation. *Etc.,*
1964, *21,* 456-466.

Krasner, L. Studies of the conditioning of verbal behavior. *Psychol. Bull.*, 1958, 55, 148-170.

Krasner, L., & Ullmann, L. P. *Research in behavior modification: New developments and implications.* New York: Holt, Rinehart, & Winston, 1965.

Krech, D., & Crutchfield, R. S. *Theory and problems of social psychology.* New York: McGraw-Hill, 1948.

Kroeber, A. L., & Kluckhohn, C. Culture, a critical review of concepts and definitions. *Papers of the Peabody Museum of American Archaeology and Ethnology,* 47 (1). Cambridge, Mass.: Harvard Univer., 1952, 1-223.

Kroeber, A. L., & Parsons, T. The concepts of culture and of social system. *Amer. sociol. Rev.,* 1958, 23, 582-583.

Kubany, A. J. Evaluation of medical student clinical performance: A criterion study. *Dissert. Abstr.,* 1957, 17, 1119-1120.

Kutner, B., Wilkins, Carol, & Yarrow, Penny R. Verbal attitudes and overt behavior involving racial prejudice. *J. abnorm. soc. Psychol.,* 1952, 47, 649-652.

Lambert, W. W., & Lambert, W. E. *Social psychology.* Englewood Cliffs, N. J.: Prentice-Hall, 1964.

Lambert, W. W., Solomon, R. L., & Watson, P. D. Reinforcement and extinction as factors in size estimation. *J. exp. Psychol.,* 1949, 39, 637-641.

Landecker, W. S. Types of integration and their measurement. In P. F. Lazarsfeld & M. Rosenberg (Eds.), *The language of social research.* Glencoe, Ill.: The Free Press, 1955. Pp. 19-27.

LaPiere, R. T. Attitudes versus actions. *Social Forces,* 1934, 13, 230-237.

Lazarsfeld, P. F., & Rosenberg, M. (Eds.) *The language of social research.* Glencoe, Ill.: Free Press, 1955.

Lazarsfeld, P. F., Berelson, B., & Gaudet, Hazel. *The people's choice.* (2nd ed.) New York: Columbia Univer. Press, 1948.

Lazarus, R. S. *Personality and adjustment.* Englewood Cliffs, N. J.: Prentice-Hall, 1963.

Leavitt, H. J. Some effects of certain communication patterns on group performance. *J. abnorm. soc. Psychol.,* 1951, 46, 38-50.

LeBon, G. *The crowd: A study of the popular mind.* (2nd ed.) London: T. F. Unwin, 1897.

Leiderman, P. H., & Shapiro, D. (Eds.) *Psycho-biological approaches to social behavior.* Stanford: Stanford Univer. Press, 1964.

Lenneberg, E. H., & Roberts, J. M. The language of experience: A study in methodology. *Int. J. Amer. Linguistics,* 1956, 22, Memoir No. 13.

Lependorf, S. The effects of incentive value and expectancy on dissonance resulting from attitude-discrepant behavior and disconfirmation of expectancy. Unpublished doctoral dissertation, State Univer. of New York at Buffalo, 1964.

Lerner, D. *The passing of traditional society.* Glencoe, Ill.: Free Press, 1958.

Lesser, G. S. Relationships between various forms of aggression and popularity among lower-class children. *J. educ. Psychol.*, 1959, *50*, 20-25.

Leventhal, H., & Niles, P. A field experiment on fear-arousal with data on the validity of questionnaire measures. *J. Pers.*, 1964, *32*, 459-479.

Levine, L. S. *Personal and social development: The psychology of effective behavior.* New York: Holt, Rinehart, & Winston, 1963.

Levine, R., Chein, I., & Murphy, G. The relation of the intensity of a need to the amount of perceptual distortion. *J. Psychol.*, 1942, *13*, 283-293.

Levinger, G. Task and social behavior in marriage. *Sociometry*, 1964, *27*, 433-448.

Lewin, K. *Principles of topological psychology.* New York: McGraw-Hill, 1936.

Lewin, K. Group decision and social change. In T. M. Newcomb & E. L. Hartley (Eds.), *Readings in social psychology.* New York: Holt, 1947. Pp. 330-344.

Lewin, K., Lippitt, R., & White, R. K. Patterns of aggressive behavior in experimentally created "social climates." *J. soc. Psychol.*, 1939, *10*, 271-299.

Lewis, O. The culture of poverty. *Trans-action*, 1963, *1*, 17-19.

Libo, L. M. *Measuring group cohesiveness.* Ann Arbor: Univer. of Michigan, Research Center for Group Dynamics, Institute for Social Research, 1953.

Likert, R. A technique for the measurement of attitudes. *Archives of Psychol.*, 1932, No. 4.

Likert, R. Motivation and productivity. *Mgmt. Rec.*, 1956, *18*, 128-131.

Likert, R. *New patterns of management.* New York: McGraw-Hill, 1961.

Lindesmith, A. R., & Strauss, A. L. *Social psychology.* (2nd edition.) New York: Dryden Press, 1956.

Lindzey, G. (Ed.) *Handbook of social psychology.* Reading, Mass.: Addison-Wesley, 1954.

Lindzey, G., & Aronson, E. (Eds.) *Handbook of social psychology.* (Revised edition.) Cambridge, Mass.: Addison-Wesley, 1967.

Lindzey, G., & Borgatta, E. F. Sociometric measurement. In G. Lindzey (Ed.), *Handbook of social psychology.* Reading, Mass.: Addison-Wesley, 1954. Pp. 405-448.

Linn, L. S. Verbal attitudes and overt behavior: A study of racial discrimination. *Social Forces*, 1965, *43*, 353-364.

Linton, Harriet, & Graham, Elaine. Personality correlates of persuasibility. In C. I. Hovland & I. L. Janis (Eds.), *Personality and persuasibility.* New Haven: Yale Univer. Press, 1959. Pp. 69-101.

Linton, R. *The cultural background of personality.* New York: Appleton-Century-Crofts, 1945. (Also published as a paperback by Appleton-Century-Crofts.)

Linton, R. A concept of national character. In A. H. Stanton &. S. E. Perry (Eds.), *Personality in political crisis.* Glencoe, Ill.: Free Press, 1951. Pp. 133-150.

Lippitt, R., & White, R. K. An experimental study of leadership and group life. In T. M. Newcomb & E. L. Hartley (Eds.), *Readings in social psychology*. New York: Holt, 1947.

Lippitt, R., Polansky, N., & Rosen, S. The dynamics of power. *Hum. Relat.*, 1952, 5, 37-64.

Lippitt, R., Watson, Jeanne, & Westley, B. *The dynamics of planned change.* New York: Harcourt, Brace & World, 1958.

Lippmann, W. *Public opinion.* New York: Harcourt, Brace, 1922.

Lipset, S. M. *Political man.* Garden City, N. Y.: Doubleday, 1960.

Lipset, S. M., & Bendix, R. *Social mobility in industrial society.* Berkeley: Univer. of Calif. Press, 1959.

Loomis, J. L. Communication, the development of trust and cooperative behavior. *Hum. Relat.*, 1959, 12, 305-315.

Lorenz, K. *On aggression.* New York: Harcourt, Brace, & World, 1966.

Lorge, I., Fox, D., Davitz, J., & Bremer, M. A survey of studies contrasting the quality of group performance and individual performance, 1920-1957. *Psychol. Bull.*, 1958, 55, 337-372.

Lorimer, F. *The growth of reason.* New York: Harcourt Brace, 1929.

Lorr, M., & McNair, D. M. Expansion of the interpersonal behavior circle. *J. Pers. soc. Psychol.*, 1965, 2, 823-830.

Luchins, A. S., & Luchins, Edith H. On conformity with judgments of a majority or an authority. *J. soc. Psychol.*, 1961, 53, 303-316.

Lynd, R. S., & Lynd, Helen M. *Middletown: A study in contemporary American culture.* New York: Harcourt Brace, 1929.

McCandless, B. R., Bilous, C., & Bennett, H. Peer popularity and dependence on adults in preschool-age socialization. *Child Development*, 1961, 32, 511-518.

McCarthy, Dorothea. A comparison of children's language in different situations. *J. genet. Psychol.*, 1929, 36, 583-591.

McClelland, D. C. *Personality.* New York: Dryden, 1951.

McClelland, D. C. The use of measures of human motivation in the study of society. In J. W. Atkinson (Ed.), *Motives in fantasy, action, and society*. Princeton: Van Nostrand, 1958. Pp. 518-552.

McClelland, D. C. *The achieving society.* Princeton: Van Nostrand, 1961.

McClelland, D. C., Atkinson, J. W., Clark, R. A., & Lowell, E. L. *The achievement motive.* New York: Appleton-Century-Crofts, 1953.

Maccoby, Eleanor. The taking of adult roles in middle childhood. *J. abnorm. soc. Psychol.*, 1961, 63, 493-503.

McDougall, W. *An introduction to social psychology.* London: Methuen, 1908. (23rd ed., 1936.)

McDougall, W. *The group mind.* New York: G. P. Putnam's Sons, 1920. (Rev. ed., 1928.)

McGrath, J. E. *Social psychology: A brief introduction.* New York: Holt, Rinehart & Winston, 1964.

McGrath, J. E., & Altman, I. *Small group research: A critique and synthesis of the field.* New York: Holt, Rinehart & Winston, 1966.

McGrath, J. E., & Julian, J. W. Interaction process and task outcome in experimentally-created negotiation groups. *J. psychol. Studies*, 1963, *14*, 117-138.

McGuire, W. J. Order of presentation as a factor in "conditioning" persuasiveness. In C. I. Hovland (Ed.), *The order of presentation in persuasion*. New Haven: Yale Univer. Press, 1957. Pp. 98-114.

McGuire, W. J. Inducing resistance to persuasion. In L. Berkowitz (Ed.), *Advances in experimental social psychology*. Vol. I. New York: Academic Press, 1964. Pp. 191-229.

McGuire, W. J. Attitudes and opinions. In P. R. Farnsworth (Ed.), *Annual review of psychology*. Vol. 17. Palo Alto, Calif.: Annual Reviews, 1966. Pp. 475-514.

McGuire, W. J., & Papageorgis, D. Effectiveness of pre-warning in developing resistance to persuasion. *Publ. Opin. Quart.*, 1962, *26*, 24-34.

McGuire, W. J., & Millman, Susan. Anticipatory belief lowering following forewarning of a persuasive attack. *J. Pers. soc. Psychol.*, 1965, *2*, 471-479.

Maclay, H. S. Language and nonlinguistic behavior: An experimental investigation. *Dissert. Abstr.*, 1956, *16*, 1039.

McNeil, E. (Ed.) *The nature of human conflict*. Englewood Cliffs, N. J.: Prentice-Hall, 1965.

Malinowski, B. *Sex and repression in savage society*. New York: Harcourt Brace, 1927.

Mandelbaum, D. G. *Soldier groups and Negro soldiers*. Berkeley: Univer. of Calif. Press, 1952.

Mann, R. D. A review of the relationships between personality and performance in small groups. *Psychol. Bull.*, 1959, *56*, 241-270.

Marcus, P. M. Expressive and instrumental groups: Toward a theory of group structure. *Amer. J. Sociol.*, 1960, *66*, 54-59.

Marshall, Helen R. Prediction of social acceptance in community youth groups. *Child Development*, 1958, *29*, 173-184.

Marshall, Helen R. Relations between home experiences and children's use of language in play interactions with peers. *Psychol. Monogr.*, 1961, 75, No. 5 (Whole No. 509).

Marshall, Helen R., & McCandless, B. R. Relationships between dependence on adults and social acceptance by peers. *Child Development*, 1957, *28*, 413-419.

Marshall, S. L. A. *Men against fire*. Washington, D. C.: Combat Forces Press, 1951.

Maslow, A. H. The authoritarian character structure. *J. soc. Psychol.*, 1943, *18*, 401-411.

Maslow, A. H. *Motivation and personality*. New York: Harper, 1954.

Mausner, B. Studies in social interaction: III. Effect of variation in one partner's prestige on the interaction of observer pairs. *J. appl. Psychol.*, 1953, *37*, 391-393.

Mausner, B. The effect of prior reinforcement on the interaction of observer pairs. *J. abnorm. soc. Psychol.*, 1954a, *49*, 65-68.

Mausner, B. The effect of one partner's success in a relevant task on the interaction of observer pairs. *J. abnorm. soc. Psychol.*, 1954b, *49*, 557-560.

Mead, Margaret. *Male and female.* New York: William Morrow & Co., 1949. (Also available as Penguin Paperback.)

Mead, Margaret. *New lives for old.* New York: William Morrow & Co., 1956. (Also available as a Mentor Book, New York, 1961.)

Medow, H., & Zander, A. Aspirations for the group chosen by central and peripheral members. *J. Pers. soc. Psychol.*, 1965, *1*, 224-228.

Merton, R. K. *Social theory and social structure.* Glencoe, Ill.: Free Press, 1957.

Milburn, T. The concept of deterrence. *J. Social Issues*, 1961, *17*, 3-11.

Milgram, S. Liberating effects of group pressure. *J. Pers. soc. Psychol.*, 1965, *1*, 127-134.

Miller, D., & Swanson, G. E. *The changing American parent.* New York: Wiley, 1958.

Miller, G. A. *Language and communication.* New York: McGraw-Hill, 1951.

Miller, G. A. The psycholinguists. *Encounter*, 1964, *23*, 29-37.

Miller, L. K., & Hamblin, R. L. Interdependence, differential rewarding, and productivity. *Amer. sociol. Rev.*, 1963, *28*, 768-778.

Miller, N., & Campbell, D. T. Recency and primacy in persuasion as a function of the timing of speeches and measurements. *J. abnorm. soc. Psychol.*, 1959, *59*, 1-9.

Miller, N. E., & Dollard, J. *Social learning and imitation.* New Haven: Yale Univer. Press, 1941.

Miller, R. E., Murphy, J. V., & Mirsky, I. A. Modification of social dominance in a group of monkeys by inter-animal conditioning. *J. comp. physiol. Psychol.*, 1955, *48*, 392-396.

Millman, Susan. The relationship between anxiety, learning and opinion change. Unpublished doctoral dissertation. Columbia Univer., 1965.

Mills, J. Opinion change as a function of the communicator's desire to influence and liking for the audience. *J. exp. soc. Psychol.*, 1966, *2*, 152-159.

Mills, J., & Aronson, E. Opinion change as a function of the communicator's attractiveness and desire to influence. *J. Pers. soc. Psychol.*, 1965, *1*, 173-177.

Mills, T. M. Power relations in three person groups. *Amer. sociol. Rev.*, 1953, *18*, 351-357.

Minard, R. D. Race relationships in the Pocahontas coal field. *J. soc. Issues*, 1952, *8*, 29-44.

Mintz, A. Non-adaptive group behavior. *J. abnorm. soc. Psychol.*, 1951, *46*, 150-159.

Moede, W. *Experimentelle Massenpsychologie.* Leipzig: S. Hirzel, 1920.

Moeller, G., & Applezweig, M. H. A motivational factor in conformity. *J. abnorm. soc. Psychol.*, 1957, 55, 114-120.

Montagu, A. *The biosocial nature of man.* New York: Grove Press, 1956.

Montagu, A. *Human heredity.* New York: New American Library, Mentor Book, 1960.

Moreno, J. L. Foundations of sociometry, an introduction. *Sociometry*, 1941, 4, 15-38.

Moreno, J. L. *Who shall survive?* (Rev. ed.) Beacon, N. Y.: Beacon House, 1953.

Moreno, J. L. (Ed.) *The sociometry reader.* Glencoe, Ill.: The Free Press, 1960.

Morgan, C. T. *Introduction to psychology.* (2nd ed.) New York: McGraw-Hill, 1961.

Morris, C. *Signs, language, and behavior.* New York: Prentice-Hall, 1946.

Morris, C. *Varieties of human value.* Chicago: Univer. of Chicago Press, 1956.

Mouton, Jane S., Bell, R. L., & Blake, R. R. Role playing skill and sociometric peer status. *Group Psychotherapy*, 1956, 9, 7-17.

Mowrer, O. H. *Learning theory and personality dynamics.* New York: Ronald, 1950.

Mowrer, O. H. Hearing and speaking: An analysis of language learning. *J. Speech & Hear. Disorders*, 1958, 23, 143-152.

Mowrer, O. H. *Learning theory and behavior.* New York: Wiley, 1960.

Mumford, L. *The conduct of life.* New York: Harcourt, Brace, & World, 1951.

Mumford, L. *The highway and the city.* New York: Harcourt, Brace, & World, 1963.

Münsterberg, H. *Psychology, general and applied.* New York: D. Appleton & Co., 1914.

Muraskin, Judith, & Iverson, M. A. Social expectancy as a function of judging social distance. *J. soc. Psychol.*, 1958, 48, 11-14.

Murphy, G. *Personality: A biosocial approach to origins and structure.* New York: Harper, 1947.

Murphy, G. *Historical introduction to modern psychology.* (Rev. ed.) New York: Harcourt, Brace and Company, 1949.

Murphy, G. *In the minds of men.* New York: Basic Books, 1953.

Newcomb, T. M. *Personality and social change.* New York: Dryden, 1943.

Newcomb, T. M. *Social psychology.* New York: Holt, Rinehart, and Winston, 1950.

Newcomb, T. M. Social psychological theory: Integrating individual and social approaches. In J. Rohrer & M. Sherif (Eds.), *Social psychology at the crossroads.* New York: Harper & Row, 1951. Pp. 31-49.

Newcomb, T. M. An approach to the study of communicative acts. *Psychol. Rev.*, 1953, 60, 393-404.

Newcomb, T. M. The prediction of interpersonal attraction. *Amer. Psychologist*, 1956, 11, 575-586.

Newcomb, T. M. Individual systems of orientation. In S. Koch (Ed.), *Psychology: A study of a science*. Vol. 3. New York: McGraw-Hill, 1959.

Newcomb, T. M. *The acquaintance process*. New York: Holt, Rinehart, & Winston, 1961.

Newcomb, T. M. Persistence and regression of changed attitudes: Long-range studies. *J. soc. Issues*, 1963, *19*, 3-14.

Newman, H. H., Freeman, F. N., & Holzinger, K. J. *Twins: A study of heredity and environment*. Chicago: Univer. of Chicago Press, 1937.

Niles, P. The relationship of susceptibility and anxiety to acceptance of fear-arousing communications. Unpublished doctoral dissertation, Yale Univer., 1964.

Nunnally, J. C. *Tests and measurements*. New York: McGraw-Hill, 1959.

Nuttin, J. M., Jr. Attitude change after rewarded dissonant and consonant "forced compliance." *Int. J. Psychol.*, 1966, *1*, 39-57.

Ogilvy, D. *Confessions of an advertising man*. New York: Dell, 1963.

Olmsted, M. S. *The small group*. New York: Random House, 1959.

Orlansky, H. Infant care and personality. *Psychol. Bull.*, 1949, *46*, 1-48.

Orne, M. T. On the social psychology of the psychological experiment: With particular reference to demand characteristics and their implications. *Amer. Psychologist*, 1962, *17*, 776-783.

Orwell, G. *1984*. New York: Harcourt, Brace & Co., 1949. (Also available as a Signet Book, New York, 1950.)

Osgood, C. E. The nature and measurement of meaning. *Psychol. Bull.*, 1952, *49*, 197-237.

Osgood, C. E. Cognitive dynamics in the conduct of human affairs. *Publ. Opin. Quart.*, 1960, *24*, 341-365.

Osgood, C. E. *An alternative to war or surrender*. Urbana: Univer. Illinois Press, 1962.

Osgood, C. E., & Tannenbaum, P. H. The principle of congruity in the prediction of attitude change. *Psychol. Rev.*, 1955, *62*, 42-55.

Osgood, C. E., Suci, G. J., & Tannenbaum, P. H. *The measurement of meaning*. Urbana: Univer. of Illinois Press, 1957.

Osgood, C. E., Ware, E. E., & Morris, C. Analysis of the connotative meanings of a variety of human values as expressed by American college students. *J. abnorm. soc. Psychol.*, 1961, *62*, 62-73.

Parsons, T. Personality and social structure. In A. H. Stanton & S. E. Perry (Eds.), *Personality and political crisis*. Glencoe, Ill.: The Free Press, 1951. Pp. 61-80.

Parsons, T., Bales, R. F., & Shils, E. A. (Eds.) *Working papers in the theory of action*. Glencoe, Ill.: Free Press, 1953.

Patchen, M. A conceptual framework and some empirical data regarding comparison of social rewards. *Sociometry*, 1961, *24*, 136-156.

Paul, J., & Laulicht, J. *In your opinion: Leaders' and voters' attitudes on defence and disarmament*. Vol. 1. Clarkson, Ontario: Canadian Peace Research Institute, 1963.

Pei, M. *The story of language*. New York: New American Library, Mentor Books, 1960.

Pelz, D. C. Influence: A key to effective leadership in the first-line supervisor. *Personnel*, 1952, *29*, 209-217.

Pepinsky, Pauline N. Social exceptions that prove the rule. In I. A. Berg & B. M. Bass (Eds.), *Conformity and deviation*. New York: Harper & Bros., 1961. Pp. 424-434.

Pepinksy, Pauline N., Hemphill, J. K., & Shevitz, R. N. Attempts to lead, group productivity, and morale under conditions of acceptance and rejection. *J. abnorm. soc. Psychol.*, 1958, *57*, 47-54.

Pepitone, A. Attributions of causality, social attitudes, and cognitive matching processes. In R. Tagiuri & L. Petrullo (Eds.), *Person perception and interpersonal behavior*. Stanford, Calif.: Stanford Univer. Press, 1958. Pp. 258-276.

Pepitone, A., & Kleiner, R. The effects of threat and frustration on group cohesiveness. *J. abnorm. soc. Psychol.*, 1957, *54*, 192-199.

Perlmutter, H. V. Stereotypes about Americans and Europeans who make specific statements. *Psychol. Reps.*, 1957, *3*, 131-137.

Petrullo, L., & Bass, B. M. (Eds.) *Leadership and interpersonal behavior*. New York: Holt, Rinehart & Winston, 1961.

Pettigrew, T. F. The measurement and correlates of category width as a cognitive variable. *J. Pers.*, 1958, *26*, 532-544.

Pettigrew, T. *A profile of the Negro American*. Princeton: Van Nostrand, 1964.

Phares, E. J. Expectancy changes in skill and chance situations. *J. abnorm. soc. Psychol.*, 1957, *54*, 339-342.

Piaget, J. *The language and thought of the child*. London: Kegan Paul, Trench, Trubner & Co., 1926.

Piaget, J. *The moral judgment of the child*. New York: Harcourt Brace, 1932.

Plant, J. S. *The envelope: A study of the impact of the world upon the child*. New York: Commonwealth Fund, 1950.

Pool, I. Effects of cross-national contact on national and international images. In H. C. Kelman (Ed.), *International behavior: A socio-psychological analysis*. New York: Holt, Rinehart, and Winston, 1965. Pp. 106-129.

Proshansky, H., & Seidenberg, B. (Eds.) *Basic studies in social psychology*. New York: Holt, Rinehart & Winston, 1965.

Rabinowitz, W. A note on the social perceptions of authoritarians and non-authoritarians. *J. abnorm. soc. Psychol.*, 1956, *53*, 384-386.

Radke, Marian J., & Klisurich, Dayna. Experiments in changing food habits. *J. Amer. Dietetics Assn.*, 1947, *23*, 403-409.

Rapoport, A. Rules for debate. In Wright, Q., Evan, W. M., & Deutsch, M. (Eds.), *Preventing World War III: Some proposals*. New York: Simon & Schuster, 1962. Pp. 246-262.

Raven, B. H., & Eachus, H. T. Cooperation and competition in means-interdependent triads. *J. abnorm. soc. Psychol.*, 1963, *67*, 307-316.

Raven, B. H., & French, J. R. P. Group support, legitimate power, and social influence. *J. Pers.*, 1958, *26*, 400-409.

Raven, B. H., & Rietsema, J. The effects of varied clarity of group goal and group path upon the individual and his relation to his group. *Hum. Relat.*, 1957, *10*, 29-45.

Reese, H. W. Relationships between self-acceptance and sociometric choices. *J. abnorm. soc. Psychol.*, 1961, *62*, 472-474.

Rhine, R. J. The effect of peer group influence upon concept-attitude development and change. *J. soc. Psychol.*, 1960, *51*, 173-179.

Ribble, Margaret A. Infantile experience in relation to personality development. In J. McV. Hunt (Ed.), *Personality and the behavior disorders*. Vol. II. New York: Ronald Press, 1944. Ch. 20.

Richardson, L. F. *Statistics of deadly quarrels*. Pittsburgh: Boxwood Press, 1960.

Riecken, H. W. The effect of talkativeness on ability to influence group solutions to problems. *Sociometry*, 1958, *21*, 309-321.

Riesman, D., Glazier, N., & Denny, R. *The lonely crowd: A study of the changing American character*. New Haven: Yale Univer. Press, 1950.

Riley, Matilda W., Riley, J. W., Jr., & Moore, Mary E. Adolescent values and the Riesman typology. In S. M. Lipset & L. Lowenthal (Eds.), *Culture and social character*. New York: Free Press, 1961. Pp. 370-386.

Rivers, W. H. R. Vision. In A. C. Haddon (Ed.), *Reports of the Cambridge anthropological expedition to the Torres Straits*. Vol. II. Cambridge: Cambridge Univer. Press, 1901.

Rivers, W. H. R. Observations on the senses of the Todas. *Brit. J. Psychol.*, 1905, *1*, 321-396.

Rohrer, J., & Sherif, M. (Eds.) *Social psychology at the crossroads*. New York: Harper-Row, 1951.

Rokeach, M. The nature and meaning of dogmatism. *Psychol. Rev.*, 1954, *61*, 194-205.

Rokeach, M. *The open and closed mind*. New York: Basic Books, 1960.

Rokeach, M. The organization and modification of beliefs. *Centennial Rev.*, 1963, *7*, 375-395.

Rokeach, M. The nature of attitudes. East Lansing: Michigan State University, Department of Psychology, 1966. (Mimeo of paper to appear in *The international encyclopedia of the social sciences.*

Rokeach, M. & Rothman, G. The principle of belief congruence and the congruity principle as models of cognitive interaction. *Psych. Rev.*, 1965, *72*, 128-142.

Rose, A. M. Reference groups of high school youth. *Child Develpm.*, 1956, *27*, 351-363.

Rosen, B. C. Conflicting group membership: A study of parent-peer group cross-pressures. *Amer. sociol. Rev.*, 1955, *20*, 155-161.

Rosenberg, M. J. Cognitive structure and attitudinal affect. *J. abnorm. soc. Psychol.*, 1956, *53*, 367-372.

Rosenberg, M. J. A structural theory of attitude dynamics. *Publ. Opin. Quart.*, 1960a, *24*, 319-340.

Rosenberg, M. J. An analysis of affective-cognitive consistency. In C. I. Hovland & M. J. Rosenberg (Eds.), *Attitude organization and change*. New Haven: Yale Univer. Press, 1960b. Pp. 15-64.

Rosenberg, M. J. Cognitive reorganization in response to the hypnotic reversal of attitudinal affect. *J. Pers.*, 1960c, *28*, 39-63.

Rosenberg, M. J. When dissonance fails: On eliminating evaluation apprehension from attitude measurement. *J. Pers. soc. Psychol.*, 1965, *1*, 28-42.

Rosenberg, M. J., & Abelson, R. P. An analysis of cognitive balancing. In C. I. Hovland & M. J. Rosenberg (Eds.), *Attitude organization and change.* New Haven: Yale Univer. Press, 1960. Pp. 112-163.

Rosenthal, F. Some relationships between sociometric position and language structure of young children. *J. educ. Psychol.*, 1957, *48*, 483-497.

Rosow, I. Issues in the concept of need complementarity. *Sociometry*, 1957, *20*, 216-253.

Ross, E. A. *Social psychology.* New York: Macmillan, 1908.

Rotter, J. B. *Social learning and clinical psychology.* Englewood Cliffs, N. J.: Prentice-Hall, 1954.

Rotter, J. B. Generalized expectancies for internal vs. external control of reinforcement. *Psychol. Monogr.*, 1966, *80*, 1-28.

Rotter, J. B., & Mulry, R. C. Internal versus external control of reinforcement and decision time. *J. Pers. soc. Psychol.*, 1965, *2*, 598-604.

Ryan, F. J., & Davie, J. S. Social acceptance, academic achievement, and academic aptitude among high school students. *J. educ. Res.*, 1958, *52*, 101-106.

Sabath, G. The effect of disruption and individual status on person perception and group attraction. *J. soc. Psychol.*, 1964, *64*, 119-130.

Samelson, F. The relation of achievement and affiliation motives to conforming behavior in two conditions of conflict with a majority. In J. W. Atkinson (Ed.), *Motives in fantasy, action and society.* New York: Van Nostrand, 1958. Pp. 421-433.

Sampson, E. E. Status congruence and cognitive consistency. *Sociometry*, 1963, *26*, 146-162.

Sanford, F. H. *Authoritarianism and leadership.* Philadelphia: Institute for Research in Human Relations, 1950.

Sapir, E. Language and environment. *Amer. Anthropologist*, 1912, *14*, 226-242.

Sapir, E. *Language: An introduction to the study of speech.* New York: Harcourt, Brace & Co., 1921. (Also available in a paperback as a Harvest Book, New York, 1949.)

Sargent, S. S. Emotional stereotypes in the Chicago Tribune. *Sociometry*, 1939, *2*, 69-75.

Schachter, S. Deviation, rejection, and communication. *J. abnorm. soc. Psychol.*, 1951, *46*, 190-207.

Schachter, S. *The psychology of affiliation.* Calif.: Stanford Univer. Press, 1959.

Schachter, S., & Singer, J. Cognitive, social and physiological determinants of emotional state. *Psychol. Rev.*, 1962, *69*, 379-399.

Schachter, S., Ellertson, N., McBride, Dorothy, & Gregory, Doris. An experimental study of cohesiveness and productivity. *Hum. Relat.*, 1951, *4*, 229-238.

Schaffner, B. *Fatherland*. New York: Columbia Univer. Press, 1948.

Schanck, R. L. A study of a community and its groups and institutions conceived of as behaviors of individuals. *Psychol. Monogr.*, 1932, *43*, No. 2.

Schuman, F. L. *The nazi dictatorship*. (2nd ed.) New York: Knopf, 1939.

Schutz, W. C. The interpersonal underworld. *Harvard Business Rev.*, 1958, *36*, 123-135.

Schutz, W. C. The ego, FIRO theory and the leader as completer. In L. Petrullo & B. M. Bass (Eds.), *Leadership and interpersonal behavior*. New York: Holt, Rinehart, & Winston, 1961. Pp. 48-65.

Scodel, A. Induced collaboration in some non-zero-sum games. *J. Confl. Resol.*, 1962, *6*, 335-340.

Scodel, A., & Mussen, P. Social perception of authoritarians and nonauthoritarians. *J. abnorm. soc. Psychol.*, 1953, *48*, 181-184.

Scott, J. P. Implications of infra-human social behavior for problems of human relations. In M. Sherif & M. O. Wilson (Eds.), *Group relations at the crossroads*. New York: Harper & Bros., 1953.

Sears, R. R. A theoretical framework for personality and social behavior. *Amer. Psychologist*, 1951a, *6*, 476-482.

Sears, R. R. Effects of frustration and anxiety on fantasy aggression. *Amer. J. Orthopsychiat.*, 1951b, *21*, 498-505.

Sears, R. R. The 1958 summer research project on identification. *J. nursery Educat.*, 1960, *16*, (2).

Sears, R. R., Maccoby, Eleanor, & Levin, H. *Patterns of child-rearing*. Evanston, Ill.: Row, Peterson, 1957.

Secord, P. F., & Backman, C. W. Personality theory and the problem of stability and change in individual behavior: An interpersonal approach. *Psychol. Rev.*, 1961, *68*, 21-33.

Seeman, M., & Morris, R. T. *A status factor approach to leadership*. Columbus: Ohio State Univer. Research Foundation, 1950.

Segall, M. H., Campbell, D. T., & Herskovits, M. J. Cultural differences in the perception of geometrical illusions. *Science*, 1963, *139*, 769-771.

Segall, M. H., Campbell, D. T., & Herskovits, M. J. *The influence of culture in visual perception*. New York: Bobbs Merrill, 1966.

Selltiz, Claire, Jahoda, Marie, Deutsch, M., & Cook, S. W. *Research methods in social relations*. (Rev. ed.) New York: Holt, Rinehart, & Winston, 1959.

Seward, Georgene. *Psychotherapy and culture conflict*. New York: Ronald, 1956.

Shapiro, H. L. (Ed.) *Man, culture & society*. New York: Oxford Univer. Press, 1956.

Sharp, L. Steel axes for stone-age Australians. *Human Organization*, 1952, *11*, 17-22.

Shartle, C. L., & Stogdill, R. M. *Studies in naval leadership*. Columbus: Ohio State Univer. Research Foundation, 1952.

Shaw, F. J., & Ort, R. S. *Personal adjustment in the American culture.* New York: Harper, 1953.

Shaw, Marjorie E. Comparison of individuals and small groups in the rational solution of complex problems. *Amer. J. Psychol.*, 1932, *44*, 491-504.

Shaw, Marvin E. Some effects of unequal distribution of information upon group performance in various communication nets. *J. abnorm. soc. Psychol.*, 1954, *49*, 547-553.

Shaw, Marvin E. Some motivational factors in cooperation and competition. *J. Pers.*, 1958, *26*, 155-169.

Shaw, Marvin E. Acceptance of authority, group structure and the effectiveness of small groups. *J. Pers.*, 1959a, *27*, 196-210.

Shaw, Marvin E. Some effects of individually prominent behavior upon group effectiveness and member satisfaction. *J. abnorm. soc. Psychol.*, 1959b, *59*, 382-386.

Shaw, Marvin E. A note concerning homogeneity of membership and group problem solving. *J. abnorm. soc. Psychol.*, 1960, *60*, 448-450.

Sherif, Carolyn W., Sherif, M., & Nebergall, R. E. *Attitude and attitude change: The social judgment-involvement approach.* Philadelphia: Saunders, 1965.

Sherif, M. A study of some social factors in perception. *Arch. Psychol.*, 1935, *27*, No. 187.

Sherif, M. *The psychology of social norms.* New York: Harper, 1936.

Sherif, M. Superordinate goals in the reduction of intergroup conflict. *Amer. J. Sociol.*, 1958, *63*, 349-358.

Sherif, M. Conformity-deviation, norms, and group relations. In I. A. Berg & B. M. Bass (Eds.), *Conformity and deviation.* New York: Harper, 1961. Pp. 159-198.

Sherif, M. (Ed.) *Intergroup relations and leadership.* New York: Wiley, 1962.

Sherif, M., & Cantril, H. *The psychology of ego-involvements.* New York: Wiley, 1947.

Sherif, M., & Sherif, Carolyn W. *Groups in harmony and tension: An integration of studies on intergroup relations.* New York: Harper, 1953.

Sherif, M., & Wilson, M. O. (Eds.) *Group relations at the crossroads.* New York: Harper, 1953.

Sherif, M., & Hovland, C. I. *Social judgment.* New Haven: Yale Univer. Press, 1961.

Sherif, M., & Sherif, Carolyn W. *Reference groups: Exploration into the conformity and deviation of adolescents.* New York: Harper & Row, 1964.

Sherif, M., & Sherif, Carolyn W. (Eds.) *Problems of youth: Transition to adulthood in a changing world.* Chicago: Aldine, 1965.

Sherif, M., Harvey, O. J., White, B. J., Hood, W. R., & Sherif, Carolyn W. *Intergroup conflict and cooperation: The Robbers Cave experiment.* Norman, Oklahoma: Univer. of Oklahoma Book Exchange, 1961.

Shibutani, T. Reference groups as perspectives. *Amer. J. Soc.*, 1955, *60*, 562-570.

Shils, E. A. Class. In *Encyclopedia Britannica*, 5, 1960. Pp. 766-68.

Showel, M. Interpersonal knowledge and rated leader potential. *J. abnorm. soc. Psychol.*, 1960, *61*, 87-92.

Shrauger, S., & Altrocchi, J. The personality of the perceiver as a factor in person perception. *Psychol. Bull.*, 1964, *62*, 289-308.

Simmel, G. *The sociology of Georg Simmel.* (Trans. and edited by K. H. Wolff.) Glencoe, Ill.: Free Press, 1950.

Sims, V. M., & Patrick, J. R. Attitude toward the Negro of Northern and Southern college students. *J. soc. Psychol.*, 1936, *7*, 192-204.

Skinner, B. F. *Verbal behavior.* New York: Appleton-Century-Crofts, 1957.

Slater, P. E. Contrasting correlates of group size. *Sociometry*, 1958, *21*, 129-139.

Smelser, W. T. Dominance as a factor in achievement and perception in co-operative problem solving interactions. *J. abnorm. soc. Psychol.*, 1961, *62*, 535-542.

Smith, M. B., Bruner, J. S., & White, R. W. *Opinions and personality.* New York: Wiley, 1956.

Spector, A. J. Expectations, fulfillment, and morale. *J. abnorm. soc. Psychol.*, 1956, *52*, 51-56.

Spitz, Rene. Hospitalism: An inquiry into the genesis of psychiatric conditions in early childhood. *Psychoanalytic Study of the Child*, 1945, *1*, 53-74.

Spock, B. *The common sense book of baby and child care.* New York: Duell, Sloan, & Pearce, 1946.

Steiner, I. D. Interpersonal behavior as influenced by accuracy of social perception. *Psychol. Rev.*, 1955, *62*, 268-274.

Steiner, I. D., & Rajaratnam, N. A model for the comparison of individual and group performance scores. *Behavioral Science*, 1961, *6*, 142-147.

Steiner, I. D., & Johnson, H. H. Authoritarianism and conformity. *Sociometry*, 1963, *26*, 21-34.

Steiner, I. D., & Fishbein, M. (Eds.) *Current studies in social psychology.* New York: Holt, Rinehart & Winston, 1965.

Stoetzel, J. *Without the chrysanthemum and the sword.* London: Heinemann, 1955.

Stogdill, R. M. Personal factors associated with leadership. *J. Psychol.*, 1948, *25*, 35-71.

Stogdill, R. M. Leadership, membership and organization. *Psychol. Bull.*, 1950, *47*, 1-14.

Stogdill, R. M. *Individual behavior and group achievement.* New York: Oxford Univer. Press, 1959.

Stott, L. H. Persisting effects of early family experiences upon personality development. *Merrill-Palmer School Quarterly* (Detroit), 1957, *3*, No. 3.

Stouffer, S. A., Suchman, E. A., DeVinney, L. C., Star, Shirley A., & Williams, R. M. Jr. *The American soldier: Adjustment during army life.* Vol. I. Princeton, N. J.: Princeton Univer. Press, 1949.

Strauss, A. Concepts, communication, and groups. In M. Sherif & M. O. Wilson (Eds.), *Group relations at the crossroads.* New York: Harper & Bros., 1953.

Strodtbeck, F. L. Husband-wife interaction over revealed differences. *Amer. sociol. Rev.*, 1951, *16*, 468-473.

Strodtbeck, F. L. The family as a three-person group. *Amer. sociol. Rev.*, 1954, *19*, 23-29.

Strodtbeck, F. L. Family interaction, values, and achievement. In D. C. McClelland, A. L. Baldwin, U. Bronfenbrenner, & F. L. Strodtbeck (Eds.), *Talent and society.* Princeton, N. J.: Van Nostrand, 1958. Pp. 135-194.

Strodtbeck, F. L., James, Rita M., & Hawkins, C. Social status in jury deliberations. In Eleanor E. Maccoby, T. M. Newcomb, & E. L. Hartley (Eds.), *Readings in social psychology.* (3rd ed.) New York: Holt, 1958. Pp. 379-388.

Suchman, E. A. The intensity component in attitude and opinion research. In S. A. Stouffer, L. Guttman, E. A. Suchman, P. F. Lazarsfeld, Shirley A. Star, & J. A. Gardner (Eds.), *Measurement and prediction.* New Jersey: Princeton Univer. Press, 1949.

Sulzberger, C. L. "Sound and fury signifying nothing?" In *St. Louis Post Dispatch*, March 15, 1960, Section B, page 5.

Sumner, W. G., & Keller, A. G. *The science of society.* Vol. 1. New Haven: Yale Univer. Press, 1927.

Tagiuri, R. Relational analysis: An extension of sociometric method with emphasis upon social perception. *Sociometry*, 1952, *15*, 91-104.

Tagiuri, R. Introduction to R. Tagiuri & L. Petrullo (Eds.), *Person perception and interpersonal behavior.* Stanford, Calif.: Stanford Univer. Press, 1958. Pp. ix-xvii.

Tajfel, H. Value and the perceptual judgment of magnitude. *Psychol. Rev.*, 1957, *64*, 192-204.

Tajfel, H. Social and cultural factors in perception. In G. Lindzey & E. Aronson (Eds.), *Handbook of social psychology.* (Rev. ed.) Cambridge, Mass.: Addison-Wesley, 1967.

Talland, G. A. The assessment of group opinion by leaders and their influence on its formation. *J. abnorm. soc. Psychol.*, 1954, *49*, 431-434.

Tarde, G. *The laws of imitation.* (Trans. from 2nd French edition by Elsie C. Parsons.) New York: Holt, 1903.

Taylor, Janet A. A personality scale of manifest anxiety. *J. abnorm. soc. Psychol.*, 1953, *48*, 285-290.

Taylor, Janet A. Drive theory and manifest anxiety. *Psychol. Bull.*, 1956, *53*, 303-320.

Terman, L. M. *The measurement of intelligence.* Boston: Houghton Mifflin, 1916.

Thibaut, J. W., & Riecken, H. W. Some determinants and consequences of the perception of social causality. *J. Pers.*, 1955, *24*, 113-133.

Thibaut, J. W., & Kelley, H. H. *The social psychology of groups.* New York: Wiley, 1959.

Thomas, E. J. Effects of facilitative role interdependence on group functioning. *Hum. Relat.*, 1957, *10*, 347-366.

Thompson, W. R., & Melzack, R. Early environment. *Scientific Amer.*, Jan., 1956, 38-42.

Thorndike, E. L. *Man and his works.* Cambridge, Mass.: Harvard Univer. Press, 1943.

Thurstone, L. L., & Chave, E. J. *The measurement of attitudes.* Chicago: Univer. of Chicago Press, 1929.

Titmuss, R. M. *Problems of social policy.* London, England: His Majesty's Stationery Office and Longmans, Green, 1950.

Titus, H. E., & Hollander, E. P. The California F scale in psychological research: 1950-1955. *Psychol. Bull.*, 1957, *54*, 47-65.

Tönnies, F. *Gemeinschaft und Gesellschaft. Abhandlung des Communismus und des Socialismus als empirische Culturformen.* Leipzig: Fues Verlag, 1887.

Trans-action. Roundup of current research, 1966, *3* (5), 3.

Tuckman, J., & Lorge, I. Individual ability as a determinant of group superiority. *Hum. Relat.*, 1962, *15*, 45-51.

Tuma, E., & Livson, N. Family socioeconomic status and adolescent attitudes toward authority. *Child Development*, 1960, *31*, 387-399.

Turk, H. Instrumental and expressive ratings reconsidered. *Sociometry*, 1961, *24*, 76-81.

Tylor, E. B. *Primitive culture. Researches in the development of mythology, philosophy, religion, language, art, and custom.* Vol. 1. New York: Henry Holt, 1877.

Uesugi, T. K., & Vinacke, W. E. Strategy in a feminine game. *Sociometry*, 1963, *26*, 75-88.

UNESCO. *Human rights, comments and interpretations; a symposium edited by UNESCO, with an introduction by J. Maritain.* London: Wingate, 1950.

UNESCO. *The race concept; results of an inquiry.* Paris: 1952.

United States Bureau of the Census. *Statistical abstract of the United States.* Washington, D. C.: Govt. Printing Office, 1964.

Upshaw, H. S. The effect of variable perspectives on judgments of opinion statements for Thurstone scales: Equal-appearing intervals. *J. Pers. soc. Psychol.*, 1965, *2*, 60-69.

Vaughan, G. M. The trans-situational aspect of conformity behavior. *J. Pers.*, 1964, *32*, 335-354.

Vaughan, G. M., & Mangan, G. L. Conformity to group pressure in relation to the value of the task material. *J. abnorm. soc. Psychol.*, 1963, *66*, 179-183.

Verba, S. *Small groups and political behavior: A study of leadership.* Princeton, N. J.: Princeton Univer. Press, 1961.

Verplanck, W. S. The control of the content of conversation: Reinforcement of statements of opinion. *J. abnorm. soc. Psychol.*, 1955, *51*, 668-676.

Vidulich, R. N., & Kaiman, I. P. The effects of information source status and dogmatism upon conformity behavior. *J. abnorm. soc. Psychol.*, 1961, *63*, 639-642.

Vigotsky, L. S. Thought and speech. *Psychiatry*, 1939, *2*, 29-54.

Vinacke, W. E. Sex roles in a three-person game. *Sociometry*, 1959, *22*, 343-360.

Vinacke, W. E., & Arkoff, A. An experimental study of coalitions in the triad. *Amer. sociol. Rev.*, 1957, *22*, 406-414.

Von Frisch, K. *The dancing bees.* New York: Harcourt Brace, 1955.

Walker, E. L., & Heyns, R. W. *An anatomy for conformity.* Englewood Cliffs, N. J.: Prentice-Hall, 1962.

Wallach, M. A., & Kogan, N. Aspects of judgment and decision making: Interrelationships and changes with age. *Behav. Sci.*, 1961, *6*, 23-26.

Wallin, P. Cultural contradictions and sex roles: A repeat study. *Amer. Sociol. Rev.*, 1950, *15*, 288-293.

Walster, Elaine. The effect of self-esteem on romantic liking. *J. exp. soc. Psychol.*, 1965, *1*, 184-197.

Walster, Elaine, & Festinger, L. The effectiveness of "overheard" persuasive communications. *J. abnorm. soc. Psychol.*, 1962, *65*, 395-402.

Walters, R. H., & Karol, P. Social deprivation and verbal behavior. *J. Pers.*, 1960, *28*, 89-107.

Walters, R. H., Marshall, W. S., & Shooter, J. R. Anxiety, isolation, and susceptibility to social influence. *J. Pers.*, 1960, *28*, 518-529.

Waly, Patricia, & Cook, S. W. Effect of attitude on judgments of plausibility. *J. Pers. soc. Psychol.*, 1965, *2*, 745-749.

Watson, G. Do groups think more effectively than individuals? *J. abnorm. soc. Psychol.*, 1928, *23*, 328-336.

Watson, Jeanne. A formal analysis of sociable interaction. *Sociometry*, 1958, *21*, 269-281.

Weiner, H., & McGinnies, E. Authoritarianism, conformity, and confidence in a perceptual judgment situation. *J. soc. Psychol.*, 1961, *55*, 77-84.

Weinstein, E. A., & Deutschberger, P. Tasks, bargains, and identities in social interaction. *Soc. Forces*, 1964, *42*, 451-456.

Weiss, W. Opinion congruence with a negative source on one issue as a factor influencing agreement on another issue. *J. abnorm. soc. Psychol.*, 1957, *54*, 180-186.

White, R. W. Motivation reconsidered: The concept of competence. *Psychol. Rev.*, 1959, *66*, 297-334.

Whorf, B. L. *Language, thought, and reality.* Edited by, and with an introduction by John B. Carroll. Cambridge, Mass.: Technology Press, 1956. (Also available in an MIT Press Paperback Edition, 1964.)

Whyte, W. F. *Street corner society.* Ill.: Univer. Chicago Press, 1943.

Whyte, W. H. *The organization man.* New York: Simon & Schuster, 1956.

Wiggins, J. A., Dill, F., & Schwartz, R. D. On "status-liability." *Sociometry,* 1965, *28,* 197-209.

Williams, Meta F. Acceptance and performance among gifted elementary-school children. *Educ. Res. Bull.,* 1958, *37,* 216-220, 224.

Williams, R. M. *American society: A sociological interpretation.* New York: Knopf, 1951. (2nd ed., 1960.)

Willis, R. H. Two dimensions of conformity-nonconformity. *Sociometry,* 1963, *26,* 499-513.

Willis, R. H. Conformity, independence, and anti-conformity. *Hum. Relat.,* 1965, *18,* 373-388.

Willis, R. H., & Hollander, E. P. An experimental study of three response modes in social influence situations. *J. abnorm. soc. Psychol.,* 1964a, *69,* 150-156.

Willis, R. H., & Hollander, E. P. Supplementary note: Modes of responding in social influence situations. *J. abnorm. soc. Psychol.,* 1964b, *69,* 157.

Wilson, E. Conformity revisited. *Trans-action,* 1964, *2,* 28-32.

Winch, R. F. The theory of complementary needs in mate selection: Final results on the test of the general hypothesis. *Amer. sociol. Rev.,* 1955, *20,* 551-555.

Winch, R. F. *Mate-selection: A study of complementary needs.* New York: Harper and Row, 1958.

Winch, R. F., Ktsanes, T., & Ktsanes, Virginia. The theory of complementary needs in mate selection: An analytic and descriptive study. *Amer. sociol. Rev.,* 1954, *19,* 214-249.

Winch, R. F., Ktsanes, T., & Ktsanes, Virginia. Empirical elaboration of the theory of complementary needs in mate selection. *J. abnorm. soc. Psychol.,* 1955, *51,* 508-514.

Withey, S. B., & Katz, D. The social psychology of human conflict. In E. McNeil (Ed.), *The nature of human conflict.* Englewood Cliffs, N. J.: Prentice-Hall, 1965. Pp. 64-90.

Wolff, W. *The expression of personality: Experimental depth psychology.* New York: Harper & Bros., 1943.

Wright, P. H. Personality and interpersonal attraction: Basic assumptions. *J. indiv. Psychol.,* 1965, *21,* 127-136.

Wyer, R. S. Effects of incentive to perform well, group attraction, and group acceptance on conformity in a judgmental task. *J. Pers. soc. Psychol.,* 1966, *4,* 21-26.

Zajonc, R. Social facilitation. *Science,* 1965, *149,* 269-274.

Zander, A., & Havelin, A. Social comparison and interpersonal attraction. *Hum. Relat.,* 1960, *13,* 21-32.

Zimbardo, P. Involvement and communication discrepancy. *J. abnorm. soc. Psychol.,* 1960, *60,* 86-94.

Zipf, G. K. *The psycho-biology of language.* Boston: Houghton Mifflin, 1935.

Znaniecki, F. *Social relations and social roles.* San Francisco: Chandler, 1965.

Name index

502

7

Subject index